CHRISTOLO
THE GOSPE

Exploring the i … hip within the apocalyptic … ses on six passages: Mark 1:16–20; 3:13–15; 4:… ; 6:45–52. Together, these passages indicate that the disciples failed to understand not just Jesus' messianic identity *per se* but the apocalyptic nature of his messiahship, as well as its implications for their own participation in God's coming reign.

The implications of this for Mark's gospel as a whole are to situate Mark's Christological claims within the broader context of the apocalyptic "gospel of God." This lends coherence to Mark's bifocal interest in miracle and passion. It also illuminates the relationship between Mark's Jesus and his followers as those who carry forward his own mission: to demonstrate the coming kingdom of God, which is fully assured if not yet fully in view.

SUZANNE WATTS HENDERSON is Assistant Professor of Religion at Salem College, Winston-Salem.

SOCIETY FOR NEW TESTAMENT STUDIES

MONOGRAPH SERIES

General Editor: John Court

135

CHRISTOLOGY AND DISCIPLESHIP IN THE GOSPEL OF MARK

SOCIETY FOR NEW TESTAMENT STUDIES

MONOGRAPH SERIES

Recent Titles in the series

122. An Aramaic Approach to Q
MAURICE CASEY
0 521 81723 4
123. Isaiah's Christ in Matthew's Gospel
RICHARD BEATON
0 521 81888 5
124. God and History in the Book of Revelation
MICHAEL GILBERTSON
0 521 82466 4
125. Jesus' Defeat of Death
PETER G. BOLT
0 521 83036 2
126. From Hope to Despair in Thessalonica
COLIN R. NICHOLL
0 521 83142 3
127. Matthew's Trilogy of Parables
WESLEY G. OLMSTEAD
0 521 83154 7
128. The People of God in the Apocalypse
STEPHEN PATTEMORE
0 521 83698 0
129. The Exorcism Stories in Luke–Acts
TODD KLUTZ
0 521 83804 5
130. Jews, Gentiles and Ethnic Reconciliation
TET-LIM N. YEE
0 521 83831 2
131. Ancient Rhetiric and Paul's Apology
FREDRICK J. LONG
0 521 84233 6
132. Reconstructing Honor in Roman Philippi
JOSEPH H. HELLEMAN
0 521 84909 8
133. Theological Hermenautics and 1 Thessalonians
ANGUS PADDISON
0 521 84983 7
134. Greco-Roman Culture and the Galilee of Jesus
MARK A. CHANCEY
0 521 84647 1

Christology and Discipleship in the Gospel of Mark

SUZANNE WATTS HENDERSON

CAMBRIDGE
UNIVERSITY PRESS

CAMBRIDGE UNIVERSITY PRESS
Cambridge, New York, Melbourne, Madrid, Cape Town, Singapore, São Paulo, Delhi

Cambridge University Press
The Edinburgh Building, Cambridge CB2 8RU, UK

Published in the United States of America by Cambridge University Press, New York

www.cambridge.org
Information on this title: www.cambridge.org/9780521859066

First published 2006
This digitally printed version 2008

A catalogue record for this publication is available from the British Library

ISBN 978-0-521-85906-6 hardback
ISBN 978-0-521-09139-8 paperback

To my father

CONTENTS

PREFACE

This book represents the culmination of a project begun some fifteen years ago during my Masters of Divinity program at Princeton Theological Seminary. There, in my final semester, I enjoyed the privilege of participating in a doctoral seminar on Mark's gospel led by Professor Joel Marcus. My seminar paper for that course addressed the topic of the disciples' incomprehension.

Nearly a decade after finishing at Princeton I enrolled in the doctoral studies program at Duke, still convinced there was more work to be done on the topic of the Markan disciples. By God's providence – or sheer good fortune – Professor Marcus joined the faculty at Duke just in time to supervise my dissertation. In the meantime he had completed his Anchor Bible commentary on Mark 1–8, which along with his earlier writings proved invaluable for my grounding of discipleship in the soil of apocalyptic thought.

The abnormally lengthy gestation period of this work has benefited from the cumulative wisdom of innumerable friends and colleagues, terms that apply equally to those I name here. To begin with, my gratitude to Professor Marcus simply could not be more profound. His example of rigorous scholarship and his free-flowing red ink have strengthened my work immeasurably; his profound kindness, persistent encouragement, and refreshing good humor have strengthened my soul even more. My thanks go also to Richard B. Hays, E. P. Sanders, and James L. Crenshaw – the other members of my dissertation committee whose careful reading and constructive feedback have contributed significantly to this work.

I also wish to thank those who have shared my journey at Duke. The Graduate Program in Religion has offered an abundantly hospitable and collegial setting for my studies. I am most grateful for the other students and faculty whose gifts of friendship and vigorous conversation have made my days in Durham so invigorating. The New Testament & Judaic Studies Colloquium provided a helpful forum for the discussion of much of chapter 2. In particular, Rick Stone has shared not only commuting expenses but also keen exegetical insights that have bolstered my arguments at every turn. Rick is this book's "sous chef," and words cannot express my gratitude for his vast contribution to this effort. In addition, Dustin Ellington, now at the Evangelical Theological Seminary in Cairo, Egypt, has read and responded to much of the work contained here with characteristic depth and sensitivity. Along the way, my community of faith, Westminster Presbyterian Church in Greensboro, has served as a living example of the ideals of discipleship presented in this book.

Institutionally, I would like to thank the administration, faculty, and students of Salem College, where I now teach Religion, for an environment that has supported this publication effort. Thanks also go to Father Michael McGarry and the staff at Tantur Ecumenical Institute in Jerusalem for the gift of time and space to complete the book's index during my stay as Scholar-in-Residence. My editorial contacts at Cambridge University Press, Kate Brett, Jackie Warren, and Jan Chapman, have dealt most graciously with me, as I navigate this process for the first time.

Finally, my husband Bob and our children Abbie, Hannah, and Will have provided the foundation of unqualified love and enthusiastic support that makes a sustained effort such as this possible. They have tolerated my frequent disappearance to the computer screen with patient grace. They are truly God's greatest gift to me.

Five years ago today my father, Thomas Ellington Watts, Jr., lost a valiant fight against cancer. Though he did not live to see the completion of this project, he was its greatest inspiration, and it is to him that I dedicate this book. The power of his unfailing love has outlasted his life on this earth; his reach does indeed exceed his grasp. May he rest from his labors.

ABBREVIATIONS

AB	Anchor Bible
ACNT	Augsburg Commentary on the New Testament
AnBib	Analecta biblica
ATANT	Abhandlungen zur Theologie des Alten und Neuen Testaments
b.	Babylonian Talmud
BAGD	Bauer, Arndt, Gingrich, and Danker, *A Greek–English Lexicon of the New Testament and Other Early Christian Literature*
BETL	Bibliotheca ephemeridum theologicarum lovaniensium
BHT	Beiträge zur historischen Theologie
Bib	*Biblica*
BibInt	*Biblical Interpretation*
BibLeb	*Bibel und Leben*
BNTC	Black's New Testament Commentaries
BZ	*Biblische Zeitschrift*
BZNW	Beihefte zur Zeitschrift für die neutestamentliche Wissenschaft
CBQ	*Catholic Biblical Quarterly*
CBQMS	Catholic Biblical Quarterly Monograph Series
CGTC	Cambridge Greek Testament Commentaries
EKKNT	Evangelisch-katholischer Kommentar zum Neuen Testament
ETL	*Ephemerides theologicae lovanienses*
EvQ	*Evangelical Quarterly*
EvT	*Evangelische Theologie*
ExpT	*Expository Times*
HNT	Handbuch zum Neuen Testament
HTKNT	Herders theologischer Kommentar zum Neuen Testament
HTR	*Harvard Theological Review*
Int	*Interpretation*

IRT	Issues in Religion and Theology
JAAR	*Journal of the American Academy of Religion*
JBL	*Journal of Biblical Literature*
JJS	*Journal of Jewish Studies*
JR	*Journal of Religion*
JSNT	*Journal for the Study of the New Testament*
JSNTSup	Journal for the Study of the New Testament Supplement Series
JSOTSup	Journal for the Study of the Old Testament Supplement Series
JSSSup	Journal of Semitic Studies Supplement Series
JTS	*Journal of Theological Studies*
LEC	Library of Early Christianity
LSJ	Liddell, Scott, and Jones, *A Greek–English Lexicon with a Supplement*
LQ	*Lutheran Quarterly*
LXX	Septuagint
m.	Mishnah
MT	Masoretic text
NICNT	New International Commentary on the New Testament
NovT	*Novum Testamentum*
NTS	*New Testament Studies*
OG	Old Greek version of the Septuagint
OT	Old Testament
PC	Proclamation Commentaries
QL	Qumran literature
RB	*Revue biblique*
RNTS	Reading the New Testament Series
SANT	Studien zum Alten und Neuen Testament
SBB	Stuttgarter biblische Beiträge
SBLDS	Society of Biblical Literature Dissertation Series
SBM	Stuttgarter biblische Monographien
SBT	Studies in Biblical Theology
SNTSMS	Society for New Testament Studies Monograph Series
SNTW	Studies in the New Testament and Its World
t.	Tosefta
TDNT	*Theological Dictionary of the New Testament*
THKNT	Theologischer Handkommentar zum Neuen Testament
TZ	*Theologische Zeitschrift*
WBC	Word Biblical Commentary

WUNT	Wissenschaftliche Untersuchungen zum Neuen Testament
ZAW	*Zeitschrift für die alttestamentliche Wissenschaft*
ZNW	*Zeitschrift für die neutestamentliche Wissenschaft*
ZTK	*Zeitschrift für Theologie und Kirche*

PART I

Introduction

1

JESUS' MISSION AND THEIRS: CHRISTOLOGY AND DISCIPLESHIP IN LIGHT OF MARK'S APOCALYPTIC GOSPEL

As Etienne Trocmé has observed, "in Mark, more than any of the other gospels, Jesus is everywhere in the company of his disciples."[1] Summoned at the outset of his ministry, those who "come after" Jesus repeatedly bear witness to activities that characterize his earthly mission. But they are also, in this gospel story, more than mere bystanders, as they benefit from Jesus' private counsel and even participate actively in his demonstration of God's dominion breaking into the human sphere. In light of their narrative significance, then, John Donahue goes so far as to claim that, while Mark "has an obvious Christological thrust . . . the story of the disciples occupies a strong second position."[2]

Yet in addition to their narrative prominence, the disciples in Mark have garnered such vigorous exegetical interest partly due to another, and less salutary, Markan emphasis: the motif of the disciples' incomprehension. Precisely the evangelist's willingness to highlight the failures of those most closely aligned with Jesus has stimulated the imaginations of a

[1] Etienne Trocmé, *The Formation of the Gospel According to Mark*, trans. P. Gaughan (Philadelphia: Westminster Press, 1975), 142.

[2] John R. Donahue, *The Theology and Setting of Discipleship in the Gospel of Mark* (Milwaukee, WI: Marquette University Press, 1983), 2. Recent scholarship has devoted ample attention to Mark's portrait of the disciples, producing a wide range of studies on topics including the following: the precise makeup of "the Twelve/disciples" (see Robert P. Meye, *Jesus and the Twelve: Discipleship and Revelation in Mark's Gospel* [Grand Rapids, MI: Eerdmans, 1968] and Gunter Schmahl, *Die Zwölf im Markusevangelium* [Trier: Paulinus, 1974]); Jewish and Greco-Roman backgrounds (see Hans Dieter Betz, *Nachfolge und Nachahmung Jesu Christi im Neuen Testament*, BHT 37 [Tübingen: Mohr (Siebeck) 1967]; Martin Hengel, *The Charismatic Leader and His Followers*, trans. J. Grieg, SNTW [New York: Crossroad, 1981]; Vernon K. Robbins, "Mark 1.14–20: An Interpretation at the Intersection of Jewish and Graeco-Roman Traditions," *NTS* 28 [1982]: 220–36); and the implied relationship between the disciples in the gospel and Mark's audience (see Mary Ann Beavis, *Mark's Audience: The Literary and Social Setting of Mark 4.11–12*, JSNTSup 33 [Sheffield: Sheffield Academic Press, 1989]; Ernest Best, *Following Jesus: Discipleship in the Gospel of Mark*, JSNTSup 4 [Sheffield: JSOT Press, 1981]; Robert C. Tannehill, "The Disciples in Mark: The Function of a Narrative Role," *JR* 57 [1977]: 386–405; Joseph B. Tyson, "The Blindness of the Disciples in Mark," *JBL* 80 [1961]: 261–8; Theodore J. Weeden, "The Heresy that Necessitated Mark's Gospel," *ZNW* 59 [1968]: 145–58).

host of interpreters who have attempted to decipher Mark's increasingly negative portrayal of the disciples.

To propose yet another study of Markan discipleship – and the incomprehension motif in particular – may seem like the retracing of well-worn tracks along the path of NT research. The literature in the field is vast, yet, as I shall demonstrate, its findings remain unsatisfactory. This study thus returns to Mark's complex depiction of the disciples to inquire about the nature of their incomprehension. What is it that the disciples do not understand? On what grounds are they culpable? Rather than beginning with thematic interest in the disciples' failures, the approach here will be *first* to examine the intended relationship forged between Jesus and his followers from the story's outset and only *then* to assess the disciples' lapses according to the intended scope of that relationship.

As we shall see, Mark's Jesus forges a relationship with his followers that is characterized by both *presence* and *practice*. In the first place, they are summoned to remain in Jesus' presence as they bear witness to his Christological mission, which entails the proleptic demonstration of God's coming kingdom; what is more, through their physical and relational proximity to Jesus, these select followers receive privileged instruction concerning the nature of that kingdom.

Yet a frequently overlooked facet of their calling in Mark is Jesus' insistence that the disciples are meant to continue Jesus' *practice* of wielding the power associated with God's apocalyptic reign. In this sense, Jesus here authorizes them as collective participants in the Christological mission that characterizes his own purpose and destiny. Just as Mark's Jesus demonstrates the in-breaking dominion of God, he deliberately summons and equips his followers to carry this program forward. And while Mark's story frequently alludes obliquely to Jesus' messianic identity, the second evangelist clearly forges that identity within the fires of Jesus' messianic mission: to give advance notice of God's decisive victory over the powers of the present evil age.

Only within this broader horizon – the assertion of God's coming dominion – can we fully grasp not just Jesus' messiahship but also his deliberate involvement of followers in the regime change he institutes. As a result, this study will maintain that even the Markan motif of incomprehension must be examined within the context of this original design for discipleship, a design that features both presence and practice. Where the disciples fail in the second gospel, they have not trusted the power of God unleashed in their midst, preeminently in the person of Jesus but also, by extension, in their own authorization to implement his apocalyptic assertion of God's coming kingdom. Their incomprehension thus derives from a failure to grasp both the apocalyptic nature of Jesus' power – he is more than a "divine man" – and its implications for those entrusted with that power.

To set the terms of the subsequent exegetical investigation, this opening chapter features several preliminary steps. First, a review of the dominant approach of Markan research over the past century will highlight the sharp Christological focus that has largely defined true discipleship in terms of correct appraisal of Jesus' messiahship. Second, a discussion of inherent weaknesses in such an unnecessarily circumscribed study of Markan discipleship will reveal a set of artificial dichotomies that have been imposed upon the text. A final step will chart the "way forward" proposed in this study, with attention to working assumptions, method, interpretive payoff, and exegetical focus.

State of the question

In many respects, William Wrede's monumental work *The Messianic Secret* laid the groundwork for Markan exegesis spanning the last century. In his study of the secrecy motif in the second gospel, Wrede not only detects doctrinal concerns underlying the evangelist's efforts but also focuses attention squarely on Jesus' messiahship as the motivating force behind the gospel. According to Wrede, "the idea of the secret arose at a time when as yet there was no knowledge of any messianic claim on the part of Jesus on earth."[3] In Wrede's view, Mark incorporates traditions about Jesus' injunctions to silence in order to reconcile post-resurrection views about his messiahship with an apparent ignorance of it in Jesus' own day. The second gospel's claim that Jesus "ordered them to tell no one about what they had seen [that is, the transfiguration], until after the Son of Man had risen from the dead" (Mk. 9:9), Wrede maintains, reveals Mark's notion of the "resurrection as the dividing-line between two periods."[4] Since Mark writes on this side of that dividing-line, Wrede finds that the evangelist's purpose is to enfold every aspect of Jesus' ministry and destiny within the framework of his suffering and vindicated messiahship, even as he attributes to Jesus a desire that that messiahship remain a "mystery" until the season of disclosure – the post-Easter epoch.[5]

[3] William Wrede, *The Messianic Secret*, trans. J. C. Grieg (Cambridge: James Clarke, 1971; orig. 1901), 228.

[4] Ibid., 72.

[5] Ibid., 80. Wrede identifies Jesus' wonder-working and teaching, as well as his suffering, dying, and rising, as constituent parts of his messiahship.

The impact of Wrede's approach on subsequent Markan scholarship can hardly be overstated. While many interpreters have taken issue with particular assertions about the scope and significance of the messianic-secrecy motif,[6] the "Wredestrasse" has led to an undeniably dominant interest in Mark's Christology. Thus Joel Marcus can offer this late twentieth-century claim: "That Mark's Gospel was written primarily to establish a particular understanding of Jesus' identity is scarcely disputed."[7] Further, William Telford claims, "The Gospel, as it now stands, invites the reader to view the Jesus of history (or at least of the tradition) in a certain light."[8]

Of course, the "certain light" to which Telford refers is the passion story, which casts long shadows over the rest of Mark's gospel, extending from the cross itself back into the gospel's central section, which is dominated by three predictions of Jesus' fate (Mk. 8:31; 9:31; 10:33–4). It is this destiny, in the view of many scholars, that decisively shapes Mark's Christology, so that interpreters generally take for granted Ben Witherington's claim that "Mark makes evident that it was not until after Jesus' death, and by precisely reflecting on that death, that Jesus was seen to be who he really was."[9] Even Robert Gundry, who overtly disavows the messianic-secrecy motif and disallows a Markan emphasis on Jesus' suffering messiahship, nonetheless maintains that the gospel serves a Christological purpose: to "make the passion itself a success-story."[10] Under the sway of Wrede's work as well as in contentious reaction against it, then, interpreters have consistently probed the second gospel's depiction of Jesus' identity. Whether they infer Mark's dominant Christology to be defined by the term Son of God,[11] Davidic messiah,[12] or apocalyptic

[6] Among those who have questioned the scope of the messianic-secret motif are Ulrich Luz, "Das Geheimnismotif und die markinische Christologie," *ZNW* 56 (1965): 9–30; Heikki Räisänen, *The "Messianic Secret" in Mark's Gospel*, trans. Christopher Tuckett, SNTW (Edinburgh: T. & T. Clark, 1990); see also Trocmé, *Mark*, 124 n. 1.

[7] Joel Marcus, *The Way of the Lord: Christological Exegesis of the Old Testament in the Gospel of Mark* (Louisville: Westminster/John Knox Press, 1992), 6.

[8] William R. Telford, ed., *The Interpretation of Mark*, 2nd edn., IRT 7 (Edinburgh: T. & T. Clark, 1999; orig. 1977), 16.

[9] Ben Witherington, III, *The Gospel of Mark: A Socio-Rhetorical Commentary* (Grand Rapids, MI: Eerdmans, 2001), 53.

[10] Robert H. Gundry, *Mark: A Commentary on His Apology for the Cross* (Grand Rapids, MI: Eerdmans, 1993), 1–3.

[11] Rudolf Bultmann understands this title in terms of the Hellenistic "divine man" and believes it is central for Mark's Christology (*Theology of the New Testament*, 2 vols. [New York: Charles Scribner's Sons, 1951–5], I:130–1). Representative of the view that the "Son of God" epithet conveys an obedient servant within a messianic Jewish framework is Jack Dean Kingsbury, *The Christology of Mark's Gospel* (Philadelphia: Fortress Press, 1994; orig. 1983), 47–155.

[12] See, e.g., John R. Donahue, "Temple, Trial, and Royal Christology (Mark 14:53–65)," in *The Passion in Mark*, ed. Werner H. Kelber (Philadelphia: Fortress Press, 1976), 72–8.

Son of Man,[13] most contemporary readers of the second gospel would agree that the key to understanding this εὐαγγέλιον Ἰησοῦ Χριστοῦ can be obtained only through determining Jesus' precise Christological identity.

This sharply Christological understanding of the second gospel has provided an almost universally accepted template for studies of the Markan disciples, so that the conduct of Jesus' followers has come to be assessed according to the accuracy of their Christology.[14] For if the gospel narrative recounts the disclosure of Jesus' messiahship, it follows quite naturally that Mark's mixed review of the disciples would concern their own deficient Christology.[15]

But what faulty views does this motley band of followers represent? The variety of verdicts on the issue of failed discipleship mirrors the wide-ranging claims about Mark's Christology, as well as motives interpreters impute to the evangelist.[16] Among pioneers addressing this topic, Theodore J. Weeden identifies the disciples as exponents of flawed views about Jesus' identity – and thus as objects of the evangelist's scathing review. Turning on its head Bultmann's benign assessment of the Hellenistic "divine man" type, Weeden argues vigorously that Jesus'

[13] A host of interpreters have focused on "Son of Man" as the only title the evangelist finds adequate to convey Jesus' true identity. Chief among proponents of this view is Norman Perrin, "The Christology of Mark: A Study in Methodology," in *A Modern Pilgrimage in New Testament Christology* (Philadelphia: Fortress Press, 1974), 104–21; also M. Eugene Boring, "The Christology of Mark: Hermeneutical Issues for Systematic Theology," *Semeia* 30 (1984): 131–3. Cf. Werner Kelber, *The Kingdom in Mark: A New Place and a New Time* (Philadelphia: Fortress Press, 1974), *passim*, who finds that Mark was correcting a false Son of Man Christology associated with Jewish apocalyptic hopes.

Throughout this book I shall defer to the prevailing use of "Son of Man" to translate the phrase ὁ υἱὸς τοῦ ἀνθρώπου, despite the fact that this gender-specific language misrepresents the more inclusive thrust of the Greek. My exegetical observations, though, will attempt to promote a broader understanding of this term, which I translate "son of humanity."

[14] In his appendix called "Mark's Perspective on the Disciples," Witherington writes, "Mark does want to leave us with the impression that at the end of the day, true discipleship, based on true understanding of Jesus and his mission, was only possible after Easter" (*Mark*, 441). Yet he acknowledges in the next paragraph that, in the gospel's opening chapters, "they are presented as responding for the most part in the right way, though their comprehension level is low." It is just this inherent contradiction – that the disciples are able to function faithfully *even before* post-Easter Christological disclosure – that this study investigates.

[15] But cf. Rikki Watts, *Isaiah's New Exodus and Mark* (Tübingen: Mohr Siebeck, 1997), who notes the opposite: it is "not a matter of whether or not one fully understands but instead whether one repents, has faith, and follows Jesus" (207). Still, owing to his focused interest in Jesus' Christological role, Watts does not pursue the implications of this important observation for our understanding of the Markan portrait of the disciples.

[16] C. Clifton Black has cited the variegated findings on this issue as evidence of the inherently subjective approach of redaction criticism. See *The Disciples According to Mark: Markan Redaction in Current Debate*, JSNTSup 27 (Sheffield: JSOT Press, 1989). I would only add that the assumption of Mark's sharply Christological agenda has further skewed our understanding of the Markan disciples.

followers in the second gospel represent those who have infiltrated Mark's community and are attempting to infuse it with a "theologia gloriae." In response, Weeden maintains, Mark crafts a story that charts in three stages (imperceptivity, misconception, rejection) the disciples' downward spiral; the nearer they come to the "theologia crucis," the more they resist, and ultimately turn away from, Jesus' suffering destiny.[17] Thus Weeden understands the gospel's early emphasis on Jesus' miraculous powers as the platform against which Mark polemicizes.

Other interpreters have adopted Weeden's basic construal concerning Markan polemic even as they have detected a different Christological emphasis the evangelist intends to supplant. For instance, Joseph Tyson thinks Mark espouses a gentile Christian perspective and so means to subvert, through his portrait of the disciples, the kind of Son of David Christology that would have characterized the Jerusalem church.[18] In a similar vein, Werner Kelber detects within the gospel a tension between a northern (Galilean) and southern (Jerusalem-based) tradition; it is their failure to grasp the true nature of God's kingdom – a kingdom aligned with Galilee – that leads the Jerusalem contingent to the tragedy of the Jewish War, where their mistaken "[k]ingdom hopes . . . had gone up in the flames of the temple."[19]

Notably, even scholars who commend a more pastoral reading of the Markan disciples have not abandoned this tendency to lay heavy interpretive weight on the "way of the cross" discipleship teachings as the authoritative window into Mark's Christology. Ernest Best introduces his study on Markan discipleship with the claim that, in this gospel, "the nature of discipleship becomes apparent only in light of the cross, and not in the light of Jesus' mighty acts."[20] To demonstrate the pivotal importance of the gospel's central section (Mk. 8:27–10:45), Best launches his investigation *in medias res*, as it were, focusing his hermeneutical gaze squarely on the gospel's presentation of the Danielic Son of Man as a suffering messiah.

While his methodological approach differs from Best's in that it follows the gospel's own narrative development, Robert C. Tannehill arrives at much the same conclusion: Mark has constructed the gospel account so as to lure those who are readily impressed with Jesus' deeds of power into a narrative snare where they must face head-on Jesus' "cost of discipleship" teachings.[21] For Cilliers Breytenbach, too, though other aspects

[17] This view was originally advanced in Weeden, "Heresy," and developed more fully in his *Mark – Traditions in Conflict* (Philadelphia: Fortress Press, 1971).

[18] Tyson, "Blindness," 261–8.

[19] Kelber, *Kingdom*, 138.

[20] Best, *Following Jesus*, 13–14.

[21] Tannehill, "Disciples," *passim*.

of discipleship are important for Mark's community, it is preeminently the motif of self-sacrifice modeled in the initial call but crystallized in the way of the cross that reflects the essence of following Jesus; moreover, the disciples cannot understand Jesus prior to the resurrection.[22] Despite their differing approaches, then, even scholars inclined toward a more pastoral reading of Mark's gospel agree with those who view the work as sheer polemic on this point: the gospel's first half serves a decidedly subordinate role in Mark's portrait of Christology, and thus of discipleship.

Put simply, a broad consensus of scholarship maintains that only in light of the cross do the disciples (and thus the readers) gain full disclosure of Jesus' identity, which is that of a crucified and raised messiah. Taken a step further, scholars generally agree that it is only when Jesus' followers have endorsed this proper Christological understanding that they are fully enabled to serve as Jesus' disciples.[23] In this view, not only does Mark's gospel itself primarily intend to advocate "Christological correctness," but it also assesses the disciples' faithfulness according to their grasp of who this Jesus really is.

Splitting Mark open: the problem of false dichotomies

The intent here is not to supplant either a Christological reading of Mark's gospel or an interpretive emphasis on the cost of discipleship. Mark *does* tell the story of Jesus in a manner that underscores God's special designation of this "beloved son" (Mk. 1:9; 9:7), and the path of suffering and death *is* one that cannot be circumvented, in Mark's view, by either the Christ or his followers. Yet recent scholarship has focused so narrowly on the gospel's depiction of Jesus as suffering messiah that it has failed to account adequately for several complementary features found in the narrative. A brief summary of the weaknesses of such a sharply Christological approach will lay the foundation for this study, which intends to expand Christological inquiry beyond the question of Jesus' messianic identity *per se*. As we shall see, interpreters who assume that Mark's overarching

[22] Cilliers Breytenbach, *Nachfolge und Zukunftserwartung nach Markus: Eine methodenkritische Studie*, ATANT 71 (Zurich: Theologischer Verlag Zurich, 1984), 335–8.

[23] Other interpreters who maintain that Mark employs the discipleship theme as a pastoral attempt to promote correct Christology, albeit with differing emphases, include Karl-Georg Reploh, *Markus – Lehrer der Gemeinde: Eine redaktionsgeschichtliche Studie zu den Jüngerperikopen des Markus-Evangliums*, SBM 9 (Stuttgart: Katholisches Bibelwerk, 1969); Klemens Stock, *Boten aus dem Mit-Ihm-Sein: Das Verhältnis zwischen Jesus und den Zwölf nach Markus*, AnBib 70 (Rome: Biblical Institute, 1975); and Elizabeth Struthers Malbon, "Fallible Followers: Women and Men in the Gospel of Mark," *Semeia* 28 (1983): 29–48.

interest lies in portraying Jesus' suffering messiahship repeatedly impose artificial dichotomies that in turn make the gospel's depiction of the disciples less, rather than more, comprehensible.

Mark's two "halves"

First, such an interpretive emphasis on the suffering messiah, combined with a post-Enlightenment disdain for miracles and the demonic sphere, has led many modern readers of Mark's gospel to detect in the first eight chapters a blurry vision (at best) of Jesus' nature and purpose.[24] As noted above, some interpreters find in the gospel's first half a portrait of Jesus as "divine man" that functions as a foil to the emerging portrait of Jesus as suffering messiah; others view the wonder-working of the first half as a merely preparatory, and wholly insufficient, rendering of Jesus the Christ. In either case, interpreters have identified Mk. 8:27 as the turning point at which the possibility of seeing clearly begins in earnest.

Yet, as Tannehill has pointed out, such a reading "cannot explain the positive aspects of the Marcan portrayal of the disciples,"[25] nor does it account for the fact that Mark repeatedly casts Jesus' proclamation and wonder-working in a positive light. Even Weeden himself concedes that Mark's inclusion of this material means it must not have been "completely offensive to him."[26] Moreover, Jesus' deeds of power continue more or less unabated into the gospel's second half, where, among other things, Jesus rids a boy of an unclean spirit (Mk. 9:14–29), heals blind Bartimaeus (Mk. 10:46–52) and curses a fig tree, with supernatural results (Mk. 11:12–14; 20–2).

Together, these observations compel us to pursue a reading of Mark's narrative that finds coherence, rather than competing claims, in Jesus' office of wonder-worker and his foreboding destiny. For if the second gospel was deliberately crafted as a "passion narrative with extended introduction,"[27] our interpretive challenge may well be to detect the evangelist's sense of continuity between Jesus' ministry (all of it) and his death. The first aim of this study, then, will be to read Mark's gospel

[24] A commonplace interpretation of the two-stage healing found in Mk. 8:22–6 finds the miracle story to serve as a "hinge" from the obscured portrait of Jesus in the gospel's first half to the clearer depiction of him in the ensuing stories of sacrifice and death. See, e.g., Frank J. Matera, "The Incomprehension of the Disciples and Peter's Confession," *Bib* 70 (1989): 163–71, for a representative example of this reading.

[25] Tannehill, "Disciples," 141. [26] Weeden, "Heresy," 153.

[27] Martin Kähler, *The So-Called Historical Jesus and the Historic Biblical Christ*, trans. Carl E. Braaten (Philadelphia: Fortress Press, 1964; orig. 1892), 80, n. 11.

as a unified message that makes sense of both miracle and passion as interwoven strands of Jesus' mission.[28]

Pre- and post-Easter Christologies

A second vulnerability of the current view, in my estimation, stems from the very paradox Wrede attempted to address: if Mark tells this story for the purpose of disclosing Jesus' messianic identity, why does Jesus emerge as an enigmatic figure who often evades efforts to identify him – and even silences those who recognize his Christological status (e.g. Mk. 1:34; 3:11)? Even as he conceals his own identity, moreover, Mark's Jesus does reveal an impulse toward revelation, as he freely proclaims the new age of God's dominion and deliberately demonstrates its powers unleashed in the world. Indeed, a fundamental problem with Wrede's proposed reconstruction is that the emphasis on pre-Easter hiddenness flies in the face of passages Mark includes, such as the command for the healed leper to "show yourself to the priest" (Mk. 1:44) and Jesus' parabolic instruction to show forth God's kingdom (Mk. 4:21–5).[29]

To be sure, Christological innuendo does suggest itself throughout the Markan narrative. In the disciples' inquiry about Jesus' identity after the stilling of the first storm at sea ("Who then is this, that even the wind and the sea obey him?," Mk. 4:41), the reader catches the evangelist's wink in the direction of Jesus' God-like command over natural forces; in conversation with his disciples ("Who do people say that I am?," Mk. 8:27), Jesus takes apparent delight in the street talk about his identity, even as he manifests a desire to set the record straight; and when asked point-blank by the High Priest, "Are you the Χριστός, the son of the Blessed One?" (Mk. 14:61), Jesus delivers a response that is startling and, to his inquisitor, blasphemous: "I am." In each case, the evangelist does seem to presuppose a level of Christological affirmation on the reader's part that lends a twist of irony to the gospel story.

Yet despite these implicit claims about Jesus' messianic identity, we should also note that the second gospel devotes much greater attention

28 The goal is similar to Breytenbach's search for a global theme that unites Mark's compositional efforts; for a discussion of narrative theory underlying this pursuit, see *Nachfolge*, 85–132. His view of the evangelist's "Zukunftsperspektive" seems helpful as far as it goes – clearly there is an eschatological impulse here – but his limited choice of focus texts does not take into full account the role of miraculous deeds within an eschatological framework.

29 Wrede himself acknowledges this tension and explains it by appeal to Mark's redactional approach: the "evangelist has taken over traditional material in which the idea of the secret messiahship was not present" (*Messianic Secret*, 125). This "conservative redactor" view, though, undermines Wrede's own claims about Mark's dogmatic interests.

to the *nature* of Jesus' messiahship than it does to the claim *that* Jesus is the Christ. Indeed, Jesus' recurrent efforts to suppress promulgation of his identity (cf. Mk. 1:34, 44; 3:11–12; 5:43; 7:36; 8:30; 9:9, 30) may reflect not so much a gap between the pre- and post-Easter Christology but, more simply, Jesus' resolute determination to situate his own mission within the context of the "gospel" of God's rule. In this light, the secrecy motif is no longer in tension with Jesus' active dissemination of the good news of God's kingdom.[30] Instead, Jesus' selective silencing can be seen as a calculated strategy, running throughout Mark's gospel, to ensure that Jesus' mission is understood within the framework of God's apocalyptic incursion into the world.

Mark's Christology, and especially Mark's exposition of Jesus' "gospel" context, drives another somewhat evasive feature of the narrative: the frequently unmodified term πίστις. To be sure, Mark's Jesus compels others to "trust" the reliability of his witness to God's kingdom, rather than to "believe that Jesus is the Christ, the Son of God" (cf. Jn. 20:31).[31] From the "faith" exhibited by the paralytic's friends (Mk. 2:1–12), to its debilitating absence in Jesus' hometown (Mk. 6:1–6), to Jesus' instructions to "have faith in God" (Mk. 11:22) as the basis for efficacious prayer, πίστις serves consistently in the second gospel to distinguish between those who become vessels of God's apocalyptic power unleashed on the earth and those who question, deny, or subvert it.[32] Thus, in contrast to the claims of John's gospel, the dividing line in Mark's gospel concerns not the precise affirmation of Jesus' identity (belief that Jesus *is* the Christ) but, rather, a resolute affirmation that, through Jesus, God's dominion is taking hold of the world (trust in the messianic mission he embodies).

[30] One episode that offers a glimpse of this revelatory thrust occurs after Jesus exorcises the Gerasene demoniac (Mk. 5:1–20). Refusing the man's request for discipleship status, Jesus urges him, "Go home to your friends, and announce to them what the Lord has done for you" (Mk. 5:19). When he then proclaims "how much *Jesus* had done for him" (Mk. 5:20), thus interpreting Jesus' command "expansively but not wrongly" (Joel Marcus, *Mark 1–8: A New Translation with Introduction and Commentary*, AB 27 [Garden City, NY: Doubleday, 2000], 346, against Wrede, *Messianic Secret*, 140–1), the man bears witness to the nature of Jesus' messianic mission, which entails God's decisive victory even over Legion.

[31] In his monograph *Faith as a Theme in Mark's Narrative*, SNTSMS 64 (New York: Cambridge University Press, 1989), Christopher D. Marshall concludes his excursus on the terms "faith in" and "belief that" with the following observation: "For Mark, faith is rooted in belief (or, better, in insight into God's presence in Jesus) and fructifies in trusting reliance upon him" (56). In my estimation, Marshall's parenthetical formulation preserves the broader horizon of faith reflected in Mark's gospel, where faith is never explicitly described as faith "in Jesus."

[32] This apocalyptic rift can be seen clearly in Mk. 4:11–12, where Jesus contrasts his hearers (ὑμῖν) with those outside (τοῖς ἔξω). On this, see below, chapter 4, as well as Joel Marcus, "Mark 4:10–12 and Marcan Epistemology," *JBL* 103 (1984): 557–74.

All of these observations lead us to maintain that the evangelist's portrait of Jesus' messiahship has less to do with Christological status than with Christological mission, as Mark emphasizes Jesus' role within the world-altering schema of God's coming kingdom. To the extent that we recognize that more expansive horizon, we can more accurately assess several apparent contradictions in Mark's narrative. As I shall discuss in greater detail in chapter 2, Jesus' opening proclamation identifies as the content of the "gospel of God" that "the time has been fulfilled, and the kingdom of God has drawn near" (Mk. 1:15). Later, in his parabolic teaching found in Mk. 4:1–34, Mark's Jesus reminds his disciples that to them has been given the μυστήριον . . . τῆς βασιλείας τοῦ θεοῦ (Mk. 4:11), a mystery which certainly carries implications for understanding Jesus as its herald but which points to God's encroaching dominion. Even in the key discipleship instruction of Mk. 8:35, Jesus exhorts those who would follow him to lose their lives "for my sake and for the sake of the gospel," a distinction which at least begs a measure of caution in assuming a strict equation between the two.

By establishing Jesus' messiahship in terms of the broader "gospel" context, Mark provides an important framework within which to understand Jesus' Christological purpose, and it is a framework that encompasses both Jesus' deeds of power and his suffering messiahship. For, once we begin to affirm the interpretive importance of Isaianic "gospel" language (see, e.g., Isa. 40:9; 41:27; 52:7), we begin to understand Mark's Christological portrait of Jesus as the paradigmatic "servant" through whom God's rule upon the earth gains disclosure. Against this backdrop, Jesus' mission is defined by the dawning rule of God, characterized not precisely by his identity as the Christ but through his Christological demonstration of God's power at work to reclaim the world from a present evil age.

Jesus and the disciples

Finally, the two weaknesses I have named to this point – a rather dismissive approach to the gospel's first half and an overemphasis on Jesus' identity *per se* – combine to expose a third weakness that goes to the heart of this study: the tendency to forge a sharp distinction between the disciples and Jesus.[33] As we shall see, the disciples are not flat foils to Jesus but

[33] Expanding Wrede's claim that the disciples' incomprehension "acts as a foil to Jesus' eminence and greatness" (*Messianic Secret*, 106), Mary Ann Tolbert overstates the case when she calls the disciples themselves "constant foils to Jesus' words and actions" (*Sowing the Gospel: Mark's World in Literary-Historical Perspective* [Minneapolis: Fortress Press, 1989], 222).

active, though faltering, participants in the kingdom reality that Jesus both proclaims and enacts.[34] When the present Christological inquiry into Mark's gospel expands beyond issues surrounding Jesus' identity as God's anointed one to consider the wider horizon of his kingdom-of-God mission, the disciples emerge as companions and collaborators in that mission, even if imperfectly so. In other words, by taking seriously the gospel's claims about the high calling of discipleship, we can better assess their undeniable shortcomings.

Without a doubt, the disciples in Mark's gospel prove increasingly incapable of grasping the full ramifications of Jesus' apocalyptic worldview. Especially as the stakes of Jesus' encounter with the "seeming rulers" of the world (Mk. 10:42) rise exponentially, the disciples seem intent on circumventing the pathway through suffering and death that Mark's Jesus so knowingly walks. Yet to focus exclusively on their misapprehension of Jesus' messiahship – and particularly his suffering messiahship – is both to define the disciples' incomprehension too narrowly and to ignore the more positive elements of the gospel's portrait of them.

Notably, within the gospel's first half, the disciples exhibit laudable tendencies.[35] When they appear at the outset of Jesus' ministry, they respond faithfully to his summons to discipleship (Mk. 1:16–20). Atop a mountain in Galilee, Jesus formally establishes the Twelve and commissions them for significant work, work that mimics his own activity of kingdom proclamation in word and deed (Mk. 3:13–19). Indeed, at the precise point where Jesus' powers are compromised, Mark recounts the apostles' missionary success achieved in his absence (Mk. 6:7–13). In each case, Jesus' followers have yet to ponder, let alone grasp, the full implications of Jesus' messiahship; what they have been given is the "mystery of the kingdom of God" (Mk. 4:11). Entrusted with the "good news" of God's dominion, they appear to respond faithfully to their calling, at least in some instances. Moreover, their faltering gains momentum *prior* to Jesus' teachings about the necessity of his impending suffering (see Mk. 6:52; 8:17–21). Thus to infer that their later failings derive from their deficient understanding of Jesus' suffering messiahship either leaves out of account these earlier instances of success and failure or views them as merely provisional. Only by casting Jesus' Christological mission within the context of God's coming reign can we make sense of such a complex

[34] Whitney Taylor Shiner rightly notes that "Jesus continues with his progressive commissioning of the disciples in spite of their incomprehension" (*Follow Me! Disciples in Markan Rhetoric*, SBLDS 145 [Atlanta: Scholars Press, 1995], 200).

[35] Marshall has recognized that "they are given the same essential message and the same sphere of action that Jesus adopts at the beginning" (*Faith*, 40).

depiction of these followers who readily affirm and disclose that reign in some instances and fail to lay claim to it in others.

In sum, these three vulnerabilities reflect artificial dichotomies that interpreters have imposed upon the text of Mark. By severing the gospel's first half from its second, we relegate Mk. 1:1–8:21 to a subordinate role rather than viewing it as Mark's effort to establish the platform of apocalyptic showdown that culminates in the ensuing passion material. By assuming that Mark's gospel primarily intends to disclose the fact that Jesus *is* the suffering messiah, we crop out of that Christological portrait the broader landscape of God's apocalyptic dominion which frames Jesus' identity and thus lends coherence to his powerful engagement with "the powers" in miracle and in death. And, most pressing for this study of discipleship in Mark, by forging a sharp divide between an obedient Jesus and his "fallible followers," we overlook the more nuanced, even pastoral, appeal the evangelist makes through this gospel tale. Ultimately, these fissures call into question the very possibility of detecting a coherent claim that might hold together the gospel's two halves, its reports of glory and suffering, and its complex portrait of discipleship as both faithful and fumbling.

A way forward

Proposal

In response to this set of interrelated weaknesses, this study proposes to chart a new course forward in the study of Markan discipleship. Rather than beginning the investigation with the question of their failures, I shall consider six passages in the gospel's first half, where the disciples respond to an initial call-to-follow and achieve some measure of success in their role. The view here is that the unfolding narrative itself contains indispensable – though often overlooked – clues about the nature of discipleship in its intended form. Indeed, a close exposition of those episodes that sketch Jesus' relationship to his followers from the outset of the story in turn provides the basis for an assessment of their increasing ineptitude.[36] In the end, the cumulative findings of the following study

[36] This approach stands in contrast to the approach of Ernest Best, who maintains that, "in thought if not in history, a consideration of the disciple's attitude to the world properly follows a consideration of his attitude to the cross" (*Following Jesus*, 164). The view here is just the opposite: to appreciate the role of the cross in Mark's version of Jesus' paradigmatic path, we must first take full account of the material Mark presents as foundational for the ensuing passion emphasis.

will lead to a synthetic understanding of the gospel's two halves, its interest in Jesus' messiahship and God's rule, and, ultimately, the relationship it establishes between Jesus' mission and that of his disciples, both in the story and in Mark's community.

Working assumptions

(1) Mark's construal of "gospel" can best be understood in terms of Jewish hopes for God's apocalyptic rectification of the world, hopes engendered especially by Isaianic prophecy concerning God's coming kingdom and developed throughout Jewish literature. As Mary Ann Beavis writes, "Mark's Gospel is an apocalyptic work, concerned with the kingdom of God, the fulfilment of the scriptures, and the parousia of the son of man."[37] In this respect, the following exegetical enterprise proceeds on terrain plowed fruitfully in recent work by Joel Marcus[38] and Rikki Watts.[39] Though their work proceeds along different lines – Marcus emphasizes Mark's apocalyptic interpretation of Isaianic hopes, while Watts suggests a more typological reading of Mark's gospel – both scholars have argued convincingly that Israel's prophetic expectation for God's rule on the earth permeates the language of Mark's story from beginning to end.[40]

Several key features can be detected within the overarching schema of God's coming kingdom. First, the incursion of God's reign entails a *cosmic apocalyptic showdown* between the opposing forces that animate human existence. The dynamics of conflict evident to some degree in Isaianic prophecy (see, e.g., Isa. 51:13; 53:7) only gained intensity over time, as can be seen in later Jewish apocalyptic writing such as the Qumran War Scroll (e.g. 1QM 1:1–7). As Watts observes, there was a "growing association in the intertestamental period of demons with idols where the

[37] Beavis, *Mark's Audience*, 170. Though differing in their interpretive emphases and methods, a variety of Markan scholars join Beavis in this view of an apocalyptic gospel; representative examples include Willi Marxsen, *Mark the Evangelist: Studies on the Redaction History of the Gospel*, trans. James Boyce, Donald Juel, and William Poehlmann (Nashville: Abingdon Press, 1969); Kelber, *Kingdom*; Adela Yarbro Collins, *The Beginning of the Gospel: Probings of Mark in Context* (Minneapolis: Fortress, 1992); Marcus, *Way*; also *Mark 1–8*; and Howard Clark Kee, *Community of the New Age: Studies in Mark's Gospel* (Philadelphia: Westminster Press, 1977).

[38] In *The Way of the Lord*, Marcus examines the second evangelist's Christological exegesis of the Isaianic Jewish tradition as a backdrop for understanding Mark. His views are carried forward in his commentary on Mark's gospel.

[39] Watts, *Isaiah's New Exodus, passim.*

[40] Richard Schneck has also undertaken a study of Mark's thematic and linguistic ties with Isaiah in his monograph, *Isaiah in the Gospel of Mark, I–VIII*, BIBAL Dissertation Series 1 (Vallejo, CA: BIBAL Press, 1994).

former are progressively understood as the reality behind the latter."[41] Within Mark's gospel, both the presence of demons and the very cross itself can be seen as signs of the present evil age, which is being thwarted by the power of God unleashed by Jesus, as well as by others in his name. As we shall see, Mark recounts the story of Jesus' life and death as the "binding of the strong man" (Mk. 3:27) – the decisive subduing of the adversarial powers whose grip on the world is being loosened.[42]

Secondly, this imminent kingdom of God constitutes a radical *reversal of power*, which Jesus as messianic agent graphically demonstrates in life and death. On the one hand, Mark reports the restoring of "power to the faint" (Isa. 40:29) in a host of healing stories (e.g. Mk. 1:29–31; 2:1–12; 5:21–43), as well as abundant provision for those "without money" (Isa. 55:1; cf. Mk. 6:34–44). On the other hand, in line with the Isaianic Suffering Servant (Isa. 52:13–53:12), Jesus suffers apparent defeat at the hands of an executioner, yet that "defeat" occurs at the very instant that God's power slits the temple veil (Mk. 15:38) and death only prevails until "very early on the first day of the week" (Mk. 16:2). Along the way, the very nature of Jesus' power, as well as the power he imparts to others, derives not from self-promotion but from self-sacrifice, from a disposition to serve rather than to be served (see Mk. 9:35; 10:42–5).

Thirdly, to be found within the sphere of God's dominion entails not simply the passive affirmation of either God's kingship or Jesus' messiahship but the *vital, collective witness* to God's triumph. As in the case of the Danielic Son of Man,[43] Jesus serves as the preeminent vice regent of God's apocalyptic dominion (Dan. 7:14); yet just as Daniel foresees the extension of that dominion to the "holy ones of the Most High" (see Dan. 7:18, 27), so too does Jesus gather around himself an elect community in which God's rule is to be manifest.[44] As they trust in the "gospel" of God's approaching dominion, these followers prepare the "way of the Lord."

[41] Watts, *Isaiah's New Exodus*, 157, who cites the LXX of both Ps. 95:5 and Isa. 65:3, 11, texts which apply the term δαιμόνια to foreign gods.

[42] In his discussion of Jesus' expulsion of Legion (Mk. 5:1–20), Gerd Theissen points out that, in Jesus' (and Mark's) milieu, the "presence of a foreign political power was always the presence of a threatening numinous power, a pollution of the land," and he suggests that the epithet "Holy One of God" serves as an allusion to the "messianic task of freeing the land from all uncleanness and restoring its holiness" – a task assigned, for instance, in *Pss. Sol.* 17:45 (*The Miracle Stories of the Early Christian Tradition*, trans. Francis McDonagh, ed. John Riches, SNTW [Philadelphia: Fortress Press, 1983], 255–6).

[43] See below, chapter 3, for a discussion of this Danielic backdrop for Mark's understanding of Jesus' relationship to his followers.

[44] In a similar fashion, Marcus detects a link between individual and communities in the Righteous Sufferer psalms as well as the QL (see 1QH 2:8–9, 20–30) (*Way*, 184–5).

Fourthly, ultimately God will bring about the full disclosure (or apocalypse) of God's rule, which is *fully assured if not yet fully in view*. Only in the context of a guaranteed apocalyptic outcome does the provisional reality of continued resistance, portrayed vividly in Mark's narrative, lose its force. Only in light of the persistent hope for God's decisive victory does Mark's Jesus engage others in the apocalyptic drama at hand. While God's dominion remains completely veiled to some and barely discernible to others, the outcome of God's coming rule has been, in Mark's view, decisively secured.

(2) A second assumption of this work proceeds from the first: Mark's depiction of discipleship is rooted in this apocalyptic soil, as the earliest followers assume the role of the elect community called to trust the hopeful promise of God's coming rule.[45] If Jesus serves as the focal point and decisive spokesperson for that kingdom, he purposefully enlists those who would follow him in its proclamation through both word and deed. Thus the sharp distinction between Jesus and his disciples that has prevailed in the view of many Markan scholars should be abandoned in favor of a more mimetic understanding of their calling (see Mk. 8:35; 9:35).

The view of an elect community is central to Israel's self-understanding as God's chosen people; frequently in Jewish scriptures the individual merges with the collective. That the Danielic Son of Man is an individual figure with collective dimensions provides an important template for our understanding of Jesus' relationship to his community, both within the gospel and within Mark's community. Interpreters of the second gospel who forge a divide between the faithful figure of Jesus and the flawed community gathered around him have failed to recognize that, at least by design, Jesus' disciples are called to emulate his own messianic agenda.

True, in Mark's rendering, the disciples are often an obdurate group. Yet their failures derive not simply from their mistaken perception of Jesus' identity, but from their inconsistent practice of exemplifying the kingdom reality he proclaims. Fallible as they can be in the narrative, the Markan disciples embody the elect community gathered to follow and imitate Jesus' apocalyptic showdown in ways that vividly demonstrate the "binding of the strong man" (including wonder-working), thus ushering in a way of suffering inherent in any conflict with the powers that be (the way of the cross).

(3) As a result, I maintain that the portrait of Jesus' (and the disciples') mission in the first half of Mark's gospel serves a complementary rather

[45] This claim can be taken to the extreme, as in the case of Kee's view of the Markan community as a band of charismatic apocalyptic preachers (*Community*, 87–97); his is a mirror reading that offers a clearer image than the original image itself yields.

than a subordinate role to that of the second half. Read in an integrated and synthetic manner, the first half's emphasis on wonder-working relates to the second half's emphasis on the way of the cross as component parts of the same kingdom reality: the Markan "good news" of God's ultimate dominion.[46] Further, closer scrutiny of the first six chapters detects key dynamics within the wonder-working ministry that link it closely to the way of the cross. In both phases, the elect enact a radical assault on cosmic forces of evil (evident, for instance, in demon-possession, illness, hunger, misappropriated religious and political power, and natural forces), and they mount their assault by the power that comes from self-giving rather than self-preservation.[47] Ultimately, just as the healings and nature miracles demonstrate that God's priorities prevail, so too the empty tomb proclaims that the way of suffering, and even death, is not the last word in this "gospel."

(4) Because Mark's "gospel" signifies the larger reality of God's kingdom come, its Christological claims carry an urgent ecclesiological calling originally addressed to Mark's own community.[48] In this work, Mark interprets the ministry and destiny of Jesus for post-resurrection followers who continue the disciples' work in the "meantime" between Jesus' earthly presence and the full disclosure of God's sway over the world. In Mark's community, the present "disciples" are not meant to wait idly for Christ's impending return; they are meant to set out from the vindication of the empty tomb, following the one who continues to "go before" them and living the kingdom reality that Jesus' resurrection ultimately proclaims: life out of death. Thus the wider implications of Mark's Christological claims ("Truly, this man is the Son of God," Mk. 15:39) shed important light on Mark's portrait of discipleship, which sounds a clarion call for the community's collective demonstration of the kingdom reality Jesus has inaugurated.

[46] In her discussion of the second gospel as an apocalyptic history, Collins offers a helpful summary of what Mark accomplished: "The result was that the various insights into the 'presence of God in Jesus' were incorporated into a vision of the significance of God's activity in Jesus for history and for the world" (*Beginning of the Gospel*, 37). "God's activity in Jesus" thus encompasses traditions of his miraculous powers as well as his destiny of suffering.

[47] This impulse is admittedly more evident in some "miracles" than in others, but it does appear: to wit, Mk. 2:1–12, where the paralytic's companions go to great lengths not for their own maladies to be addressed, but on behalf of another; Mk. 5:30, which reports that Jesus' power "had gone out" from him; and Mk. 6:37, where Jesus issues a pointed command for the disciples to provide food for the masses from their own resources.

[48] This claim is not new; as discussed briefly above, a wide range of interpreters believe that Mark addresses his contemporaries through his portrait of the disciples. The present study attempts to expand earlier findings to take into account the gospel's positive assessment of the disciples' active role in Jesus' mission.

Method

This study intends to be primarily exegetical in nature, organized around a set of passages that feature the disciples as prominent players in the gospel drama. Along the way, various exegetical tools and strategies will be deployed in order to elucidate the text at hand. In general terms, the method will proceed along the following lines:

(1) Final form as exegetical starting point: careful exegesis begins with an analysis of the text as we have it, noting attentively its own structure and intratextual linguistic relationships. At this initial stage of close reading, the tactics of narrative criticism lead to careful detection of the second gospel's language and imagery.[49] In this study, Mark's gospel constitutes not primarily a haphazard collection of traditional material but a holistic literary entity with a voice of its own[50] – a voice initially articulating the view of the second evangelist (thus questions of authorial intent retain significance) but a voice that has found new expression in changing places and times (and thus is not exhausted by authorial intent).

(2) Text as interpretation of tradition: exegetical interest in the text's final form by no means precludes the investigation of background material that has helped to shape the gospel as we have it today.[51] Indeed, close attention to the text itself *requires* that we probe the context within

[49] This approach is in evidence in David Rhoads and Donald Michie, *Mark as Story: An Introduction to the Narrative of a Gospel* (Philadelphia: Fortress Press, 1982). To admit the deficiencies of their exclusively narrative approach does not require that we jettison an appreciation for Mark's final form as the *starting point* of the present investigation. For a contextual discussion of narrative criticism as one sub-discipline within the broader designation of "literary criticism" – especially as it arises out of "profound disgruntlement with the hegemony of historial criticism" (7) – see Stephen D. Moore, *Literary Criticism and the Gospels: The Theoretical Challenge* (New Haven: Yale University Press, 1989). Also reflecting this "profound disgruntlement" is Hans W. Frei, *The Eclipse of Biblical Narrative: A Study in Eighteenth and Nineteenth Century Hermeneutics* (New Haven: Yale University Press, 1993; orig. 1974).

[50] Interestingly, Frank Kermode also examines the final form but warns against detecting a coherent unity in the text, looking with disdain upon the interpretive impulse to explain problematic texts by imagining "something *behind* it rather different from what we have in front of us" (*The Genesis of Secrecy: On the Interpretation of Narrative* [Cambridge, MA: Harvard University Press, 1979], 79). Sometimes, though, it is the reading *behind* the text that introduces more difficulties than are present in the final form itself.

[51] As those who labor in the fields of text criticism would readily point out, this is an oversimplified way of speaking of "the" Markan text, which does not, precisely speaking, actually exist. My intent here is not to diminish the importance of text criticism but, rather, in large measure to take for granted the immense contribution of such works as Bruce M. Metzger, *A Textual Commentary on the Greek New Testament: A Companion Volume to the United Bible Societies' Greek New Testament*, 3rd edn. (London, New York: United Bible Societies, 1971). I shall consider text-critical issues as they arise in and impinge upon the exegetical enterprise, as is the case already in Mk. 1:1 (see below, 35 n. 13).

which it was written. Since Mark primarily represents a hermeneutical activity, the interpretation found in this study depends on a foundational understanding of the literary, theological, and historical contexts in which Mark wrote.

Mark's interpretive storytelling involves his interaction with at least two layers of tradition, and I shall attempt to investigate both layers in this study of the Markan text. As the first written gospel,[52] Mark inherited Jesus-tradition material, which he reshaped, even as he transmitted it. On this level, questions of form- and redaction-criticism come into play, as I attempt to detect Mark's editorial fingerprints in the narrative choices reflected in the gospel.

On another level, this creation of a "gospel" story also proceeds from the evangelist's dynamic interaction with first-century Jewish thought.[53] Obviously, our most accessible source for this line of investigation is Jewish scripture, along with intertestamental writings such as the Qumran literature and various apocryphal and pseudepigraphical works. Because of the difficulties associated with dating its underlying traditions, rabbinical literature will generally be cited only where it confirms a growing interpretive tradition. Taken together, these sources provide an important treasury of witnesses to topics that were on the mind of our evangelist, such as the coming kingdom of God and related expectations surrounding God's coming messiah(s). In essence, we may deem Mark's gospel an exegetical enterprise of its own,[54] as the evangelist interprets traditions concerning the life and death of Jesus in light of both biblical and extrabiblical texts.

(3) Text as interpreted tradition: not only has the text interpreted prior tradition, but it has also become the object of interpretation from earliest days (and even earliest scribal activities). Thus we enhance our understanding of Mark's gospel through an account of its meaning as "negotiated" through the later centuries and in particular times and places. As part of its exegetical enterprise, this study will take note of the twists and turns in the history of Markan interpretation and will engage prior views

[52] This view is widely held despite recent attempts to revive the Griesbach hypothesis of Matthean priority (see, e.g., William R. Farmer, *The Synoptic Problem: A Critical Analysis* [Mercer, GA: Mercer University Press, 1981; orig. 1964]; cf. Christopher M. Tuckett, *The Revival of the Griesbach Hypothesis: An Analysis and Appraisal*, SNTSMS 44 [Cambridge: Cambridge University Press, 1983]).

[53] For a thorough rehearsal of key findings with respect to Mark's use of OT scripture, see Watts, *Isaiah's New Exodus*, 9–28; also, more succinctly, Marcus, *Way*, 2–5.

[54] On the term "inner biblical exegesis" as it applies to the Hebrew Bible, see Michael Fishbane, *The Garments of Torah: Essays in Biblical Hermeneutics* (Bloomington, IN: Indiana University Press, 1989), ch. 1.

as conversation partners. The point is not to control the exegesis through prior interpretation but to appreciate, and interact with, the interpretation of Mark in ever-changing times and places.[55]

(4) Intelligible unity of the text: such an array of critical approaches would be of little use if they did not work together to illuminate the Markan text as an intelligible unity. Only to the extent that they make more, rather than less, sense out of the whole gospel will this eclectic set of exegetical questions bear the intended fruit. So the aim here is not to provide a comprehensive synthesis of competing methodologies applied to the first half of Mark; rather, it is to engage in dialogue with the text, the traditions it interprets, and its later interpreters, all in a concerted effort to draw the claims of the second gospel – and specifically its treatment of Jesus' disciples – into sharper focus, that we might "see clearly" (Mk. 8:25).

Interpretive payoff

(1) In taking primary clues from the text, this study avoids interpretive dependence on precise historical reconstruction that finally can be neither confirmed nor denied. To be sure, historical probing of the gospel's provenance as well as its Jewish and Greco-Roman literary setting sheds important light on the evangelist's hermeneutical aims. Less helpful are elaborate historical proposals that require a more complex reading than the text itself commends. For instance, while Wrede and others have explained the "messianic secret" motif by appeal to the dogmatic interests of the Markan community, Jesus' injunctions to silence make sense in their narrative context if Mark's message is not, precisely speaking, about Jesus' messianic identity. Similarly, in his eucharistic reading of the feeding of the five thousand as well as the oblique reference to "the loaves" in Mk. 6:52, Quesnell interprets these suggestive Markan texts with reference to early Christian practices that are not clearly evinced in the passages themselves.[56] By leaving aside the assumption that Mark's gospel aims to advance the claim *that* Jesus is the Christ, we open the possibility of reading the text as a window into the Markan community's

[55] Thus I would not go so far as to call pre-critical exegesis "superior" (see David C. Steinmetz, "The Superiority of Pre-critical Exegesis," *Theology Today* 37 [1980]: 27–38), since even such language belies an interpretive hegemony uncharacteristic of ancient exegetes. Still, Steinmetz's insistence that modern readers have much to learn from our exegetical forebears is correct; we should, and I shall, draw them into the interpretive conversation.

[56] See Quentin Quesnell, *The Mind of Mark: Interpretation and Method Through the Exegesis of Mark 6,52* (Rome: Pontifical Biblical Institute, 1969).

view of Jesus' Christological mission, rather than relying on elaborate presuppositions about the Markan community's dogmatic views to determine our reading of the Markan text.

(2) Externally, this study's chosen set of exegetical lenses makes room in the discussion for both Jesus' and Mark's Jewish apocalyptic worldview and affirms in large measure the continuity between prior hermeneutical traditions (both biblical and extrabiblical) and the mission and purpose of Jesus. To view Jesus' proclamation of God's kingdom as rooted in the increasingly apocalyptic perspective of certain streams of Jewish thought takes seriously the progress of scholarship in this field over the last century.[57] Even Mark's Christological affirmation of Jesus' status can be most fully understood only in light of the earlier traditions' witness about the nature of his mission within Jewish apocalyptic thought and its implications for the faithful elect.

(3) Internally, our understanding of the entire second gospel can be enhanced by eclipsing the dichotomies identified above. Indeed, the overarching claim of God's coming kingdom lends striking unity to the gospel's relationship between Christology and discipleship from beginning to end: in both his earthly mission and in his path of suffering, Jesus calls others to carry forward his demonstration of God's dominion. And though the gospel features an awkward tension between faithful and faithless following, Mark consistently affirms that, despite dogged opposition from within and without, God's eschatological triumph will bring life out of death. Indeed, only when the way of suffering is viewed as a constituent part of a more comprehensive whole can we read Mark's gospel not as tragedy but as victory, a victory that depends finally on God's radically transforming power.

(4) Finally, this study both acknowledges and joins an ongoing hermeneutical conversation. On the one hand, the approach here respects the interpretive tradition with its decidedly Christological lens; on the other hand, it examines questions both historical and literary that shape our understanding of that Christology. By noticing the ways in which Mark's account of the "gospel of Jesus Christ" appropriates and reshapes traditions at his disposal, we can better detect how the evangelist formulated a gospel addressed to a historically conditioned time and place. And

[57] For helpful discussions about first-century Jewish thought as definitive for understanding Jesus and his message, see, e.g., E. P. Sanders, *Jesus and Judaism* (Philadelphia: Fortress Press, 1985); Geza Vermes, *Jesus the Jew: A Historian's Reading of the Gospels* (Philadelphia: Fortress Press, 1981); John P. Meier, *A Marginal Jew: Rethinking the Historical Jesus*, 3 vols. (Garden City, NY: Doubleday, 1991–2001); Dale C. Allison, *Jesus of Nazareth: Millenarian Prophet* (Minneapolis, MN: Fortress Press, 1998).

in the gospel's own interpretive moves, we find evidence of the nature and purpose of that gospel that can be reaffirmed (and reinterpreted) for the believing community today.

Outline

This text-based study will investigate the topic of discipleship as depicted from the outset of Mark's gospel up to the narrative moment when the evangelist first ascribes explicit incomprehension to the disciples (Mk. 6:52). As we shall see, the intended pattern of discipleship established early in the gospel provides a vital framework for the narrative's unfolding account of the relationship between Jesus and his disciples. By combining the followers' call to be in Jesus' *presence* and with the expectation that they will *practice* the demonstration of God's coming kingdom, the evangelist sets the terms for understanding the gospel's account of the disciples' mounting incomprehension. Together, the six episodes of discipleship that constitute the exegetical focus of this work provide a cumulative portrait of successes and failures, all of which can be traced to the vital relationship that Mark's Jesus forges with his companions.

The first major section of this study – Part II: Patterns of discipleship – examines the relationship that Mark's Jesus establishes with those who "come after" him. Chapter 2 examines Jesus' initial call to discipleship, which is found in Mk. 1:16–20. Following immediately on the heels of Jesus' programmatic proclamation of God's coming kingdom (Mk. 1:14–15), this cryptic interchange between Jesus and four fishers establishes their vital role in Jesus' "gospel of God" mission. In terms of context, I shall consider both the placement of this story within the Markan narrative and the history-of-religions background of Jesus' "gospel" message; both perspectives sharpen our awareness of the eschatological community that Jesus assembles in preparation for God's fully disclosed rule upon the earth. Moreover, the call passage deftly balances Jesus' summons to "follow me" with his promise to (re)create these four characters as "fishers of humans." That is, from the outset, their loyalty to Jesus entails not just acquiescence to his leadership but also active engagement in his own mission.

Chapter 3 examines the mountaintop commissioning of the Twelve, found in Mk. 3:13–19. On the one hand, the encounter preserves the same core components of what it means to be involved with Jesus, as he calls his followers "to be with him" and "to be sent out." Yet the rhetorical weight of the passage lends due emphasis to the apostolic aspects of the disciples' mission, as Jesus elaborates in great detail the purpose and the authority that characterize his sending out of his followers. Like Jesus, their mission will entail both proclamation (κηρύσσειν, Mk. 3:14) and deeds of power (ἔχειν ἐξουσίαν ἐκβάλλειν τὰ δαιμόνια, Mk. 3:15). By nature, then, Jesus' authority, which consistently amazes his onlookers, extends to those whom he appoints as his agents in the campaign against the forces of the present evil age. Together, these call and commissioning passages establish clear standards for the nature of faithful discipleship; notably absent from both pericopes is any mention of correct Christological affirmation.

The second major section of this work – Part III: Discipleship in action – explores the disciples' development as practitioners of their calling to both presence and practice. Based on the expectations set forth in Mk. 1:16–20 and 3:13–15, to what extent do Jesus' followers faithfully execute the kingdom-of-God mission for which they have been drafted? Chapter 4 focuses attention on Jesus' special instruction in Mk. 4:1–34 as paradigmatic for what it means to be "with him." Through the parabolic discourse, Mark's Jesus conveys to his disciples the hope that, even in face of prevalent obstacles, God's kingdom will take root and yield fruit. Significantly, Mark conjoins the interpretation of the sower parable and the additional teachings concerning God's kingdom in a manner that encourages the disciples to disseminate the good news of God's rule, trusting the sometimes surprising results to God's sovereign care. Thus even this glimpse of discipleship as presence provides Jesus with a forum for instructing his followers about their active stewardship of God's coming kingdom.

Mark's account of the disciples' missionary journey appears in Mk. 6:7–13 and constitutes the focus of Chapter 5 in this study. Having continued in Jesus' presence through his dramatic disclosure of God's dawning dominion, the disciples are now poised to fulfill the second facet of their calling: to be sent out by him. Mark positions this story so that it follows the report of Jesus' own compromised activity in Nazareth, where he was "not able to do many deeds of power" (Mk. 6:5) due to the lack of faith (ἀπιστία) he found there (Mk. 6:6). Thus the apostles carry forth Jesus' enterprise as designated agents, empowered with "authority over unclean spirits" (Mk. 6:7). In the end, this passage presents the missionary journey as an unqualified success (Mk. 6:12–13); here the disciples have effectively wielded their authority as they have performed the very tasks that have characterized Jesus' mission to this point in the Markan story.

Chapter 6 examines a second passage that portrays discipleship as presence, the story of the miraculous feeding found in Mk. 6:30–44. Once again, though, close attention to the narrative details of this pericope reveals that even to be "with him" entails active involvement in Jesus' own mission. In this story, it is the disciples who diagnose the crowd's physical hunger, the disciples who provide the means for the crowd to be fed, and even the disciples who distribute the loaves. Despite his companions' repeatedly insufficient appraisal of their circumstance, Jesus does not cast them aside or dispense with their perspective; instead he transforms it. In the end, Jesus and the disciples collaborate to supply God's kingdom provision – a provision of eschatological abundance – to those in need. While the disciples appear in this passage as flawed vessels, in the end they are God's vessels, put to effective use nonetheless.

As this work's final exegetical study, chapter 7 considers the outright failure of the disciples in the second sea-crossing story (Mk. 6:45–52). The cumulative claims of the preceding chapters establish a helpful framework for grasping the nature of the disciples' shortcomings. In the first place, the text itself suggests that Jesus intends to "send out" his disciples on a second tour of missionary duty. Just as Jesus has wielded God's kingdom authority over the sea in the first sea-crossing story (Mk. 4:35–41), so here he expects his followers, endowed with his very power, to quell the demonic force they encounter in an adverse wind. When they fail to do so, he offers an epiphanic reminder to prompt the disciples' recollection of the authority Jesus has conferred upon them. In the end, when the disciples defer to and marvel at Jesus' own miraculous abilities, they have misunderstood both the apocalyptic showdown that this windstorm represents and their own part in it.

Once we have followed the contours of the Markan text to discern the disciples' calling as collaborators in Jesus' gospel witness to God's coming rule, their increasing failures in the second gospel can be seen in a new light. This study's concluding chapter considers the broader implications of the findings as they apply to the landscape of Mark's gospel. With respect to the motif of incomprehension, I find that to assess the disciples' grasp of Jesus' identity in and of itself leaves out of account much of the Markan narrative which deliberately skirts that very issue; only when we expand the Christological inquiry to consider the nature and scope of Jesus' messianic mission can we begin to make sense of the disciples' failure to grasp it.

On the other hand, once we construe Mark's "gospel" as the apocalyptic history of God's coming kingdom, we have identified a theme which lends an interpretive unity to the gospel's two halves, since both deeds of power and the plight of suffering represent a frontal assault on the "seeming powers" that must be unseated for God's rule ultimately to take hold of the world. And finally, this apocalyptic lens makes sense of Mark's message to his own community, situated in close proximity to the tumult surrounding the Jewish War, as he seeks to remind his hearers both of the empowering presence of Jesus and of their resulting call to demonstrate as vividly as he has the final victory of God.

In sum, the final stage of this study suggests a reconsideration of the gospel's two halves and detects between them a more consistent and integrated set of claims than is often maintained. The consistent reality of the second gospel is the power of God's coming kingdom, expressed through miracle and cross. The consistent dynamic that links the two halves concerns self-giving for the sake of others. The consistent calling of discipleship entails active participation rather than bystander status (not consumer but provider of gospel). Yet, despite this urgent summons, the gospel also offers the consistent hope that God's coming reign will not be finally thwarted by human failure; it is, after all, *God's* victory (Mk. 16:7).

PART II

Patterns of discipleship

2

THE CALLING OF THE FISHERS IN MARK 1:16–20

Introduction

Perhaps because of the explicit and weighty discipleship instructions affixed to its three passion predictions, the second gospel's central section (Mk. 8:27–10:45) has often been deemed the appropriate starting point for grasping Mark's view of what it means to follow Jesus.[1] From this widely held perspective, Mark's "way of the cross" teachings (Mk. 8:34–9:1; 9:35–7; 10:42–5) provide interpretive keys to the evangelist's claims about the nature and calling of discipleship within his community. In turn, the gospel's defining trait of true discipleship has come to be seen in terms of a follower's willingness to suffer, and even to lose life, for the sake of the gospel (Mk. 8:35), a willingness derived from a correct Christological understanding of Jesus' own passion.

The preceding discussion has examined this approach in detail, assessed its limitations, and proposed a more synthetic reading of Mark's gospel as a whole, as well as Mark's portrait of discipleship in particular. If Mark's theological innovation is to cast the gospel kerygma within a historical framework[2] – if indeed the gospel presents a "passion narrative with extended introduction" – we draw closer to its original thrust by taking seriously that introductory framework. In other words, this study of discipleship in the gospel of Mark begins not with the gospel's central section but instead where Mark begins, that is, with his portrait of discipleship as it appears prior to the cross in both narrative and

[1] Donahue calls this section a "gateway to Mark's major theological concerns" (*The Theology and Setting of Discipleship in the Gospel of Mark* [Milwaukee, WI: Marquette University Press, 1983], 2). See also Best, *Following Jesus: Discipleship in the Gospel of Mark*, JSNTSup 4 (Sheffield: JSOT Press, 1981), 164.

[2] Willi Marxsen, *Mark the Evangelist: Studies on the Redaction History of the Gospel*, trans. James Boyce, Donald Juel, and William Poehlmann (Nashville: Abingdon Press, 1969), 216, asserts that Mark's effort consists in tying together the "two 'strands' of primitive Christian preaching: the Pauline kerygma and the (so-called) synoptic tradition." See also Rudolf Bultmann, *Theology of the New Testament*, 2 vols. (New York: Charles Scribner's Sons, 1951–5), I:86.

history.[3] Thus I affirm, with Tannehill, the function of the gospel's first section: "to establish the role relationships which are basic to the rest of the story."[4]

But what is the nature of those "role relationships," and what light do they shed on the "rest of the story"? These are the questions addressed in Part II as I probe two passages that expose the gospel's intended pattern of discipleship: the call of the fishers in Mk. 1:16–20 and the commissioning of the Twelve in Mk. 3:13–15. Together, these stories combine two discrete but interrelated aspects of the gospel's view of discipleship, which entails both remaining in Jesus' *presence* and participating in the *practice* of his own mission. In turn, this pattern of the relationship that Jesus initially forges with his followers will provide an indispensable benchmark against which the disciples might be assessed at both the narrative level of the story and the historical level of Mark's own community. As we shall see, Mark's readers discover in the unfolding story not just the nature of Jesus' Christological agenda, portrayed in his life and in his death, but also its implicit expectation that his followers will carry that mission forth. Rather than driving a wedge between the naive pre-resurrection viewpoint of the story's characters and the more discerning post-resurrection audience, the second gospel reminds its readers of their enduring ties to Jesus' first followers – and to their intended role in his kingdom-of-God proclamation. In this respect, the gospel's interest in Jesus' Christological identity and mission provides the framework for understanding its decidedly mixed review of Jesus' first disciples.

Narrative context

The gospel's opening call to discipleship (Mk. 1:16–20) will serve as a critical launching point for examining the intended function of "following

[3] To give heed to the story's own twists and turns along the way to Jerusalem also respects what was likely its original function of being read aloud within the Markan community, a claim long advocated by form critics such as Bultmann and Dibelius and carried forward by modern critics such as Beavis (*Mark's Audience: The Literary and Social Setting of Mark 4.11–12*, JSNTSup 33 [Sheffield: Sheffield Academic Press, 1989], 18–20), but more recently challenged by Witherington, who assigns the gospel to the genre of *bios* and claims that "Mark is not meant to be heard, but rather to be taken in through the act of reading" (*The Gospel of Mark: A Socio-Rhetorical Commentary* [Grand Rapids: Eerdmans, 2001], 10–11). Low literacy levels in the first-century Mediterranean world, along with the early Christian community's variegated socio-economic makeup, undermine this position. On the latter view, see Harry Y. Gamble, *Books and Readers in the Early Church: A History of Early Christian Texts* (New Haven: Yale University Press, 1995), 40: "These writings envisioned not individual readers but gathered communities, and through public, liturgical reading they were *heard* by the whole membership of the churches."

[4] Robert C. Tannehill, "The Gospel of Mark as Narrative Christology," *Semeia* 16 (1979): 68.

Jesus" in the second gospel. Yet, as we shall see, Mark's redactional placement and handling of the traditional account clearly relate its claims about discipleship to Jesus' own Christological mission as depicted in Mk. 1:1–15. Only after tracing out the contours of Jesus' identity and purpose as sketched in these opening verses (Mark's Christology) are we positioned to examine the gospel's first glimpse of discipleship, in which Jesus deliberately summons others to join the ranks of his own apocalyptic regime (discipleship).

In several respects, Mk. 1:1–15 sets the stage for understanding not only Jesus' identity as harbinger of a new apocalyptic age, but also his followers' intended role in that in-breaking dawn of God's dominion.[5] For at the very heart of Jesus' Christological purpose lies the hope, and the full expectation, that God's coming rule will become patently evident within the human realm, among those who "repent and trust" in God's sovereignty.

To be sure, this introduction[6] positions Jesus as protagonist of the story; from the gospel's opening line, through his wilderness encounters with John the Baptist and with Satan, and finally in his public debut in Galilee, Jesus emerges as the figure who will dominate the landscape of Mark's gospel. Along the way, the story's initial snapshot of Jesus features titular language that telegraphs Jesus' messianic identity, as Mark designates him as the Christ (Ἰησοῦ Χριστοῦ, Mk. 1:1), the stronger one (ὁ ἰσχυρότερος, Mk. 1:7),[7] and God's beloved son (ὁ υἱός μου ὁ ἀγαπητός, Mk. 1:11).[8]

[5] Kee expresses the relationship in this way: "The christological titles . . . are employed in the Markan tradition to highlight the continuity between Jesus' inaugural role in the redemptive purpose of God . . . and the work in his name that the community has been commissioned to carry forward" (*Community of the New Age: Studies in Mark's Gospel* [Philadelphia: Westminster Press, 1977], 144).

[6] We should not overstate the significance of the different expressions that scholars use to characterize Mark's opening verses, which range from "prologue" (e.g. William L. Lane, *The Gospel According to Mark*, NICNT [Grand Rapids, MI: Eerdmans, 1974], 39; Joel Marcus, *Mark 1–8: A New Translation with Introduction and Commentary*, AB 27 [Garden City, NY: Doubleday, 2000], 137; Rudolf Pesch, *Das Markusevangelium*, HTKNT 2 [Freiburg: Herder, 1976], I:71–2), to "introduction" (e.g. Leander E. Keck, "The Introduction to Mark's Gospel," *NTS* 12 [1965–6]: *passim*, but see 368–9, where he calls it a "prologue" to the entire work; Vincent Taylor, *The Gospel According to Saint Mark*, 2nd edn. [Grand Rapids, MI: Baker, 1981; orig. 1950], 151), to "beginning" (e.g. Joachim Gnilka, *Das Evangelium nach Markus*, 2 vols., EKKNT 2 [Zurich: Benziger, 1978–9], I:39; Eduard Schweizer, *The Good News According to Mark* [Atlanta: John Knox Press, 1970], 28). Despite these discrepancies, commentators generally concur that the gospel's opening sheds important light on the claims of its ensuing narrative.

[7] On the term as a possible messianic epithet, see W. D. Davies and Dale C. Allison, *A Critical and Exegetical Commentary on the Gospel According to Saint Matthew*, 3 vols. (Edinburgh: T. & T. Clark, 1988–97), I:314–15.

[8] The combination of "sonship" and "beloved" status here may reflect Mark's tendency to conflate scriptural allusions, in this case to Psalm 2 and Deutero-Isaiah, respectively

Yet weighty as these claims prove to be for our understanding of Jesus' Christological role, the gospel's introduction deliberately frames Jesus' messiahship within the wider horizon of God's coming eschatological victory. As we shall see, the passage's use of "gospel" language, linked explicitly to Jewish scriptural hopes and confirmed through both the Elijah-like portrait of John and Jesus' initial encounter with Satan, establishes the story of Jesus' life and death firmly within the claim that, in the words of Mark's Jesus, "the dominion of God has drawn near" (Mk. 1:15).[9] In turn, Mark presents his story of Jesus as the advance agent of that encroaching rule who will emerge not as a solitary hero-warrior but as a battalion commander enlisting others in his mission.

An apocalyptic "gospel"

The investigation begins with the term εὐαγγέλιον, which frames Mk. 1:1–15 (vv. 1, 14, 15). Not only does this *inclusio* lend structural support to the passage's introductory thrust,[10] but it also highlights the term's thematic significance for Mark's opening scene.[11] On the one hand, the evangelist both announces the "beginning of the gospel" (ἀρχὴ τοῦ εὐαγγελίου, Mk. 1:1) and reports that Jesus came "preaching the gospel" (κηρύσσων τὸ εὐαγγέλιον, Mk. 1:14); on the other hand, Jesus' own opening proclamation ends with the injunction for his hearers to "trust in the gospel" (πιστεύετε ἐν τῷ εὐαγγελίῳ, Mk. 1:15). Clearly the word plays a defining role for Mark's view of Jesus' ministry, but what dimensions of that mission does the substantive εὐαγγέλιον signify?

The text's first interpretive clue both clarifies and confuses the issue, since two of the word's three occurrences here carry genitive modifiers which seem to make distinctive – perhaps even competing – claims. In

(Joel Marcus, *The Way of the Lord: Christological Exegesis of the Old Testament in the Gospel of Mark* [Louisville: Westminster/John Knox Press, 1992], 54). The somewhat tenuous case for a messianic understanding of either term grows more convincing through their convergence in this phrase (see Rikki Watts, *Isaiah's New Exodus and Mark* [Tübingen: Mohr Siebeck, 1997], 110–14; Marcus, *Way*, 48–79).

[9] All translations of passages found in the gospel of Mark are my own.

[10] Among those who note this *inclusio* are Keck, "Introduction," 359, John Painter, *Mark's Gospel: Worlds in Conflict*, New Testament Readings, ed. John Court (New York: Routledge, 1997), 35, and Witherington, *Mark*, 68. Watts, *Isaiah's New Exodus*, 91–5, provides a helpful summary of positions in the debate about whether Mk. 1:14–15 constitutes the end of the prologue or the beginning of the next unit. He concludes that "the prologue hinges upon verses 14–15" (95), thus detecting in these verses both the consummation of the introduction and the segue to Mark's report of Jesus' Galilean ministry.

[11] Marxsen, *Mark the Evangelist*, 125, maintains that the term reflects Mark's redactional contribution throughout the text, since his is the only gospel to use the absolute εὐαγγέλιον.

Mk. 1:1, the evangelist announces the beginning of the gospel Ἰησοῦ Χριστοῦ ("of Jesus Christ"), a phrase which many commentators throughout the centuries have understood in an objective sense as the gospel concerning Jesus Christ.[12] From this influential perspective, Mark opens with a bold affirmation of the story's strong Christological focus, which is only enhanced by the (probable) scribal addition of the phrase υἱοῦ θεοῦ.[13] A review of internal and external evidence both supports and qualifies this objective reading of the genitive, a reading which leads to the view that for Mark, the "proclaimer has become the proclaimed."[14]

In large measure, the objective sense of the genitive follows from the verse's own narrative context as Mk. 1:1 introduces both the ensuing episode, in which John the Baptist points to Jesus, and the gospel's overarching plotline, which retraces the story of Jesus' life, death, and resurrection. For instance, in John's preaching *about* Jesus as the "stronger one than I (ὁ ἰσχυρότερός μου)" (Mk. 1:7), Gundry locates the "Christocentric nature of John's preaching," which identifies the content of the "beginning of the gospel."[15]

Yet to view the "gospel of Jesus Christ" through the lens of John's deferential treatment of Jesus leaves out of account the evangelist's own – and rather elaborately crafted – interpretive horizon portrayed in the ensuing verses. In the first place, Mk. 1:2 introduces the scriptural landscape within which this gospel is to be understood: "Just as it is written (καθὼς γέγραπται) in Isaiah the prophet . . ." As many interpreters readily admit, the citation formula functions epexegetically to bind what follows – a

[12] Among interpreters who emphasize the objective sense, see, e.g., Taylor, *Saint Mark*, 152, Morna D. Hooker, *A Commentary on the Gospel According to St. Mark*, BNTC 2 (London: A. & C. Black, 1991), 34. Marcus is less emphatic: "the subjective nuance cannot be excluded" (*Mark 1–8*, 147).

[13] See Bart D. Ehrman, "The Text of Mark in the Hands of the Orthodox," *LQ* 5 (1991): 143–56, who bases this conclusion on factors such as the phrase's absence from Sinaiticus (original hand), the unlikelihood of parablepsis at this early point in the text, and the plausibility of a scribal emendation in response to heresies in early Christianity. Cf. T. Alec Burkill, *Mysterious Revelation: An Examination of the Philosophy of St. Mark's Gospel* (Ithaca, NY: Cornell University Press, 1963), 9–10, for a less persuasive defense of the phrase's originality.

[14] The phrase is Bultmann's description of the transformation that has taken place between the life of the historical Jesus and the written gospels (*Theology*, I:33).

[15] Robert Gundry, *Mark: A Commentary on His Apology for the Cross* (Grand Rapids, MI: Eerdmans, 1993), 32. Similarly, Marxsen, *Mark the Evangelist*, 33, maintains that "the Baptist has no significance in himself . . . Rather the statements concerning the Baptist are christological." Aloysius M. Ambrozic, *The Hidden Kingdom: A Redaction-Critical Study of the References to the Kingdom of God in Mark's Gospel* (Washington: Catholic Biblical Association of America, 1972), 19, claims that the "beginning of the gospel" can be specifically identified as John's ministry (against, e.g., Keck, "Introduction," 359, 367, who calls Jesus the "beginning").

conflated array of scriptural texts from Isaiah, Exodus, and Malachi – to the "gospel of Jesus Christ" that has been announced in the work's opening line.[16]

The citation itself has been examined closely in recent scholarship, especially with an eye to Jewish interpretation of its verses. Several critical findings shed important light on our understanding of the "gospel of Jesus Christ" and may be summarized here. First, the attribution of these verses to "Isaiah the prophet" points many interpreters to the context within which the precise Isaianic citation (Isa. 40:3) is located,[17] which serves as "a *locus classicus* for Isaianic salvation" within first-century Jewish thought.[18] Toward the end of this opening oracle, the bearer of "good news" addresses the forlorn holy city as a collective beneficiary of the "gospel" content:

> Get you up to a high mountain, the one "gospeling" Zion (ὁ εὐαγγελιζόμενος Σιων); lift up in strength your voice, the one "gospeling" Jerusalem (ὁ εὐαγγελιζόμενος Ιερουσαλημ). Lift up; do not fear. Say to the cities of Judah behold your God (ἰδοὺ ὁ θεὸς ὑμῶν). (Isa. 40:9)[19]

In this word of exilic prophecy, the announcement of "good news" heralds the arrival of God himself, which in turn precipitates the long-awaited return of God's people to the land by the hand of Yahweh (Isa. 40: 10–11).[20]

In turn, later Jewish interpretation of this announcement of "good news" consistently conveys the hope of God's coming kingdom.[21] The Qumran Community Rule, for instance, speaks of the separation of "holy ones" who will "walk in the desert to open there his path" (1QS 8:11, 13),

16 See, e.g., Watts, *Isaiah's New Exodus*, 55–77; Ambrozic, *Hidden Kingdom*, 18–20; Richard Schneck, *Isaiah in the Gospel of Mark, I–VIII*, BIBAL Dissertation Series 1 (Vallejo, CA: BIBAL Press, 1994), 29–31.

17 See Schneck, *Isaiah*, 42, who calls the citation of Isa. 40:3 a "pointer to the larger section (Isa. 40:1–11) in which the verse was found." Here he supports C. H. Dodd's view of Isa. 40:1–11 as belonging to early Christian *testimonia*, on which see *According to the Scriptures* (London: Fontana, 1965; orig., 1957), 28–9; 84–5.

18 Watts, *Isaiah's New Exodus*, 84.

19 My own rather wooden translation of this LXX passage intends to demonstrate the linguistic ties between Mark and Isaiah.

20 It is in this respect that Peter Stuhlmacher has called the Deutero-Isaianic prophet the "father of apocalyptic" (*Das paulinische Evangelium. Vorgeschichte* [Göttingen: Vandenhoeck & Ruprecht, 1968], I:116–22).

21 See K. R. Snodgrass, "Streams of Tradition Emerging from Isaiah 40:1–5 and Their Adaptation in the New Testament," *JSNT* 8 (1980): 31 and *passim*.

an act based on the interpretation of Isa. 40:3.[22] Similarly, *T. Moses* 10:1–5 announces the appearance of God's kingdom "throughout his whole creation" by claiming that "the high mountains will be made low" (see Isa. 40:4).[23] Other Jewish traditions that carry forward this expectant thrust include *Pss. Sol.* 11 and *Tg. Isaiah* 40:3, which anticipate the eschatological culmination of Israel's salvation and ultimate return from the ends of the earth. Thus Isaiah's "gospel" promise engenders Israel's eschatological longing for "the triumphant march of the holy warrior, Yahweh, leading his people through the wilderness to their true homeland in a mighty demonstration of saving power."[24]

This purposeful depiction of the "gospel of Jesus Christ" within the context of apocalyptic hope makes sense, too, in light of subsequent features of the Markan introduction. For example, even Mark's portrayal of the "one crying out in the wilderness" (Mk. 1:3) describes John's message as "a baptism of repentance for the forgiveness of sins" (κηρύσσων βάπτισμα μετανοίας εἰς ἄφεσιν ἁμαρτιῶν, Mk. 1:4). In other words, if Mark casts John in the prophetic role of the messenger who will "prepare the way" (Mk. 1:2, 3), the initial report of his message concerns not Jesus himself but the call to repentance and forgiveness that is characteristic of prophetic exhortation in preparation for God's coming redemption.[25] Moreover, many have attributed to Mark's redaction the wilderness motif shared by John and Jesus,[26] a motif that apparently has in view "specifically the Deutero-Isaianic . . . hope of eschatological victory in the wilderness."[27] In addition, John's reference to Jesus as the "stronger

[22] Unless otherwise indicated, translations of the QL come from Florentino García Martínez and Eibert J. C. Tigchelaar, eds., *The Dead Sea Scrolls: Study Edition*, 2 vols. (Grand Rapids, MI: Eerdmans, 1997–8).

[23] Translations of pseudepigraphical works come from James H. Charlesworth, ed., *The Old Testament Pseudepigrapha*, 2 vols. (Garden City, NY: Doubleday, 1983, 1985).

[24] Marcus, *Way*, 29. Watts expands the purview by close attention to both Exod. 23:20 and Mal. 3:1 which introduce the "spectre of Yahweh's purging judgement which hangs over Jerusalem's . . . Temple" (*Isaiah's New Exodus*, 90). He notes that the verses had already been combined in some Jewish literature; on this, see Howard Clark Kee, "The Function of Scriptural Quotations and Allusions in Mark 11–16," in *Jesus und Paulus*, ed. E. Earle Ellis and E. Grässer (Göttingen: Vandenhoeck & Ruprecht, 1975), 180ff.

[25] This observation coheres, too, with Marcus's claim that the phrase "way of the Lord" (Mk. 1:3) should be construed in its subjective sense as a reference to "Yahweh's *own* way through the wilderness" (*Way*, 29).

[26] E.g. Marxsen, *Mark the Evangelist*, 35, relying on the work of K. L. Schmidt. The significance of the Exodus wilderness motif for Mark has been developed further by Ulrich Mauser, *Christ in the Wilderness: The Wilderness Theme in the Second Gospel and Its Basis in the Biblical Tradition* (London: SCM Press, 1963). As we have seen, both Marcus and Watts have advanced the view that Mark adumbrates the Isaianic New Exodus.

[27] Marcus, *Way*, 26. See also Watts, *Isaiah's New Exodus*, 90.

one" resonates both with Isaiah's frequent reference to Yahweh's strength (e.g. Isa. 40:11; 42:13) and with contemporary Jewish hope centered on the successor of an Elijah figure.[28] In short, John's encounter with Jesus points toward the "good news" of God's coming dominion that Jesus will authoritatively proclaim.[29]

Further, in Jesus' baptism itself, Mark describes the rending of the heavens, a "common feature of apocalyptic thought,"[30] which graphically conveys the divine penetration of the human realm. Even the voice that designates God's beloved son (Mk. 1:11) aligns Jesus with Israel's king as specially designated leader (Ps. 2:7) whose service is committed exclusively toward Yahweh (Ps. 2:11).[31]

Finally, Jesus' showdown with Satan (Mk. 1:12–13) dramatizes the anticipated combat between God and God's adversaries as the inaugurating event of God's salvation (see *T. Levi* 18:12).[32] Moreover, Mark's succinct account combines narrative details, including the presence of wild animals, angels, and Satan, that resonate with *T. Naph.* 8:4, 6, where "my children" are enjoined to achieve good in the context of the appearance of God's kingly power (*T. Naph.* 8:3).[33] In all these ways, then,

[28] The literature on this topic is vast. For a recent contribution to the discussion, with up-to-date bibliographic information, see Markus Öhler, "The Expectation of Elijah and the Presence of the Kingdom of God," *JBL* 118 (1999): 461–76, who concludes: "since Elijah, the eschatological forerunner of God, had come, the next phase of the apocalyptic schedule had commenced: the coming of the βασιλεία τοῦ θεοῦ" (476).

[29] Marxsen identifies as a "gulf between Mark and his successors" the distance that Matthew and Luke establish between John the Baptist and Jesus. In both cases, John is no longer understood within the "gospel" but instead precedes it (*Mark the Evangelist*, 48–51). Yet, even if Mark's gospel retains close ties between John and Jesus, they still proclaim the gospel sequentially; that is, Jesus begins his public preaching only after John has been "handed over" (Mk. 1:14).

[30] Taylor, *Saint Mark*, 160.

[31] To infer that Mark's Jesus functions as a prototype of God's hope for God's people seems more fitting than the view that he assumes, in an exclusive way, the role of "true" Israel (see, e.g., Watts, *Isaiah's New Exodus*, 112, 119; Witherington, *Mark*, 73; Lane, *Mark*, 47–51), since the latter designation rules out any collective expression of that embodiment by others. Put differently, as the present investigation of discipleship passages in Mark will demonstrate, Jesus is no faithful substitute for errant followers but a servant-leader who points the way for others to follow, even in the wake of their own failures.

[32] Though this battle is by no means universal within Jewish apocalyptic thought, it certainly figures prominently in Mark's account of the coming kingdom. Cf. Keck, who calls this encounter a "power-struggle in which Jesus is victorious" ("Introduction," 361). Yet if it is the "gospel of God" that he proclaims, perhaps the victory is rather God's, achieved through the agency of Jesus.

[33] See Jeffrey B. Gibson, "Jesus' Wilderness Temptation According to Mark," *JSNT* 53 (1994): 21–3, who cites, in addition to *T. Naph.* 8.4, 6, Ps. 91, *T. Iss.* 7.7, *T. Benj.* 5.2. Gibson helpfully underscores the "testing" aspect of this wilderness encounter but neglects its apocalyptic context.

Mark's prologue establishes Jesus' leading role in the drama of God's victory, which he subsequently proclaims in Mk. 1:14–15.[34]

In a similar way, Mark's large-scale narrative about Jesus, extending from his baptism by John through his resurrection, can be called "Christocentric" only insofar as we recognize the story's poignant paradox: if Mark's story is about Jesus, it is about a Jesus who consistently points away from himself and toward "what the Lord has done" (Mk. 5:19).[35] Thus it seems more accurate to speak of the entire gospel content as God's decisive activity "on the earth," as evinced in and through the life of Jesus. In sum, internal evidence certainly links the person and destiny of Jesus, understood in messianic terms, with the content of the "gospel" announced by Mark in 1:1; to define "gospel" solely in terms of Jesus' identity, though, obscures the evangelist's efforts to establish Jesus' messiahship firmly within the apocalyptic hope for God's in-breaking dominion.[36]

Outside the scope of Mark's gospel, the abundant use of the substantive εὐαγγέλιον in early Christian writings indicates to many interpreters that the word refers to the "Apostolic message of salvation in Christ."[37] In this reading, when Mark refers to the "gospel of Jesus Christ," he has in view the redemptive significance of Jesus' life and death for his own community.[38] If the gospel was written around the time of the Jewish War, the Pauline mission had already proclaimed the "gospel" to Jews and Gentiles alike, and the term had apparently come to be closely associated with Jesus himself.[39] So the gospel's post-resurrection setting, the

[34] As Donahue puts it, "Jesus is here portrayed as the eschatological herald of God's rule in history" (*Theology and Setting of Discipleship*, 14).

[35] This irony seems frequently lost on interpreters, to wit, Gundry, *Mark*, 32: "Mark devotes the bulk of his book to Christology rather than to theology . . . [yet] Jesus will not proclaim himself." Witherington identifies Jesus' reticence as a "key historical element from the actual ministry of Jesus" (*Mark*, 54), though he attributes it more to a desire for selective revelation than to Jesus' theocentric focus.

[36] Marcus presents a nicely balanced view: "Mark's composition is not only the good news about Jesus but also the good news that Jesus himself proclaims through Mark" (*Mark 1–8*, 147).

[37] Taylor, *Saint Mark*, 152. Cf. Johannes Weiss, *Jesus' Proclamation of the Kingdom of God*, trans. and ed. R. H. Hiers and D. L. Holland (Philadelphia: Fortress Press, 1971), 29–42.

[38] Robert A. Guelich, *Mark 1–8:26*, WBC 34A (Dallas: Word, 1989), 43, speaks of the evangelist's appropriation of "terminology drawn from the Church's mission situation to describe Jesus' activity in Galilee."

[39] Ibid., 46: "For Mark, Jesus was both the one who proclaimed the good news from God in terms of the coming of God's promised redemptive rule and the one through whom this good news was effected in history." Similarly, Watts, *Isaiah's New Exodus*, 98, claims that, "as Jesus' words and deeds became the content of the verb εὐαγγελίζω, the substantive

argument goes, dictates that the "good news" must be equated with "the person of Jesus, his message and above all his ministry."[40]

Yet, under careful scrutiny, the broader NT witnesses themselves portray an early Christian understanding of "gospel" that again fixes Jesus' role in salvation history firmly within the wider horizon of God's activity upon the earth. A leading case in point is Paul's apparent use of an existing traditional "gospel" affirmation in 1 Cor. 15:3b–5.[41] When Paul specifies the very "gospel that I preached" (1 Cor. 15:1), he intentionally refers not just to the life, death, and resurrection of Jesus, but to the way in which those events represent the *fulfillment of OT prophecy*: "that Christ died for our sins *according to the scriptures*, and that he was buried, and that he arose on the third day *according to the scriptures*" (1 Cor. 15:3b–4).[42]

In a similar vein, Paul begins his letter to the Romans with a traditional "gospel" affirmation that retains the same scriptural context, as he claims to have been "set apart for the gospel of God (εἰς εὐαγγέλιον θεοῦ), which was prepromised through his prophets in holy scriptures" (Rom. 1:1). Even if the next verse modifies the "gospel of God" with the qualifying phrase "concerning his son," for Paul the origin and goal of that "gospel" – including the obedience of faith in all the nations (Rom. 1:5) – is clearly presaged in Israel's prophetic witness.[43] In other words, Paul's reference to the "gospel of God" relates specifically to Christ as he embodies that "gospel," yet Paul consistently appeals to Israel's sacred writings as the literary and conceptual setting which interprets the term.[44]

appears to have become similarly understood." The distinction I intend to forge is between Jesus as an agent of the "gospel" and Jesus as the exclusive content of it.

40 Watts, *Isaiah's New Exodus*, 99, n. 46. This sharply Christological perspective is evident in G. Friedrich, "εὐαγγελίζομαι," in *TDNT* 2 (1964): 707–37, who claims that, if Jesus "realised that He was the Son of God who must die and rise again, then He also realised that He was Himself the content of the message of His disciples" (728).

41 Gordon D. Fee, *The First Epistle to the Corinthians*, NICNT (Grand Rapids, MI: Eerdmans, 1987), 722, notes that "most scholars consider [vv. 3b–5] to be an expression of a very early Christian creed," a claim based on the transmission-of-tradition language in v. 3a as well as the "bare bones" form of the gospel expression.

42 Richard B. Hays, *First Corinthians*, Interpretation (Louisville, KY: John Knox Press, 1997), 255, deems it "highly significant that the story of Jesus' passion and resurrection must be interpreted in light of Scripture."

43 Richard B. Hays, *Echoes of Scripture in the Letters of Paul* (New Haven: Yale University Press, 1989), speaks of Romans as an "intertextual conversation between Paul and the voice of Scripture" (35), implying the kind of dynamic, two-way interaction that militates against Hays' own reading of Rom. 1:2–4 as pointing toward a "christocentric exposition of Scripture" (85) – an expectation that, Hays admits, the "letter to the Romans does not carry through" (ibid.).

44 Stuhlmacher concludes that the early church coined the substantive to cast its understanding of Jesus Christ within the horizon of OT promise (*Das paulinische Evangelium*, I:209–44).

As a result, an inquiry into Mark's use of the word εὐαγγέλιον would be incomplete without a brief discussion of its background in the Jewish scriptures. We should note first of all that the related Hebrew noun בשרה is used in the MT only in a secular sense as a "reward for good news"[45] or as the expression of "good news" associated with deliverance from an enemy.[46] Consistently, though, the root belongs to the lexicon of the battlefield, an observation supported also by the uses of the verb בשר, which heralds both triumph over an opposing military force (e.g. 1 Kgs. 1:42; 1 Sam. 4:17) and, in later prophetic appropriation of that metaphor, God's victorious reign (e.g. Isa. 52:7; 61:1).[47]

The Greek translation of Israel's scriptures yields similar findings. Although the neuter singular substantive never appears in the LXX,[48] its cognate verb εὐαγγελίζω typically portends military victory – victory attributed not just to Israel's military prowess but also to *Yahweh's* triumphant strength in the face of *Yahweh's* adversaries.[49] And as in the Hebrew Bible, the LXX frequently employs εὐαγγέλ- terminology in its depiction of Yahweh as Victorious Warrior, especially in the prophecy of Isaiah.[50] Above I have noted the importance of Deutero-Isaiah's opening oracle for Mark's gospel; here I shall explore only briefly the term's nuance in subsequent passages.

For example, Isa. 52:7 casts in poetic parallel the content of the prophet's "good news":

> How beautiful upon the mountains are the feet of the one
> announcing a message of peace (εὐαγγελιζομένου ἀκοὴν εἰρήνης)
> as one announcing good [news] (ὡς εὐαγγελιζόμενος ἀγαθά):
> I make known your salvation,
> saying, 'Zion, your God reigns' (λέγων Σιων βασιλεύσει σου ὁ θεός).

[45] 2 Sam. 4:10; 18:22. [46] 2 Sam. 18:20, 25, 27; 2 Kgs. 7:9.

[47] See M. Eugene Boring, "Mark 1:1–15 and the Beginning of the Gospel," *Semeia* 52 (1990): 43–81, who translates the term as "good news of victory from the battlefield" (56).

[48] The neuter plural substantive (εὐαγγέλια) does appear in 2 Sam. 4:10, where it conveys news of military victory. The feminine singular εὐαγγελία occurs in 2 Sam. 18:20, 25, 27, and 2 Kgs. 7:9.

[49] The Samuel/Kings narrative employs the verb nine times, most often with reference to battlefield triumph. See, e.g., 2 Sam. 18:31: "Good tidings (εὐαγγελισθήτω) for my lord the king! For the LORD has vindicated you this day, delivering you from the hand of all who rose up against you." Within this particular pericope, the verb appears five times as the translational equivalent of בשר in conjunction with Yahweh's direct intervention on behalf of the Israelite army (2 Sam. 18:19, 20 [2x], 26, 31).

[50] LXX: 40:9 (2x), 52:7 (2x), 60:6, 61:1. The MT also includes the participle מבשר in Isa. 41:27.

In this case, the "good news" encompasses both the (post-exilic) salvation of Zion and the ultimate sovereignty of Zion's God. Notably, the Qumran pesher on this verse (11QMelch 2:15–25) ascribes to the messiah the role of announcing the "good news" that God rules (and thus Belial has been defeated).[51] Further, Isa. 60 expands the purview of the "gospel": the eschatological ingathering will include the "nations" (ἔθνη, Isa. 60:3) as well as "Israel's sons" (οἱ υἱοί σου, Isa. 60:4). Taken together, then, these Isaianic texts articulate an elaborate vision of God's "good news," which entails *promised salvation* by the intervening hand of Yahweh, *Israel's restoration* as the people on whom "the glory of the Lord has risen" (Isa. 60:1), and ultimately the universal *ingathering of the nations* who will in turn proclaim that glory. Significantly, the prophetic "gospel" hopes consistently focus expectation on the universal acclaim of Yahweh's dominion.

On the basis of the foregoing study, we are well positioned to consider again the thrust of Mk. 1:1's designation of the "gospel of Jesus Christ," a designation which, in Mark's time, did not yet indicate a recognized literary genre.[52] Certainly Guelich is correct in his claim that "εὐαγγέλιον in 1:1 refers at least to the content of the literary work that follows."[53] Yet to construe this work as a "gospel" in the generic sense that it has since assumed obfuscates the Markan message, which is primarily about the εὐαγγέλιον signaled in the life and death of Jesus as it inaugurates the coming age of God's reign. In other words, to exhaust our reading of "gospel" content as this Markan story about Jesus, we miss Mark's (and Mark's Jesus') wider horizon for understanding εὐαγγέλιον.

In light of these findings, the genitive construction of Mk. 1:1 can best be understood as the "good news" both personified and heralded by Jesus Christ, a reading that encompasses the phrase's objective ("about Jesus Christ") as well as subjective ("that Jesus Christ enacts") senses.[54] This gospel, as Mark reports it, primarily announces what God is doing to reclaim the world, precisely as Jesus both articulates and dramatizes the claim that "God rules." Thus with respect to the question of Jesus' identity and purpose, Mark's gospel presents Jesus as a "proclaimed proclaimer" – "proclaimed" in that the evangelist identifies him as the designated agent

[51] See David E. Aune, "A Note on Jesus' Messianic Self-Consciousness and 11QMelchizedek," *EvQ* 45 (1973): 163–5.

[52] Schweizer credits the evangelist with the "theological accomplishment" of creating the literary gospel genre, in contrast to the early church's gospel proclamation ("Die theologische Leistung des Markus," *EvT* 19 [1964]: 339).

[53] Guelich, *Mark 1–8:26*, 9.

[54] In this respect, Marxsen seems on target when he claims, "For Mark Jesus is the subject and object of the gospel" (*Mark the Evangelist*, 148).

of God's good news, yet still a "proclaimer" because his own words and deeds consistently point not toward himself but toward the impending reign of God.

To determine that the gospel's opening phrase signals "good news" embodied in the story of Jesus but not exclusively defined by him in turn preserves Mk. 1:1's own rhetorical link with Mk. 1:14–15 mentioned above. Those who assume that Mark has introduced his writing as the "gospel about Jesus Christ" find themselves somewhat puzzled over the summary of Jesus' opening proclamation as the εὐαγγέλιον τοῦ θεου (Mk. 1:14).[55] Contrary to what we might expect, Hooker notes that Mark's "Jesus says nothing at all about himself or his own position."[56] It is *God's* good news to which Jesus points and which Jesus will dramatize throughout the Markan narrative.

Jesus' "gospel" proclamation

Because Mk. 1:14–15 provides a programmatic summary of Jesus' message, interpreters have devoted significant attention to Mark's rather cryptic account of Jesus' emergence on the Galilean preaching circuit.[57] At a minimum, the verses establish the focal point of Jesus' mission, which Mark casts once more within the context of the "gospel of God":

> After John was handed over, Jesus went into Galilee proclaiming the ***gospel of God*** (τὸ εὐαγγέλιον τοῦ θεοῦ) and saying: the season has been fulfilled (πεπλήρωται ὁ καιρός), and the rule of God has approached (ἤγγικεν ἡ βασιλεία τοῦ θεοῦ); Repent and trust in the ***gospel*** (τῷ εὐαγγελίῳ). (Mk. 1:14–15)

Close attention to Mark's account of this proclamation confirms that, for this evangelist, Jesus' "gospel" announcement resonates with its prophetic roots.

55 Guelich warns against a "misplaced emphasis on 1:14 from which 1:1 has been interpreted rather than interpreting 1:14 in terms of 1:1" (*Mark 1–8:26*, 9). Gundry approaches the issue differently, forging quite a distinction between John's Christocentric message and the "theocratic content" of Jesus' preaching (*Mark*, 32).

56 Hooker, *Mark*, 54.

57 Though scholars have debated whether Mk. 1:14–15 belongs to the prologue (Mk. 1: 1–15) or to the ensuing section on Jesus' ministry (beginning with Mk. 1:14), this brief episode functions as a bridge from Mark's introduction of Jesus to the gospel's narrative portrayal of his mission. Despite Guelich's insistence that "1:14–15 does represent a summary of Mark's Gospel, but not as a 'programmatic summary' or an 'opening statement'" (*Mark 1–8:26*, 42), the narrative position of this proclamation at the outset of Jesus' public ministry may well indicate its "programmatic" function (see Matt. 5–7; Lk. 4:16–30).

If Mark describes the content of Jesus' initial preaching enterprise as the "gospel of God," Jesus' words themselves also confirm the above findings, as he first announces the anticipated arrival of God's reign upon the earth[58] and then summons his hearers to participate in that reign. The programmatic function of this pithy proclamation raises the stakes for the present reading of the entire second gospel. The discussion will briefly consider first Jesus' indicative pronouncement of the "gospel of God" and then his imperative call to "turn and trust" in it.

The two clauses that compose Jesus' "gospel" proclamation have raised a host of thorny interpretive issues, particularly with respect to their chronology. Cast in synthetic parallel, the claims that the "time has been fulfilled" and the "rule of God has drawn near" employ perfect-tense verbs πεπλήρωται and ἤγγικεν to indicate both the past and present dimensions of the "good news" Jesus proclaims,[59] while the verbs' subjects, καιρός and βασιλεία τοῦ θεοῦ, introduce temporal futurity as they connote the eschatological day of the Lord. In light of this temporal polyvalence, the precise claims of Jesus' "gospel" proclamation have proven particularly elusive.

With respect to the first clause, Marcus has argued that the "fulfillment of time" should be understood in an extensive,[60] rather than punctiliar,[61] sense, and further, that the term καιρός designates the epoch of Satan's rule, which has been "fulfilled" – or brought to completion – with the advent of Jesus as herald of God's rule.[62] On the first point, Marcus confirms the dominant linear sense of the verb πληρόω but does not directly address the force of the perfect-tense construction. His reading of the clause with reference to a protracted "span of time" seems to downplay the "decisive moment" conveyed through the verb's tense; that

58 Guelich, *Mark 1–8:26*, 43: "The content of this 'gospel' is set forth in the message of 1:15 that is epexegetic to 1:14."

59 Adela Yarbro Collins preserves both past and present senses when she summarizes the claim of the phrase in this way: "the good news that God *has acted* and *is acting* in history to fulfill the promises of Scripture and to inaugurate the new age" (*The Beginning of the Gospel: Probings of Mark in Context* [Minneapolis: Fortress Press, 1992], 36–7, emphasis added). On the use of the perfect tense to emphasize the "state of affairs resultant upon the action," see Maximilian Zerwick, *Biblical Greek*, trans. Joseph Smith (Rome: Pontifical Institute, 1963), 97.

60 Developing the argument of F. Mussner, "Gottesherrschaft und Sendung Jesu nach Mk. 1,14f. Zugleich ein Beitrag über die innere Struktur des Markusevangelium," in *Praesentia Salutis. Gesammelte Studien zu Fragen und Themen des Neuen Testaments* (Düsseldorf: Patmos, 1967), 88.

61 This is the position of G. Delling, "πλήρης," in *TDNT* 6 (1968):287, 309.

62 Joel Marcus, "'The Time Has Been Fulfilled!' (Mark 1.15)," in *Apocalyptic and the New Testament*, ed. Joel Marcus and Marion L. Soards (JSNTSup 24; Sheffield, England: JSOT Press, 1989), 49–68.

is, if the fulfillment has been a process rather than an isolated instance – on this point I follow Marcus – the language of Mk. 1:15a draws attention to the claim that that process has, at some point, reached its completion.[63]

On the claim that καιρός here specifically refers to the epoch of Satan's dominion, now supplanted by God's, I find Marcus's reading attractive but not finally compelling. Certainly *part* of what this proclamation heralds is God's triumph over Satan, as both the immediate and broader contexts indicate (see Mk. 1:12–13, 24, 39; 3:23–7). Yet less convincing is the view that the "time" that has been fulfilled can be precisely identified as the dominion of the demonic. First, the prophetic backdrop of Mark's gospel frequently associates the term καιρός with the season of God's saving action, and only rarely with the era of God's adversaries.[64] For instance, Isa. 49:8 casts the phrase καιρῷ δεκτῷ in equipoise with the phrase ἐν ἡμέρᾳ σωτηρίας, while Isa. 60:22 concludes the song of Zion's triumph with Yahweh's promise that, κατὰ καιρὸν συνάξω αὐτούς. In addition, Danielic prophecy frequently designates the epoch of God's coming vindication through the phrase ἕως καιροῦ συντελείας (Dan. 12:4; see also 8:19; 9:27; 11:35; 12:7).[65]

Secondly, Marcus adduces Mk. 10:30 to support his reading of καιρός as the present evil age, yet the point of that verse seems to be just the opposite: there, "this age" is imbued with the rewards typically granted ἐν τῷ αἰῶνι τῷ ἐρχομένῳ. This age, then, cannot be the same one that has been entirely supplanted; we might say instead that it has been reclaimed and rejuvenated by the imminence of God's rule. As Hooker puts it, Jesus' proclamation heralds the "hope of a time when God would assert his authority in such a way that rebellion against him would be defeated."[66] Implementing that defeat will constitute much of Jesus' ministry, his crucifixion and resurrection, and ultimately the work of his followers in Mark's post-resurrection age.

The time frame of God's coming kingdom has been the subject of vigorous debate revolving around the second in this verse's pair of perfect-tense indicative verbs: ἤγγικεν. At one end of the spectrum is the view, championed especially by C. H. Dodd, that locates the force of the verb in the arrival of God's kingdom in Jesus' own life (and death), with

[63] This emphasis appears to be supported, by negative example, in Jn. 7:8, where Jesus claims that his time has "not yet been fulfilled (οὔπω πεπλήρωται)." That is, the decisive moment has not yet arrived. See Marcus, "Time," 51–2.

[64] The latter can be claimed for Dan. 7:25 (OG), which describes the duration of the power of the fourth beast.

[65] Interestingly, in his discussion of Jn. 19:28, 30, Marcus has noted the family resemblance between language of "fulfillment" and "accomplishment" ("Time," 52).

[66] Hooker, *Mark*, 55.

John the Baptist as the historical dividing line.[67] Dodd thinks it is Jesus' radical appropriation of Jewish apocalyptic eschatology that allows him to announce the arrival of God's dominion based not on the conventional expectation of a cataclysmic end but rather on what Dodd calls "the divineness of the natural order."[68] Probably because he drives such a sharp wedge between Jesus' language (as expressed here by Mark) and first-century Jewish thought, Dodd's reading has not carried the day.

Rebuttals to Dodd's "realized eschatology" view have come from many corners. Both Kümmel[69] and Marxsen[70] have favored reading ἤγγικεν not as "arrival" but as "nearness," thus preserving greater continuity with Jewish eschatological hopes. Bearing the influence of Weiss and Schweitzer, these interpreters and their successors locate the coming dominion of God at a temporal remove; the announcement of Jesus, in this view, conveys an approaching reality which casts both a hopeful and an ominous shadow across the narrative moment of Jesus' emergence on the Galilean preaching scene.

Perhaps the most helpful way forward is to acknowledge the language's inherent ambiguity.[71] On the one hand, Dodd's reading seems to reflect accurately Mark's sense that, in Jesus, God's engagement with the world has reached a critical juncture. After all, the claim that the "time has been fulfilled" indicates that the apocalyptic age has indeed dawned.[72] Thus Jesus can proclaim the reality of God's dawning dominion as an outcome that is fully assured.

On the other hand, both the language of Jesus' proclamation and the subsequent gospel story indicate that while God's rule may already be guaranteed, its culmination remains not yet in full view. As Marxsen puts it, the kingdom of God "has already begun and . . . only the finale remains."[73] Jesus' proclamation that God's dominion "has drawn near," then, exposes the charged nature of the meantime, the intervening era in which the rule of God is taking root upon the earth (see, e.g., Mk. 4:26–9).

[67] C. H. Dodd, *The Parables of the Kingdom* (New York: Scribner's, 1961), 48. He finds in Jesus' "realized eschatology" a dramatic departure from traditional Jewish thought, in that the "thought of Jesus passed directly from the immediate situation to the eternal order lying beyond all history, of which He spoke in the language of apocalyptic symbolism" (207).

[68] Ibid., 22.

[69] W. G. Kümmel, *Promise and Fulfillment: The Eschatological Message of Jesus*, trans. Dorthea M. Barton, SBT 23 (London: SCM Press, 1961), 19–25, maintains that NT uses of the verb and its cognate ἐγγύς convey a sense of "nearness" rather than "arrival."

[70] Marxsen, *Mark the Evangelist*, 132–4.

[71] So Ambrozic, *Hidden Kingdom*, 23.

[72] See, e.g., Gnilka, *Evangelium*, I:66.

[73] Marxsen, *Mark the Evangelist*, 176.

That urgent sense of God's impending arrival can be detected too in the verse's second set of parallel phrases, which shift from indicative to imperative mood: "Repent, and trust in the gospel" (Mk. 1:15b). As becomes clear throughout the second gospel, God's coming incursion evokes wildly differing – even differentiating – responses; Jesus' blanket summons to repentance and trust sounds something of a battle call, stirring his hearers to display active allegiance to God's (winning) forces in the apocalyptic showdown.

Notice the phrase's significant shift toward the implications within the human realm of the "good news" of God's coming kingdom. In the stark second-person-plural call to "repent," Jesus' words echo and carry forward his precursor's proclamation of a baptism of "repentance for the forgiveness of sins" (Mk. 1:4) – words which resonate too with various Jewish streams of thought linking community repentance to God's eschatological advent (see, e.g., 4QpPs37 3:1).

The second imperative to "trust in the gospel" further elaborates the realignment of human life according to the reality of God's coming kingdom. The rather exceptional use of the preposition ἐν (instead of εἰς) to introduce the object of πιστεύετε[74] leads Ambrozic to conclude that ἐν should "be given its full force by being translated 'on the basis of.' "[75] Thus, rather than soliciting "belief" or even "trust" in his own identity, Jesus invites his hearers "to recognize the new world in which they live."[76] Guelich understands the two commands to work in tandem, as he observes, "Thus one 'repents,' turns in total surrender to God, as one 'believes the gospel' about God's rule."[77] Together these actions constitute the response to, not the prerequisite of, the imminent dramatization of God's dominion. In other words, Mark's Jesus asserts *first* the assured nearness of God's kingdom and only *second* the reordering of life it evokes, rather than stipulating human action as a prerequisite to residence in that kingdom. Thus the εὐαγγέλιον τοῦ θεοῦ serves rhetorically as the first and last word of Jesus' initial proclamation.

According to Mark's account, then, Jesus begins his public ministry by aligning himself and his mission with the "gospel of God," a proclamation that entails both cosmic divine victory and its accompanying implications

[74] Only Mk. 1:15 in the entire New Testament features the construction πιστέυω ἐν.

[75] Ambrozic, *Hidden Kingdom*, 26. See BAGD, 660 1aε, which cites Sir. 32:21 to support the translation "put one's trust in."

[76] Marcus, "Time," 56. For further discussion on human participation in the impending regime change, see also his "Entering into the Kingly Power of God," *JBL* 107 (1988): 663–75.

[77] Guelich, *Mark 1–8:26*, 45.

on the earthly sphere. The phrase's immediate context in Mark's prologue, its use in Paul's writings, and its wider backdrop in OT prophecy and Jewish exegesis together reveal the content of the word εὐαγγέλιον that will be foundational for the developing portrait of Jesus' life and death but is not yet precisely equated with it. As a result, even the Markan prologue's Christological identification of Jesus as the messiah (Mk. 1:1), as the "stronger one" (Mk. 1:7), and as the "beloved son" (Mk. 1:11) can be best understood within this context of God's decisive incursion into the time and space of human existence.

In summary, this "gospel" entails the promise of a fully assured dominion of God, a promise which has in view the restoration of God's people in repentance and trust, the ingathering of the nations, and ultimately the universal acclaim of Yahweh's Lordship. It is at the intersection of the divine and human realms, where the cosmic and the social realities collide, that Jesus stakes his claim as both leading harbinger and protagonist of the promised "dominion of God."

To understand this proclamation of God's gospel, of God's imminent reign, against the backdrop of OT prophecy not only subsumes Jesus' mission under the overarching hope of God's apocalyptic dominion but also paves the way for understanding his disciples as participants in that mission. Once the stage has been set by Jesus' pronouncement of the "gospel of God," Mark's narrative moves swiftly to enlist other players in its vivid dramatization.[78]

The initial call: Mark 1:16–20

Immediately after his first public pronouncement of the εὐαγγέλιον τοῦ θεοῦ (Mk. 1:14–15), Jesus summons first Simon and Andrew, then James and John, and enlists them in his work (Mk. 1:16–20). Because it lies sandwiched between Mark's introduction of Jesus (Mk. 1:1–15) and the launch of his Galilean ministry (Mk. 1:21–3:12), the initial call to discipleship functions to align the first disciples with Jesus' own mission.[79] Thus from its earliest days, the "good news" that Mark's Jesus embodies involves not only Jesus himself but also the company of followers who

[78] Such a priority in Mark's storytelling has not been overlooked by exegetes. Matera, for example, finds the disciples' starring role in the gospel to be self-evident (*What Are They Saying about Mark?* [New York: Paulist Press, 1987], 38).

[79] Guelich notes the connection in this way: "The disciples will not only accompany Jesus but he will enable them to share his ministry and eventually continue it . . . [Mark] places them with Jesus 'from the beginning' as witnesses to and participants in his ministry" (*Mark 1–8:26*, 53). See also Ambrozic, *Hidden Kingdom*, 26: "The 'good news of God' proclaimed by Jesus Christ should infuse courage into the hearts of the disciples."

will surround him and engage in his work, since their Janus-like narrative setting links these four fishers both to Jesus' initial "gospel" message and to the flurry of following episodes that will demonstrate the kingdom come "in power" (cf. Mk. 9:1).

Especially in contrast with the other synoptics' treatment of this summons to follow (Matt. 4:18–22; Lk. 5:1–11),[80] Mark's mention of the disciples from the outset may highlight a keen pastoral motivation, as the evangelist intends for his contemporary "followers of Jesus" to understand that their forebears in discipleship have been with the Lord from the beginning.[81] They represent not some afterthought or appendage to this account of Jesus' ministry; at least in this gospel, Jesus' work will not proceed without them.[82]

Kingdom proclamation and discipleship call

The lines of continuity between Mk. 1:14–15 as a summary statement of Jesus' mission and Mk. 1:16–20 as the incipient act of that mission are both grammatical and thematic.[83] In the first place, this call story may be construed as a closely related sequel to Jesus' gospel proclamation because of its opening conjunction, καί (Mk. 1:16). Especially in contrast with the μετὰ δέ that begins Mk. 1:14 and which suggests a narrative break or change of scene, we may infer that Mark's use of καί to begin the call narrative not only reflects the evangelist's typically paratactic style but also implies some sense of the story's sustained development.[84] Further,

[80] Matthew follows Mark's placement of this episode immediately after Jesus begins his Galilean proclamation (Matt. 4:17), but the first gospel's inclusion of Jesus' genealogy and the birth and infancy stories keeps narrative attention squarely focused on Jesus as protagonist. Luke further relegates – and adapts – the initial call-to-discipleship story, basing the followers' allegiance on Jesus' miraculous provision of fish (Lk. 5:9).

[81] Tannehill argues that Mark's placement of this pericope deliberately capitalizes on the reader's early identification with the disciples so as to "speak indirectly through the disciples' story" ("The Disciples in Mark: The Function of a Narrative Role," *JR* 57 [1977]: 393). One of the more convincing conclusions of Meye's *Jesus and the Twelve: Discipleship and Revelation in Mark's Gospel* (Grand Rapids, MI: Eerdmans, 1968) is that it affirms continuity between discipleship in Jesus' day and its extension into Mark's age. Less compelling is his claim that, in contrast to Luke and John, Mark emphasizes that the "disciples" are the Twelve, and exclusively so. Cf. Donahue's more elastic reading (*Theology and Setting of Discipleship*, 8–9).

[82] Shiner calls it "striking that the creation of community has primacy over both teaching and christological confession in the Gospel of Mark" (*Follow Me! Disciples in Markan Rhetoric*, SBLDS 145 [Atlanta: Scholars Press, 1995] 190–1).

[83] So Taylor, *Saint Mark*, 165, who refers to *Sammelberichte* which form the backbone of the Markan narrative. Cf. Alfred Firmin Loisy, *L'Evangile selon Marc* (Paris: Emile Nourry, 1912), 67.

[84] Taylor, *Saint Mark*, 165.

the designated setting of the opening discipleship story παρὰ τὴν θάλασσαν τῆς Γαλιλαίας (Mk. 1:16) carries forward what Gundry calls "the topographical movement begun in v. 14."[85] Even these rather minor narrative links between the two scenes indicate that, for Mark, Jesus' recruitment of the fishers constitutes an inaugural – and thus momentous – step in his enactment of God's dominion, which Mark begins to stage in Galilee.

Besides in matters of redactional word choice, the very placement of this pericope – which a broad consensus of scholarship attributes to Mark[86] – further underscores the close thematic relationship between Jesus' identity and purpose (Mark's Christology) and that of his followers (Mark's discipleship).[87] As I have argued above, Jesus enters the public domain announcing a message of God's approaching reign; in turn, he follows this "gospel" proclamation with an apocalyptic summons to radical reorientation of human life. For, just as Israel's scriptures anticipate the collective expression of that divine sovereignty through Yahweh's chosen people,[88] Jesus' heralding of God's apocalyptic victory includes a call to bear collective witness to that "gospel" through repentance and trust.[89] In other words, Jesus' initial proclamation and his subsequent call to follow constitute two facets of the same Markan theme: the dominion of God eliciting clear allegiance within the human sphere. As we shall see, Jesus' initiative toward his followers continues his "gospel" proclamation by both promising God's imminent rule and evoking an active witness to that dominion. Thus our first glimpse of Markan discipleship, as portrayed in Mk. 1:16–20, develops out of Jesus' "gospel" vision articulated in Mk. 1:14–15.[90]

Seeing and summoning

Once I have affirmed grammatical and broad thematic ties between Jesus' opening preaching and the first discipleship call I can begin to examine

[85] Gundry, *Mark*, 62, though he is probably correct to deny Mark's influence on the Galilean setting, arguing instead that its theological value (asserted by Marxsen and others) is "much overestimated in modern scholarship" (71).

[86] See, e.g., Best, *Following Jesus*, 169; Guelich, *Mark 1–8:26*, 49; Marcus, *Mark 1–8*, 182.

[87] See Rudolf Pesch, "Ein Tag vollmächtige Wirkens Jesu in Kapharnaum (Mk. 1, 21–34.35–39)," *BibLeb* 9 (1968): 114–95, who identifies a pre-Markan source of miracle stories that may have served as a "community-founding tradition."

[88] See, e.g., the so-called Servant Songs of Deutero-Isaiah (Isa. 42:1–9; 49:1–6; 50:4–11; 52:13–53:12), as well as other Isaianic texts that portray Israel as the embodiment of God's glorious victory (e.g. Isa. 41:8–10; 44:1–2; 44:21).

[89] As Witherington puts it, "when others came under [God's] reign there began to be a realm, a community where the dominion was manifest" (*Mark*, 78).

[90] Marcus, *Mark 1–8*, 182, finds that the "preaching of the gospel is *somehow* linked to the appearance of the disciples" (emphasis added). This study intends to trace out some of the particulars of the "somehow."

in detail the nature and purpose of the relationship Jesus forges with the four fishers – a relationship that will in turn serve as the backbone of the gospel's subsequent discipleship passages (esp. Mk. 3:13–19; 6:7–13). The investigation will take note of the particular narrative contours of Mk. 1:16–20, especially as they derive from the "gospel" reality that Jesus has proclaimed, as well as in the passage's relationship to extant models of discipleship in first-century Palestine. By detecting Mark's "intermingling of tradition and convention,"[91] we may identify the evangelist's hermeneutical moves that together point to what it means to follow Jesus.

From the passage's beginning verse, Jesus continues in the role of protagonist that he has assumed in the gospel prologue. Grammatically, Jesus is the (implied) subject of verse 16's opening participial phrase παράγων παρὰ τὴν θάλασσαν τῆς Γαλιλαίας as well as its finite verb εἶδεν, thus underscoring his command of the story. It is Jesus' movement beside the sea that sets the stage for the encounter, and it is Jesus' act of "seeing" that inspires his interaction with the fishers. Indeed, as the verse's first finite verb, εἶδεν conveys the driving action behind the discipleship summons that will ensue. For Mark, ophthalmic imagery will emerge as a dominant motif in his gospel narrative, as Jesus' action will so often be preceded and motivated by his vision.[92]

The synoptic treatment of this call story in Lk. 5:1–11 provides an interesting foil to the Markan perspective indicated in Mk. 1:16. As Luke tells the story, before the fishers respond to Jesus' summons, Jesus provides proof of his divine power by promising an abundant catch. Especially striking is Luke's description of Simon Peter's response to the overflowing nets: ἰδὼν δὲ Σίμων Πέτρος προσέπεσεν τοῖς γόνασιν Ἰησοῦ (Lk. 5:8). As it turns out, "seeing" plays just as pivotal a role in the Markan call to discipleship, but as Marcus puts it, here it is "not principally the brothers' detection of some special quality in Jesus" that establishes this disciple–teacher relationship, but rather "his perception of them."[93] Within this pericope, Mark presents Jesus as a compelling leader with a keen eye.

Despite this narrative emphasis on Jesus' prominence from the story's outset, we should note in passing at least two features of the verse that indicate Mark's strong interest in those who will become disciples. In the first place, the verse explicitly names "Simon and his brother Andrew."

[91] See Vernon K. Robbins, *Jesus the Teacher: A Socio-Rhetorical Interpretation of Mark* (Philadelphia: Fortress Press, 1984), 197.

[92] Among examples of this narrative pattern are the healing of the paralytic (Mk. 2:5), the feeding of the multitude (Mk. 6:34), and the second sea-crossing story (Mk. 6:48). A notable exception occurs when the hemorrhaging woman's touch (Mk. 5:32) elicits Jesus' power *before* he recognizes her need. Despite the import of these instances, Schweizer probably goes too far in his estimation of "seeing" as an elective act (*Good News*, 48).

[93] Marcus, *Mark 1–8*, 183.

Though such overt mention of those who will form the inner circle of Jesus' cohort may simply reflect the fact that, for Mark's community, they were well-known apostles, Mark's mentioning them by name ascribes to them at least a measure of honor in the narrative itself.

Even more significantly, however, Mark includes in this verse quite an elaborate description of their life situation prior to Jesus' call. Commentators frequently emphasize Jesus as the verbal subject of this verse,[94] yet the brothers serve both as referents of the participial phrase ἀμφιβάλλοντας ἐν τῇ θαλάσσῃ and as subjects of the accompanying finite verb ἦσαν (Mk. 1:16). And while scholars frequently attribute the explanatory γὰρ-clause to Mark's redactional interpretation of a traditional (and somewhat obscure) participle,[95] in any case the verse gives as much narrative attention to the circumstances of those whom Jesus will call as it does to Jesus himself. The initiative in the leader–follower relationship may, in Mark's account, lie with Jesus. Yet the brothers' deliberate identification by name and profession renders them as characters who are by no means incidental to the ensuing encounter.

God's gospel and its human response

As I turn to the form of the summons itself, as found in Mk. 1:17, I shall consider the way in which this succinct expression of the discipleship pattern relates both to Jesus' "gospel" proclamation in Mk. 1:15 and to extant Jewish and Hellenistic literature. Already I have traced both grammatical and thematic ties that link Jesus' enlistment of the four fishers to his own kingdom proclamation. Here we observe that even the language of Jesus' summons to discipleship echoes the content of his programmatic preaching. Notice, for instance, how Jesus' first utterance to Peter and Andrew by the Sea of Galilee reverses the elements of his initial public pronouncement:

Mark 1:15			Mark 1:17
time has been fulfilled + dominion has drawn near	(indicative)	(imperative)	come after me
repent + trust in the gospel	(imperative)	(indicative)	I will make you fishers of people

In the first place, the indicative statements that begin Mk. 1:15 and end Mk. 1:17 serve a bracketing function in which this "good news" of

[94] See ibid., 182: "The prospective followers are introduced in a rather incidental way, by means of a participial phrase."

[95] E.g. Best, *Following Jesus*, 166–74; Gundry, *Mark*, 71–2.

God's dominion reaches temporally from past accomplishment through future promise. For, on the one hand, Jesus' double declaration that "the time has been fulfilled and God's dominion has drawn near" (Mk. 1:15) employs double perfect-tense verbs to convey a past act with continuing repercussions; as the divine incursion into human history has *already* dawned, it casts a new hue over the landscape of the present.

Yet the closing promise of Mk. 1:17 to make of his followers "fishers of people" leaves nothing either to chance or to the whims of human loyalty. In this future-tense claim, the task of transforming the disciples' vocation depends not on their own strength or insight, but on God's creative power unleashed in the life of Jesus. Both Jesus' kingdom proclamation of Mk. 1:15 and his promise to the fishers in Mk. 1:17 thus testify to the same Markan claim: the "gospel" is God's good news, carried out on God's terms, and through precisely the means God has chosen.

It is only within this framework – a framework that grounds human life in the context of divine sovereignty – that the imperatives standing at the center of this chiastic structure can be considered. The commands – to "repent and trust in the gospel" (Mk. 1:15) and to "come after me" (Mk. 1:17) – intend to bring Jesus' hearers on board with the "good news" of God's assured victory.[96] In a sense, Jesus' "gospel" proclamation penetrates the human realm like a magnetic force field marked by the polarities of the old age and the new. Those whose lives become reoriented toward the reality of God's good news will thus find salvation and life, while those who sustain the old age's status quo will remain within the sway of its judgment and death. There cannot be, either in Mark's or in the OT prophetic understanding, any divine "good news" apart from human response. Thus the call of the first disciples reflects and reiterates the dramatic tension between the "good news" of God's assured victory and its drastic implications for human life.

"Come after me"

If we construe the pithy imperative δεῦτε ὀπίσω μου in its narrative context as a more specific reiteration of Jesus' sweeping invitation to "repent and trust in the gospel," we gain further insight into the relationship Mark's Jesus establishes in this passage by considering the broader context of the Jewish and Greco-Roman framework that certainly would

[96] Marcus's characterization of "entering the kingdom" in Mk. 10:15 applies here as well: it is "an incorporation of [the disciple] into God's powerful invasion of this world" ("Kingly Power," 674).

have influenced both Jesus and the second evangelist. Secondary literature exploring this theme of discipleship in background literature is vast and cannot be weighed exhaustively here. The modest aim of the present inquiry, then, is to touch on key assertions of the scholarly discussion as it has evolved in the last century and then to suggest ways in which the history-of-religions perspective can elucidate Mark's hermeneutical purposes.

One view championed in the last century is that of Anselm Schulz and Hans Dieter Betz, whose investigations of the motif of "following after" Jesus link discipleship in the gospels to "the Palestinian Jewish relationship of the teacher of the Torah to his pupil."[97] It is true that by the end of the first century, the Jewish tradition had assimilated Hellenistic patterns of teacher–student relationships so that rabbinic literature is replete with references to those who "follow after" a rabbi.[98] For instance, *b. 'Erub.* 30a, *b. Ketub.* 66b, and *b. Yoma* 37a all speak of students "going after" the instructor, and many who emphasize Jesus' own Jewishness as well as the teaching component of his ministry assert that rabbinic reports of students following at a distance behind their teacher provide the closest analogy for understanding Jesus' relationship to his disciples.[99]

Such an emphasis on Jesus as rabbi has been challenged by scholars such as Hengel, who notes many aspects of the gospel discipleship accounts that are at odds with this portrait. Chief among them, with respect to Mk. 1:16–20, is the fact that rabbinic literature typically stresses the initiative of would-be students who petition a respectable rabbi for the privilege of his tutelage.[100] As Hengel points out, nowhere "did the summons 'follow me' resound from any rabbinical teacher *in respect of entry* into a teacher–student relationship."[101]

[97] Hans Dieter Betz, *Nachfolge und Nachahmung Jesu Christi im Neuen Testament*, BHT 37 (Tübingen: Mohr Siebeck, 1967), 27. See also Anselm Schulz, *Nachfolgen und Nachahmen: Studien über das Verhältnis der neutestamentlichen Jüngerschaft zur urchristlichen Vorbildethik*, SANT 6 (Munich: Kösel-Verlag, 1962), 127, who attributes to Jesus a "konkrete Gestalt eines spätjüdischen Gesetzeslehrers."

[98] Also, both Philo and Josephus employ teacher–student language to describe relationships between such biblical figures as Moses and Elijah. See, e.g., Robbins, *Jesus the Teacher*, 97, who claims that Josephus's writings "contain teacher–disciple language that pervades the narratives of biblical stories themselves."

[99] Among those who stress Jesus' role as teacher are Meye, *Jesus and the Twelve*, 97, who claims that the "teacher–disciple relationship appears in an institutional form and has a definitely intellectual aspect," and Betz, *Nachfolge*, 3.

[100] So Robbins, *Jesus the Teacher*, 101.

[101] Martin Hengel, *The Charismatic Leader and His Followers*, trans. J. Grieg, SNTW (New York: Crossroad, 1981), 50–1 (emphasis added). Though the "following" terminology is lacking, we should note that Sir. 51:23 does feature an invitation to "draw near . . . and lodge in the house of instruction."

Further, that the rabbi–talmid relationship was devoted to Torah instruction reflects a purpose quite inconsistent with what Schweitzer called the "dogmatic, eschatological considerations" that inspired Jesus' decision to call the disciples.[102] In Mark's gospel, Jesus' teaching ministry figures as a constituent part of his apocalyptic proclamation; as I shall explore below in chapter 4, even where Mark emphasizes Jesus' teaching (Mk. 4:1–34), the content of that teaching generally concerns not Torah interpretation (cf. Matt. 5:1–7:29) but the approach of God's dominion.[103] Indeed, where Jesus *does* engage topics related to Torah (e.g. Mk. 7:1ff.; 10:1ff.), he does so in response to others' exegesis, which he deems flawed. Despite a common portrait of a group "going after" a leading figure, then, the Jewish model of rabbi–student relationships fails to account in full measure for Mark's emphatic portrait of Jesus' initiative, for Jesus' relatively mitigated teaching role in Mark's gospel, or even for the content of the instruction Jesus does convey.

The Greco-Roman milieu of first-century Palestine supplies other examples of leader–follower relationships that exhibit important points of contact with Jesus' summons to "come after me." Robbins argues that a central function of discipleship in the gospels is patterned after the transmission of religio-philosophical wisdom as exemplified, for instance, in Greek literature such as Plato's *Theaetetus* and *Meno* and Philostratus' *Life of Apollonius*.[104] In both instances, he maintains, "the religio-ethical teacher . . . gathers disciple companions in order to transmit to them the system of thought and action that he himself embodies."[105] And in the case of Plato's work this "eventually leads to the arrest, trial, and death of the teacher."[106]

Yet this paradigm also includes noteworthy divergences from the Markan discipleship pattern. Though Greco-Roman literature features philosopher-teachers who actively recruit followers, they do so on the basis of remarkable words or deeds that inspire their pupils' loyalty; only after much convincing proof do the leaders earn the right to be surrounded

[102] Albert Schweitzer, *The Quest of the Historical Jesus: A Critical Study of Its Progress from Reimarus to Wrede* (Baltimore: Johns Hopkins University Press, 1998; orig. 1906), 357. Hooker likewise notes that following Jesus involved far more "than learning a particular form of teaching" (*Mark*, 60).

[103] While not all of the parables in Mk. 4 are explicitly identified with the "kingdom," nor does the text stipulate all of the teachings as "parables," the unifying theme of material in that "parables chapter" is its illustrative representation of God's kingdom. Guelich, *Mark 1–8:26*, 51, claims that the disciples' function was "not to learn and transmit [Jesus'] teaching of the Law . . . but to become 'fishers of men.' " See also Shiner, *Follow Me!*, 192: "Discipleship is primarily an attachment to Jesus and only secondarily involves learning from him."

[104] Robbins, *Jesus the Teacher*, 136. [105] Ibid., 54–5. [106] Ibid., 147.

by those who would learn from and espouse their teachings.[107] Further, the case of Apollonius of Tyana seems representative in its depiction of the leading figure as a "lone hero rather than a member of a community."[108] At least to some degree, the role ascribed to followers in the Greek pattern of discipleship intends to showcase the exemplary human wisdom of the teacher.

A third possible, and more convincing, construal of Jesus' summons to "come after me" identifies Jesus' imperative as a call to eschatological holy war. In the first place, in OT traditions leaders employ the phrase to incite followers to rise up and defend the cause of Yahweh (e.g. Judg. 6:34; 1 Sam. 11:6–7).[109] Indeed, this theocratic notion of combat is cloaked in eschatological fervor in later writings such as Dan. 11:33–5 and *1 Enoch* 90:9–19, where the impending showdown between God's chosen ones and the idolatrous ruling powers occurs as a prelude to God's restoration of cosmic sovereignty – that is, in the "interval until the time appointed" (Dan. 11:35). As Hengel observes, "*The charismatic and the eschatological element are here conjoined.*"[110]

To see Jesus' call to "come after me" through this eschatological lens, then, enables us to recognize an urgent and compelling summons to participate "in the eschatological event which taking its beginning in him was moving powerfully towards the complete dawn of the rule of God."[111] Especially on the heels of Jesus' proclamation of God's imminent dominion (Mk. 1:14–15), this model of "coming after" resonates with the pulse of apocalyptic expectation detected in Mark's account of Jesus' mission and purpose. To the extent that it refines that model by depicting a leader "not interested in placing himself at the head of an enthusiastic crowd"[112] as well as one whose theater of war remains outside the political sphere, we may affirm again Mark's hermeneutical melding of Jesus tradition material in light of his own contemporary setting.

Finally, in its rather urgent and abrupt account of Jesus' initiative as well as the fishers' response, this passage finds an important literary antecedent in the 1 Kgs. 19 account of Elijah's "call" of Elisha, a story which offers in broad outline several striking parallels with

107 I have already noted this significant discrepancy between Mark's and Luke's initial call stories, which may reflect the latter's more Hellenistic provenance. In contrast with the Markan portrait of Jesus' summons to discipleship, Shiner's study of Hellenistic parallels yields "no example of such an unmotivated call story" in comparable literature (*Follow Me!*, 183).

108 Ibid., 125.

109 Marcus, *Mark 1–8*, 183, points out the further parallel to Mark in that, in these texts, "the call of the leader for followers is preceded by the coming of the Spirit upon him."

110 Hengel, *Charismatic Leader*, 20. 111 Ibid., 73. 112 Ibid., 59.

Mk. 1:16–20.[113] The two stories share significant feaures that can easily be enumerated: (1) both accounts feature divinely authorized leaders who have just emerged from the wilderness; (2) both offer succinct reports of a "prophetic" leader's compelling initiative in recruiting one or more follower(s); (3) both emphasize that the positive act of "following after" also dictates a negative impulse to leave behind family and career; and (4) in both stories, those who follow do so passively and without apparent warrant.[114] The narrative effect in each case is to focus attention not on the followers' existential "crisis of decision" but on the driving impulse behind the call itself.

Beneath these surface points of contact, we may detect several contextual features that link both Elisha and the four fishers to their leaders' own mission and purpose. To sharpen the reading of Mk. 1:16–20, then, I turn first to the wider narrative context of 1 Kgs. 19, which supplies a helpful key to unlocking the nature of the Elijah–Elisha relationship.[115] The chapter opens with Queen Jezebel's death threat to Elijah, which inspires his fearful flight "a day's journey into the wilderness (ἐν τῇ ἐρήμῳ)" (1 Kgs. 19:4). Despite a miraculous provision of food, which supplies enough strength for a forty-day journey toward Horeb, Elijah articulates his deep despair to Yahweh through the repeated complaint, "I alone am left, and they are seeking my life, to take it away" (1 Kgs. 19:10, 14). The first time Elijah utters these words, Yahweh responds with the divine self-disclosure of a "sound of sheer silence" (1 Kgs. 19:12), but even God's presence does not restore Elijah's spirits. So his pathetic cry goes up a second time, and Yahweh answers with a rather pointed command to

[113] Above I have noted the Elijah-like role of John the Baptist, and much recent scholarship has focused on the early Christian view of Jesus as the new Elisha (on this see, e.g., Raymond E. Brown, "Jesus and Elisha," *Perspective* 12 [1971]: 85–104; D. Gerald Bostock, "Jesus as the New Elisha," *ExpT* 92 [1980]: 39–41; and Thomas L. Brodie, "Jesus as the New Elisha: Cracking the Code," *ExpT* 93 [1981]: 39–42). But to view Jesus' relationship to John in this context does not preclude detecting the literary parallels discussed here; after all, in light of the fluidity of scriptural interpretation, the equation is not meant to be restrictive but, rather, evocative.

[114] Hengel notes that "Mark and Q [share] the reduction of the [call] form to a minimum, the lack of any psychological justification – and clear parallels in form and content to the call of Elisha by Elijah" (*Charismatic Leader*, 5). Donahue calls Mark's language "remniscent" of 1 Kgs. 19 (*Theology and Setting of Discipleship*, 14). Cf. Meye, *Jesus and the Twelve*, 95, who finds the parallel lacking because it is "not at all clear that a dominant part of Elisha's course was the reception of a teaching from Elijah." Also, Gundry, *Mark*, 70, puts it bluntly: "This model of prophetic call does not work." Gundry and Meye seem impaired by an apparent dogmatic refusal to consider the nuanced interaction between the Markan account and its OT backdrop.

[115] While interpreters frequently mention the Elijah–Elisha parallel itself, to my knowledge this broader contextual study is unprecedented.

anoint kings over Aram and Israel, and then to anoint Elisha as a "prophet in your place" (1 Kgs. 19:15). Further, undermining Elijah's solitary claim to loyalty, Yahweh promises to leave "seven thousand in Israel, all the knees that have not bowed to Baal" (1 Kgs. 19:18).

Despite Elijah's musings to the contrary, then, the 1 Kings portrait of his interaction with Yahweh indicates that prophecy constitutes neither a private nor an isolated affair. Not only does the prophetic office involve those who give ear to this authorized "word of the Lord," but it also entails the transmission of that authority from one charismatic leader to another. The story itself even affirms Elijah's sense of his own insufficiency to the task when God sets him on a course to involve others in proclaiming the divine claim on the people of Israel. According to the 1 Kings account, the call of Elisha follows from Yahweh's relentless determination to ensure that the prophetic display of divine power and authority will continue in strength.

Although in Mark's gospel it is the figure of John the Baptist – not Jesus – who seems most closely aligned with Elijah as the one who "must come first" (especially in Mk. 1:2–8), only an overly strict typological reading would dismiss the interpretive assistance that the 1 Kgs. 19 call story lends to investigation of the nature and function of discipleship in Mk. 1:16–20. Even if the evangelist's post-resurrection community views Jesus as more than "one of the prophets" (cf. Mk. 8:27–9), the Elijah–Elisha encounter still provides a template for Mark's account of Jesus' call of his first disciples, a story in which Jesus assumes the narrative role of a familiar, and eschatologically oriented, OT prophet.[116]

But what does this analogous story contribute to the understanding of Jesus' relationship with his disciples? Primarily, it elucidates the durable ties between Jesus' own mission and his recruitment of followers. Like Elijah, Jesus has just emerged from a defining wilderness experience lasting forty days and nights. Like Elijah's, Jesus' words and deeds pertain in the story not to himself but to the wider audience before whom he will dramatize God's kingdom as well as to those he will involve in his mission, beginning with the four fishers. Finally like Elijah's (remarkably so), Jesus' earthly ministry will eventually end and so will require that his mantle of authority be extended to others.[117] These narrative points

[116] Hengel, *Charismatic Leader*, 17, cites as "one essential difference between the call to follow Jesus and the story of Elijah and Elisha" the fact that in Mark, "the person who calls is ultimately God himself." Yet in light of the fact that Yahweh instructs Elijah to anoint Elisha, the difference may not be as "essential" as Hengel maintains.

[117] We might add that, as that authority is imparted from Elijah to Elisha, its effectiveness is doubled (2 Kgs. 2:9; cf. Sir. 48:12 [Syr]).

of contact, I propose, underscore the vital purpose that Jesus and Elijah share as "man of God"/"son of God," a mission which by nature extends beyond the individual toward others enlisted in that mission.[118]

Fishers of people

To this point, I have considered the language of "coming after" (and "following") as employed in the first half of Mk. 1:17's summons to discipleship. But the summons, compelling as it is, also carries Jesus' promise: ποιήσω ὑμᾶς γενέσθαι ἁλιεῖς ἀνθρώπων. If Jesus sounds a pointed "call to arms" in his command to "come after me," in the present clause he vows to transform their calling in life (see Mk. 1:16) as he "makes" them to be "fishers of people." Indeed, this second element of Jesus' summons is to be understood not primarily as a prediction made in order "to display Jesus' power of foretelling the future"[119] but rather as a reiteration of God's creative powers unleashed when humans trust the reality of God's "gospel."

The prevalent use of fishing imagery in antiquity has been thoroughly explored by Wilhelm Wuellner, who finds the motif spanning a rich and variegated array of literary settings. For instance, both the Qumran community (e.g. CD 4:15–16) and Rabbi Gamaliel (*'Abot R. Nat.* A40) depict the gathering of followers as a fishing enterprise, a use that parallels at least to some degree Plato's metaphoric use of fishing in his portrait of the teacher–student relationship.[120] Similarly, the association of the fishing motif with the establishment of justice spans a wide variety of literary traditions ranging from the Egyptian *Book of the Dead* to the OT prophetic traditions (to which I return below) to Lucian's essay *The Fisherman.*[121] In light of the polyvalent thrust of this metaphor, then, what sense might we make of Jesus' promise in Mk. 1:17 to "make you to be fishers of people"?

[118] Marcus deems "important to Mark" both the "theme of prophetic authority" and "the notion that Jesus shares authority" (*Mark 1–8*, 183). To take this observation a step further, with respect to both Elijah and Jesus, prophetic authority necessarily *becomes* shared authority.

[119] So Gundry, *Mark*, 67.

[120] See Wilhelm Wuellner, *The Meaning of "Fishers of Men"* (Philadelphia: Westminster Press, 1967), 64, where he calls *The Sophist* the "first example from pre-Christian times of the metaphoric use of fishing activities in the description of teacher–student relationships." See also ibid., 112, where he discusses the rabbis' adoption of composite "Biblical and Hellenistic traditions," and 127–31, where he discusses the Qumran covenanters' adoption of fishing imagery (e.g. 1QH 5:7, which uses the term "many fishermen" to describe followers of the Qumran leader).

[121] Ibid., 73.

Weaving together the strands of his disparate findings, Wuellner maintains that Jesus' use of the fishing metaphor in connection with his disciples links them to the prophetic tradition which envisions God's apocalyptic rectification of the world, carried out through Israel as authorized agent, and entailing both universal salvation and accompanying judgment.[122] As they become, through no power or initiative of their own, "fishers of people," Jesus' disciples in Mark are transformed into agents of God's apocalyptic rectification of the world and so participate in the "gospel" reality Jesus proclaims. Wuellner puts it this way:

> The crucial issue . . . is not the fact that Jesus permitted the Twelve to share in his mission, but rather how this indubitable mission and partnership came to be interpreted not only after Easter, but even before then.[123]

The nature of this mission and partnership becomes even clearer when we consider the frequently cited OT prophecy that Mk. 1:17 most closely parallels. Though the fishing image occurs in various prophetic and wisdom texts (e.g. Amos 4:2; Hab. 1:14–15; Eccl. 9:12), Jer. 16:16 employs the motif in a way that links it explicitly with the prophetic hope for God's dominion, which will be dramatized in Israel's return to its own land – a vision influential on Mark's expression of his gospel. In the first place, the prophet states Yahweh's promise to "send many fishers" as a preparatory step in the implementation of the new world order announced in this passage. The LXX reads: ἰδοὺ ἐγὼ ἀποστέλλω τοὺς ἁλεεῖς τοὺς πολλοὺς λέγει κύριος καὶ ἁλιεύσουσιν αὐτούς. Typically, readers of this prophecy focus interpretive attention on the motivating cause cited in ensuing verses: "For my eyes are on all their ways . . . and I will doubly repay their iniquity and their sin" for the proliferation of idol worship (Jer. 16:17–18). In this light, the fishing metaphor conveys the prospect of decisive judgment against the people of Israel.[124] Certainly, read together

[122] Wuellner notes that the rabbinic tradition's use of the fishing metaphor to describe the process of 'catching' students of Torah contrasts with early Christianity, which "conceived of the 'fishing of men' as a radically new manifestation of God in history which would not vindicate the old, but create or reconstitute an altogether new covenant, New Israel, new creation" (ibid., 123). Wuellner's radical discontinuity, though, seems forced, especially in light of Mark's use of Israel's scriptural tradition as the "thought world" which itself conceived of a "new thing" (e.g. Isa. 43:19).

[123] Ibid., 160.

[124] Thus C. W. F. Smith, "Fishers of Men: Footnotes on a Gospel Figure," *HTR* 52 (1959): 188–203, argues that the phrase in its Markan setting indicates as a primary function of discipleship the summoning of people for judgment.

with other biblical and non-biblical references to fishing and nets, the ominous threat of judgment looms large.[125]

Yet within its biblical context, and particularly within the context of exilic prophecy, the specter of judgment cannot be severed from its durable literary and theological ties to the larger, and more promising, theme of God's sweeping sovereignty on earth. To read Jer. 16:16 in its more expansive context is to glimpse the hope of that victory, which entails restoration for God's people:

> Therefore, the days are surely coming, says the LORD, when it shall no longer be said, "As the LORD lives who brought the people of Israel up out of the land of Egypt," but "As the LORD lives who brought the people of Israel up out of the land of the north and out of all the lands where he had driven them." For I will bring them back to their own land that I gave to their ancestors. (Jer. 16:14–15)

Thus the fishing imagery of Jer. 16:16 can best be construed not exclusively as judgment in the narrow sense but as the activity of a God who gathers the people of Israel out of all the lands where he had driven them and whose judgment is enacted within the broader context of restorative salvation.[126] Indeed, following the language of judgment cited in Jer. 16:17–18, the passage's concluding verses expand the promise of Israel's restoration until it is cosmic in scope. When the suppliant triumphantly predicts, "To you shall the nations [not just Israel] come from the ends of the earth," Yahweh responds with an equally triumphant promise: "Therefore I am surely going to teach them . . . and they shall know that my name is the Lord."[127]

In view of these findings we may more fully understand the hermeneutical moves found within the tradition itself as well as Mark's appropriation of it. Since I have already suggested the prophetic vision of God's coming dominion as the generative hope for the Markan Jesus' initial apocalyptic pronouncement of God's good tidings, his promise to make of his followers "fishers of people" exposes their significant, divinely

[125] As Witherington notes, "always [in the Old Testament] this metaphor is used in the context of a discussion about judgment" (*Mark*, 85).

[126] Jack R. Lundbom, *Jeremiah 1–20*, AB 21A (Garden City, NY: Doubleday, 1999), views as "unlikely" the modern claim that "vv. 14–15 are a later insertion" (766).

[127] John Bright, *Jeremiah*, AB 21 (Garden City, NY: Doubleday, 1965), notes that though the "poetic fragment" of Jer. 16:19–21 is "frequently denied to Jeremiah on the grounds that it shows dependence on the thought of later prophecy . . . [indeed it] swarms with Jeremianic expressions, and the idea of the turning of the nations to Yahweh rests on very old tradition" (113).

ordained role within the schema of God's ultimate reign over even "the nations from the ends of the earth."[128] To understand the image as one of judgment certainly is consistent with its prophetic usage; to understand it *only* as judgment is to bracket out the broader context of God's imminent dominion. For in the OT prophetic backdrop, as well as its hermeneutical translation in Mark's gospel, the threat of judgment is only one negative ramification of the broader hope of salvation by the hand of Yahweh.[129]

Leaving and following

So far I have focused attention on Jesus as the initiator of this first discipleship encounter and, more precisely, on the nature and function of the relationship he establishes with Simon and Andrew, as well as James and John. Jesus' compelling relational authority is apparent throughout the passage[130] – but so too is the full eschatological agency to which he calls those who would come after him. So, just as the followers' response to Jesus relates closely to his purpose in summoning them, so too does the study of this incipient call to discipleship require due attention to that response, which further forges a link between the Christology of Mk. 1:14–15 and the discipleship of Mk. 1:16–20.

It is interesting to note that, within the doublet of summons to discipleship found in Mk. 1:16–18 and 1:19–20, Jesus' words of command and promise which expose his purpose for the followers appear only once (Mk. 1:17), as they are summarized rather than restated in the second encounter by the terse report, καὶ εὐθὺς ἐκάλεσεν αὐτούς (Mk. 1:20). What *is* repeated within the narrative is the fishers' response. In the case of Simon and his brother Andrew, Mark reports, καὶ εὐθὺς ἀφέντες τὰ δίκτυα ἠκολούθησαν αὐτῳ (Mk. 1:18). Significantly, the two verbs in

[128] Wuellner captures the importance of the community within this schema when he identifies the collective people of Israel as "the human agent appointed to be the medium of God's eschatological revelation" (*Meaning*, 155).

[129] Page H. Kelley has missed the interrelationship between judgment and salvation when he contrasts Mark's use of fishing with Jeremiah's: "When Jesus used the metaphor of fishermen to describe the mission of his disciples . . . he was reversing its meaning from that intended by Jeremiah. Jeremiah's fishers caught men for judgment; Jesus' fishers caught them for salvation" (Peter C. Craigie, Page H. Kelley, and Joel F. Drinkard, Jr., *Jeremiah 1–25*, WBC 26 [Dallas: Word Books, 1991], 219). Similarly, Hooker, *Mark*, 60, and Best, *Following Jesus*, 170.

[130] As Origen puts it, "There can be no doubt that it is not by human strength or resources that the word of Christ comes to prevail with all authority . . . in the minds and hearts of all humanity" (*On First Principles*, trans. G. W. Butterworth [London: SPCK, 1936; reprint, Gloucester, MA: Peter Smith, 1973], 4.1.2).

this verse answer, in reverse order, both Jesus' injunction to "come after me" (as "they followed him") and his promise to transform their fishing enterprise (as they trust his promise in "letting go of their nets"). Such a dramatic, wholehearted response only gains intensity as Mark's sparse language gives way to an elaborately detailed balance sheet of just what it is that James and John forfeit in order to follow Jesus: καὶ ἀφέντες τὸν πατέρα αὐτῶν Ζεβεδαῖον ἐν τῷ πλοίῳ μετὰ τῶν μισθωτῶν ἀπῆλθον ὀπίσω αὐτοῦ (Mk. 1:20). This piling up of particulars underscores the full weight of the verb ἀφέντες: not just nets are left behind, but a named father, a boat, and indeed an entire enterprise.

In its dual expression of the disciples' "leaving" and "following," this reaction to Jesus' initiative also answers Jesus' early – and more universally proclaimed – imperative to "repent and trust in the gospel" (Mk. 1:15). The verb μετανοεῖτε certainly implies a turning away, a reorientation, a departure from the former way of life, all of which occurs as the four men "leave" their current endeavors. Further, their "coming after" Jesus constitutes a willingness to trust in the "gospel" reality of God's provision. As Tertullian puts it, "None of those whom the Lord chose said to him, 'I have no means to live.' "[131]

This double dynamic of turning away from current circumstance and following after a charismatic leader provides another point of contact with the 1 Kgs. 19 call story considered above. Yet despite the two narratives' parallel accounts of leaving and following, they exhibit one key difference, as Elisha briefly interrupts his initial "running after" Elijah by insisting on both a ceremonial parting from his parents and the slaughter of his oxen as a feast for the people (1 Kgs. 19:20–1). Only after he has appropriately commemorated those relationships of family and business does he part with them. Because of the underlying similarities discussed above, this sharp divergence underscores the urgency of Jesus' command, the compelling authority of this herald of God's kingdom, and the utter abandon of those summoned to participate in that kingdom.

According to Mark's account, the two opening scenes of Jesus' public ministry together lay an important foundation for understanding the relationship between Christology and discipleship. As we have seen, when read together as parallel expressions of Jesus' inaugural word and deed, Mk. 1:14–15 and Mk. 1:16–20 bear witness to Mark's delicately balanced assertion: the unilateral and assured dawning of God's reign carries

[131] Tertullian, *On Idolatry* 12, in *The Ante-Nicene Fathers: Translations of the Writings of the Fathers down to AD 325*, 5th edn., ed. A. Menzies (Grand Rapids, MI: Eerdmans, 1978), 3:68.

a concomitant call to the collective participation in that dominion. While Mark's transmission of the tradition deliberately asserts that success of God's dominion does not hang on proper human expression of it, the evangelist does seem to affirm the momentous eschatological role to be played by Jesus' followers. In their coming after Jesus, the disciples are to imitate the pattern of his life and to be "engaged in the work or mission of the one who calls."[132] Eusebius describes the call episode this way:

> When he had thus called them as his followers, he breathed into them his divine power, and filled them with strength and courage . . . With this empowerment God sent them forth to be workers and teachers of holiness to all the nations, declaring them heralds of his own teaching.[133]

Conclusion

This opening chapter has explored episodes at the outset of Mark's gospel that portray Jesus and his followers against the literary and theological backdrop of Israel's prophetic, and ultimately apocalyptic, hopes for God's coming rule. As the interpretive focus of this study, the pattern of discipleship that Mark's Jesus establishes at the beginning of his ministry will have important bearings on the reading of subsequent interaction between Jesus as agent of God's coming new age and those he has summoned into his company. Let me summarize principal findings that expose that pattern of discipleship as depicted in Mk. 1:16–20:

(1) The topic of Mark's portrait of the disciples cannot be extracted from its narrative and theological grounding in Jesus' apocalyptic pronouncement of the good news of God's dominion. Mk. 1:1–15 serves an important foundational role as it introduces Jesus against the backdrop of Israel's prophetic hopes for God's rule and reports his opening proclamation of the approach of that rule. Mark's Christology, as presented in the gospel's opening pericope, must be understood primarily as a function of this apocalyptic gospel. Jesus is its divinely sanctioned herald and advance agent, but the "gospel" content defines his role, rather than the reverse.

(2) Both in Mark's account and in the Jewish scriptures that inform it, the dawning reality of God's reign carries ponderous implications

[132] Donahue, *Theology and Setting of Discipleship*, 15.

[133] Eusebius, "The Proof of the Gospel," in *Thesaurus linguae graecae: Canon of Greek Authors and Works*, 2nd edn., ed. L. Berkowitz and K. Squiter (Oxford: Oxford University Press, 1986), 2018.005, 3.7.10–1.

for human life; the study of Jesus' messianic identity, then, cannot be extracted from a study of the community called to participate in the messianic age. Thus, as Mark's Jesus summons his hearers to "repent and trust in the gospel," and then to "come after me," he solicits their direct involvement in the assured reality of God's dominion. From the outset, then, Mark's Jesus – the Christ – enlists his followers in the campaign for regime change that he is launching "on the earth."

(3) We have seen that the intended pattern of their relationship includes both *presence* – here taking the specific form of "coming after" Jesus as observers and recipients of his instruction – and their *practice* as active agents – "fishers" – in God's apocalyptic restoration of the world. We shall see, in the scrutiny of later texts, how the two thrusts often work in tandem to maintain both the pivotal role of Jesus and the full empowerment of his disciples.

3

THE COMMISSIONING OF THE TWELVE IN MARK 3:13–15

Introduction

The pattern of discipleship etched in Mk. 1:16–20 – a pattern featuring both *presence* and *practice* – gains more elaborate expression as Jesus calls those whom he wishes up to the mountain and there establishes the Twelve (Mk. 3:13–19). As the second passage in Mark to feature significant direct interaction between Jesus and his followers, this detailed exposition of the group's own mission and purpose builds on their increasing narrative prominence in a way that signals their significant partnership with Jesus.[1] An examination of the context, setting, and structure of this succinct mountaintop encounter will demonstrate that in their twofold commission to "be with" Jesus and to be "sent out" by him, the Twelve assume a vital role as divinely appointed administrators of the in-breaking kingdom of God that has been the focus of Jesus' ministry up to this point in the gospel. In other words, if Jesus has emerged in the second gospel as God's specially designated emissary, in this passage he explicitly extends his power and authority to the Twelve who surround him. For Mark's audience, the Twelve thus provide a paradigm for the practice of that divinely sanctioned role even in a post-resurrection age,[2] perhaps particularly at a time when the cosmic showdown between the "powers that

[1] As Martin Hengel observes, Mark's inclusion of both 1:16–20 and 3:13–19 undermines the view that the disciples' activity "falls wholly into the background over against that of Jesus" (*The Charismatic Leader and His Followers*, trans. J. Grieg, SNTW [New York: Crossroad, 1981], 79).

[2] Joel Marcus's claim that the appointment of the Twelve is "probably paradigmatic for all disciples" thus highlights the way in which the Markan community's calling encompasses both the way of the cross and the "life of empowerment that is found as they tread that difficult and treacherous path" (*The Way of the Lord: Christological Exegesis of the Old Testament in the Gospel of Mark* [Louisville: Westminster/John Knox Press, 1992], 123). On Matthew's "transparent" rather than "historicizing" depiction of the disciples, and thus their connection with Matthew's community, see Ulrich Luz, "The Disciples in the Gospel According to Matthew," trans. Robert Morgan, in *The Interpretation of Matthew*, ed. Graham Stanton (Edinburgh: T. & T. Clark, 1995): 115–48. Notably and regrettably, though he allows for some transparency in the pre-Markan community (see 134–5), Luz dispenses with the

be" and the kingdom of God seems to have come to a head (see, e.g., Mk. 13:14).

Narrative context

From the juncture at Mk. 1:20, where Simon, Andrew, James, and John have left behind their nets to follow Jesus, this core group of disciples has lived out the first imperative of their initial summons to "come after" him (Mk. 1:17). For the most part, it is Jesus himself who plays the protagonist in this dramatic depiction of God's rule on earth. When he rids a man in Capernaum of an unclean spirit (Mk. 1:21–8), raises Simon's mother-in-law from a fever (Mk. 1:30–1), heals a man of skin disease (Mk. 1:40–5), and in various ways arouses the increasing ire of his foes (Mk. 2:1–3:6), Jesus strides forward as the figure through whose life the dominion of God reaches out to take hold of individuals and the world at large. In Jesus' words as well as in his deeds, the powers of the Evil One have met their match in a man whom they acclaim as God's advance agent (Mk. 1:24, 34; 3:11).

Jesus' authority in word and deed

In his programmatic report of Jesus' mission,[3] Mark introduces Jesus' Galilean activity with an episode that adeptly intertwines Jesus' teaching and wonder-working activity so as to emphasize their apocalyptic bearings. In the first place, Mark begins and ends the initial Capernaum encounter with references to Jesus' "authority" (Mk. 1:22, 27).[4] The summary found in Mk. 1:22 attributes the people's amazement to Jesus' teaching "as one having authority" (ὡς ἐξουσίαν ἔχων), an observation

second gospel itself in one sentence, claiming it "provides no material for our question because here the disciples are made to serve the christological conception of the messianic secret" (136).

[3] The passage's significant position has been noted, for example, by John P. Meier, *A Marginal Jew: Rethinking the Historical Jesus*, 3 vols. (Garden City, NY: Doubleday, 1991–2001), I:409.

[4] On thematic, stylistic, and lexical grounds, interpreters frequently ascribe these two references to Jesus' authoritative teaching to Mark's redactional activity (see Rudolf Bultmann, *The History of the Synoptic Tradition*, trans. John Marsh, rev. edn. [Peabody, MA: Hendrickson, 1994; orig. 1921], 209; also Robert A. Guelich, *Mark 1–8:26*, WBC 34A [Dallas: Word, 1989], 55; but cf. Vincent Taylor, *The Gospel According to Saint Mark: The Greek Text with Introduction, Notes, and Indexes*, 2nd edn. [Grand Rapids, MI: Baker, 1981; orig.1950], 171, who follows Johannes Weiss, *Jesus' Proclamation of the Kingdom of God*, trans. and ed. R. H. Hiers and D. L. Holland [Philadelphia: Fortress, 1971], 143–6, in asserting the traditional basis of the material.

reiterated in Mk. 1:27 as they marvel at "a new teaching with authority" (διδαχὴ καινὴ κατ' ἐξουσίαν).[5] While Daube has suggested that this emphasis implies distinction from local religious leaders based on Jesus' erudition,[6] Mark's use of the language resonates more fully with the apocalyptic vision of Daniel, where the word frequently conveys the sovereignty either of God (e.g. LXX/OG Dan. 4:17, 27; 5:4) or a human ruler authorized by God (e.g. LXX/OG Dan. 4:31; 7:14).[7]

The connection between Jesus' authority and the eschatological establishment of God's dominion only grows clearer when an exorcized demon addresses Jesus as the "Holy One of God" (Mk. 1:24). As many have pointed out,[8] the epithet applies in the Old Testament to a variety of figures[9] but never explicitly to a messianic one.[10] Yet especially in conjunction with the pericope's dominant interest in "authority," the phrase "Holy One of God" seems strikingly close to the Dan. 7 vision of "one like a son of man"[11] whose dominion will be inherited by the "holy ones of the Most High" (Dan. 7:18, 22, 25, 27). Further, Marcus cites various Qumran texts (e.g. 1Q30; 1QM 13:2–6) as examples of the apocalyptic mindset that associates "holiness" with the establishment of God's rule.[12] Thus the phrase denotes more than what Guelich calls a "special relationship, though unspecified here, between Jesus and God":[13] Jesus

[5] Some interpreters (including Joachim Gnilka, *Das Evangelium nach Markus*, 2 vols, EKKNT 2 [Zurich: Benziger; Neukirchen: Neukirchener Verlag, 1978–9], I:77, following Gerd Theissen, *The Miracle Stories of the Early Christian Tradition*, trans. Francis McDonagh, ed. John Riches, SNTW [Philadelphia: Fortress Press, 1983], 164–5) have questioned Mark's influence here, detecting instead early church missional language (Acts 17:19). Yet the evangelist weaves repeated mention of both Jesus' "newness" (Mk. 2:21, 22; 14:25) and his "authority" (Mk. 1:22; 2:10; 3:15; 6:7; 11:28 [2x], 29; 11:33; 13:34) throughout the narrative.

[6] David Daube, "ἐξουσία in Mk. i. 22 and 27," *JTS* 39 (1938): 45–59, effectively refuted by William L. Lane, *The Gospel According to Mark*, NICNT (Grand Rapids, MI: Eerdmans, 1974), 72, n. 111.

[7] Joel Marcus notes that since the word "authority" is particularly linked to God's eschatological victory, it is "no accident that it appears most frequently in the eschatologically oriented books of Daniel in the Old Testament and Revelation in the New" (*Mark 1–8: A New Translation with Introduction and Commentary*, AB 27 [Garden City, NY: Doubleday, 2000], 191).

[8] E.g. Robert H. Gundry, *Mark: A Commentary on His Apology for the Cross* (Grand Rapids, MI: Eerdmans, 1993), 82.

[9] Among those the Old Testament identifies as a "holy one of God" are Aaron (Ps. 106:16), Elisha (2 Kgs. 4:9), and Samson (Judg. 16:17).

[10] But cf. Walter Grundmann, *Das Evangelium nach Markus*, THKNT 2 (Berlin: Evangelische Verlagsanstalt, 1977), 60, on the possible link with the messianic priest described in *T. Levi* 18:11–12 who will bear a "spirit of holiness" even as "Beliar shall be bound by him."

[11] As mentioned above, the Greek ἀνθρώπου translates more accurately as "humanity."

[12] Marcus, *Mark 1–8*, 193.

[13] Guelich, *Mark 1–8:26*, 57.

functions, at the very least, as an exemplary denizen of God's apocalyptic kingdom.

Together, then, the language of Jesus' teaching "with authority" and his identity as the "Holy One of God" contribute to Mark's eschatological framing of Jesus' ministry. Further, the battery of exorcisms and healings that follows the initial episode only confirms the apocalyptic nature of that gospel mission.[14] But on what evidence does Jesus' wonder-working ministry signal the encroaching reign of God? In the first place, Watts argues that Mark's portrait of Jesus as "Yahweh-Warrior who delivers the captives from demonic bondage, as Israel's healer, and as the one who forgives her sin"[15] replaces the Isaianic focus on removing idol worship with an emphasis on the demons' demise.[16] Yet such a shift can also be found in the eschatological hope of Zech. 13:2 for Yahweh's removal of "the unclean spirit"[17] as well as in the Qumran community's curse on Belial who embodies opposition to God (1QM 13:4–5). Thus Mark's depiction of Jesus as one who subdues the resistance forces of the present evil age can best be understood against the backdrop of Jewish literature, which sometimes anticipates such activity as evidence of God's coming reign on earth.

If Mark's narrative so closely aligns Jesus with God's impending rule, what role does the evangelist ascribe to Jesus' followers throughout this rapid-fire enactment of God's apocalyptic victory? In many cases the loose coalition of Jesus' companions remains in the story's backdrop; they figure primarily as "silent partners" in the unfolding plot. Notably, those with Jesus have not yet been labeled "disciples" (a term not used until Mk. 2:15), and their actions are scarcely noted.

Yet Mark does appear to insert references to Jesus' followers in his introductory frames throughout this section, mentioning them only obliquely through third-person plural pronouns. For example, immediately after Jesus enlists the four fishers, Mark reports that "*they* went to Capernaum" (Mk. 1:21), indicating that this newly minted entourage accompanies Jesus as he wages his campaign for God's dominion. A similar use of an implied third-person subject which suggests the disciples' presence occurs in Mk. 1:29, where Mark writes, "And immediately,

[14] Modern scholarship can credit Weiss, *Jesus' Proclamation*, 74ff., with early recognition of the eschatological nature of Jesus' conflict with Satan. Among others, Rikki E. Watts has carried forward this emphasis by detecting the influence of Isaiah's depiction of Yahweh-Warrior as "agent of the N[ew] E[xodus]" (*Isaiah's New Exodus and Mark* [Tübingen: Mohr Siebeck, 1997], 140).

[15] Watts, *Isaiah's New Exodus*, 140. [16] Ibid., 164.

[17] Marcus, *Mark 1–8*, 193, points out that rabbinic traditions construe this text in association with exorcisms (e.g. *Num. Rab.* 19.8).

when they had gone out from (ἐξελθόντες) the synagogue, they went into the house (ἦλθον εἰς τὴν οἰκίαν) . . ."[18]

Moreover, Mark's redactional tendency to draw the disciples onto the scene opens the possibility that we should infer their continued presence where traditional material mentions an unspecified "they." After the healing of Simon's mother-in-law, Mk. 1:31 reports that she "began to serve *them*," a pronoun whose antecedent must on the basis of Mk. 1:29 include Simon, Andrew, James, and John along with Jesus. Even in the subsequent scene, where Mark apparently transmits a traditional report that "*they* brought to him" those to be healed or exorcized, the narrative setting at least preserves the possibility that the four men named earlier serve as the verb's collective subject.[19] Thus, repeatedly, Mark involves the group as witnesses to Jesus' activity even if they remain otherwise in the backdrop; though the effect is a subtle one, Jesus' mission in Mark emerges not as a strictly individual enterprise but as one enacted alongside his followers, since they remain "with him" throughout his Galilean activity.[20]

Besides these more veiled references to the company of Jesus' followers, Mark's narrative also mentions his companions by name and even finds them engaging with their leader in plot-shaping ways. It has been noted above that the four fishers who leave their nets to follow Jesus by Mk. 1:20 are overtly named when Jesus enters Simon's house in Capernaum to cure Simon's mother-in-law (Mk. 1:29). Of even greater significance is the episode later in the first chapter, when Jesus has removed himself to a "deserted place" (εἰς ἔρημον τόπον) to pray (Mk. 1:35). As Mark tells the story, Jesus' solitude is abruptly interrupted when Σίμων καὶ οἱ μετ' αὐτοῦ pursue Jesus to advise him of his increasing notoriety (πάντες ζητοῦσίν σε, Mk. 1:37). In response to their report, Jesus announces a change in their itinerary, as he resolves to expand his mission beyond its base in Capernaum: ἄγωμεν ἀλλαχοῦ εἰς τὰς ἐχομένας κωμοπόλεις (Mk. 1:38).[21] Moreover, the verse nicely balances the collective nature of the journey (through the first-person plural ἄγωμεν) with

[18] A few MSS (B λ φ al bo) instead supply a singular verb and participle, so that Jesus remains the exclusive subject. Yet the Markan framing tendencies noted here, along with the larger context in which Jesus proceeds along with his unnamed group of companions, support the more widely attested plurals.

[19] I discuss below this possibility for the disciples' role in Mk. 2:1–12.

[20] See Klemens Stock, *Boten aus dem Mit-Ihm-Sein: Das Verhältnis zwischen Jesus und den Zwölf nach Markus*, AnBib 70 (Rome: Biblical Institute, 1975), 188–9, who notes their presence throughout Mk. 1:21–39.

[21] Guelich, *Mark 1–8:26*, 70–1, detects in Jesus' detour a faint hint of a pre-Markan "messianic secret" motif, though he rightly concludes that the evangelist's emphasis lies not with Jesus' silence but with his ensuing proclamation in Galilee.

a redactional emphasis on Jesus' own mission: "for this is why I have come" (Mk. 1:38).[22] Still, we should not overlook the textual nuance that accords "Simon and those with him" a formative role in the direction and scope of that mission.

Controversy dialogues

Narrative attention to Jesus' disciples gains momentum in the series of controversy dialogues featured in Mk. 2:1–3:6.[23] Within this sub-unit the disciples are first named as such (Mk. 2:15), and as the story unfolds, their actions begin to attract the interest – and inspire the vigorous objections – of the religious authorities. To be sure, Mark's account stops short of giving full voice to the disciples; Jesus remains their mouthpiece as he rises to their defense in two key instances (Mk. 2:19–20, 25–8).

Still, these episodes of verbal sparring between Jesus and religious leaders widen the gospel's focus from Jesus' own Christological role to its collective expression in the practices of those who "come after" him. What is more, as the disputes intensify and culminate here in the plotting of Jesus' demise (Mk. 3:6), the disciples gain increasing notice. In particular, four discrete episodes crescendo toward the formal commissioning of the Twelve (Mk. 3:13–19).

The unit's opening pericope, the healing of the paralytic (Mk. 2:1–12), begins with the narrative spotlight squarely on Jesus himself. In contrast with the earlier verses that take note of the companionship of an unspecified group, Mk. 2:1 employs third-person singular verbs to set the stage: "And when *he* returned (εἰσελθών) again to Capernaum after some days, it was reported that *he* was (ἐστίν) at home."[24] Only after "many"

[22] Rudolf Pesch, *Das Markusevangelium*, 2 vols., HTKNT 2 (Freiburg: Herder, 1976), I:137–8. While some interpreters infer the verb ἐξῆλθον as a tacit theological statement of Jesus' "coming out from God" (e.g. Gnilka, *Markus*, I:89), Marcus, *Mark 1–8*, 204, is probably correct to point out the verb's possible military connotation as an expression meaning "coming out to battle" (see LSJ, 591 [1c]).

[23] Both form and rhetorical critics have argued, from differing perspectives, for the unity of this constellation of passages. Bultmann, *Synoptic Tradition*, 12–27, and others have assigned Mk. 2:1–3:6 to prior tradition on form-critical grounds, arguing that Mark has adopted wholesale the material reflecting early disputes between the nascent Christian community and Jewish authorities. Subsequent studies have identified at least Mark's redactional hand in the shaping of the material. For instance, Guelich, *Mark 1–8:26*, 82–3, excavates a pre-Markan source (Mk. 2:13–28) which the evangelist has framed by the inclusion of Mk. 2:1–12 and Mk. 3:1–6. In any case, the material in this section holds together well as a literary unit, as Joanna Dewey has argued on the basis of the passage's structure (*Markan Public Debate: Literary Technique, Concentric Structure, and Theology in Mark 2:1–3:6*, SBLDS 48 [Chico, CA: Scholars Press, 1980]).

[24] If, as scholars generally agree, Mk. 2:1 belongs to the evangelist's redactional frame (see, e.g., Bultmann, *Synoptic Tradition*, 14; Guelich, *Mark 1–8:26*, 83; Marcus, *Mark 1–8*,

gather around him does the story mention again the ambiguous "them" – a term that often at least includes the disciples – to identify those to whom Jesus was "speaking the word" (Mk. 2:2).[25]

But rather than elaborating the content of Jesus' address, the story takes a dramatic turn as an unnamed group launches an initiative that interrupts Jesus' proclamation with an episode of controversial healing. Mark recounts the group's bold move in this way: καὶ ἔρχονται φέροντες πρὸς αὐτὸν παραλυτικὸν αἰρόμενον ὑπὸ τεσσάρων (Mk. 2:3). Most interpreters infer that those bearing the paralytic to Jesus are simply friends motivated by the hope of healing.[26] Yet several features of the passage may suggest cryptically that Jesus' followers instigate the healing episode.

In the first place, the awkward syntax may designate the "four" as a common subject for both the finite verb ἔρχονται and the participle φέροντες; up to this point in the gospel, precisely four men have been named as Jesus' inner circle of followers. The very omission of such a detail in both synoptic parallel accounts (Matt. 9:2; Lk. 5:18) reflects the subsequent evangelists' dominant concern to showcase Jesus' remarkable healing power even as they tone down the story's interest in these supporting characters. Moreover, since Mk. 2:1 positions Jesus alone "at home," it may imply that some of his companions are otherwise disposed, perhaps concerned with an unnamed paralytic. In this reading, the healing begins when, "[his followers] came, bringing to [Jesus] a paralytic lifted up by four [of them]" (Mk. 2:3).

Finally, and most compellingly, Mark's account reports that only *after* fixing his gaze on "their faith" (ἰδὼν . . . τὴν πίστιν αὐτῶν, Mk. 2:5) does Jesus address the paralytic with a word of forgiveness. But what is this "faith," and how does it lead to the healing/forgiveness pronouncement? In line with an underlying Christological approach to Mark's gospel, many interpreters understand this word in terms of a trust in Jesus' healing abilities,[27] while others view it more broadly as a trust in Mark's message about Jesus.[28]

219), the singular focus on Jesus suggests that Mark here emphasizes Jesus' physical distance from his followers. I explore one possible explanation for this below.

25 We should probably construe the absolute τὸν λόγον, found here as in Mk. 4:14–20, 33, in light of the summary proclamation of Mk. 1:14–15: the gospel word of God's dominion. Guelich unnecessarily cites Mk. 1:45 as an exception to this notion of Jesus' message (*Mark 1–8:26*, 84); what the cleansed leper proclaims need not be essentially different from the good news that Jesus announces, namely, the word of God's salvation.

26 E.g. Marcus, *Mark 1–8*, 215: "namely the four friends of the paralytic."

27 E.g. Pesch, *Markusevangelium*, I:158; Taylor, *Saint Mark*, 194.

28 E.g. Gnilka, *Markus*, I:99. Similarly, Marcus points out that the early church had, by the time of Mark's writing, adopted "faith" and its verbal forms "as technical terms for believing in Jesus and in the God who had raised him from the dead" (*Mark 1–8*, 220).

On the other hand, just as I have asserted in chapter 1 that Jesus' summons to "trust in the gospel" (Mk. 1:15) encompasses the larger reality of God's dominion established on earth, here too the "faith" Jesus perceives may be more accurately viewed as their acknowledgment, through action, of the reality of God's coming rule. Thus, "their faith" sets this healing in motion in the sense that it provides a way around an apparent obstacle.[29] Moreover, in Jesus' response to that faith, the present passive ἀφίενται may imply his recognition of a pre-existing condition rather than his pronouncement of their forgiveness.[30] In other words, the incipient moment of the paralytic's healing can be located in the group's resolute trust in God's victory over the evil alliance of sin and disease.

Further, in his pronouncement that the "son of man has authority on earth to forgive sins" (Mk. 2:10), Mark's Jesus once again correlates implicit claims about his own Christological status (if the phrase alludes to the authoritative Danielic Son of Man) with their implications for the messianic community he is establishing. Certainly the fluid oscillation between the individual figure and his collective representatives "on earth" can be found in Dan. 7, which promises that the "holy ones of the Most High shall receive the kingdom (βασιλείαν)" (Dan. 7:18).[31] Thus the ability to proclaim God's act of forgiveness, pronounced here with authority by Jesus, is also implicitly conferred upon those whose "trust" in God's kingdom.[32] In this respect, those who lift up the pallet must be

[29] Based on its appearance in Markan healing narratives, Theissen calls faith "a boundary-crossing motif " (*Miracle Stories*, 129). Similarly, Guelich emphasizes faith as an "attitude expressed in conduct" (*Mark 1–8:26*, 85).

[30] Among those who identify the verb as conveying a divine passive are Joachim Jeremias, *New Testament Theology*, part I, *The Proclamation of Jesus* (London: SCM Press, 1971), 114; Eduard Schweizer, *The Good News According to Mark* (Atlanta: John Knox Press, 1970), 61; and Pesch, *Markusevangelium*, I:156. Cf. Marcus, *Mark 1–8*, 216, 222–3.

[31] Precisely who is meant by the term "holy ones of the Most High" has been widely debated in the secondary literature ever since Martin Noth argued that the term meant not faithful Israelites but celestial beings (see "The Holy Ones of the Most High," in *The Laws in the Pentateuch and Other Studies*, trans. D. R. Ap-Thomas [Edinburgh: Oliver & Boyd; Philadelphia: Fortress Press, 1966]: 215–28). Subsequent studies offering variations on Noth's theme include John J. Collins, *The Apocalyptic Imagination: An Introduction to Jewish Apocalyptic Literature*, 2nd. edn. (Grand Rapids, MI: Eerdmans, 1998; orig. 1984), 104–7, who understands the figures to be angelic, and John Goldingay, "'Holy Ones on High' in Daniel 7:18," *JBL* 107 (1988): 495–7, who finds the phrase to suggest "beings who are celestial in some way – angels or glorified Israelites" (497). Yet, in its depiction of the earthly "fourth kingdom," the Danielic vision seems to imply earthly persecution for the "holy ones" (see Dan. 7:25). Thus, while the term may refer precisely to the Maccabean martyrs (so L. F. Hartman and A. A. Di Lella, *The Book of Daniel*, AB 23 [Garden City, NY: Doubleday, 1978], 85–102), its function within an apocalyptic work probably implies a broader frame of reference, so that readers are inspired to read themselves into the term.

[32] As an early interpreter of Mark, the first evangelist has latched onto this extension of authority (see Matt. 16:19, where Peter inherits the keys to the kingdom and the authority to bind and to loose, an authority extended to the church in Matt. 18:18).

seen as Jesus' followers at least in the broadest sense, since they have both come after Jesus and engaged in the "fishing" enterprise.

If the increasing stature of discipleship is adumbrated in the healing of the paralytic, the ensuing passage returns to an explicit calling to discipleship in its report of the enlisting of Levi, son of Alphaeus (Mk. 2:13–14). The fact that Levi never again appears in Mark's gospel (or, apart from Luke's parallel, in the entire New Testament) raises questions about the story's origin as well as its function in Mark's narrative. Though some have argued that Mark has constructed the account after the pattern of Mk. 1:16–20,[33] Levi's subsequent omission from the list of the Twelve as well as any other extant early Christian literature indicates that the story probably derived from an earlier tradition adopted, with some editorial influence, by Mark.[34]

More pertinent to this study is Mark's deliberate inclusion, as well as his redactional handling, of the account. Certainly Mk. 2:13–14 rehearses in miniature the initial call to discipleship of Mk. 1:16–20:

Setting: "beside the sea"	Mk. 1:16	Mk. 2:13
Initial action: Jesus' "seeing"	Mk. 1:16, 19	Mk. 2:14
Initial summons: ἀκολούθει μοι	Mk. 1:17	Mk. 2:14
Response: ἠκολούθησεν αὐτῷ	Mk. 1:18, 20	Mk. 2:14[35]

Such striking verbal similarity closely links the character of Levi with the four previously called and demonstrates that a vital part of Jesus' mission is the inclusion of others – even those beyond the bounds of acceptably pious lifestyles – in his work. Moreover, Levi's name and his profession introduce an ironic twist, combining allusive hope for a figure "from Levi and Judah" as eschatological leader (e.g. *T. Dan* 5:10; *T. Gad* 8:1; *T. Benj*. 4:2) with one whose way of life constitutes a "despised trade" in first-century Jewish thought.[36]

Alongside the escalating conflict between Jesus and the Jewish leaders, the narrative role of Jesus' followers only gains momentum as the "disciples" are recognized as such for the first time (Mk. 2:15) and then become

[33] E.g. Rudolf Pesch, "Levi-Matthäus (Mc 2,14/Mt 9,9; 10,3). Ein Beitrag zur Lösung eines alten Problems," *ZNW* 59 (1968): 43–5.

[34] Ernest Best, *Following Jesus: Discipleship in the Gospel of Mark*, JSNTSup 4 (Sheffield: JSOT Press, 1981), 176.

[35] The only glaring omission from Mk. 1:17 to 2:14 is the promise of Jesus to make of the follower a "fisher of humans," an omission that may derive from the fact that Mark did not consider Levi to be one of the Twelve (Best, *Following Jesus*, 177).

[36] See Joachim Jeremias, *Jerusalem in the Time of Jesus: An Investigation into Economic and Social Conditions during the Time of Jesus* (Philadelphia: Fortress Press, 1969), 303–12; also E. P. Sanders, *Jesus and Judaism* (Philadelphia: Fortress Press, 1985), 177–8 and *passim*.

the object of the Pharisees' scrutiny in two instances. In the first place, the discussion of fasting practices etches a sharp demarcation between disciples of John and the Pharisees on the one hand, and Jesus' disciples on the other, as an unspecified "they" pose a contentious question: "Why do the disciples of John and the disciples of the Pharisees fast, but your disciples do not fast?" (Mk. 2:18).[37] In response, Jesus appeals to wedding imagery that resonates with prophetic passages that liken God's joy over Zion's to that of a bridegroom: "As the bridegroom rejoices over the bride, so shall your God rejoice over you" (Isa. 62:5).[38]

What is more, both Mk. 2:19 and Isa. 62:5 assign to "sons" a participatory role in the wedding feast. Significantly, both the MT and the LXX of Isa 62:5 assert, "For as a young man marries a young woman, so shall your sons (בָּנָיִךְ /οἱ υἱοί σου) marry you."[39] Thus, in calling the disciples "sons of the bridegroom" (οἱ υἱοὶ τοῦ νυμφῶνος),[40] Jesus effectively grants his followers a similar stake in this eschatological celebration.[41] In both cases, the impending reality of God's dominion and the salvation it brings (cf. Isa. 62:11) offer due cause for delight. According to Jesus, as long as the "bridegroom" remains present, his "sons" share in the celebratory feast; only "in that day" (Mk. 2:20) when the bridegroom has been "taken away," and the final judgment is at hand, will the disciples fast.[42] Even this brief dialogue, then, casts Jesus' disciples as participants in Jesus' mission, since their actions signal the eschatological timetable he has come to proclaim.

In the grainfield encounter with the Pharisees (Mk. 2:23–8), we can detect the disciples' further strides toward full participation in Jesus' mission. As in the preceding controversy, it is the *disciples* – not Jesus – who

[37] See David C. Daube, "Responsibilities of Master and Disciples in the Gospel," *NTS* 19 (1972–3): 4–5, for a full explanation of the appropriate implication that "Jesus is responsible for this infringement of the law" (5).

[38] This eschatological hope draws on other prophetic uses of the imagery in Israel's scriptures, including Jer. 2, Hos. 2, and Ezek. 16. In turn, various NT traditions appropriate the imagery to depict the church in Israel's role as bride and Jesus in God's role as bridegroom (e.g. Matt. 25:1–3; Eph. 5:23–33; Rev. 19:7–9).

[39] NRSV translators have deemed the MT corrupt and translated the term as "so shall your *builder* marry you."

[40] The common translation "wedding guests" parallels the equivalent Talmudic expression found, for example, in *b. Sukk.* 25b and *t. Ber.* 2:10 but obscures the linguistic ties to the prophetic literature discussed here.

[41] Relational language that confers a leading figure's destiny on sons/children is ubiquitous, but see, for example, *T. Levi* 18:12–13, in which the children of the "new priest" are granted authority to trample wicked spirits and become the object of the Lord's rejoicing.

[42] Based on the substantial parallels between Jesus' healings and the promises of Isaiah, Watts concludes that "Mark's presentation of Jesus' healing ministry can be understood as evidence, not of some generalised 'messianic time', but particularly as 'iconic' indicators associated with the inauguration of the Isaianic N[ew] E[xodus]" (*Isaiah's New Exodus*, 177).

offend the sensitivities of their onlookers as they pluck heads of grain on the Sabbath.[43] Again, Jesus functions primarily as their spokesman and interpreter of their actions when he answers the Pharisees' query about the lawfulness of the practice.[44] In rabbinic style, he appeals to the precedent of David and his companions (οἱ μετ' αὐτοῦ), who entered the house of God and nourished their own hunger with the bread of the presence (Mk. 2:25–6) – an act patently "not lawful" (οὐκ ἔξεστιν, Mk. 2:26).

What is most striking about this retort is its reshaping of biblical tradition, as Mark's Jesus exercises bold interpretive license in a way that elevates the stature of Jesus' followers.[45] First, the rather clumsy addition of the phrase αὐτὸς καὶ οἱ μετ' αὐτοῦ (Mk. 2:25) expands 1 Sam. 21's cast of characters to include David's companions. Thus while David remains the story's protagonist (τί ἐποίησεν Δαυὶδ ὅτε χρείαν ἔσχεν καὶ ἐπείνασεν, Mk. 2:25), Jesus defends his followers by applying David's deed to his entire cohort.

A second enhancement to the Davidic story reflects a similarly maladroit expansion. As Jesus enumerates David's actions and their offense, he claims not only that David "went into the house of God" and "ate the loaves of presentation," but also that "he gave them also to those who were with him (τοῖς σὺν αὐτῷ οὖσιν)" (Mk. 2:26). In this story, then, Jesus invokes the authority displayed by David *and his companions* as a precedent for his own license while, even more provocatively, it claims that authority for those who are "with him."

The passage's closing couplet – a notorious crux for interpreters of Mark – goes even further as it ascribes authority to humanity as the collective beneficiary of the Sabbath, which has been created διὰ τὸν ἄνθρωπον (Mk. 2:27). As a result (ὥστε), Jesus claims, "the son of man is lord even of the Sabbath" (Mk. 2:28), an assertion through which Jesus' authority is clearly intertwined with that of his companions.[46]

[43] Many interpreters attribute this detail to the controversy's origin in the early church, not Jesus' historical ministry (see, e.g. Bultmann, *Synoptic Tradition*, 16). Yet if the point were to justify the church's position over against Jewish objections of the day, the appeal could have been made stronger by ascribing grain-plucking activity to Jesus himself, a worthy enough target of censure elsewhere in the gospel. On the fluid lines of responsibility between master and disciple, see Daube, "Responsibilities," 11–12.

[44] In typically variegated fashion, Jewish halakah on this issue includes Philo's interpretation of Exod. 20:10 (*Life of Moses*, 2.22), which denies the lawfulness of plucking or cutting any kind of fruit, tree, or plant, as well as the Talmud's provision for plucking grain in order to create a path through a field on the Sabbath (*b. Šabb*. 127a).

[45] Daube posits that in an earlier version of the encounter, Jesus' reply was more faithful to the 1 Samuel narrative and mentioned only David's actions; Mark's introduction of the disciples' daring initiative, he maintains, necessitated an apparently unprecedented adaptation of the biblical tradition ("Responsibilities," 6).

[46] The debate about the identity of the Son of Man in this passage has been vigorous. One position that has garnered ample support is the view that the phrase merely derives

Finally, it is important to note that, within the plot development of Mark, the mounting tension between Jesus and the authorities necessarily ropes his followers into the conflict at hand. As long as Jesus makes his way through the Galilean countryside healing and teaching, his mission may raise a few eyebrows, but it does not fundamentally threaten the existing power base. But, as Jesus exhibits increasing pretense to authority, both on his own behalf and on behalf of his followers, the Jewish leaders show increasing signs of exasperation. In this respect, the ensuing showdown appears inevitable; within Mk. 2:1–3:6, it reaches a crest in the concluding controversy episode about the man with a withered hand, a story which ends with the first overt mention of the incipient plot by the Pharisees and Herodians against Jesus (Mk. 3:6). Although Jesus becomes the focal point of these ominous plans, Mark's account makes it clear that this vehement opposition has escalated at least partly in response to his involvement of others in his authoritative expression of God's dominion.

Transition to the Twelve

In the wake of the controversy conclusion, the story of the multitude at the seaside (Mk. 3:7–12) provides an important transitional summary which also lays narrative groundwork for the appointment of the Twelve in Mk. 3:13–19.[47] In this case, Mark names Jesus' disciples (Mk. 3:7) as a distinct group that has emerged from the πολὺ πλῆθος. The geographical reach of Jesus' repute, according to Mark, is far-flung; the multitudes have gathered in response to all they have heard him to

from the Aramaic idiom for "human," a claim sustained in this case by the previous verse's explanation of the Sabbath's creation διὰ τὸν ἄνθρωπον. On the other hand, those who emphasize Mark's frequent allusion to Dan. 7 claim that the phrase must here refer to the individual figure of Jesus. Yet, as I have maintained with respect to Mk. 2:10, and indeed as Marcus discusses (see especially *Way*, 167–71), the Daniel context itself presumes a close relationship between the individual and the "holy ones," who like the disciples in Mark's gospel and Mark's community itself, inherit the dominion first established by the representative figure. See also Marcus's treatment of Mk. 2:10 and 2:27–8 in "Son of Man as Son of Adam. Part II: Exegesis," *RB* 110 (2003): 370–86, where he demonstrates that hopes for the eschatological transformation of humanity sometimes found their focus in Jewish traditions about the first, and prototypical, man.

[47] Opinions predictably divide over the origin of this material, but the high incidence of *hapax legomena* (five terms found within three of the passage's verses), together with the passage's concentration of terminology generally ascribed to pre-Markan tradition make it likely that the evangelist has at least adapted existing material (see, e.g. Leander E. Keck, "Mk. 3,7–12 and Mark's Christology," *JBL* 84 [1965]: 346–7). But the positioning is Mark's and functions both to encapsulate the preceding material (cf. ibid., 344–5; also Gnilka, *Markus*, I:135) and to introduce what follows (see Lane, *Mark*, 126; Wilhelm Egger, *Frohbotschaft und Lehre: Die Sammelberichte das Wirkens Jesu im Markusevangelium* [Frankfurt am Main: Knecht, 1976], 93; Schweizer, *Good News*, 78).

be doing (Mk. 3:8), with particular emphasis on Jesus' healing ability (Mk. 3:10).

Perhaps most striking is Jesus' response to these unsolicited masses. In contrast to other passages in Mark where he remains captive to the whims of the crowds (Mk. 2:1–12; 5:21–43) and even preemptively supplies their needs (Mk. 4:1ff.; 6:34), Jesus here exhibits remarkable self-preservation when he asks the disciples to prepare an escape route so that the crowds might not crush him (ἵνα μὴ θλίβωσιν αὐτόν, Mk. 3:9).[48] At this point in the story, Jesus removes himself from center stage, it seems, in order that his own mission might not be thwarted. It is this desire to prolong his witness to God's incursion on earth that appears to motivate Jesus' rebuke to the spirits concerning his identity as Son of God (Mk. 3:11). The injunction to secrecy intends to stem the tide of Jesus' fame, which has begun to encroach upon his freedom and may threaten his very life.[49] Jesus has proclaimed the dawn of God's reign through word and deed, mounting a frontal assault on palpable forces of evil to claim victory for the Yahweh-Warrior portrayed in OT prophecy. Thus this passage offers a striking example of Jesus' demurral, as he diverts attention from himself and redirects it toward the kingdom reality that, in the company of his followers, he so poignantly demonstrates.

The making of the Twelve: Mark 3:13–15

If Mark's story has increasingly highlighted the disciples' presence as well as their actions, the way has been paved for more formal attention to their relationship to their master. In Mk. 3:13–19, Mark's protagonist calls his companions away from the action, up to a mountaintop, to designate and equip them for further service in this drama of the new age. The passage serves as a hinge between the initial call to discipleship (Mk. 1:16–20) and its culmination in their successful "fishing" activity (Mk. 6:7–13, 30), as it both echoes the twofold pattern of presence

[48] Guelich, *Mark 1–8:26*, 147, downplays the boat as a means of escape by pointing to its use in Mk. 4:1 as a means of teaching the crowds. Yet it serves no such purpose here; rather it provides a "way out" from the press of the multitudes (see Karl-Georg Reploh, *Markus – Lehrer der Gemeinde: Eine redaktionsgeschichtliche Studie zu den Jüngerperikopen des Markus-Evangeliums*, SBM 9 [Stuttgart: Katholisches Bibelwerk, 1969], 39).

[49] Tolbert understands Jesus' commands to silence as "his steadfast rejection of personal renown and glory" (*Sowing the Gospel: Mark's World in Literary-Historical Perspective* [Minneapolis: Fortress Press, 1989], 227) – a feature which she contends buys "time for sowing the word" (229). I would maintain, as Tolbert does elsewhere, that the Markan Jesus' demurral also expresses a core dynamic of that "word," which culminates in the self-emptying act of the cross.

and practice and lays rhetorical emphasis on their coming missionary endeavors.[50]

To determine this pericope's particular claims about the pattern of discipleship, I shall consider three facets of this brief but significant episode: its mountaintop setting, the "making" of the Twelve, and the dual purpose of their designation. Individually, each of these components appeals either directly or indirectly to first-century hopes for the restoration of Israel as the assurance of God's end-time victory. Their convergence here only accentuates Mark's portrayal of discipleship against the backdrop of Israel's apocalyptic anticipation. As we shall see, this discipleship passage portrays a "high Christology" in the intimate connections it forges between Jesus and the God whose final sovereignty the people of Israel so desperately awaited. Yet in myriad ways, the making of the Twelve establishes a similarly lofty view of discipleship, as Jesus' followers are summoned to enact, through authoritative word and deed, the same kingdom reality that has characterized Jesus' mission to this point in Mark's gospel.

Mountaintop calling

Commentators have frequently recognized in this passage's opening verse distinct intertextual allusion to instances of divine disclosure found in the Old Testament.[51] Perhaps most prominent among these precursor texts is Moses' ascent to Mount Sinai as recounted in Exod. 19:3–7, an episode that in many respects underscores the significance of Jesus' ascent to the mountaintop in Mk. 3:13. Particularly striking are the verbal links between Exod. 19:3 (LXX) and Mk. 3:13:

Exodus 19:3	Mark 3:13
καὶ Μωυσῆς ἀνέβη	Καὶ ἀναβαίνει
εἰς τὸ ὄρος τοῦ θεοῦ	εἰς τὸ ὄρος
καὶ ἐκάλεσεν αὐτὸν ὁ θεός	καὶ προσκαλεῖται οὓς ἤθελεν αὐτός

[50] John R. Donahue, *The Theology and Setting of Discipleship in the Gospel of Mark*, The 1983 Père Marquette Theology Lecture (Milwaukee, WI: Marquette University, 1983), 16, notes this difference between Mk. 1:16–20 and 3:13–9: "the 'call' dimension is condensed while the mission aspect is expanded."

[51] E.g. Grundmann, *Markus*, 101; Lane, *Mark*, 132; Schweizer, *Good News*, 81; but cf. Gundry, *Mark*, 166; Guelich, *Mark 1–8:26*, 156, who calls this encounter "hardly a divine revelation." Dale Allison, *The New Moses: A Matthean Typology* (Edinburgh: T. & T. Clark, 1993), 174–5, points out that the phrase ἀναβαίνειν εἰς τὸ ὄρος occurs some twenty-four times in the LXX, mostly in the Pentateuch and mostly with Moses as its subject. Also abundant are references to τὸ ὄρος in Samuel and Kings as a place where God encounters God's chosen one(s) (e.g. 1 Kgs. 19:11). Obviously, the biblical language reflects, to some extent, the topography of the area; yet the pattern is consistent enough to support the more metaphorical view that associates the mountain with divine revelation.

Such distinctive echoes establish Israel's Sinai story as foundational for Mark's account of this commissioning narrative in several respects. In the first place, the close literary resemblance highlights the tension inherent in Mark's portrait of Jesus, which casts him in the double role of Moses and of God. On the one hand, each story's protagonist serves as subject of the verb ἀναβαίνω, so that Jesus plays the part of Moses when he "goes up to the mountain." In this respect, Jesus assumes Moses' position as intermediary between God and the people whom God has chosen.[52]

Yet this role correspondence shifts dramatically in the verse's next verb, προσκαλεῖται, which speaks of Jesus' summons to "whom he wanted" (Mk. 3:13). According to Exod. 19:3, it is not Moses but God who serves as the subject of the related verb: ἐκάλεσεν αὐτὸν ὁ θεός. Indeed, such language of divine election reverberates throughout Israel's scriptures. For instance, Isa. 41:8–9 addresses "Israel, my servant" as the one "whom I took from the ends of the earth, and called (ἐκάλεσα) from its farthest corners." When Jesus "calls" from the mountaintop, then, he assumes a similar mantle of sovereign authority, an authority confirmed rhetorically in the verse's pleonastic construction, which combines the middle-voice verb προσκαλεῖται with the pronoun αὐτός, as well as in the verb ἤθελεν.[53] Finally, once Jesus summons his followers,[54] it is they who become designated and entrusted leaders among God's people.

Another interpretive clue that the Exodus passage supplies for our understanding of this mountaintop setting derives from its wider narrative context. For Moses' Sinai encounter with God entails more than an instance of divine self-disclosure; it formalizes a covenant relationship that will equip God's people for faithful living. It is on the mountaintop that God speaks the ten words, the Decalogue, which will constitute the heart of Israel's code of conduct and establish the relationship that

[52] Further, W. Horbury, "The Twelve and the Phylarchs," *NTS* 32 (1986): 503–27, cites Josephus, *Ant.* 3.47, 219–22 and *Num. Rab.* 13.2 to support the connection in later Jewish thought between Moses and the twelve tribal leaders.

[53] Reploh, *Markus*, 44, notes the "souveräne Ruf Jesu in die Nachfolge, der hier in οὓς ἤθελεν αὐτός seinen Ausdruck findet." Guelich, *Mark 1–8:26*, 157, adds that the pronoun αὐτός indicates that the choice was "Jesus' alone," and in it he detects a "faint echo of the OT references to God's sovereign call." I submit that the "echo" would have been at least faintly audible to Mark's first-century audience.

[54] Leading the way for subsequent exegetes, Matthew and Luke interpret quite differently the relationship between the group whom Jesus initially calls and the Twelve named later in the passage. For Luke (6:13; followed, e.g., by Marcus, *Mark 1–8*, 266; Taylor, *Saint Mark*, 230), the Twelve are selected from among a larger group initially summoned; for Matthew (10:1; followed, e.g., by Robert P. Meye, *Jesus and the Twelve: Discipleship and Revelation in Mark's Gospel* [Grand Rapids: Eerdmans, 1968], 147; Pesch, *Markusevangelium*, I:204; Lane, *Mark*, 132), the two groups are synonymous. Since Mark's account offers no clear mention of a secondary selection process, the latter view seems more likely.

ensures its status as a "treasured people" (Exod. 19:5). In other words, to affirm God's presence on the mountain is only the starting point for the intended revelation, which itself inspires the people's active participation in the way of life designated through that revelation.

In Mark's story, too, this mountaintop episode derives its significance not just from epiphany itself – or even from the "high Christology" that ascribes divine authority to Jesus – but also from its function in the drama of God's dawning kingdom. As I have already observed, this passage occurs in Mark's gospel at a point where Jesus' followers are first stepping forward as agents of that kingdom in their own right. Like the Exodus encounter, this divine disclosure further fortifies them for a mission that reflects God's dominion. Yet, as we shall see, Mark's account diverges from the Exodus paradigm in a remarkable way. While both mountaintop encounters establish a framework for living in relationship to God, the Torah given to guide Israel's religious and ethical practice contrasts with the authority given to equip the Twelve in their end-time warfare against the δαιμόνια.

Finally, the narrative timing of Moses' Sinai encounter parallels in a significant way the timing of Mark's mountaintop story. Moses ascends Mount Sinai in the middle of Israel's "meantime" wilderness experience, as the people of God wander in limbo between their miraculous deliverance from Egyptian captivity and their arrival in the Promised Land. The mountaintop gift of Torah offers the people of Israel a framework for their identity forged out of this "meantime" perspective, as the covenant constitutes both a grateful response to God's rescue in the Exodus event and the foundation for community life across the Jordan. From Mark's perspective, Jesus and his disciples (and even Mark's audience) also reside in a charged "meantime" between the dawn of God's dominion and its full disclosure. Thus Jesus' equipping of the disciples on the Galilean mountaintop occurs at a similar juncture in the life of this eschatological community, between God's active intervention in the world, specifically in the person of Jesus, and the "promised land" of God's coming kingdom.

Complementing this mountaintop tradition of Sinai in Mark's Jewish landscape is the expectation that Mount Zion will serve as the locus for God's coming kingdom.[55] As Frank Moore Cross has demonstrated,

[55] I should note that while Sinai and Zion are certainly different mountains associated with different biblical traditions, they share prominence as specific locations where God repeatedly intervenes in the life of God's people. For the purposes of understanding Mark's language and imagery, the interpretation is enhanced through consideration of both mountaintop experiences. On the relationship between the two traditions in first-century Jewish thought, see Jon D. Levenson, *Sinai and Zion: An Entry into the Jewish Bible*,

several passages in Deutero-Isaiah reflect a convergence in thought of the Deuteronomic way through the wilderness (e.g. Isa. 40:3–5) and the Zion psalms heralding God's enthronement on the holy mountain (e.g. Pss. 2, 110).[56] A prime example can be found in Isa. 51:10–11, which speaks of the "way for the redeemed to cross over / So the ransomed of the Lord shall return, and come to Zion with singing." As a backdrop to this encounter in Mk. 3, such a "proto-apocalyptic" vision depicts the mountaintop as the setting in which God's kingship will be established.

The prophetic hope that God's rule will gain a decisive foothold upon a mountain carries implications that are both universal in scope (eliciting the response of the nations) and particular in focus (the reassembly of the twelve tribes).[57] The vision articulated in Isa. 2 establishes the "mountain of the Lord's house" as the place where that restoration will take place:

> Many nations (ἔθνη πολλά) shall come and say,
> "Come and let us go up to the mountain of the Lord (δεῦτε καὶ ἀναβῶμεν εἰς τὸ ὄρος κυρίου) . . ."
> For out of Zion shall go forth instruction (νόμος) and the word of the Lord (λόγος κυρίου) out of Jerusalem. (Isa. 2:3)

In this depiction, as in its similar expression in Mic. 4:2, the mountaintop has taken on an eschatological role, in the "days to come" (Isa. 2:2), as the locus to which all nations shall stream (Isa. 2:2) and from which both νόμος and λόγος κυρίου shall emanate. Such a vision motivates the prophet, in Isa. 56:7, to identify that mountain inclusively as a "house of prayer for all nations (πᾶσιν τοῖς ἔθνεσιν)." The universal, even cosmic, scope of God's dominion thus entails procession to the mountain of the Lord, where that dominion will become fully evident in the "days to come."

Later writings confirm and reiterate this view of the mountain as locus for the end-time ingathering. While it lacks mention of a mountain *per se*, *Pss. Sol.* 17 anticipates a messianic king who "will glorify the Lord

New Voices in Biblical Studies (Chicago, New York, Minneapolis: Winston Press, 1985), especially 187–217, where Levenson explores what he calls the "pluriform" nature of that relationship.

[56] Frank Moore Cross, *Canaanite Myth and Hebrew Epic: Essays in the History of the Religion of Israel* (Cambridge, MA: Harvard University Press, 1973), 108, maintains that the "procession to Zion and the feast on the holy mountain . . . have . . . redirected the route of the Exodus and Conquest to lead to Zion."

[57] On the relationship between Israel and the Gentiles in the coming kingdom, see Joachim Jeremias, *Jesus' Promise to the Nations* (Philadelphia: Fortress Press, 1982), *passim*, who argues that Jesus restricted his mission to Israel even while he anticipated the eschatological incorporation of the Gentiles into the people of God.

in (a place) prominent (above) the whole earth," a place to which nations will "come from the ends of the earth to see [the Lord's] glory" (*Pss. Sol.* 17:30–1). A similar mountaintop setting is linked more explicitly, in 4 Ezra 13:6, to the eschatological deliverer who "carved out for himself a great mountain, and flew up upon it." Indeed, the vision's subsequent interpretation promises that this figure "will stand on the top of Mount Zion [and that] Zion will come and be made manifest to all people" (4 Ezra 13:35–6). Significantly, both texts combine motifs of an eschatological leader and a mountaintop setting to depict the full manifestation of God's reign.

When Jesus calls his disciples εἰς τὸ ὄρος in Mk. 3:13, then, the second evangelist evokes the richly symbolic function of mountaintop encounters found in Jewish scripture. Jesus serves as both Moses (God's special intermediary) and God himself; the mountaintop setting hints at both divine disclosure and divine empowerment; and it both recalls God's decisive intervention in Israel's history and anticipates the apocalyptic hope for God's universal sovereignty. Taken together, all of these nuances establish the terms for understanding Mark's view of his own community as those "called" by Jesus at the turn of the ages.

The "making" of the Twelve

While Mark's commissioning story evokes the hope of God's universal sovereignty, Jesus' "making" of the Twelve reflects the widespread view of Israel's restoration as a constituent part of God's eschatological victory. Moreover, the nature of the Twelve's commissioning, as depicted in these verses, confirms their role as participants in that apocalyptic drama.

I begin the discussion of these verses with the cryptic clause that introduces the commissioning itself: "And he made the Twelve" (καὶ ἐποίησεν δώδεκα, Mk. 3:14a).[58] As I shall demonstrate below, the verb ἐποίησεν combines with the eschatologically charged term δώδεκα as a proleptic glimpse of end-time restoration, when the twelve tribes converge upon the mountain to acclaim God's sovereignty established on earth. At issue here are both the historical understanding of this oblique reference to a New Israel and its theological weight for Mark's audience.

In the first place the choice of the aorist active indicative ἐποίησεν to express Jesus' inaugural action upon this mountain echoes Jesus' initial

[58] The additional phrase οὓς καὶ ἀποστόλους ὠνόμασεν found in several key witnesses (including ℵ, B, and Θ) is more easily explained as an effort to harmonize the passage with Matt. 10:1–4 and Lk. 6:12–16 than as a deliberate omission in another manuscript tradition (see, e.g., A, C^2, D, K).

promise to "make" his followers fishers of people (Mk. 1:17).[59] After a period of "coming after" him, the disciples are poised to embark on the other half of their calling. Within its narrative context, the verb ἐποίησεν carries forward Jesus' intention to "make" those who will come after him into active agents of God's ingathered kingdom.

Yet the verb resonates, too, with LXX language surrounding God's creative acts reported in Genesis. Certainly the verb ποιέω is a common one carrying a wide range of semantic connotations,[60] yet the fact that in this passage Jesus assumes the God-like role of calling others to himself, combined with the apocalyptic expectation otherwise suggested, points to the likelihood that the encounter on the mountain signifies the promise of new creation.[61]

Worth noting too is that, besides the use of ποιέω to characterize God's incipient creative act,[62] the verb figures prominently in another pivotal Genesis story of divine initiative: God's call and promise to Abram. While the Gen. 12 encounter begins with the command for Abram to "go out" (ἔξελθε), it grounds the imperative in Yahweh's assurance: ποιήσω σε εἰς ἔθνος μέγα. Together, these two scriptural antecedents from the LXX of Genesis converge to connote, in Mark's story, the "making" of a new creation in the form of a new Israel. Just as Jesus has assumed God's role as the one who "calls" atop the mountain, here too he "makes" the Twelve as an act of new creation which, as we shall see, envisages the restoration of the "many nations" first promised to Abram.

What Jesus "makes" is just as significant for our understanding of this mountaintop encounter. For when Mark reports Jesus' designation of Twelve (δώδεκα, Mk. 3:14a), he attributes to Jesus a clear eschatological vision. As Sanders has argued, historical probability supports the notion that Jesus himself promoted an understanding of his followers as the core members of the New Israel.[63] Several complementary findings

59 See Meye, *Jesus and Twelve*, 105, who maintains that the verb refers to an act endowed with a particular purpose.

60 See BAGD, 680–3.

61 Gunther Schmahl, *Die Zwölf im Markusevangelium* (Trier: Paulinus, 1974), 55; Pesch, *Markusevangelium*, I:204. Commentators often rely on the verb's use in both LXX and NT passages (e.g. 1 Kgdms. 12:6; Heb. 3:2) for the sensible translation "appoint." As Guelich observes, the translational choice "is not without significance" (*Mark 1–8:26*, 157). He argues in favor of "appointed" as the "more natural reading" (158), mainly because he believes it lends proper emphasis to the purpose clauses (see also Stock, *Boten*, 16–17). In my view, those clauses only gain weightier significance through their dependent relationship – in structure and content – to Jesus' creative act.

62 The verb appears fifteen times in the opening Genesis creation story: Gen. 1:1, 7, 11, 12, 16, 21, 25, 26, 27 (3x), 31; Gen. 2:2 (2x), 3.

63 Sanders, *Jesus and Judaism*, *passim*, esp. 95–106. Meye also finds "momentous support" for the accuracy of Mark's depiction of the Twelve, *Jesus and the Twelve*, 192–209,

support Jesus' establishment of the Twelve as belonging to the category of "(almost) indisputable facts."[64] First, a variety of early Christian writings mention a group of twelve followers and thus suggest a historical basis on the grounds of multiple attestation.[65] Second, the embarrassing tradition of Judas's betrayal finds resolution in a variety of ways, but in each case the original group of twelve is maintained.[66] Finally, after Acts 1:15–26 reports the replacement of Judas by Matthias, the prominence of the Twelve seems only to wane. The combined weight of evidence thus confirms the historical likelihood that Mark preserves Jesus' own eschatological impulse in the making of the Twelve.

The significance of the "Twelve" within Jesus' ministry, and within Mark's gospel, grows transparent in light of first-century Jewish thought. The number's correlation to the tribes of Israel finds widespread expression in both biblical and post-biblical Jewish writings. While the passages that articulate this concrete hope are too vast to mention here, I shall note examples that demonstrate the breadth of the tradition that leads scholars to maintain that "the expectation of the reassembly of Israel was so widespread, and the memory of the twelve tribes remained so acute, that 'twelve' would necessarily mean 'restoration.'"[67]

First, Ezekiel's vision of the restoration of Israel combines images of a new temple with "the boundaries by which you shall apportion the land for inheritance among the twelve tribes of Israel of Ezekiel" (Ezek. 47:13). Within the wisdom tradition, a cry for deliverance from foreign oppression calls for the gathering of "all the tribes of Jacob" (Sir. 36:13) which leads both to the eradication of the enemy (Sir. 36:11) and to the ultimate hope that "all who are on the earth will know that you are the Lord, the God of the ages" (Sir. 36:22). Moreover, remarkably consistent claims found both in the QL (e.g. the 4Q164 fragment) and in the Sibylline

though he views the relationship from a more didactic rather than an apocalyptic perspective. On the other hand, others (e.g. Rudolf Bultmann, *Theology of the New Testament*, 2 vols. [New York: Charles Scribner's Sons, 1951–5] I:37, and Günther Klein, *Die zwölf Apostel: Ursprung und Gehalt einer Idee* [Göttingen: Vandenhoeck & Ruprecht, 1961]) consider the "Twelve" as a post-Easter fabrication that Mark inserts into the tradition.

64 Sanders, *Jesus and Judaism*, 101.

65 In addition to the synoptic gospels, John's gospel as well as 1 Cor. 15:5 preserve remnants of the widespread memory of this body of "Twelve."

66 Sanders observes that Matt. 19:28's claim that "you yourselves will be seated upon the twelve thrones judging the twelve tribes of Israel" would have been particularly embarrassing (*Jesus and Judaism*, 99–100).

67 Ibid., 98. Despite the frequent mention of ten "lost tribes," extant tribes in first-century Palestine included Levi, Judah, and Benjamin (named in 1QM 1:2 as "the exiled of the desert (נולת המדבר)," and claimed by Paul [Rom. 11:1; Phil. 3:5]). Both *T. Jos.* 19:1–2 and *1 Enoch* 89:72 also divide the tribes into nine and three.

Oracles (e.g. 2.170–6) confirm the expansive theological and geographic range of this set of expectations associated with the Twelve. What is more, the active part played by this eschatological community, entailing both judgment and salvation, coheres fittingly with Mark's portrait of the discipleship calling.

Appropriately, then, Guelich calls the appointment of the Twelve "commensurate with [Jesus'] announcement of the 'fulfillment of time' and his proclaiming of the coming of the kingdom (1:15)."[68] It is the Twelve who collectively bear witness to the triumph of God over the cosmic adversary. And as we shall see below, it is the Twelve who join Jesus as vessels through whom that triumph is to be enacted.[69]

I have finally to consider briefly two related issues that have long concerned Markan scholarship: the narrative relationship between the "Twelve" and Jesus' "disciples," and the relationship between the Markan community and both groups. First, does Mark mean to distinguish the "Twelve" from a wider group of Jesus' followers? The question is complicated rather than resolved by the recognition that, in many instances, Mark has drawn references to the "Twelve" from tradition, while the mention of "disciples" is often attributed to his own redactional contribution[70] – a claim that serves arguments for *and* against an intentional distinction.[71] Perhaps the clearest resolution emerges when we perceive not a dichotomy but a progressive continuity between the particular symbolism surrounding the "Twelve" and the more expansive nature of the

[68] Guelich, *Mark 1–8:26*, 158, though he exercises caution in the use of the term "New Israel" because of its supersessionist thrust and its implicit claim to continuity with Old Israel. He wants to stress, instead, the apocalyptic expectation of the restoration of "*all* God's people." Lane, *Mark*, 133, calls the Twelve the "proleptic form . . . of the Messianic community, the eschatological creation of God."

[69] Among those who deny this apocalyptic thrust are Donahue, *Theology and Setting of Discipleship*, 10, and Best, *Following Jesus*, who contrasts the role given here with the more "apocalyptic role they possess" in the Matthew and Luke parallels. In addition he maintains (1) that the group is not presented as the "core of the New Israel" and (2) that their identity within Mark's community is "the consecration of a group as full-time missionaries" (184). What Best fails to recognize is the "apocalyptic" nature of the missionary authority given to the disciples, which I shall consider below in greater detail.

[70] This is the view of Best, "Mark's Use of the Twelve," *ZNW* 69 (1978): 32. Also, Marcus, *Mark 1–8*, 265, finds that Mark appropriated from tradition the appointment of the Twelve.

[71] Among those espousing such a distinction in the case of Mk. 3:13–19 are Best, *Following Jesus*, 184 (though cf. "Role of the Disciples," 380) and Stock, *Boten*, 200, who construes the disciples as "eine größere Gruppe." On the other hand, Meye, *Jesus and the Twelve*, 147, Seán Freyne, *The Twelve: Disciples and Apostles: A Study in the Theology of the First Three Gospels* (London: Sydney, Sheed & Ward, 1968), 107–19, and Pesch, *Markusevangelium*, I:204, all consider the twelve in this passage to be indistinguishable from the group whom Jesus calls together.

group designated as Jesus' followers. As we shall see, Mk. 3:35 reports Jesus' deliberate alignment of familial ties according to the criterion of doing "the will of God," while Mk. 4:10 designates as "insiders" both the core group of "Twelve" and "those around him." For Mark, then, the mountaintop commissioning of the Twelve functions as an "initial point of departure" for his own community's missionary activity rather than an exhaustive, or even privileged, designation of Jesus' followers.[72]

The purpose of the Twelve

In the preceding chapter, I have identified components of presence and practice within Jesus' initial call to discipleship found in Mk. 1:17, as he summons four fishers to "come after" him and to be made "fishers of humans." Here I intend to demonstrate the extent to which Mk. 3:14b–15 both echoes and carefully elaborates the core pattern of that original encounter.[73] Already, I have suggested that this commissioning encounter serves as an identity marker for Jesus' companions as well as for their heirs in Mark's audience. The passage's ensuing verses complete the picture, as their deliberate structure supplies the content of that identity – an identity which also finds its foundation in Israel's anticipation of God's decisive power at work in the world.

To specify the purpose motivating Jesus' formation of the Twelve (ἐποίησεν δώδεκα), Mark employs two parallel ἵνα clauses that assert, with some degree of tension, the group's relational tether to Jesus as well as their deliberate removal from him:

> καὶ ἐποίησεν δώδεκα
> ἵνα ὦσιν μετ᾽ αὐτοῦ
> καὶ ἵνα ἀποστέλλῃ αὐτοὺς
> κηρύσσειν καὶ ἔχειν ἐξουσίαν ἐκβάλλειν τὰ δαιμόνια.
> (Mk. 3:14–15)

[72] Hengel, *Charismatic Leader*, 88. Also Donahue, *Theology and Setting of Discipleship*, 10, believes that Mark here roots his community's own missionary self-understanding in "the period of its origin." These views contrast sharply with Best, *Following Jesus*, 184: "As distinct from the missionary activity of every Christian we find here the consecration of a group of full-time missionaries."

[73] In his comparison of the two call/commissioning pericopes, Stock, *Boten*, 42–50, finds that Mk. 3:13–19 represents a "freie Form" (50) departure from the structure of Mk. 1:16–20 and emphasizes instead the preparation of the Twelve for their missionary journey. While I grant the missionary emphasis (see below), I simply view it as the elaboration of the previous call.

These two foundational components of the Twelve's mission – being with him and being sent out – together constitute a benchmark against which the disciples' developing role in the gospel might be assessed.

In the first purpose clause, Jesus appoints the Twelve ἵνα ὦσιν μετ' αὐτοῦ, a phrase that both *echoes* the δεῦτε ὀπίσω μου from Mk. 1:17 by emphasizing presence and subtly *redefines* the disciples' role from followers to companions.[74] Just as in the initial call narrative, the command to "come after me" precedes the promise to be made "fishers of humans," Jesus' appointment of the Twelve here names their close proximity to Jesus as a prerequisite to advancing his agenda. The mantle of authority has not yet been transferred from the leader to his followers; indeed, just as in the prophetic model of Elijah and Elisha, the ones "coming after" Jesus must in the first instance accompany him, as witnesses and participants in his own mission.[75] For the disciples, "being with" Jesus provides a foundation for any other function they may be given.[76]

Yet a parallel ἵνα clause indicates a second, equally important, and even more detailed aspect of the commissioning: Jesus appoints the Twelve ἵνα ἀποστέλλῃ αὐτούς. This succinct phrase both echoes and develops Jesus' promise, in Mk. 1:17, to make his followers "fishers of people." In the first place, the prophet Jeremiah employs the same verb ἀποστέλλω to convey Yahweh's promised restoration of the people to their land: ἰδοὺ ἐγὼ ἀποστέλλω τοὺς ἁλεεῖς τοὺς πολλούς (Jer. 16:16). The fishers, in both Jeremiah's and Mark's accounts, will be divinely ordained for service in the "days that are coming" (Jer. 16:14). As investigation of Jer. 16 in the previous chapter has shown,[77] Yahweh's act of sending many fishers constitutes a vital, preparatory step in the eschatological ingathering of Israel "back to their own land" (Jer. 16:15) – a particular mission that will culminate on a universal scale when the nations return to Yahweh "from the ends of the earth" (Jer. 16:19). Similarly, just as this commissioning passage establishes the Twelve as an eschatological community of Israel's

[74] Stock argues against such a reading when he maintains, "Zwischen ihnen [that is, Jesus and his disciples] besteht kein partnerschaftliches Verhältnis. Jesus ist der bestimmend Herr" (*Boten*, 193). Such emphasis on (hierarchical?) Lordship, though, both seems beside the point for Mark's Jesus (see, e.g., Mk. 10:45) and diminishes the narrative development of the disciples' part in the story.

[75] Because this presence is denied to the Gerasene demoniac in Mk. 5:18, Guelich finds this phrase to denote a "special personal relationship whereby [the disciples] shared in his life and ministry (*Mark 1–8:26,* 158).

[76] Stock views the purpose of this presence as an opportunity to grasp Jesus' identity, an understanding intended to be preliminary to mission work (*Boten*, 70). In the narrative itself, though, the disciples are sent out long before Jesus' identity is clear in their minds.

[77] See above, chapter 2, 60–2.

restored tribes, their "sending" will signal an indispensable act in the establishment of God's sovereignty.

Even as we acknowledge the momentous role the Twelve are commissioned to play, though, we should not fail to notice the verse's emphasis on Jesus as subject of the verb ἀποστέλλῃ. We have already seen that the Twelve's "being with" Jesus precedes and thus prepares them for their participation in this eschatological event. Further, as Donahue notes, the awkward grammatical shift from the plural verb ὦσιν to the singular ἀποστέλλῃ "stresses that the mission originates with Jesus."[78] It is Jesus who engages the Twelve in the task at hand; only out of their relationship to him do the Twelve bear a significant part in Jesus' mission. Thus the narrative's double ἵνα clauses suggest the complementary nature of these two facets of the commissioning: neither the followers' "being with" Jesus nor his "sending them out" can be understood apart from the other.[79]

Once we affirm the Twelve's dependence on Jesus, both rhetorically and theologically, we turn attention to the purpose associated with their being "sent out." For while the succinct phrase "to be with him" remains unmodified grammatically, the passage affixes two distinct actions, expressed by two present indicative infinitives, to explicate Jesus' intent in sending out the Twelve. The observation that these infinitive phrases' language and style seem to reflect Mark's redaction[80] underscores the evangelist's editorial interest in depicting Jesus' followers in a manner that corresponds closely with Jesus' own mission.

The first activity to characterize the mission of the Twelve is one that has already been associated with Jesus' ministry: κηρύσσειν. Early in Mark, John the Baptist's proclamation has elicited a baptism of repentance for the forgiveness of sins (Mk. 1:4) even as it has heralded a "stronger one than I coming after me" (Mk. 1:7). Indeed, in the wake of this precursor's message – and only after John has been handed over – Jesus himself begins to proclaim τὸ εὐαγγέλιον τοῦ θεοῦ (Mk. 1:14). Already I have noted that the content of that "gospel" extends beyond Jesus' own precise Christological identity to encompass the "good news" of God's coming apocalyptic victory.[81] For instance, when Jesus resolves to expand his mission into the neighboring towns, he names his intent to "proclaim" as the express purpose of his coming out: εἰς τοῦτο γὰρ ἐξῆλθον (Mk. 1:38). In the following verse, Mark summarizes Jesus' activity in this way:

[78] Donahue, *Theology and Setting of Discipleship*, 17.

[79] Even if, as Donahue emphasizes, the "being with" Jesus is preparatory for the missionary service of the Twelve, neither is it complete without his "sending them out."

[80] See, e.g., Gnilka, *Markus*, I:137.

[81] See above, chapter 2, esp. 34–40.

κηρύσσων εἰς τὰς συναγωγὰς αὐτῶν . . . καὶ τὰ δαιμόνια ἐκβάλλων (Mk. 1:39).

As the story continues, Mark employs the verb κηρύσσειν to describe the proclamation not only of Jesus but also of various figures who interact with him. In Mk. 1:45 – and despite Jesus' injunction to "say nothing to anyone" (Mk. 1:44) – a healed leper "began to proclaim (κηρύσσειν)" and to spread word of his cure. Later, the Gerasene demoniac responds similarly, when according to Mark he "began to proclaim (κηρύσσειν) . . . the things Jesus had done for him" (Mk. 5:20). Indeed, the summary of Mk. 7:36 reports that however much Jesus commanded to the contrary, those who witnessed his healing "more abundantly proclaimed (ἐκήρυσσον) it." Together these uses of the verb characterize proclamation as an act that proceeds quite naturally – indeed it cannot be stopped[82] – from the dramatic demonstration of God's victory over evil as enacted by Jesus' healing ministry. Significantly, though these instances of proclamation often draw further attention to the person of Jesus (cf. Mk. 1:45; 5:20; 7:37), in each case they emerge from an apocalyptic showdown in which Jesus has vividly enacted God's sovereign victory.

What, then, is the content of the message that Jesus commissions the Twelve to proclaim? On the basis of the word's use elsewhere in Mark's gospel, we may infer that they will proclaim the same as Jesus has proclaimed, namely the "gospel of God" (Mk. 1:14). And though Jesus' Christological role as specially designated mediator of that gospel lies at the heart of the proclamation, especially for Mark's community, its wider claims consist in the world-altering hope of God's dominion. In other words, for Mark, Jesus' life (including his healing ministry), his death, and his resurrection vividly demonstrate the promises of God's coming rule, but they do so in an expansive rather than an exclusive manner.[83] Indeed, as Mark's Jesus purposefully confers upon his followers the proclamation task, he anticipates their full perpetuation of his own gospel mission articulated at the story's outset.

That the Twelve's proclamation entails their explicit witness to the nearness of God's kingdom only grows clearer in light of the second purpose affixed to their being sent out: ἔχειν ἐξουσίαν ἐκβάλλειν τὰ δαιμόνια

[82] What Wrede's messianic-secret thesis (*The Messianic Secret* [Cambridge: James Clark, 1971; orig. 1901]) overlooks is the nuanced difference, in the Markan account, between Jesus' willingness to proclaim – and have others proclaim – the good news of God's kingdom and his reticent redirection of any acclaim that would herald his own wonder-working abilities instead of "what the Lord has done" (Mk. 5:19).

[83] Guelich, *Mark 1–8:26*, 159, argues similarly that the content of both Jesus' and the disciples' proclamation is the "message of the Kingdom" given in Mk. 1:14–15.

(Mk. 3:15). As Jesus gives them this type of authority (ἐξουσίαν), he endows the Twelve with traits that have characterized Jesus' own ministry to this point. Already the disciples have been commissioned to proclaim God's coming dominion; here Jesus extends to them the authority to demonstrate that dominion by casting out demons.[84] And just as Mark's gospel exhibits an ascending interest in the authority that God has conferred on humanity (e.g. Mk. 2:10, 27–8), this aspect of the Twelve's commissioning squarely aligns their power with Jesus' own demonstration of God's rule.[85]

We should note that the weight of that mantle is not insignificant in the story, as the issue of Jesus' vast authority has emerged early on as a trademark of his ministry.[86] From the gospel's outset, both Jesus' instruction and his deeds have been attributed to his remarkable "authority." When Jesus begins to teach in the Capernaum synagogue, he does so, in the estimation of onlookers, "as one having authority" (ὡς ἐξουσίαν ἔχων, Mk. 1:22); when he then rids a man of an unclean spirit, observers marvel at his authority, asking τί ἐστιν τοῦτο; διδαχὴ καινὴ κατ᾽ἐξουσίαν (Mk. 1:27).

Above I have discussed the possible conferral of that authority on humanity in Mk. 2:10, where the "son of man has authority (ἐξουσίαν) to forgive sins upon the earth (ἐπὶ τῆς γῆς)." What is implicit in the healing of the paralytic gains specificity when Jesus defends his companions' Sabbath infraction by pronouncing that the "son of man is lord even of the Sabbath" (Mk. 2:28). Pertinent in both cases, I have maintained, is the Danielic vacillation between an individual figure who mediates between the divine throne room and the earthly sphere on the one hand, and the "holy ones" who inherit his authority on the other. Against this backdrop, the endowment of the Twelve with "authority" only etches deeper lines of continuity between Jesus' "authority" and theirs.

Several features of Daniel buttress the claim that this apocalyptic vision provides an interpretive backdrop for Mark's apocalyptic scheme. In the

[84] Rather interestingly, Wrede links Jesus' "warring with the demonic realm" with his messiahship (e.g. *Messianic Secret*, 21, 49). Yet if Mark construed Jesus' miracles as "manifestations of the Messiah" (17), might we not safely gather that the disciples' similar authority entails their participation in his messiahship?

[85] Ben Witherington, III, *The Gospel of Mark: A Socio-Rhetonical Commentary* (Grand Rapids, MI: Eerdmans, 2001), 426, construes this authorization in terms of what he calls the "Jewish concept of agency." I submit that the authorization also draws on an understanding of the collective embodiment of a representative figure (e.g. "my servant Israel").

[86] Whitney Taylor Shiner, *Follow Me! Disciples in Markan Rhetoric*, SBLDS 145 (Atlanta: Scholars Press, 1995), 186, notes that Mark's characterization of Jesus rests on his remarkable authority rather than his rational powers.

first place, both Dan. 7 and Mark envision the coming kingdom of God as the culmination of a season of open conflict (Dan. 7:23; Mk. 13:8); indeed God's judgment stands at the cusp of this coming age (Dan. 7:26; Mk. 1:15). Moreover, just as the Son of Man approaches the throne of God, thus bridging the human and divine spheres (Dan. 7:13), so too in Mark, a voice from heaven twice designates Jesus as God's beloved son (Mk. 1:11; 9:7). And perhaps most significantly, both representative figures serve as conduits through whom divinely apportioned authority is conferred, as Daniel puts it, upon "the people of the holy ones of the Most High" (Dan. 7:27). For if the Danielic vision of a coming kingdom focuses authority in the individual Son of Man, that figure retains a collective scope in which authority extends to the "people of the Holy Ones."[87] In the same manner, Jesus serves as the prototypical focus of God's reign, which ultimately becomes dramatized not just through his life but through the collective witness of those who become swept up in its current.

Read in this light, the specific authority that Jesus ascribes to the Twelve – authority "to cast out demons" (Mk. 3:15) – must be understood within the context of the cosmic showdown between the divine and demonic realms that the gospel has repeatedly related.[88] At Jesus' behest are the powers of the "present evil age" whose contrary forces Jesus has already begun to unseat and who now will meet with a new battalion of opposition. As Hengel has pointed out, the goal of Jesus' followers in Mark is not to align themselves with tradition but "to prepare for the service of the approaching rule of God."[89] Yet if that rule is "approaching," its sway can already be detected in Mark's unfolding story; the strong man is being bound as a part of God's search and seizure mission that aims to reclaim the earth.

To be sure, both Jesus' general "authority" and his vigorous combat against the demonic realm have already earned him a reputation that draws swarming crowds and threatens the power structure. Why then would Mark's Jesus share center stage with those whom he calls to the mountaintop? Why would he confer upon the Twelve the very authority he has wielded effectively, and to this point exclusively? After all, as Shiner has observed, Jesus' transfer of his own authority – rather than simply a

[87] For a discussion of the collective and corporate dimensions of various OT background texts, see Marcus, *Way*, 196–7.

[88] Watts, *Isaiah's New Exodus*, 164, recognizes this move as Mark's transposition of the Isaianic "evil" of idolatry into a first-century concern with the demonic "occupying legions," whose demise would signal the coming of deliverance.

[89] Hengel, *Charismatic Leader*, 81.

body of teaching – to his followers represents a teacher–student dynamic "quite alien" to contemporary philosophical and wisdom material.[90]

When Mark's Jesus endows the Twelve with the "authority to cast out δαιμόνια," he deliberately gives up exclusive rights to a central aspect of his own Christological mission. Like the Danielic Son of Man, Jesus extends the divinely sanctioned authority to those who become its stewards upon the earth. For Mark, and for Mark's post-resurrection audience, the message is clear: Jesus' authority continues on in their own collective participation in his apocalyptic agenda. Perhaps to transform them from mere bystanders awaiting full disclosure of God's promised rule, Mark reports that Jesus' followers are to be enlisted as agents in the showdown that will usher in the new age.

This mountaintop encounter establishes firm ties between Mark's Christology and his portrait of discipleship. Mark's overarching message about God's coming dominion identifies both Jesus and his followers as those enlisted to demonstrate its accompanying authority. That Jesus journeys to the mountaintop to equip his followers to carry on his mission does not diminish his own Christological mission. Instead it expands its impact and thrust.

Conclusion

As it develops the patterns of discipleship identified in the last chapter, Jesus' encounter with the Twelve in Mk. 3:13–15 elaborates several important elements of the intended relationship, in Mark's narrative, between this leader and his followers. Let me summarize the observations that have emerged from this exegetical study:

(1) Mark's placement of this traditional element within his narrative framework affirms and expands the disciples' increasing prominence in the narrative. On the one hand, Jesus' followers are beginning to play a greater role in the story, as they do in Mk. 2:23–8. On the other hand, Jesus' own ministry has come under the shadow of a plot to kill him (Mk. 3:6). That Jesus would deliberately call his disciples to the mountaintop and formally establish their own mission in relationship to his makes perfect narrative sense and highlights the significance of their intended role.

(2) In many respects, the passage clearly assigns to Jesus the initiative in this relationship with his disciples. No matter how extensive the Twelve's mission might ultimately be, it derives first and foremost from Jesus'

[90] Shiner, *Follow Me!*, 188–9.

calling them, from their being with him, and even from their being sent out by him. As I have noted, Mark rather subtly likens Jesus' narrative role to that of the One who, in Israel's scriptures, summons leaders to equip them as agents of the divine will at work in the world.

(3) Just as the mission of the Twelve must be securely anchored in their "being with" Jesus, neither will his mission proceed without the complementary activity of those whom he will "send out." Both the structure and the verbal emphasis of Mk. 3:14b–15 devote painstaking care to showcase the activities of their mission, expressed through language that aligns their own activity with Jesus' ministry. Endowed by Jesus with the same kind of authority that has characterized his own words and deeds, the Twelve thus are equipped to provide a vital collective witness to the "new thing" (Isa. 43:19) that God is doing to establish dominion over the world.

PART III

Discipleship in action

4

DISCIPLESHIP AS PRESENCE IN MARK 4:1–34

Introduction

The present study has so far examined two key call/commissioning texts (Mk. 1:16–20 and 3:13–15) and detected within these passages core components of Mark's portrait of discipleship: presence and practice. Both Jesus' initial summons, addressed to the four fishers, to "come after" him (Mk. 1:17) and his appointment of the Twelve to "be with him" (Mk. 3:14) suggest that Mark's Jesus enlists his followers primarily as companions as he proclaims God's impending reign. Only through their presence alongside their leader do the disciples gain the requisite foundation for the second facet of their calling, their practice of proclaiming God's kingdom as "fishers of humans" (Mk. 1:17) endowed with "authority to preach and to cast out the δαιμόνια" (Mk. 3:15). The investigation will proceed by following the narrative contours of Mark's gospel as it depicts Jesus' engagement with his disciples while they are "with him" as the platform for their practice.

In this chapter the probe of *discipleship as presence* focuses on a pericope that is both indispensable for our understanding of the gospel and a veritable exegetical minefield: Jesus' parabolic teaching found in Mk. 4:1–34. Though the story includes earlier reports of Jesus' teaching[1] and his use of parables,[2] in Mk. 4 the gospel's brisk narrative pace slows to a crawl as Jesus instructs his hearers through a sustained series of parables. To be sure, Mark's Jesus generally lacks the sage-like attributes depicted in Matthew's and Luke's gospels (e.g. in the Sermon on the Mount/Plain) as well as the overt Christological teachings of John's gospel. Yet at

[1] Prior to its appearance in Mk. 4:1, the verb διδάσκω occurs in Mk. 1:21, which immediately follows the first call to discipleship and where Jesus' teaching is subsequently (Mk. 1:28) linked to his command over unclean spirits, and in Mk. 2:13, where Mark reports the teaching of a "whole crowd" just prior to the call of Levi. Moreover, elsewhere Mark's gospel employs different words, especially κηρύσσω (e.g. Mk. 1:14; 1:39) and λέγω (e.g. Mk. 1:15; 2:8, 25; 3:23) to convey Jesus' instructional activity.

[2] See Mk. 3:23–7, an example discussed in greater detail below.

Mk. 4:1, the evangelist inserts a prolonged set of teachings in which Jesus instructs through his *words* what he has previously demonstrated through his *deeds*: the nature of God's dominion.[3] Perhaps it is the dramatic pause created by this complex of teachings that has led many exegetes to locate in Mk. 4:1–34 the interpretive clue to the entire gospel.[4]

Included among the myriad exegetical issues swirling around Mk. 4 are its compositional history, the origin and function of Mk. 4:10–12 (including the question of the so-called Markan Parable Theory), and the chapter's import for Mark's community. While these and other scholarly debates will be considered throughout this chapter, the inquiry will be governed by an overriding interest in discipleship. Thus this study of Mk. 4:1–34 will focus on a central question: what light does this account of Jesus' teachings shed on the topic of discipleship in Mark's gospel, at both the narrative level of the gospel story and the historical level of Mark's community? As I proceed through the chapter's sub-units, I shall consider Mark's shaping of traditional material as it elucidates both Jesus' mission and purpose and, by extension, that of his followers. As this study will reveal, Jesus' parabolic teaching in Mk. 4:1–34 further develops the evangelist's emphasis on the disciples' participation in the dawning rule of God, which features Jesus as its prototypical embodiment. Central to Jesus' exposition of that reign ("the kingdom of God") is a symbiotic effort in which a vulnerable God entrusts humanity with the task of sowing the seeds even while a sovereign God ultimately ensures victory over evil and the abundant harvest that victory promises.

Narrative context

As in each of the previous chapters, I begin by situating the passage within the second gospel. For although in Mk. 3:13–15 Jesus commissions the

[3] Paul J. Achtemeier, "'He Taught Them Many Things': Reflections on Marcan Christology," *CBQ* 42 (1980), reminds the reader that for Mark Jesus' teaching and miracle-working derive from the same power source and thus should not be severed from one another or weighed against each other (478–80).

[4] Examples of monographs that argue for the centrality of this text include Mary Ann Tolbert, *Sowing the Gospel: Mark's World in Literary-Historical Perspective* (Minneapolis: Fortress Press, 1989); Mary Ann Beavis, *Mark's Audience: The Literary and Social Setting of Mark 4.11–12*, JSNTSup 33 (Sheffield: Sheffield Academic Press, 1989); Joel Marcus, *The Mystery of the Kingdom of God*, SBLDS 90 (Atlanta: Scholars Press, 1986); and Frank Kermode, *The Genesis of Secrecy: On the Interpretation of Narrative* (Cambridge, MA: Harvard University Press, 1979). Similarly, Jan Lambrecht calls the chapter "a short synthesis of Mark's pronounced and refined theology" ("Redaction and Theology in Mk., IV," in *L'Evangile selon Marc: tradition et redaction*, ed. M. Sabbe, BETL 34 [Leuven: Leuven University Press, 1974], 307).

Twelve to "be with" Jesus and to be "sent out" by him, the ensuing story narrates their presence with him for almost three chapters before Jesus finally initiates their first missionary journey apart from him in Mk. 6:7. The parabolic instruction of Mk. 4 lies at the heart of that material as a glimpse of discipleship as presence, yet the two encounters that Mark places between the mountaintop commissioning and the seaside instruction together sharpen the gospel's claims both about Jesus' mission and about what it means to follow him. Together, several features of the Beelzebul controversy (Mk. 3:20–30) and the redefinition of family ties (Mk. 3:31–5) provide important interpretive clues for our understanding of the parabolic teaching of Mk. 4.

The Beelzebul controversy

To begin with, Jesus' response to allegations of his alliance with Beelzebul present the gospel's first mention of parables as a pedagogical tool: "And calling them (αὐτούς) together, in parables [Jesus] said to them . . ." (Mk. 3:23). In this case, his audience is described by the pronoun αὐτούς, which most likely finds its antecedent in the "scribes from Jerusalem" who have, in the previous verse, attributed Jesus' authority over demons to his "having" Beelzebul (Mk. 3:22).[5] At least three observations support the view that the scribes constitute the object of Jesus' initial parabolic instruction. First, grammatically, the text presents the definite noun γραμματεῖς as the pronoun's most proximate and thus natural antecedent. Second, the Jesus of Mark's gospel does not cower in the face of the authorities' accusations but, rather, rises up rhetorically in defense of his own (or his disciples') authority;[6] that Jesus would address his accusers directly fits well in a narrative that drives relentlessly toward a showdown with the religious leaders whose detractions eventually bring about his demise. Third, and perhaps most pertinent to the study of Mk. 4, the use of a parable as a means to implicate its hearers finds scriptural precedence in such prophetic writings, for instance, as Isa. 5, Ezek. 17, and

[5] The use of the participle προσκαλεσάμενος, which almost always in Mark characterizes Jesus' calling together of the disciples (Mk. 3:13; 6:7; 8:1; 10:42; 12:43) and/or an agreeable crowd (Mk. 7:14; 8:34) for instruction, could suggest that Jesus calls together his family/followers for this instruction. Yet, as noted by many commentators (e.g. John Drury, *The Parables in the Gospels: History and Allegory* [London: SPCK, 1985], 47; Morna D. Hooker, "Mark's Parables of the Kingdom (Mark 4:1–34)," in *The Challenge of Jesus' Parables*, ed. Richard N. Longenecker [Grand Rapids, MI: Eerdmans, 2000], 81; Robert A. Guelich, *Mark 1–8:26*, WBC 34A [Dallas: Word, 1989], 175), the other factors mentioned here seem to outweigh this Markan tendency.

[6] E.g. Mk. 2:8, 25; 3:4.

2 Sam. 12.[7] Thus, Jesus' parabolic teaching about the kingdom of God, at least in Mk. 3:23–7, aims not to confuse but to elucidate the conflict that accompanies its coming.[8] It is his opponents' unwillingness to identify themselves with God's dominion, not Jesus' use of parables *per se*, that will ultimately lead to their judgment.[9]

Redefinition of family ties

The question of eschatological allegiances becomes the topic of further discussion in Mk. 3:31–5, where we find not parabolic instruction but an overt realignment of familial ties. Already in Mk. 3:21, Jesus' own relatives have acted on the public claim that he had gone "out of his mind" (ἐξέστη), a misconstrual of Jesus' authority similar to the scribes' allegations. Here Jesus' mother and brothers reappear, yet they are the ones twice described as "outside" (ἔξω, Mk. 3:31, 32), a term that not only locates them at a physical remove from Jesus but also adumbrates the contrast, found in Mk. 4:10, between those with Jesus and those "outside." Further, when Jesus himself hears a report of family members who seek him (Mk. 3:32), he responds by naming those seated around him as his mother and brothers (Mk. 3:33–4), based on a new criterion for kinship: "Whoever does (ποιήσῃ) the will of God is my brother and sister and mother" (Mk. 3:35).[10]

Whereas Matthew here identifies Jesus' family as "the disciples" (Matt. 12:46) and Luke applies the term to those who "hear and do the word of God" (Lk. 8:21), Mark handles the tradition in a manner that highlights two important claims in this passage. First, the crowd seated around Jesus includes those who may be favorably disposed toward Jesus' proclamation of God's in-breaking reign. Second, their relationship to

[7] See Drury, *Parables*, 12, who says that these prophets "attracted their prey by concealing under their agreeable and interesting forms a biting relevance to contemporary events." In any case, the parables' ultimate purpose, beyond this concealment, was to reveal those events to their hearers.

[8] Kelber seems to go too far in his claim that from 3:23, "speaking 'in parables' becomes Jesus' habitual mode of speech reserved for the opposition" (*The Kingdom in Mark: A New Place and A New Time* [Philadelphia: Fortress Press, 1974], 25–6). Certainly the crowd of Mk. 4:1 cannot be considered "opposition"; moreover, the disciples form at least part of the audience in the parables chapter as a whole.

[9] Cf. Guelich, *Mark 1–8:26*, 175; Joachim Gnilka, *Das Evangelium nach Markus*, 2 vols., EKKNT 2 (Zurich: Benziger; Neukirchen: Neukirchener Verlag, 1978–9), I:149.

[10] Most commentators view this verse as an independent logion affixed at some point in the traditioning process to Mk. 3:31–4 (e.g. Rudolf Bultmann, *The History of the Synoptic Tradition*, trans. John Marsh, rev. edn. [Peabody, MA: Hendrickson, 1994; orig. 1921], 29–30; Ernest Best, "Mark iii. 20, 21, 31–5," *NTS* 22 [1975–6]: 315).

him is determined not so much by their "acceptance of Jesus as the one in whom God's will is at work"[11] as by their "doing" the "will of God." Rather than passive receptivity, the posture of those sitting around Jesus reflects an active openness to performing (ποιέω) the will of God, which Jesus seems driven to disclose.[12]

Taken together, these two brief episodes constitute an important narrative backdrop for the parabolic instruction of Mk. 4. In both cases, Jesus proclaims God's coming reign to ally and foe alike; that his hearers do not respond with uniform acclaim does not mute his message. Ultimately, the effectiveness of that proclamation hinges not on passive reception but on active participation, or "doing" the "will of God" (Mk. 3:35). Both of these apocalyptic elements – the freely disclosed, ineluctable reign of God together with the heightened division it entails – gain fuller expression in Mk. 4:1–34. For Jesus' followers, the parabolic instruction will assert the imminence of God's rule, even amid variegated forms of resistance. Though it may be going too far to say that the evangelist included Mk. 4 primarily to make sense of controversy and conflict in the evangelist's community,[13] certainly the teaching has been reshaped in the form of a "reflection after the fact on the conflict."[14]

Jesus' kingdom-of-God teaching: Mark 4:1–34

Even a cursory glance at Mk. 3:20–35 has provided an important backdrop for the investigation of Mk. 4:1–34. Although I shall address questions of the passage's composition history with a particular eye to Mark's redactional contributions, we most accurately grasp its relationship to

[11] So Guelich, *Mark 1–8:26*, 183. Similarly, Klemens Stock maintains that the Twelve's grasp of Jesus' identity is the primary purpose of their "being-with-him" (*Boten aus dem Mit-Ihm-Sein: Das Verhältnis zwischen Jesus und den Zwölf nach Markus*, AnBib 70 [Rome: Biblical Institute, 1975], 70).

[12] It is significant that this group is delineated above all by their physical proximity to Jesus – their "being with him." Certainly this group includes, but is not limited to, the Twelve (so Guelich, *Mark 1–8:26*, 182; contrast Robert P. Meye, *Jesus and the Twelve: Discipleship and Revelation in Mark's Gospel* [Grand Rapids: Eerdmans, 1968], 151, who finds "absolutely no reason to infer a group of disciples larger than the Twelve in this text").

[13] E.g. John Painter, *Mark's Gospel: Worlds in Conflict*, New Testament Readings, ed. John Court (New York: Routledge, 1997), 76; Ched Myers, *Binding the Strong Man: A Political Reading of Mark's Story of Jesus* (Maryknoll, NY: Orbis, 1988), 170. See also Morna D. Hooker, *A Commentary on the Gospel According to St. Mark*, BNTC 2 (London: A. & C. Black, 1991), 125, who asserts that for Mark, "the continued obduracy of the Jewish nation when confronted by the Christian gospel could be explained only as part of God's mysterious purpose."

[14] Ben Witherington, III, *The Gospel of Mark: A Socio-Rhetorical Commentary* (Grand Rapids, MI: Eerdmans, 2001), 164.

discipleship when we bear in mind various features of the story's landscape: Jesus' prior use of parables for exposure, not obfuscation; his positive engagement with the crowd in Mk. 3:34–5; and the deepening crevice between those whose lives exhibit the rule of God that Jesus proclaims and those bedeviled by it.

Jesus teaches a very large crowd

The narrative introduction itself, found in Mk. 4:1–2, contains several details that establish Jesus' teaching as a deliberately momentous event in his ministry. The evidence here of Mark's editorial hand only underscores the import the evangelist ascribes to Jesus' parabolic teaching.[15] To begin with, Mark includes, almost to the point of redundancy, three references to Jesus' teaching act. The combination of the passage's opening line, "and again he began to teach (διδάσκειν)" (Mk. 4:1), with the repetitive claim that "he taught (ἐδίδασκεν) them" and "he said to them in his teaching (ἐν τῇ διδαχῇ αὐτου)" (Mk. 4:2) sets the stage for understanding Jesus' ensuing instruction as calculated and proactive. As Drury observes, Jesus' deliberate teaching activity here exhibits interesting points of contact with the book of Deuteronomy, understood as Moses' speech that interprets the narrative that precedes and follows it.[16]

Moreover, the modifying infinitive phrase καθῆσθαι ἐν τῇ θαλάσσῃ not only establishes a spatial distinction between Jesus and the crowd (described as ἐπὶ τῆς γῆς) but also confers on him the magisterial authority frequently associated with "sitting": Ps. 29:10 depicts Yahweh's sitting enthroned over the flood;[17] various gospel passages (e.g. Matt. 5:1–2; 13:1–2; 23:2; Lk. 4:20–1; 5:3), along with *m. 'Abot* 1:4, link the act of sitting to deliberate instruction; and sitting often denotes a position of authority such as a throne (e.g. Ps. 9:7; Rev. 3:21) or judgment seat (Josephus, *Ant.* 20.130). Thus, while Mark's gospel includes a relative paucity of Jesus' teaching content (when compared with the other evangelists' accounts), at this point in the story Jesus' instruction receives the full weight of Mark's editorial emphasis.

[15] Guelich, *Mark 1–8:26*, 189, points to vocabulary, content, and style as evidence that "Mark's redactional hand appears beyond doubt in the setting of 4:1" and that the "same is likely true of 4:2, though Mark may have reworked a traditional introductory statement." See also Joachim Gnilka, *Die Verstockung Israels. Isaias 6:9–10 in der Theologie der Synoptiker* (Munich: Kösel, 1961), 57; Joel Marcus, *Mark 1–8: A New Translation with Introduction and Commentary*, AB 27 (Garden City, NY: Doubleday, 2000), 293; cf. Rudolf Pesch, *Das Markusevangelium*, 2 vols., HTKNT 2 (Freiburg: Herder, 1976), I:230.

[16] Drury, *Parables*, 49.

[17] Ibid.

A second facet of Mk. 4:1–2 that relates directly to this study is Jesus' audience, which shifts from the masses to a more select group. I have noted in chapter 2 that the initial call of the four fishers in Mk. 1:16–20 makes more specific Jesus' preceding summons to "repent and trust in the gospel" (Mk. 1:15). Similarly, Jesus' indiscriminate teaching reported in Mk. 2:13 leads to a more focused discipleship command to Levi, found in Mk. 2:14. Both instances balance Jesus' willingness to engage the public at large with his concern for particular responses among his followers.

That same balance can be seen at the opening of this chapter, where the verbal links between Mk. 2:13 and Mk. 4:1, both usually considered redactional,[18] are especially striking:

Mark 2:13	Mark 4:1
καὶ ἐξῆλθεν πάλιν	καὶ πάλιν ἤρξατο διδάσκειν
παρὰ τὴν θάλασσαν	παρὰ τὴν θάλασσαν
καὶ πᾶς ὁ ὄχλος ἤρχετο	καὶ συνάγεται
πρὸς αὐτὸν	πρὸς αὐτὸν ὄχλος πλεῖστος
καὶ ἐδίδασκεν αὐτούς	

In both passages, Mark's narrative combines the sweeping nature of Jesus' instruction with the particular response of those who repent and trust in his gospel message. In other words, as we shall see through the course of Mk. 4:1–34, this text holds in tension the universal, revelatory intent of Jesus' teaching and the differing responses it elicits, as once again, Jesus' teaching serves as a launching point for discipleship.[19]

Indeed Mark's editorial concern for the crowd only grows more transparent with the mention of the ὄχλος πλεῖστος that has gathered around Jesus. The superlative modifier conveys that the crowd's magnitude surpasses Jesus' previous audiences (cf. Mk. 3:7, 9, 20)[20] and necessitates his removal by boat so that he might teach them many things (πολλά, Mk. 4:2). At the chapter's outset, then, Jesus teaches in a manner that

[18] This widely held view is based on the verses' Markan vocabulary (e.g. paratactic καί, πάλιν, the phrase παρά τὴν θάλασσαν, and the verb διδάσκειν). See Guelich, *Parables*, 190, who calls Mk. 4:1 "reminiscent of a similar redactional seam in 2:13." See also Gnilka, *Markus*, I:104, 156.

[19] Elizabeth Struthers Malbon observes that, in Mark's gospel, the "disciples and the crowd are more complementary than competing groups" (*In the Company of Jesus: Characters in Mark's Gospel* [Louisville: Westminster John Knox, 2000], 97). I would add that the disciples' distinctive authorization, identified especially in the call narratives studied above, only binds them more closely to the masses with whom Jesus repeatedly interacts.

[20] Whether this superlative, found only here in Mark, indicates a "high point" (so Gnilka, *Markus*, I:156) or merely a "crescendo" (Marcus, *Mystery*, 15; also Guelich, *Mark 1–8:26*, 190), it at least underscores the narrative momentum of Jesus' growing appeal, which in turn occasions his deliberate instruction.

does not depend on the hearing level of his audience. In contrast to Mk. 3:9, where a boat is mentioned as a means of escape from the threat of a crushing crowd, the vessel here enables his continued ministry in their midst.[21] Just as the crowd mentioned in Mk. 3:20 does not thwart but even promotes his speaking in parables (Mk. 3:23), here too Jesus finds a way for the crowd not to impede his teaching.

Finally, Mark reports that Jesus "taught them many things in parables" (Mk. 4:2), a phrase ambiguous enough to elicit vastly different readings of Jesus' parabolic instruction. In Greco-Roman thought, the parable functioned rhetorically to persuade through the use of illustrative comparison.[22] And as Drury's survey of Jewish literature demonstrates, while the LXX word παραβολή (which translates משל) denotes various forms of figurative speech, it frequently concerns God's action within human history.[23] For instance, among OT uses, Ezek. 17, Num. 23–4, and Deut. 28:37 each represents what Drury calls a "distillation of historical experience" into a figurative expression.[24]

Certainly the literature differs when it comes to parables' opacity and the means of their interpretation. On the one hand, apocalyptic literature (e.g. Dan. 2; *1 Enoch* 43, 46; *4 Ezra* 4) features parabolic instruction requiring explanation by a divine intermediary. On the other hand, in wisdom literature (e.g. Sir. 47) humans have the ability to decipher parables on their own. Yet, despite these differences, parables ultimately serve a revelatory function, a view evident in Matthew's insertion here from Ps. 78:2: "I will open my mouth in parables, I will utter things that have been hidden since the foundation of the world."[25] Especially given its broader context in the psalm, this use of the word "parable" indicates a speech designed to unveil that which has been hidden, to expose that which has been masked. So, however the revelation is attained, parables ultimately serve in Jewish thought to bring to light what has been obscured: namely, the reality of God's sometimes covert action in the world. That Jesus addresses this "very large crowd" through parabolic discourse only confirms this view, since in Mark's account even the masses include potential recruits for Jesus' apocalyptic worldview.

21 Guelich rightly notes that the boat's primary function is as a " 'seat' for Jesus' teaching," since it serves "more as a podium than a means of escape" (*Mark 1–8:26*, 191).

22 Both Aristotle, *On Rhetoric* 2.20.1ff., and Quintilian, *Inst.* 5.11.22–30 emphasize the comparative nature of parables as an inductive teaching technique.

23 See Drury, *Parables,* chs. 1 and 2, for a survey of forms including riddles, pithy sayings, and allegorical prophecy.

24 Ibid., 15.

25 Marcus, *Mystery*, 17, calls this a "dramatic moment of revelation and of judgment."

The sowing parable taught

Once Mark has established the purposeful and widespread nature of Jesus' instruction, Jesus begins his teaching with a parable drawn from the imagery of the land. While scholars have vigorously debated whether the parable is primarily about the sower, the seeds, or the differing soil conditions and their productivity, a more prudent approach will recognize the significance of each of these narrative elements in the process of sowing that encompasses them all.[26] As it turns out, each of these features is equally essential to the illustrative story that moves from sowing to growth (or failure) to harvest. As we shall see, it is their interaction that constitutes the essence of comparison between this parable and Jesus' own interaction with his hearers.

In Mark's account, Jesus' teachings begin with a double summons to listen (ἀκούετε) and to see (ἰδού), commands that together call the audience's attention to the significance of Jesus' teaching. In the first place, as Gerhardsson has argued, the opening imperative echoes the language of Israel's *Shema* of Deut. 6:4–5, which introduces not just the oneness of God and the undivided loyalty required by "Yahweh your God" but also the encompassing summons to "think upon and do all my commandments, and be holy to your God."[27] Moreover, later Jewish exegesis implicitly links the *Shema* with the reign of God (cf. *m. Ber.* 2:2). The opening command to hear, then, seems to suggest that Jesus' ensuing instruction provides an implicit commentary on the nature of that kingdom. The parable's finale drives home its import, as the phrase Ὃς ἔχει ὦτα ἀκούειν ἀκουέτω (Mk. 4:9) marks the story's end with a resonant inclusio.

[26] The differing views fall loosely into three groups: (1) those who follow the traditional description of this passage as the parable of the sower; (2) those who view the story's main concern as the soil quality (e.g. Adolf Jülicher, *Die Gleichnisreden Jesu*, 2nd edn. [Tübingen: Mohr, 1910; orig. 1888], II:514; Tolbert, *Sowing the Gospel*, *passim*); and (3) those who claim that the seeds are the story's primary interest (Guelich, *Mark 1–8:26*, 192–7; Friedrich Hahn, "Das Gleichnis von der ausgestreuten Saat und seine Deutung (Mk. iv. 3–8, 14–20)," in *Text and Interpretation*, ed. E. Best and R. McL. Wilson [Cambridge: Cambridge University Press, 1979], 133–42; Pesch, *Markusevangelium*, I:231). Witherington combines several facets of the story to claim that "the parable is about the seed merging with the soil to produce a crop" (*Mark*, 163), though inexplicably he neglects the sower's role in the process. Marcus finds that "the sower is not at the center of the narrative" but affirms that "the sower and the fate of the seed are inextricable themes" (*Mystery*, 20–1).

[27] Birger Gerhardsson, "The Parable of the Sower and Its Interpretation," *NTS* 14 (1967–8): 165–93. Hooker affirms that "this language does, at the very least, indicate the authority with which Jesus is said to have spoken" ("Mark's Parables," 89). Contrast Guelich, *Mark 1–8:26*, 192.

The verse's second imperative, "See! (ἰδού)," expands the prior auditory appeal to include a visual command and highlights the rich scriptural (particularly prophetic) backdrop of the story Mark's Jesus will tell. Though the word appears only seven times in Mark's gospel, it consistently draws attention to what follows.[28] In the LXX, the verb εἶδον serves as the normative translational equivalent for הנה, an expression that regularly marks the beginning of a divinely ordained oracle. Indeed, the gospel's opening citation of Mal. 3:1 (Mk. 1:2) uses the summons ἰδού to attract hearers' attention to decisive action of God's making a way in the wilderness. And another prophetic passage, the eschatological vision of Isa. 55:3–5, combines imagery of hearing and seeing (in the same order) in a manner not unlike Mk. 4:3. The prophet expresses God's post-exilic invitation in this way:

> Incline your ear, and follow my ways;
> listen (ἐπακούσατε), so that you may live . . .
> See (ἰδού), I made [David] a witness to the peoples . . .
> You shall call nations (ἔθνη) that you do not know (οὐκ ᾔδεισαν),
> and peoples that do not know (οὐκ ἐπίστανται) you shall run to you.

Here we find an elaborate prophecy of God's cosmic reign that will culminate in the calling of Gentiles (ἔθνη). Such a convergence of auditory and visual language in a scriptural text notable for its vision of God's coming kingdom casts Jesus' call to attention in Mk. 4:2 as an invitation to hear and to see the ensuing parabolic illustration of that kingdom.[29]

The fact that Isa. 55 also employs agricultural imagery, including both seed and sower in Isa. 55:10, confirms its importance as a precursor text for Mk. 4:3–9.[30] And as Israel's prophetic voice gave way to apocalyptic expectation in later Jewish literature, farming continued to provide a graphic metaphor for the incursion of God's kingdom on earth. One representative example can be found in *4 Ezra* 4:28–9, which juxtaposes the present evil age with the coming age in terms of harvests reaped:

[28] Mk. 1:2; 3:23; 4:3; 10:28, 33; 14:41–2.

[29] As we shall see, Mark's portrait of that kingdom entails not just restoration but also judgment; still, in Mk. 4:11–12 as throughout the gospel, those most roundly indicted are not the Gentiles but the Jewish leaders themselves.

[30] To ascertain whether or not Mark's Jesus deliberately echoes Isa. 55 is beyond the ability or purpose of this investigation. Suffice it to say that the two passages exhibit enough intertextual resonance to claim that they derive their language and imagery from the same "thought-world."

> For the evil about which you ask me has been sown, but the harvest of it has not yet come. If therefore that which has been sown is not reaped, and if the place where the evil has been sown does not pass away, the field where the good has been sown will not come.

As Drury puts it, a range of Jewish texts share with Mk. 4:3–9 these essential features: "divine agency of sowing, the eschatological bent, and the contrast of good and bad."[31] As Jesus tells it in Mk. 4:3–9, the sowing parable adopts prevailing linguistic currency to express a set of hopes associated with the impinging reign of God.

As striking as the texts' shared imagery are the ways in which Mark's sowing parable diverges from the cited texts. In the first place, while the texts mentioned above envision sequential harvests – first the evil, then the good – the sowing parable seems squarely focused on the coexistence of the two kingdoms.[32] In a manner that resembles the QL (e.g. 1QM 14:9–10), Mark affirms the "mystery" of continuing opposition to God's reign as inaugurated by Jesus – opposition apparently in full force both at the narrative level and in Mark's community. Yet despite this persistence of evil, evinced in the parable by the three kinds of bad soils, the good seed has been sown; moreover, Mark's Jesus would contend, it is already bearing a bumper crop.

The parable itself conveys this dynamic of coexistent forces at work "on the earth" through an intricate narrative of both contrast and progression. On the one hand, many commentators have correctly cited the balanced 3:3 presentation of the seeds' fates, which Crossan calls a "formal balance and contrast between three situations of waste and failure and three situations of gain and success."[33] In this way the story drives a sharp apocalyptic wedge between the old age and the new. Yet, while the parable does depart from the view of sequential and separate sowing acts, it also retains a sense of divinely ordained momentum so that the results culminate with an abundant, albeit not unfathomable, harvest.[34] In other words, even if the present age's yields seem contradictory, they are

[31] Drury, *Parables*, 52–3. See also Marcus, *Mark*, 295.

[32] Marcus, *Mystery*, 48–9. In this way, Marcus supplants Jeremias's "eschatological"/temporal understanding of the parable with an "apocalyptic"/spatial one and thus construes the parable more as an illustrative example of the present incursion of God's kingdom than as a meantime preparation for it.

[33] John Dominic Crossan, *In Parables: The Challenge of the Historical Jesus* (New York: Harper & Row, 1973), 41. See also Hahn, "Gleichnis," 134–6, who emphasizes the triadic results of "thirty, sixty, and a hundredfold."

[34] Cf. *1 Enoch* 10:19; *2 Apoc. Bar.* 29:5, which cite eschatological yields of 1000 and 10,000.

not finally ambivalent: the parable ends on a note of success, and success that expands in each of its three measures.[35] Thus, the story affirms the eschatological hope that even the present age of resistance will culminate in the kingdom's success.

Still another detail of Mark's sowing parable stands out in sharp relief against the literary-religious backdrop that speaks of the sowing of evil. While *4 Ezra* and *2 Baruch* include in their portraits the sowing of "evil seeds" by the "evil one," Jesus' story features but one sower, who casts good seed indiscriminately on all types of soils. Both the character of the sower and the nature of the seeds remain constant; all that distinguishes the seeds' outcomes is the receptivity of the soil.[36] As a result, the sowing parable implicitly disenfranchises the "evil one" simply by omitting mention of "evil seeds" from the sowing process. In turn, the story shores up the authority of a solitary sower as the advance agent of God's kingdom on earth, even while it maintains narrative emphasis, noted in Mark's redactional introduction, on the broadcast nature of his mission.[37]

What has this brief discussion of the sowing parable contributed to our understanding of discipleship as presence? Primarily, the narrative provides an illustrative portrait of Jesus' mission, which will in turn shape the disciples' own practice in Mark's story as well as in Mark's community. In it, Jesus employs an indirect manner of self-reference to expose several core claims of his ministry. First, his is a mission devoted to disseminating the apocalyptic reign of God "on the earth." Thus while Jesus remains indispensable to the story, he is not its sole focus.[38] Second, the nature of that dissemination is deliberately universal and indiscriminate; he scatters the "seeds" of that kingdom without regard for the nature of the soil on which they will land. Third, despite horticultural obstacles to germination and fruitfulness, the success of some seeds is assured. Ultimately God's dominion does take root, producing a bountiful crop.

35 See J. Dupont, "La Parabole du semeur," *Foi et Vie* 66 (1967): 5–7.

36 Cf. Witherington, *Mark*, 165: "This strongly suggests that the point has to do with the reception of the seed."

37 Marcus, *Mystery*, 38–9, supplies a helpful summary of textual arguments that support the view of Jesus as sower. They include the following: redactional language (Mark's repeated use of "going out" to characterize Jesus: see 1:38; 2:13); the immediate and broader contexts in which Jesus instructs the crowds; the gospel's account of mixed reception to Jesus' teaching and proclamation; and the later evangelists' apparent identification of Jesus with the sower.

38 Cf. Hooker, "Mark's Parables," 89: "the parable of Jesus calls for wholehearted response to Jesus himself" – this claim despite her earlier concession that "Jesus does not announce or proclaim himself as the Christ" (88).

Yet if these claims hold true for Jesus' ministry, the same can be said of Mark's community. Precisely because the prototypical sower is no longer physically present "on the earth," his faithful followers must continue the work of sowing. Thus the parable is not so much an exhortation, for Mark's community, to ensure they are counted among the "good soil."[39] Neither does it primarily address Jesus' followers in what Kelber calls the "drought of the interregnum."[40] Rather, the parable counters the "discouragement a sower (read proclaimer or persuader) faces when so many do not, or do not for long, respond positively to the message."[41] Without denying the role of Jesus as sower, then, this reading suggests that Mark's appropriation of the parable promotes his community's identification with Jesus as sower, thus reflecting the kind of participatory Christology that I have detected in other "discipleship" texts. Indeed the sowing parable maintains the same delicate balance found throughout the second gospel: while the demonstration of God's dominion occurs within the ministry of Jesus and its continuation by his followers, God himself grants the final assurance of that dominion.[42] As we shall see, the "private audience" instruction of Mk. 4:10–12 and the parable's earliest interpretation in Mk. 4:13–20 solidify this claim, as do the collection of logia and similitudes that conclude Jesus' parabolic teaching in Mk. 4:21–32.

The mystery given

Three enigmatic verses lie at the heart of Mark's presentation of the parable with its interpretation and supply critical clues to Mark's view of this parabolic instruction. Especially because this brief exchange features those who are "with him" as Jesus' interlocutors, Mk. 4:10–12 figures

[39] Cf. Tolbert, *Sowing the Gospel*, 175, who focuses attention on the "responses that differentiate the good earth from the bad earths" and finds the disciples to fall in the latter group. The evidence of Mark's gospel, though, supports a more nuanced assessment of Jesus' followers.

[40] Kelber, *Kingdom*, 43.

[41] Witherington, *Mark*, 162. But cf. his own claim, 165, that it is "Jesus who is seen as the sower in the parable." It is this exegetical ambivalence, echoed by many commentators, that suggests the likelihood of a link between the two.

[42] See Joel Marcus, "Blanks and Gaps in the Markan Parable of the Sower," *BibInt* 5 (1997): 247–62, for a discussion of the "gap" (= "deliberate ambiguity in the narrative," 247) of the sower's identity. Marcus entertains the possibility of three different sowers (God, Jesus, and Christian preacher in Mark's community) and finds that "the sower is meant to be all three of the figures" (260). While the gospel's apocalyptic worldview certainly presupposes that divine action undergirds human activity, though, even Marcus's own discussion lends compelling credence to the text's view of the sower as Jesus and, by extension, his followers. As is the case in Isa. 55 as well as Mk. 4:26–9, God's role relates more directly to the growth than to the sowing activity.

prominently in our understanding of Markan discipleship. In this section, I shall consider in turn three exegetical issues that directly relate to the topic: the identity and function of "those around him with the Twelve" (Mk. 4:10); the assertion, in Mk. 4:11, that to them has been given the "μυστήριον of the kingdom of God"; and their contrast with "those outside," to whom "all things come in parables."

Discipleship as inquiry

A pivotal scene shift occurs at the outset of Mk. 4:10. In the first place, the ὅτε that begins this subsection introduces a significant temporal and spatial remove from the previous teaching episode.[43] If, as Mark tells the story, Jesus' audience for the sowing parable has been an ὄχλος πλεῖστος, Jesus would require ample time and space in order to find himself "alone" by the beginning of Mk. 4:10. The awkward combination here of the singular ἐγένετο as well as the phrase κατὰ μόνας on the one hand (Mk. 4:10a), and a participial phrase introducing the contemporaneous inquiry of "those around him with the Twelve" on the other hand (Mk. 4:10b), reflects Mark's redactional emphasis on Jesus' changing audience. From this point on, Jesus' parabolic teaching directly addresses those who constitute his band of followers.

But whom does Mark designate through the phrase οἱ περὶ αὐτὸν σὺν τοῖς δώδεκα? While most scholars agree that its redundancy reflects the author's reshaping of tradition, efforts to separate the original core from Mark's expansion have produced diametrically opposing views. Since Bultmann, many commentators have maintained that Mark has introduced "the Twelve" to specify the group originally identified as "those around him."[44] In part, this claim rests on the assumption that every mention of "the Twelve" in Mark is redactional, a claim that was undermined in the previous chapter. In addition, Meye contends that, in the gospel as a whole,

[43] See William L. Lane, *The Gospel According to Mark*, NICNT (Grand Rapids: Eerdmans, 1974), 155–6. Cf. Guelich, *Mark 1–8:26*, 203, whose "conservative redactor" stance leads him to the conclusion that Mark found, and simply transmitted, inconsistencies of audience and locale in the tradition. Yet, as I shall argue further below, as Mark has arranged the material, this "when"-clause seems rather to reflect a deliberate transition from public to private instruction.

[44] Bultmann, *Synoptic Traadition*, 345–6. Others following his lead have included Meye, *Jesus and the Twelve*, 152–6; Gunther Schmahl, *Die Zwölf im Markusevangelium* (Trier: Paulinus, 1974), 83–4; Karl-Georg Reploh, *Markus – Lehrer der Gemeinde: Eine redaktionsgeschichtliche Studie zu den Jüngerperikopen des Markus-Evangliums*, SBM 9 (Stuttgart: Katholisches Bibelwerk, 1969), 47–9.

Jesus never finds himself alone except with a "fixed group."[45] Yet the "fixed groups" he cites (Mk. 6:31, 32; 9:2; 13:3) are neither limited to "the Twelve" nor composed of the same characters – and so are not so "fixed" after all. Even less cogent is his insistence that "Mark simply means to say that those about Jesus are to be understood as those associated with the Twelve, *or* belonging to the Twelve."[46] If that is Mark's "simple" meaning, though, he certainly could have chosen another, more precise grammatical construction.

The view that Mark has appended "those around him" to the traditional "with the Twelve" seems more plausible on various grounds.[47] In terms of style, the proposal that the phrase originally read "when he was alone with the Twelve" makes better sense of the singular imperfect ἐγένετο. Moreover, as I have discussed in the preceding chapter, the prevalence of the "Twelve" in the tradition seems more likely in light of the gospel's awkward inclusion, for instance, of the call of Levi (Mk. 2:13). Finally, the view that Mark has expanded the tradition's narrower identification of the "Twelve" disciples also squares with Mk. 3:34–5, where Jesus includes among his true family not a precisely numbered entourage but "*whoever* does the will of God."[48] In Mark's account, the lines demarcating those loyal to Jesus are constantly shifting. While the evangelist seems intent on preserving the heritage of the "Twelve," he seems equally deliberate in reading his own community into a revised and expanded understanding of discipleship.

If the loose coalition mentioned in Mk. 4:10 cannot be decisively identified by name, what does distinguish them from the ὄχλος πλεῖστος is their inquiring response to Jesus' instruction. Along with the spatial and temporal shift noted above, Mk. 4:10 also introduces a markedly different level of engagement between Jesus and his hearers. Whereas the crowd has served as the collective recipient of Jesus' authoritative teaching, here some of its members emerge as probing interlocutors whose query evokes both a distinction between ὑμῖν and τοῖς ἔξω (Mk. 4:11–12) and the ensuing private instruction.

When "those around Jesus with the Twelve" step forward in pursuit of deeper understanding, they exhibit a disposition deemed appropriately faithful in both the QL and Jewish scripture. As Marcus has demonstrated,

45 Meye, *Jesus and the Twelve*, 152. 46 Ibid., 155.

47 Best can be credited with tracing out many of the contours of this argument ("Mark's Use of the Twelve," *ZNW* 69 [1978]: 11–35).

48 Besides Best, those who endorse this view include Hooker, *Mark*, 127; Marcus, *Mystery*, 80–1; Kelber, *Kingdom*, 31.

the Hymns Scroll assesses positively those who inquire of God and God's ways (1QH 4:23–4), while the Community Rule indicts those who have *not* sought after God (1QS 5:11–12).[49]

Yet the spirit of inquiry finds important expression much earlier in Jewish scriptures. Especially in light of the repeated use of the verb ἀκούω in Mk. 4:3 and 4:8 as a framing device for the chapter's opening parable – an echo of the *Shema* – the hearers' ensuing interrogation reflects the appropriate human response to divine pronouncement. In the Deuteronomic account, the *Shema* is followed by catechesis which begins with these words: כִּי־יִשְׁאָלְךָ בִנְךָ/ὅταν ἐρωτήσῃ σε ὁ υἱός σου (Deut. 6:20). In other words, the gift of instruction does not ensure its appropriation; only an inquiring response primes the hearers for full-fledged participation in the divine reality. That these unnamed followers exhibit both initiative and inquiry demonstrates that, in the first place, discipleship as presence entails their divinely inspired pursuit of understanding, which comes only through being "with him."

Discipleship as giftedness

After those "with Jesus" have purposefully asked about the parables, Mark's Jesus opens his reply with an explicit contrast between "you" and "those outside":

> ὑμῖν τὸ μυστήριον δέδοται τῆς βασιλείας τοῦ θεοῦ·
> ἐκείνοις δὲ τοῖς ἔξω ἐν παραβολαῖς τὰ πάντα γίνεται.
> (Mk. 4:11)

Already, we have noted the inquiring, "listening" spirit of these followers that distinguishes them from the "very large crowd." But here Jesus explicates their special relationship to him as designated recipients of the "mystery of the kingdom of God." This claim will prove central to Mark's developing portrait of discipleship as presence in this chapter.

In the first place, we may consider the verb "has been given," δέδοται. Many have noted that this word conveys a Semitic divine passive[50] and thus lays Jesus' emphasis squarely on God's free gift apart from any human achievement. On the one hand, such a view contrasts with the Wisdom of Sirach (e.g. 39:1–3, 7), which credits human endeavors enabled by the Lord's counsel with the unlocking of divine mysteries; on the other hand, Mark's claim falls more in line with apocalyptic literature such as

[49] Marcus, *Mark 1–8*, 302.
[50] E.g. Joachim Jeremias, *The Parables of Jesus*, trans. S. H. Hooke (New York: Scribner's Sons, 1972), 15.

Daniel and *1 Enoch*, which emphasize the divine initiative required for such discovery.[51] The first distinguishing trait that this phrase indicates, then, is God's free bestowal of the μυστήριον upon Jesus' hearers.[52]

Besides its emphasis on divine gift through the use of the passive voice, the perfect tense of δέδοται also signals an important facet of the giving of the μυστήριον. Since it conveys an act that has happened in the past but continues to exert influence in the present, the verb itself delimits our understanding of the gift as "something which has already put in an appearance in the Gospel."[53] So at least at the narrative level, the assertion that the μυστήριον has (already) been given to Jesus' followers precludes a strictly Christological understanding of the content of the mystery.[54] To this point in Mark's gospel, the issue of Jesus' messiahship has not yet been directly addressed by his disciples; instead, the immediate context of Mk. 4 portrays the broader reality of God's kingdom.[55] Indeed, the use of the perfect tense in such a pivotal spot in the story recalls Jesus' initial public pronouncement, which also directly concerned the βασιλεία τοῦ θεοῦ (Mk. 1:14–15). What "has been given" is the good news of God's assured dominion, a claim staked at the outset but reiterated throughout the gospel. So while Mark's Jesus plays the role of leading harbinger and even quintessential embodiment of God's reign, the "mystery" must denote a reality that is not circumscribed by him.

Finally, we gain a firmer grasp on the significance of the word δέδοται when we consider its function throughout Mark's gospel, where the word repeatedly conveys the sharing of some important attribute or authority. Notably, Matthew's interpretation of this logion adds the qualifying infinitive γνῶναι (Matt. 13:11), so that the giving of the mystery becomes specifically aligned with the acquisition of special knowledge.[56] Yet, as

51 Notably, though, Dan. 2 recounts the interpretation of the king's dream as a mystery "revealed" (Dan. 2:19, 23, 28, 30) rather than "given."

52 See Raymond E. Brown's study, *Semitic Background of the Term "Mystery" in the New Testament* (Philadelphia: Fortress Press, 1968), for a thorough exposition of the emergence of μυστήριον in Jewish literature, which I engage more fully below.

53 Marcus, *Mystery*, 44.

54 Cf. Paul J. Achtemeier, *Mark*, 2nd edn., PC (Philadelphia: Fortress Press, 1986), 69–70, who acknowledges that a precise Christological view of the "mystery" depends on the ensuing narrative.

55 See Madeleine Boucher, *The Mysterious Parable: A Literary Study*, CBQMS 6 (Washington, DC: Catholic Biblical Association, 1977), 80–1, who views Jesus' messianic role as one element of this kingdom-of-God mystery, which "has to do with the necessity of suffering."

56 Luke parallels this twofold revision (see Lk. 8:10), a move carried further, rather uncritically, by modern interpreters who interpret δέδοται to mean "has been revealed" (see, e.g., Seán Freyne, "The Disciples in Mark and the *MASKILIM* in Daniel. A Comparison," *JSNT* 16 [1982]: 16).

Boucher maintains, in Mark's gospel understanding is "not so much knowledge as faith and obedience."[57] For Mark, the verb δίδωμι regularly functions to convey the act of "giving" as a constituent part of the kingdom-of-God reality to which Jesus and his disciples bear witness.

A brief review of the verb's occurrences in Mark's gospel illustrates its diverse but complementary connotations. In several instances, the verb describes Jesus' own extension of his authority to his disciples (e.g. Mk. 2:26; 6:7, 41; 8:6; 14:23). Other uses speak of "giving" as a vital divine prerogative (e.g. Mk. 4:25; 6:2; 10:37; 11:28; 12:9; 13:11). Finally, Jesus directly commands his hearers to "give" in ways that dramatize the reality of God's reign (e.g. Mk. 6:37; 10:21, 45). More often than not in Mark's gospel, to "give" is to transmit one's own resources in service to others. For Mark, then, this distinction of those to whom the mystery has been "given" may concern special knowledge, but only to the extent that that knowledge then becomes shared, in life-giving ways, with others.[58] To follow Jesus in Mark's gospel entails being entrusted with the μυστήριον of the kingdom of God. In turn, that gift of the μυστήριον becomes a challenge of stewardship for those to whom it has been given.[59]

The precise nature of the "mystery" entrusted to Jesus' hearers (and, by extension, Mark's community) has been the source of vigorous debate. Earlier in the twentieth century, scholarship widely viewed the secret initiatory rites of Greco-Roman mystery religions as the appropriate matrix for understanding the "mystery" imparted to those around Jesus. But recently scholars have drawn increasing attention to the language of mystery in Jewish apocalyptic texts, which according to Brown contain "all the raw material . . . needed for the use of 'mystery' without venturing into the pagan religions."[60]

Brown's study traces the lineage of the term through the Hebrew words *raz* and *sod* to an early understanding of the divine council where the inexplicable course of events becomes transparent. Although the LXX at times uses μυστήριον in a purely secular sense,[61] in more apocalyptic

[57] Boucher, *Mysterious Parable*, 84.

[58] Freyne, "Disciples," 11, has detected this dynamic as a contour shared between the disciples in Mark and the *maskilim* in Daniel, whose special instruction is also for the benefit of others. See also Benoit H. M. G. M. Standaert, *L'Evangile selon Marc. Composition et genre littéraire* (Nijmegen: Stichting Studentenpers, 1978), 213, who stresses the recurrent tension in Mark between divine gift and its incumbent human responsibility.

[59] Cf. Beavis, *Mark's Audience*, 154, who infers instead a challenge for them to understand.

[60] Brown, *Semitic Background*, 32. See also Gunther Bornkamm, "μυστήριον," in *TDNT* 4 (1967): 814–17.

[61] See Tob. 12:7, 11; Jdt. 2:2, where it refers to the political confidences of the king.

texts it frequently refers to end-time mysteries.[62] Yet it is important to note that even where it refers to eschatological events, the term μυστήριον conveys a relatively wide range of meanings: it may refer to natural phenomena as cosmic mysteries; it may denote the final judgment *per se* (*1 Enoch* 68:5); it may point to a particular interpretation of Torah (1QS 11:5–8); or it may reflect the puzzling resistance of Belial to the assured victory of God (1QM 14:9–10; 1QS 3:20–3).

Especially in view of such varied nuances, two aspects of the term seem consistent throughout Jewish apocalyptic literature. First, "mystery" typically conveys the puzzlement of God's assured reign not yet fully disclosed on the earth. Second, the paradox of "mystery" maintains simultaneously the hiddenness of that dominion and its impulse toward revelation. As it becomes unveiled, then, mystery gives way to apocalypse.[63] For example, Daniel explains this revelatory thrust in his report to the king: "This mystery has not been revealed to me because of any wisdom that I have more than any other living being, but in order that the interpretation may be known to the king and that you may understand the thoughts of your mind" (Dan. 2:30). Put another way, the mystery of God's coming kingdom drives relentlessly toward disclosure.

Thus, it is important to understand the term μυστήριον in a manner that coheres with its narrative context as well as its wider setting in Jewish apocalyptic thought. Within the gospel's first three chapters, those who have remained "with Jesus" have been granted the life-shaping assurance of God's imminent dominion. At the same time, while it is evident in fits and starts as Jesus defeats the powers of the present evil age, God's sovereignty still remains enshrouded to the degree that active resistance continues; the kingdom's full acclaim is not yet accomplished. In this respect, the coexistence of good and evil forces upon the earth, even in the shadow of God's decisive victory, constitutes one "mysterious" dimension of the kingdom of God.[64]

Yet even the sowing parable addresses not so much the continued presence of both good and bad soils as it does the ultimate outcome of increasingly abundant yields. Similarly, Jesus' response about "the parables" concerns less the circumstances surrounding the coming triumph of God than the assurance of God's ultimate reign – in other words, the "mystery which is the imminence of God's kingdom."[65] And, as is the case for

[62] See Dan. 2:18–19, 22; *1 Enoch* 68:5; 103:2; 1QS 11:3–4.

[63] See Bornkamm, "μυστήριον," 820–1.

[64] So Marcus, *Mystery*, 48–9.

[65] See Rikki E. Watts, who understands the "mystery" to refer to the "mysterious way in which the kingdom is expressed and revealed in Jesus' mighty deeds, in his powerful words, and ultimately, linked to his identity" (*Isaiah's New Exodus and Mark* [Tübingen: Mohr Siebeck, 1997], 228).

the *maskilim* in Daniel, the very knowledge of this mystery serves as a catalyst for their sharing it with others, that they might be saved (Dan. 11:33).[66] Thus for Mark, the language of "giving" and of the "mystery of God's kingdom" converge to suggest this reading of the parable: like Jesus, his hearers are those who have been empowered ("given") to disseminate the word of God's coming kingdom ("the mystery") without regard to the soil type on which it falls. Indeed, the greatest mystery may be that at least some of the seeds grow, even bear fruit, while the sower knows not how (see Mk. 4:27).

Discipleship and insider knowledge

Despite its optimistic, even triumphant note, the sowing parable describes a range of soil conditions that hinder at progressive stages the seeds' germination and growth. Similarly, Jesus' response in Mk. 4:11 explains "the parables" not only with reference to his inquirers' giftedness but also in view of "those outside," to whom "all things come in parables." The stark contrast, expressed through antithetical parallelism, can be detected in several features of the clauses:[67]

Mark 4:11a	Mark 4:11b
To you	But to those, to the ones outside
	in parables
the mystery of the kingdom of God	all things
has been given.	happen.

In the first place, the verse's redundant inclusion of the demonstrative pronoun ἐκείνοις probably does reflect a Semitism[68] but also sharpens the implicit contrast between the ὑμῖν of 4:11a and the τοῖς ἔξω of 4:11b. Such a deliberately accented opposition of two groups apparently derives from a mindset of apocalyptic dualism that distinguishes unabashedly between insiders and outsiders. Certainly by the time the second gospel was written, the phrase "those outside" had been appropriated from Judaism by the early Christian movement to reflect the division between believers

[66] Freyne, "Disciples," 18. See also Marcus, *Mystery*, 122, who emphasizes that God gives the "mystery" in apocalyptic writings not just to comfort but to save God's people (see Mk. 13:13b).

[67] See the similar diagrams of J. Arthur Baird, "A Pragmatic Approach to Parable Exegesis: Some New Evidence on Mark 4:11, 33–34," *JBL* 76 (1957): 201–7; Marcus, *Mystery*, 75. This chart differs mainly in the refusal to supply an implied parallel to "in parables" (Baird: "with explanations"; Marcus: "in parables"), a gap that I shall discuss below.

[68] So Jeremias, *Parables*, 15.

and non-believers (cf. 1 Cor. 5:12; Col. 4:5; 1 Thess. 4:12),[69] yet such a phrase would already have been at home in the setting of Jesus' own eschatological ministry.

But who are "those outside" in this verse? Gnilka has argued that the word specifically refers to Israel so that its inclusion at this point in Mark relates to the problem of Israel's failure to respond positively to its messiah.[70] Yet while Mark's gospel has featured the mounting resistance of Israel's leaders, such a broad-based condemnation is not consistent with Mark's refusal to assess entire groups either favorably or unfavorably. Indeed, in light of Mk. 3:20–35, the spatial designation of "those outside" distinguishes them from those "around Jesus" (Mk. 3:34; 4:10) who both "do the will of God" (Mk. 3:35) and inquire about the parables (Mk. 4:10). Thus for Mark's community, while "those outside" may include many among "Israel," the term cannot be strictly equated with it.

Besides the identity of the hearers, the verse's other contrasting elements prove even more problematic exegetically. The clauses' subjects, the "mystery . . . of the kingdom of God" and "all things," appear to be diametrically juxtaposed, but in what respect? Interpreters who understand the phrase τὰ πάντα to designate "all things about the kingdom of God" view the parallel clauses as synonymous rather than antithetical, a move that seems strained in light of the verse's other opposing elements.[71] Another, more Christological reading confines "all things" to the realm of Jesus' ministry, understood either historically[72] or narratively.[73] But underlying each of these readings is an unnecessary delimitation of "all things," a phrase that at face value denotes a more expansive reality.[74]

To construe "all things" as a phrase designating "the cosmos" helps to delineate the epistemological divide forged through the gift of the μυστήριον. From this vantage point, the mystery given to "you" supplies more than prized or privileged knowledge; it provides an interpretive lens for viewing the world, a lens ground so that God's cosmic reign appears clearly. As Brown puts it, full understanding of the parable "will come not so much by way of added revelation, as of added perception gained

[69] Pesch, *Markusevangelium*, I:239.

[70] Gnilka, *Verstockung*, 83–4. [71] E.g. Marcus, *Mystery*, 109.

[72] C. E. B. Cranfield, *The Gospel According to Saint Mark: An Introduction and Commentary*, CGTC (New York: Cambridge University Press, 1977), 154–5.

[73] Guelich, *Mark 1–8:26*, 208.

[74] A similarly universal understanding of τὰ πάντα seems consistently in view in the Pauline corpus: see, e.g., Rom. 11:36; 1 Cor. 8:6, 15:27–8; Gal. 3:22; Phil. 3:21. Notably, each of these uses appears in a context in which Paul grapples with God's in-breaking cosmic sovereignty.

through faith,"[75] a dynamic expressed through another contrasting feature of Mk. 4:11: the verb γίνεται. Whereas the perfect passive δέδοται has conveyed God's gracious bestowal of the μυστήριον, here the deponent γίνεται removes the hand of divine gift and consigns "those outside" to experience "all things" as they "come to pass" – that is, apart from any awareness of God's sway over the universe. Put another way, the difference lies in the widely divergent perception of cosmic reality, as "those outside" remain ill-equipped to perceive "all things" other than parabolically.

This difference in perception may help to explain the rather perplexing claim of Mk. 4:11 that, to those outside, "all things come to pass *in parables*."[76] For once we identify the expansive scope of the phrase τὰ πάντα, Jesus' assertion grows more intelligible through careful consideration of the word παραβολή. Since the expression literally conveys a side-by-side comparison, perhaps the claim that "all things come in parables" refers to the side-by-side existence of apparent human reality[77] on the one hand and the kingdom-of-God reality on the other. Thus "those outside" see only the parabolic figures, so that everything (τὰ πάντα) transpires "in parables"; their impaired, "old aeon" vision distorts their clear perception of God's dominion.

Jesus' teaching "in parables," then, coheres with his hearers' varied perceptions of reality. By illustrating God's dominion through figurative speech, Jesus' parabolic teaching can be revelatory (to those already entrusted with the mystery) and at the same time incomprehensible (to those "outside" whose perception is hindered by their remove from Jesus). In any case, though, Jesus repeatedly summons even the crowds to "hear" and to "see," thus retaining the possibility that God might somehow prompt deeper perception even among those who have not yet exhibited it.[78]

Of course, this suggestion that Jesus' parabolic discourse intends to reveal God's kingdom reality seems to fly in the face of the passage's

75 Brown, *Semitic Background*, 36.

76 Marcus has aptly summarized the problem presented by the phrase "in parables" when the meaning of "all things" is limited to the arena of Jesus' ministry: "either the meaning of *ta panta* must be limited or the meaning of *en parabolais* must be stretched" (*Mystery*, 109).

77 This cosmic conflict between seeming human reality and Jesus' claims about God's true sovereignty appears again in Mk. 10:42, where Jesus speaks of οἱ δοκοῦντες ἄρχειν τῶν ἐθνῶν. Significantly, in this passage Jesus again casts these "outsiders" in contrast with ὑμῖν (Mk. 10:43).

78 As we have seen above, this tension between divine sovereignty and human decision resembles the apocalyptic thought of the Qumran community, where those who refuse to seek after God's ways (1QS 5:11–12) shoulder at least some of the blame for their decision.

ensuing ἵνα clause which introduces the "parable theory" citation from Isa. 6:9–10. Indeed, the setting of Mk. 4:11 within a complex of material that features calls to "hear" and to "see," as well as further teachings that explicitly articulate a strategy of illumination (Mk. 4:21–2), have prompted interpreters to dance gingerly around exegetical questions ranging from composition history to redactional intent. Since the aim here is not to rehearse the intricacies of the Markan parable-theory debate,[79] I shall touch only briefly on critical issues that can help to make sense of the logion in its present Markan context.

One interpretive decision dividing modern interpreters is the question of how well Mark's citation of Isa. 6:9–10 fits its narrative context, both within this chapter and within the gospel as a whole. Almost all commentators agree that the second evangelist combines both clarity and obscurity in his account of Jesus' life and death. The point of contention arises specifically with regard to Jesus' use of parables: does he employ this linguistic form, in Mark's gospel, for the express purpose of confounding "those outside"?

Those who find such a telic purpose at odds with the citation's context have employed a number of tactics either to dismiss the citation or to tame its meaning. For instance, Räisänen has argued that such a deliberate bafflement contradicts Mark's general disposition toward "the crowds" and his use of parables that outsiders *do* understand (e.g. Mk. 3:23–7; 7:14–15; 12:1–12).[80] While the "parable theory" may have its roots in the problem of Israel's failure to accept Jesus as messiah, Guelich claims that "this sharp bifurcation into two distinct groups finds little correspondence with Mark's portrait."[81] Yet, if the citation is so alien to Mark's thought, the "conservative redactor" stance required to support its inclusion also proves to be its Achilles' heel, since it must by definition bracket out appeal to "Mark's portrait."

From another angle, Manson deems "simply absurd" the notion that Jesus would have taught in a manner that deliberately prevented both insight and forgiveness.[82] He then accounts for Mark's form of the expression as a mistranslation of the Aramaic relative particle ד, which he believes originally intended to highlight the nature of "those outside,"

[79] For a thorough discussion of the various views, see, e.g., Craig A. Evans, *To See and Not Perceive: Isaiah 6.9–10 in Early Jewish and Christian Interpretation*, JSOTSup 64 (Sheffield, England: JSOT Press, 1989), 92–6.

[80] See Heikki Räisänen, *Die Parabeltheorie im Markusevangelium* (Helsinki: Finnische Exegetische Gesellschaft, 1973), esp. ch. 3.

[81] Guelich, *Mark 1–8:26*, 212.

[82] T. W. Manson, *The Teaching of Jesus: Studies of Its Form and Content* (Cambridge: Cambridge University Press, 1931), 76.

not the purpose of Jesus' parabolic teaching.[83] But besides a foundation resting on several layers of speculation (including tortuous arguments required to circumvent the telic tenor of μήποτε), this proposal still does not adequately explain *Mark's* handling of the citation.

Others have taken Mark's introduction of the Isaianic prophecy more seriously by suggesting translations that mitigate the final force of the introductory ἵνα. For instance, some interpreters construe the word in either a causal[84] or resulting[85] sense, so that the condition of seeing and not perceiving, of listening and not understanding, reflects the outcome, but not necessarily the intent, of Jesus' parabolic instruction. Another set of commentators read the ἵνα as verbal marker for scriptural citation, a type of shorthand for "in order that it might be fulfilled."[86] The effect of this move is to forge a distinction between Jesus' and God's purpose, a difference hardly sustainable in Mark's gospel. Still others have argued that the ἵνα functions epexegetically to further explain the condition, expressed in Mk. 4:11b, that "all things come in parables."[87] That is, the Isaianic citation restates, in light of prophetic scripture, the condition of "those outside" just uttered by Jesus. Despite these diverse attempts to soften the blow of the ἵνα . . . μήποτε combination, though, Mark has apparently adapted and interpreted the prophetic verse in a way that underscores the telic thrust of the claim that "all things come in parables."[88]

As we navigate this rough exegetical terrain, the interpretive challenge lies in a reading that preserves *both* the puzzling and doomful final sense of the conjunctions *and* the chapter's basically revelatory and victorious promise of God's coming kingdom. If there is a way through, it may lie in the view argued above that the statement "all things come to pass

[83] Ibid., 79–80.

[84] T. Alec Burkill, *Mysterious Revelation: An Examination of the Philosophy of St. Mark's Gospel* (Ithaca, NY: Cornell University Press, 1963), 112; Hans Windisch, "Die Verstockungsidee in Mk. 4:12 und das kausale ἵνα in der späteren Koine," *ZNW* 26 (1927): 203–9. Similarly, Richard Schneck, *Isaiah in the Gospel of Mark, I–VIII*, BIBAL Dissertation Series 1 (Vallejo, CA: BIBAL Press, 1994), 129, believes the Isa. 6 citation "indicates the effect of Jesus' ministry and teaching among the people."

[85] Carl Heinz Peisker, "Konsekutives ἵνα in Markus IV, 12," *ZNW* 59 (1968): 127, differentiates between the intention and the result of Jesus' parabolic teaching.

[86] Jeremias, *Parables*, 17; Gnilka, *Verstockung*, 45–8.

[87] Peter Lampe, "Die markinische Deutung des Gleichnisses vom Sämann, Markus 4, 10–12," *ZNW* 65 (1974): 141.

[88] Perhaps the most telling support for a telic reading comes from two of Mark's earliest interpreters, Matthew and Luke. The fact that they emend Mark's reading – Matthew replaces the ἵνα with ὅτι while Luke effaces the μήποτε phrase – probably reveals the same discomfort that still causes commentators to squirm.

in parables" (Mk. 4:11b) explains the epistemological status of "those outside"[89] rather than the specific form of Jesus' teaching. In this line of thinking, the ἵνα clause introduces the purpose of their divinely ordained misperception rather than the purpose of Jesus' parabolic instruction *per se*.

Moreover, when Mark's Jesus appeals to the Isaiah call narrative, he tacitly reminds his followers that their prophetic role neither requires nor ensures outward success. If the sown seeds encounter circumstantial impediments to growth, they do so within the framework of God's final, and abundant, harvest. Notably, Jesus here addresses not the resistant factions themselves but God's own allies; the message comes not as a word of judgment, nor as cause for gloating, but as exhortation in the face of apparent failure. To them has been entrusted the mystery of God's coming kingdom; that there continue to be "those outside" whose imperceptivity prevents their full apprehension of that good news should not deter their faithful stewardship of it.

The citation's Isaianic context further substantiates this exhortative view of Mark's prophecy citation. In the first place, if Isa. 6 is understood as a retrospective reflection on the prophet's failures from a vantage point later in life,[90] rather than an incipient "call to prophecy," it functions primarily to address the dissonance between God's word and its inefficacious results.[91] Just as Isaiah's career is not to be determined by his apparent lack of success, neither are those "with Jesus" to be deterred by a lack of uniformly positive response to their sowing of the word.

Moreover, even in Isaiah, this word of judgment contains a seed of prophetic hope, as the passage so dominated by vitriolic speech concludes with a faint echo of restoration: "the holy seed is its stump" (Isa. 6:13).[92] Judgment itself serves not as the final word but as a refiner's fire that leaves a faithful remnant.[93] Across the span of Isaianic prophecy and the wider witness of OT prophecy, God's most vehement judgment ultimately gives way to hope. Thus perception returns to God's people, for instance,

[89] 1 Cor. 2:14–15 seems to represent the same epistemological divide in terms of those who are ψυχικός rather than πνευματικός; the latter, Paul writes, discern τὰ πάντα.

[90] Hooker, *Mark*, 127.

[91] Thus, as Evans claims, the commission of judgment emerges as a sequential response to Israel's obtuseness (*To See and Not Perceive*, 24).

[92] In its emphasis on the broadcast method of kingdom dissemination, Mark's account may hint at something of a foil to the more sectarian mindset reflected, for instance, in 1QIsaiah[a], where the Qumran community aligns itself with the "holy seed" as the only true remnant of Israel. See Evans (ibid., ch. 2) for a helpful discussion of the sect's treatment of Isa. 6:9–10.

[93] Evans, ibid., 40.

in Isa. 32:3–4; 35:5; 42:7; 49:9; and 61:1, passages which often echo (and reverse) the proclamation of Isa. 6.

In its Markan context, then, the "parable theory" of Mk. 4:10–12 sharpens our understanding of discipleship in just this way: it explains the phenomenon of "poor soil conditions" as a constituent part of God's plan, a plan whose success is measured not by immediate universal acclaim but by its persistence in the face of opposition. Moreover, it affirms that, within the scope of God's universal sovereignty, the blindness and deafness encountered in pockets of resistance will not have the final word. In turn, this affirmation spurs on those who continue the indiscriminate sowing patterned by Jesus.

The sowing parable interpreted

As recounted in Mk. 4:13–20, the interpretation of the sower parable raises several exegetical issues that relate at least indirectly to this study's dominant interest in Markan discipleship. Among topics that scholars have probed, the passage's composition history, its relationship to the sowing parable itself, and its meaning both within the gospel narrative and for Mark's community together form an important backdrop for our understanding of this passage and the chapter as a whole. While many interpreters share the view that the parable and its interpretation constitute a challenge to Mark's community to "ensure that they are found in the last group,"[94] this section of the study will suggest that the interpretation develops a claim already implicit in the parable itself: as those "around Jesus" and as those "given the μυστήριον of the kingdom of God," the disciples are expected to participate actively in the sowing of that word. Thus Mk. 4:13–20 provides an unmistakable link between Jesus as sower and those in the early church who are called to continue his broadcast sowing activity. As an expanded commentary on the parable, then, the explanation offers its hearers the hope that despite the appearance of failure, God's eschatological victory will not be thwarted.

The first task is to determine the relationship between the parable and its interpretation, a question that I approach from two discrete perspectives: the interpretation's composition history and the degree to which it coheres with the sowing parable. First, what is the origin of the interpretation as found in Mk. 4:13–20? Does it belong to the original setting of the parable itself, which most scholars locate within the life of the historical Jesus? While some maintain its authenticity simply because parabolic is

[94] Hooker, *Mark*, 130; Witherington, *Mark*, 167. Cf. Guelich, *Mark 1–8:26*, 224.

so rare within traditional material, most scholars concur that Mk. 4:14–20 derives from an early church setting. Not all evidence adduced to support this view is equally compelling. On the one hand, the trend championed by Jülicher[95] that forged a sharp distinction between "parable" as simile and "allegory" as metaphor has been effectively undermined by numerous studies.[96] As a result the a priori assumption that the sowing parable's interpretation could not have originated with Jesus no longer holds sway. Indeed, Jewish literature is replete with examples of parable and allegory that elide clear distinction, as well as with interpretive commentary on an illustrative story.

Yet Mk. 4:14–20 does bear the unmistakable stylistic and lexical imprint of a setting at some remove from Jesus' own life. Especially its abundant use of language characteristic of the early church seems beyond question. For example, the following words hardly ever appear in Jesus' teachings but frequently crop up in the epistles: λόγος (in the absolute form), μέριμναι τοῦ αἰῶνος, ἀπάτη, πρόσκαιροί.[97] Moreover, the graphic language of persecution seems to point to a *Sitz im Leben* in which followers of Jesus were singled out for their faithfulness.[98] Finally, in its structural emphasis on the factors undermining the seeds' yield, the interpretation reworks the parable's balanced 3:3 comparison in a way that reflects later development. Taken together, then, the weight of these observations leads to the conclusion that, at least in its present form, the interpretation found in Mk. 4:14–20 constitutes an early Christian commentary on the sowing parable.[99] While we cannot rule out the possibility that Jesus offered his own explanation, its form and content lie beyond the

95 Jülicher, *Gleichnisreden*, *passim*. Among those following in his footsteps are C. H. Dodd, *The Parables of the Kingdom* (New York: Scribner's, 1961), 1–7; and Jeremias, *Parables*, 12–13.

96 Representative examples include Hans-Josef Klauck, *Allegorie und Allegorese in synoptischen Gleichnistexten* (Münster: Aschendorff, 1978); Boucher, *Mysterious Parable*; and Raymond E. Brown, "Parable and Allegory Reconsidered," in *New Testament Essays* (Garden City, NY: Image/Doubleday, 1968), 321–33.

97 See, e.g., Hooker, *Mark*, 129. Klauck, *Allegorie*, 200, n. 77, cites eight Markan *hapax legomena*.

98 While the reference to θλίψεως ἤ διωγμοῦ (Mk. 4:17) conveys an opposition not necessarily inconsistent with resistance that may have been brewing during Jesus' ministry, the language itself appears to derive from a setting in which persecution had more fully fomented.

99 Witherington, *Mark*, 161, plausibly contends that some form of application originated with the sower parable and was amended and edited along the way. Less viable is Witherington's particular claim that Mark is responsible for the interpretation's emphasis on sowing the "word," since his argument that one "might have expected Jesus to talk about sowing the good news of the coming dominion of God rather than the 'Word'" (n. 60) is true also of Mark.

realm of reconstruction, and we are left to consider only the interpretation as Mark has appropriated it.

To argue that the present form of Mk. 4:14–20 reflects the interpretation of the early church, though, leaves open the question of coherence mentioned above. Does the explanation expressed in these verses fundamentally distort the parable's meaning, or does it faithfully appropriate its message? Central to the interpretation is its strict equation of "the seed" with "the word" (Mk. 4:14), an allegorizing move sustained throughout the parable.[100] Even if the absolute τὸν λόγον belongs more to the lexicon of the early church than to the language of Jesus himself, its roots in OT prophecy provide a vital link with the gospel message Jesus has announced in Mk. 1:14–15.[101] In line with Jesus' earlier pronouncement, the "word" here refers to the "good news" of God's coming kingdom. If it is a word which Jesus delivers in a definitive sense in Mark's gospel,[102] it is also a word which Jesus' followers will continue to articulate in the post-resurrection age.[103] Moreover, neither Jesus nor those who carry on his mission speak autonomously; from Mark's apocalyptic Jewish perspective, the "word" must always be heard as the word that is ultimately the "word of God." The interpretation seems primarily aimed at reclaiming for the early Christian community the important task of sowing the same word that Jesus had sown in his earthly ministry. Thus a first danger is averted: the danger of a despairing powerlessness in the wake of the kingdom's apparent non-arrival.

That Mark adopts that pastoral intention becomes strikingly clear when we consider the relationship between the sowing parable material and the content of Mk. 4:10–12. If the parable and its interpretation were conjoined at an earlier stage in the chapter's composition history, Mark's apparent insertion of these verses of private instruction focuses attention not on the insiders' reception of the word but on their "giftedness" and the responsibility it brings. As I have discussed above, the point is not simply that they "understand" the mystery of God's coming kingdom

100 Interpreters routinely refer to the ensuing ambivalence between the seed as the word (the allegorization is clear at least in Mk. 4:15–16 and 18–20) and the seed as hearers (based on the reference to the "ones sown" in Mk. 4:15–16, 18, and 20).

101 Cf. Jeremias, *Parables*, 77–8, who views the absolute use as early Christian coinage. But Brown, "Parable and Allegory," 42, has linked *logos* to the prophetic use of *dabar* as "divine message entrusted to them."

102 While Marcus groups together the nine instances in which the Markan Jesus "teaches, speaks, or proclaims the word (2:2; 4:33; 8:32; 9:10; 10:22, 24; 11:29; 13:31; 14:39)" (*Mark 1–8*, 311), we should be careful to distinguish the uses that refer to the singular articulated form of the noun (only 2:2; 4:33; 8:32; 9:10).

103 The lines of continuity are forged most clearly asserted in Mk. 13:10 and 14:9, both of which express Jesus' anticipation of the cosmic proclamation of the "gospel."

at a cognitive level. Rather, the insiders have been entrusted with that mystery as its stewards, as those called to assert without apology God's firm hold on the universe, a sway that carries dramatic implications for human existence. And so, the interpretation suggests, those "with him" are expected to cast the seed of that mystery, even while God may be entrusted with the outcome.[104]

Prior to the interpretation itself, though, comes Mark's apparent editorial insertion found in 4:13, a verse that identifies Jesus' interlocutors (identified in Mk. 4:10 as "those around him with the Twelve") as insiders even as it subtly links them to "those outside." As Jesus' first response,[105] the question "Do you not comprehend (οἴδατε) this parable?" implicates his hearers for not grasping the parable thus for requiring further explanation. Yet, while a different verb conveys the insiders' uncomprehending condition, the connection is clear: both Jesus' followers and those who see but do not perceive (μὴ ἴδωσιν) lack the discernment necessary to grasp the parabolic instruction. In the end, though, the insiders' being "with Jesus" will distinguish them from "those outside," since "he explained (ἐπέλυεν) everything to them" (Mk. 4:34).

Such an interpretive dependence on Jesus gains confirmation in the verse's second question, "'How then will you know (γνώσεσθε) all the parables?' " The question indicates that the sowing parable provides a test case for Jesus' hearers. In other words, it is not the sowing parable's content that provides for the knowledge of "all parables."[106] Neither does the ensuing allegorical explanation suggest "Mark sees *all* the parables as allegories," as Hooker claims.[107] Rather, precisely because Mark uses these two questions to introduce Jesus' explanation, together they underscore the notion that any true grasp of the nature of God's kingdom derives not from human speculation but from close affiliation with Jesus, from "being with him" as followers and heirs to his mission. In this way Mark addresses a second looming danger within his community: the danger of power wielded autonomously.

Finally, the interpretation's emphasis on both active and passive resistance to the sown seed exposes a third danger that this passage addresses: despair in the face of failure. In this regard, the interpretation simply

[104] As Hooker affirms, it is "clear from the explanation that for Mark's community the word will be spoken by Christian preachers" (*Mark*, 129).

[105] Though the punctuation of Mk. 4:13 is to some extent a matter of interpretation, the designation of two separate questions, linked by the conjunction καί seems to make most sense of the grammar.

[106] Mk. 3:21–2 in no way indicates that the sowing parable is needed as an interpretive key.

[107] Hooker, *Mark*, 131.

elaborates the claims made by the sowing parable itself, namely that the appearance of opposition in no way compromises the ultimate outcome of God's victory.

As we have seen, the interpretation found in Mk. 4:13–20 develops in a coherent way many of the dynamics identified within the sowing parable, including the broadcast nature of the sowing, the present reality of resistant factors, and the ultimate assurance of an abundant yield. For this portrait of discipleship, I have detected an implicit call both to remain in Jesus' presence, where all insight and purpose originate, and to continue his sowing act, which is sustained by the One whose word is sown. The separate strands of instruction woven together throughout Mk. 4 – from the sower parable, to the private instruction, to the logia on lamp and measure, and finally to the concluding seed parables – convey not a paranetic warning to receive the kingdom message (the firm assumption is at least that those around him have already "been given the mystery"), but a resounding summons to continue Jesus' sowing of God's "good news." As the parable and its interpretation demonstrate, the "gospel" heralds an eschatological victory assured by a sovereign God but dramatized within the vulnerable human realm.

Lamp and measure teachings

The ensuing instruction reiterates the revelatory thrust of God's in-breaking kingdom detected above in the complex of sower tradition teachings.[108] Although the text does not label the sayings about the lamp and the measure as "parables," both examples employ imagery from daily life to illustrate the purpose for which the good news of the "mystery of God's kingdom" has been given, illustrations that are then interpreted by means of explanatory γάρ clauses. In a sense, both examples interpret the sower parable in a manner that underscores the disciples' broadcasting of the word.

Standaert has argued that these sayings constitute the chiastic center of the parables discourse and thus the "point de gravité de tout le chapitre."[109] In his view, not only do they separate the parable of the sower from the other two seed parables (Mk. 4:26–9), but they also preserve the chapter's tension between human responsibility and divine gift, a tension itself

[108] Marcus points to these verses (vv. 21–32) as a demonstration that the "ultimate purpose for which God designed the gospel" as "to illuminate the whole world" (*Mystery*, 231).

[109] Standaert, *Marc*, 217.

conveyed in the exhortation of Mk. 4:23: "whoever has ears to hear, let that one hear."[110]

But what do these brief teachings contribute to this study of discipleship? In the first place, the audience within Mark's narrative context has not broadened from the private instruction of Mk. 4:10–20, as Jesus still addresses those closest to him. In view of the findings about the sowing parable, both the lamp and the measure sayings shift attention from the varied effects of the sowing to its intent. In other words, just as placing a lamp under a bushel or a bed subverts its inherent purpose of illuminating the dark, so the light of God's kingdom is meant to cast its beams as broadly as possible. The blindness and confusion portrayed in Mk. 4:11–12 become reinterpreted as constituent parts of an interim reality on its way to full disclosure. If the disciples have been given the μυστήριον, it is not a prized possession to be hoarded or reserved for the sake of private knowledge; it is rather a reality whose very nature it is to shine forth, since it ἔλθῃ εἰς φανερόν (Mk. 4:22).

But whom or what does the lamp represent in this saying? Many interpreters who liken the sower to Jesus also construe the lamp as a figure for Jesus himself.[111] In this view, Mark's hearers would be compelled through this saying to proclaim the identity of Jesus as the crucified and raised Christ. Yet this Christological focus once again seems superimposed on our text.[112] To be sure, Mark's gospel does address a community shaped by the perplexing apocalyptic reality of a crucified messiah, a perspective that perceives Jesus' passion as a source of empowerment in the face of their own trials. Yet again we should recognize the wider "gospel" landscape: while Jesus serves as the unique harbinger of God's "good news," in Mark's gospel he resists serving as its exclusive focus. Thus, with Witherington, we affirm that it is "not impossible to interpret the light to be a reference to the dominion which is also said to come" in Jesus; indeed all indicators point to that reference.[113]

Yet again, this broader understanding of the saying's light/lamp imagery proceeds quite naturally from its use in both biblical and post-biblical Jewish literature, where it presents metaphorical manifestations of God's illuminating presence, sometimes mediated through human

[110] Ibid., 216.

[111] William Wrede, *The Messianic Secret*, trans. J. C. Grieg (Cambridge: James Clarke, 1971; orig. 1901), 70–1. See also, e.g., Hooker, *Mark*, 131–3, who asserts that the active sense of the verb ἔρχεται (Mk. 4:21) suggests that firm correlation; also Lane, *Mark*, 165–6.

[112] Wrede's reading depends too heavily on Mk. 9:9, which as Räisänen observes, appears rather late in the story to play such a determinative role (*Parabeltheorie*, 79–80).

[113] Witherington, *Mark*, 169. Similarly, Guelich, *Mark 1–8:26*, 231.

agents.[114] In each case, the imagery conveys God's activity within the human sphere. Moreover, while the forms likened to a lamp/light vary widely, each text emphasizes the light's function, which is to cast the human realm in shades of divine luminosity. The example of David's song of thanksgiving provides an apt illustration of just such a function (2 Sam. 22:29–30/Ps. 18:28–9): "Indeed you are my lamp, O Lord, the Lord lightens my darkness. By you I can crush a troop, and by my God I can leap over a wall." That the image here is linked to divinely empowered victory only further underscores that the lamp/light image can function in its Markan context as a reference to God's impending eschatological dominion.

If the lamp saying encourages Jesus' hearers to make God's coming kingdom visible, the saying about the measure (Mk. 4:24–5) registers a similar message through synonymous parallel.[115] Though the language is rather cryptic, certainly the use of "giving" and "having" provide important points of contact with the implicit call to stewardship detected in this reading of the sowing parable material, as both teachings counter any impulse to hoard the "gift" of God's mysterious rule. In this saying those who mete out the "good news" entrusted ("given") to them not only stand to recoup their original investment but also will accrue even more, as Jesus asserts, προστεθήσεται ὑμῖν.[116]

The language of "giving" in Mk. 4:24–5 resonates with Mk. 4:11–12 in two respects. First, within its setting in Mk. 4,[117] this saying seems to be addressed still to the inner circle of Mk. 4:10, so that it works along with the lamp saying to remind those entrusted with the μυστήριον of the apocalyptic reversal of the divine economy. Since the revelatory gift has been given for the purpose of widespread proclamation, its recipients need not fear its absence; if they "measure out" the "measure" they have been given, it will only be increased. So we may paraphrase the saying and its interpretation in this way:

[114] E.g. God (2 Sam. 22:29/Ps. 18:28); David (2 Sam. 21:17); God's "word" (Ps. 119:105); the eyes of the Lord (Zech. 4:2, 10); the people Israel (Isa. 49:6); the elect community (1QSb 4:27); Moses (*Sifre* Num. §94).

[115] Among those who forge a similar connection between Mk. 4:21–3 and 4:24–5 as implicit challenge to the community's dissemination of God's reign are Reploh, *Markus*, 70–1, and Pesch, *Markusevangelium*, I:253.

[116] Both Matt. 7:2 and Lk. 6:38 lack this additional detail, a detail which disrupts the balance of the saying. Mark's inclusion of it, though, squares with the progressively fruitful seed at the end of the sowing parable and interpretation in their claim that the kingdom payoff drives relentlessly toward abundance.

[117] Most scholars concede Mark's redactional hand at least in the placement of these sayings.

> To the extent that your lives measure out the mystery of God's coming kingdom entrusted to you, in turn it shall be measured out to you – and even more so! For to the one who has – that is, to the steward and participant in God's kingdom – it shall be given by God, just as the one who lacks – that is, the one standing outside that kingdom reality – will have taken away what s/he appears to "have."

Addressed to the same "you" identified in Mk. 4:10, then, these sayings constitute a combined affirmation of the hearers' role in extending God's gospel toward others, as well as a consolation that outsiders' apparent gains ultimately come to nothing.

More seed parables

In the two concluding seed parables, the text explicitly identifies the βασιλεία τοῦ θεοῦ as the object of the illustration: οὕτως ἐστὶν ἡ βασιλεία τοῦ θεοῦ (Mk. 4:26). Indeed, the first parable shares a great deal of common language with the sowing parable, including the casting of seed ἐπὶ τῆς γῆς (Mk. 4:26). But this time, rather than emphasizing various outcomes of scattered seed under various soil conditions, the parable highlights the means through which the sown seed is parlayed into fruit.

As in the case of the sowing parable, the sower himself scatters the seed and then awaits its outcome, but in this case the story makes explicit the sower's ignorance about what happens next: ὁ σπόρος βλαστᾷ καὶ μηκύνηται ὡς οὐκ οἶδεν αὐτός (Mk. 4:27). In stark contrast to the sower's passivity in the sprouting and growing, the parable suggests the divine sway over the seed's destiny in its claim that the earth bears fruit αὐτομάτη (Mk. 4:28).[118] The harvest comes, in the end, not as the result of a contrived act on the sower's part, but as the natural outcome of the earth's own properties. Once again, the act of sowing is a prerequisite to the outcome of God's fruitful reign; still, it is the Creator that has engendered that outcome.

Once again, to identify the sower in Mk. 4:26–9 with both Jesus and his followers seems consistent with the contours of the chapter's dominant parable discussed above. Yet this brief illustration expands the sower's role in a way that appears at first glance to threaten these findings. For

[118] Jeremias, *Parables*, 149, 151–2, may go too far in his view of this parable as an endorsement of divine activity over against human activity in the sowing and harvesting of the kingdom. More helpfully nuanced is Guelich's claim that the parable "does not repudiate human effort in favor of divine action" (*Mark 1–8:26*, 242).

in contrast to the main sowing parable, which ends with a tally of yield amounts, this succinct account draws explicit attention to the farmer's final activity: putting the sickle to the harvest. Many have observed that this added detail alludes to the portrait of God as the eschatological reaper depicted in Joel 4:13 (MT), an allusion that strictly precludes the identification of the sower as Jesus' followers.[119] Yet such a sharp distinction between divine judgment and human agency seems forced in light of claims both internal and external to Mark. In the first place, I have discussed above the gospel's initial call to discipleship (Mk. 1:16–20), which casts Jesus' followers as eschatological fishers. Outside Mark, we find explicit reference to the disciples' role as "laborers in the harvest" in Matt. 9:37/Lk. 10:2. Just as there can be no doubt that the harvest is the Lord's, human agency in the reaping process cannot be dismissed out of hand.

Finally, in the parable of the mustard seed, we encounter the complex's final illustration of God's dominion, which turns out to be vast in scope despite an initially meager appearance. Once again, the coming reign of God is explicitly likened to the sowing of a seed "upon the earth" (Mk. 4:31). The twofold repetition of the phrase ἐπὶ τῆς γῆς within this verse represents the culmination of the parable complex, which has begun in Mk. 4:1 with the staging of the "whole crowd by the sea upon the earth." In this case, Mark's language aligns the crowd, rather than the inner circle, with the "earth" upon which now the third measure of seed is cast. Above I mentioned the linkage with the Danielic vision of God's kingdom established "on earth," so that, at the very least, we have here a reiteration of this divine kingdom impinging upon the earthly reality of human existence.

But what does this mustard-seed imagery connote? Even this brief parable employs a metaphor whose various dimensions illustrate vital properties of God's reign. In the first place, the most obvious contrast in these verses is between the "almost invisible seed and the enormous bush."[120] Thus the word of exhortation for Mark's community, represented in the text by "those around Jesus with the Twelve," may well bolster their sense of the significance of the kingdom proclamation with which they have been entrusted. The words they utter and deeds they perform to demonstrate God's reign may seem paltry in their present surroundings, yet they can be assured by these words of Jesus that in due time they will witness its full fruition.

But two other potential dimensions of this imagery also portend a prosperous outcome for a kingdom likened to such a modest seed. In the

[119] See, e.g., Marcus, *Mystery*, 177.
[120] Hooker, *Mark*, 136, identifies this contrast as the "important point."

first place, the portrait of the bush as a nesting place for the birds of the air may well allude to the ingathering of the nations who ultimately return to affirm Yahweh as Lord of the universe.[121] As depicted in prophetic glimpses of that eschatological return (e.g. Ezek. 17:23; Dan. 4:12, 21), the mustard-bush imagery presents God's dominion as a refuge for those who have been lost.[122]

But there is another, less palatable dimension to this image. Following the findings of Crossan,[123] Witherington highlights the noxiousness of the mustard plant, which Pliny the Elder describes as "pungent . . . fiery . . . [and] wild."[124] Due to its rapid germination, the mustard bush threatens to encroach on existing vegetation and depicts God's kingdom as an annoying, ineradicable weed that can overtake other kingdoms sown on the earth. In a sense, then, even as God's dominion promises shelter to the birds of the heavens, so too it looms as a menace in the field where it was sown.[125] Still, the main point of the mustard-seed likeness concerns the dogged persistence of God's dominion, perhaps especially in the face of opposition from those determined to weed it out.

Parable complex conclusion

I turn at last to the teaching section's conclusion, which emphasizes the parabolic nature of Jesus' sayings through both a positive and a negative claim. In essence, these verses constitute Mark's closing argument for understanding the revelatory impulse of Jesus' teaching and its implicit commission for his hearers, especially in Mark's community.[126]

The final reference to Jesus' followers in Mk. 4:1–34 differentiates carefully between the wider audience whom Jesus addresses in parables

[121] Both Mark and Luke (13:19) preserve, through different wording, the biblically allusive language of the "birds of heaven" who "nest in its shade," while *Gos. Thom.* 20 only mentions a "shelter for the birds of heaven." In any case, the OT image seems an indispensable background to the verse.

[122] Both Dodd (*Parables*, 154) and Jeremias (*Parables*, 147) equate the "birds of heaven" specifically with Gentiles, a claim which reflects the universal cosmic scope of God's kingdom but seems, in the Markan context, too narrowly defined.

[123] John Dominic Crossan, *The Historical Jesus* (San Francisco: Harper, 1991), 277–9.

[124] Pliny the Elder, *Natural History* 19.170, cited by Witherington, *Mark*, 172.

[125] Witherington calls it a "threat to the existing garden or field of early Judaism" (ibid.).

[126] Sorting through evidence of tradition and redaction in these verses is tricky, since lexical choice and theological content do not support clearly consistent findings. For instance, the occurrence of three *hapax legomena* in Mk. 4:34 (χωρίς τοῖς ἰδίοις μαθηταῖς ἐπέλυεν), combined with the uncharacteristic use of δέ, suggest a pre-Markan origin, while the restrictive nature of Jesus' instruction seems to many interpreters to derive from Mark's own redaction (see Gnilka, *Verstockung*, 23–4). Similarly, while the language of Mk. 4:33 sounds Markan, it seems to function as a summarizing conclusion of pre-Markan material, since it describes the broad-based nature of Jesus' parabolic teaching. Rather than resolving this issue definitively, my interpretation aims to unpack the verses' implicit tension between public and private instruction, as well as their revelatory thrust.

and those to whom he makes all things clear. The deliberate (and somewhat redundant) Markan structure drives home the centrality of Jesus' use of parables in his teaching:

Mark 4:33	Mark 4:34
καὶ τοιαύταις παραβολαῖς	χωρὶς δὲ παραβολῆς
πολλαῖς ἐλάλει αὐτοῖς τὸν λόγον	οὐκ ἐλάλει αὐτοῖς
καθὼς ἠδύναντο ἀκούειν:	κατ' ἰδίαν δὲ τοῖς ἰδίοις μαθηταῖς ἐπέλυεν πάντα

The verses feature both parallel and contrasting elements that help to elucidate Jesus' relationship to his hearers. In the first place, the repeated combination of "parables" + "spoke" + "to them" – expressed both positively and negatively – deliberately depicts parabolic teaching as a trademark of Jesus' ministry (cf. Mk. 1:45). The use of imperfect verbs only enhances the repeated and thus characteristic nature of this instruction. Such deliberate teaching comports well with Mark's understanding of Jesus as sower of "the word" in Mk. 4:13, that is, as an indiscriminate dispenser of the seed (= the word, τὸν λόγον). Scattered like seed, the parable itself does not always bear fruit, nor does its initial appearance correspond to its potential significance. Yet Jesus' driving impulse, like the sower's, is to broadcast the seed, which (given salutary conditions) produces αὐτομάτη (Mk. 4:28).

But in what ways do these two closing verses advance our understanding of Mark's portrait of discipleship? On the one hand, the double emphasis on Jesus' widespread teaching in parables affirms that his mission is not restricted to those who have chosen to follow him. As noted above, his strategy may even reflect the parabolic nature of "all things" which appear in figures to those outside even while signifying God's sovereignty to those enabled to perceive it. In Mark's gospel, Jesus remains engaged with followers, detractors, and the unspecified masses in his relentless mission to demonstrate the dawning of God's dominion. He is no sectarian secluded among the ranks of a rigidly defined community; the itinerant nature of his mission reflects his impulse to extend the kingdom "good news" to as wide an audience as possible.

Further, the phrase καθὼς ἠδύναντο ἀκούειν (Mk. 4:33) qualifies Jesus' parabolic teaching in a way that affirms his hearers' ability to listen: "And in many such parables he spoke the word to them, to the degree that (καθώς) they were empowered to hear" (Mk. 4:33).[127] The etymological

[127] Both Gnilka, *Verstockung*, 51–2, and Quentin Quesnell, *The Mind of Mark: Interpretation and Method Through the Exegesis of Mark 6,52* (Rome: Pontifical Biblical Institute, 1969), 75, 85, maintain, on the basis of Mk. 4:11–12, that the ability to hear is implicitly impaired. The verse itself, however, lends more weight to the ability than it does to the impairment.

connection between the verb ἠδύναντο and the noun δύναμις implies that any "ability" has been given by God in the first place (see Mk. 2:27; 3:25–7). Underlying the summary of Mk. 4:33 is the assumption that parabolic teachings will not fall entirely on deaf ears. Rather, at least some may be empowered to heed the summons of Mk. 4:9: ὃς ἔχει ὦτα ἀκούειν ἀκουέτω. Thus Mk. 4:33 eclipses any sharp distinction between insiders whose privileged position enables their hearing and outsiders on whom the teaching is necessarily lost.

Still, we must consider the following verse, which does seem to confer a special status upon Jesus' "own disciples." In a way, the language of Mk. 4:34 reintroduces the insider/outsider division addressed in Mk. 4:10–12. Thus both passages reckon with just this perplexing reality faced by Jesus' followers (at least in Mark's day, but probably earlier as well): despite Jesus' eschatological vision of God's dominion, there remain "those outside, [to whom] all things come in parables." According to interpreters such as Gnilka, the Markan *hapax legomenon* ἐπέλυεν (Mk. 4:34) signals the exclusive nature of the disciples' understanding.[128] Only those receiving special instruction from Jesus would truly be capable of "hearing."[129] Such a two-staged revelation, coming as it does through parabolic teaching as well as private instruction, fits Mark's apocalyptic worldview in which an initial vision or teaching remains obscure until a later stage of elucidation.

Yet, as I have noted throughout this chapter, the illustrative stories found in Mk. 4 repeatedly assert a view of God's coming kingdom that is not so much a riddle to be deciphered as it is a reality to be proclaimed and dramatized. To the degree that Jesus' followers gain "understanding" (a degree notoriously limited in Mark), it entails their own participation in that reality so decisively announced by Jesus. Their being "with Jesus" does constitute their chance to become privy to his special instruction, but they can only be considered true "hearers" when they engage their very lives in his kingdom mission.

Finally, it may be helpful to summarize the findings about the shifting identity of the audience in this chapter. As we move from the crowd described in Mk. 4:2, to "those around him with the Twelve" in Mk. 4:10, to an unspecified "them" in Mk. 4:33 and "his own disciples" in Mk. 4:34, we recognize two somewhat competing thrusts within Mark's redactional

128 Gnilka, *Verstockung*, 62–4.

129 As Guelich puts it, "'Hearing' they could not understand apart from an interpretation" (*Mark 1–8:26*, 258). Even he concedes, though, that the view reflected in these verses "apparently ran at cross purposes to [Mark's] own understanding of Jesus' use of parables" – an inconsistency he explains through an appeal to the motif of the misunderstanding disciples.

activity. On the one hand, we must acknowledge the text's overarching claim, spanning from Mk. 4:1 to Mk. 4:34, that Mark's Jesus addresses a vast and unscreened audience. Further, as study of the text has demonstrated, the intent of the parables is for revelation, not for concealment. On the other hand, only those "with ears to hear" step forward from the crowd to pursue greater elucidation. In this group, identified first as "those around him with the Twelve," we can detect Mark's audience as heirs to Jesus' privileged instruction, which in turn will equip them for spreading the word about God's kingdom. This passage thus envisions a group of followers that extends beyond the boundaries of the Twelve to include those who would learn from him, τοῖς ἰδίοις μαθηταῖς (Mk. 4:34).[130]

Conclusion

Mark's fourth chapter presents an intricate complex of didactic material that has intrigued, and often confounded, its readers from earliest days. Yet it offers critical insights into Mark's view of the kingdom of God heralded and inaugurated by Jesus. In turn, it dramatizes in living color the calling of those who would be "with him" as collaborators in God's coming rule. In what respects has this chapter shaped our understanding of Mark's portrait of discipleship?

(1) The proclamation of God's dominion extends to all the earth. Rather than targeting a select group of recipients, Jesus instructs the masses in a broadcast, indiscriminate manner. Moreover, the primary thrust of Jesus' parabolic teaching is revelatory in nature; as Witherington claims, the "purpose of the parables was not obfuscation but revelation."[131] Through illustrative speech, Jesus heralds the hopeful bounty of the coming harvest, as he proclaims a kingdom that is gaining ground.

(2) Those who align themselves with God's kingdom participate actively in its disclosure. As Marcus puts it, the "clash between God's kingdom and that of Satan which occurred in the ministry, death, and resurrection of Jesus, cannot be understood by the Markan community except as that community recapitulates Jesus' way."[132] Being with Jesus engenders first and foremost not proper dogma but active embodiment of his Christological mission to sow seeds of God's dominion "upon the earth."

(3) The harsh reality, however, remains. Not everyone who sees perceives; not all who listen understand. The incursion of God's kingdom

[130] Witherington supplies a helpful distinction: "the Twelve epitomize the disciple group in Mark; they do not exhaust it" (*Mark*, 425).

[131] Ibid., 173. [132] Marcus, *Mystery*, 71.

into the human realm does not proceed without resistance. Thus this array of parables includes an exhortative word to the faithful: the problematic resistance of "those outside" will not ultimately supplant God's assured rule. As Chrysostom puts it, "Even though more seed would be lost than survive, the disciples were not to lose heart."[133] In the meantime, then, that resistance must not hinder the casting of seed or keep a lamp under a bushel.

(4) Ultimately the outcome is assured. The dominant motif of the chapter is not secrecy but growth, growth even in the face of resistance and opposition. A vulnerable God may work "on the earth" through the agency of human beings (preeminently his own son), but in the end the sovereignty of God has predetermined the outcome, which is the return of all the "birds of heaven" who nest in the shade of the branches. In that day all things will come to light.

133 Chrysostom, "The Gospel of St. Matthew, Homily 44.5.1," in *A Select Library of the Nicene and Post-Nicene Fathers of the Christian Church*, ed. P. Schaff *et al.* (Peabody, MA: Hendrickson, 1994; orig. 1887–94).

5

DISCIPLESHIP AS PRACTICE: JESUS' SENDING OUT OF THE TWELVE IN MARK 6:7–13

Introduction

This study of discipleship in the opening chapters of Mark's gospel has discerned an intimate connection between Jesus' own earthly mission and his call to "come after me." The pattern established in the initial call to discipleship (Mk. 1:16–20) and developed in the appointing of the Twelve (Mk. 3:13–19) balances two complementary thrusts: *both* remaining in Jesus' presence *and* being sent out by him as agents of God's coming rule. Moreover, even when Mark's Jesus does arrest his breathless pace to instruct those who are "with him" (Mk. 4:1–34), the second evangelist shapes traditional material so as to depict Jesus' followers as stewards of the μυστήριον . . . τῆς βασιλείας τοῦ θεοῦ. As a result, their being in Jesus' presence prepares the disciples to carry forward the practice of Jesus' own gospel enterprise, a deft move that in turn extends Jesus' sowing activity to the Markan community seeking to live out their own discipleship calling in the post-resurrection age.

As it recounts Jesus' sending out of the Twelve, Mk. 6:7–13 only continues, and etches more indelibly, the lines of continuity between Jesus' and the disciples' display of the "gospel," which is God's encroaching dominion.[1] As we shall see, Mark carefully situates this successful

[1] The relative paucity of secondary literature devoted to this passage can be explained by at least two factors: (1) the general consensus (expressed, e.g., by Friedrich Hahn, *Mission in the New Testament*, SBT 47 [London: SCM Press, 1965], 42) that the earlier (and more authentic?) form of the commissioning can be found in Q (Luke 10:2–12); and (2) the view that the passage's favorable report about the Twelve's activity presents an inconsistency in the Markan narrative, which is mainly concerned with depicting their faults. With regard to the former, whether Mark's account is dependent on (Rudolf Bultmann, *The History of the Synoptic Tradition*, trans. John Marsh, rev. edn. [Peabody, MA: Hendrickson, 1994; orig. 1921], 145) or independent of Q (B. H. Streeter, *The Four Gospels: A Study of Origins* [London: Macmillan, 1924], 190), the discrepancies between the similar reports probably reflect the second evangelist's particular hermeneutical interests, especially the New Exodus motif. With regard to the latter, the view here is that this passage is not, as Witherington claims, "but a prelude" to the gospel's true view of Jesus' and the disciples' mission *The*

discipleship venture at the precise narrative point where Jesus' own efforts have yielded patchy results (Mk. 6:5–6). In many respects, Mark's portrait of discipleship reaches its climax in this passage, as the Twelve enact with striking effectiveness their role as authorized agents of Jesus' eschatological mission. It is here that we see clearly that, for Mark, discipleship entails doing the deeds of power that characterize Jesus' mission, even – and perhaps especially – when he is "not able" (Mk. 6:5).[2]

Once again, I begin the investigation of Mk. 6:7–13 with a careful consideration of its narrative context within the second gospel: what interpretive leverage can be gained by assessing the evangelist's placement of this passage within an array of miracle stories? Next, I proceed to a close reading of the structure and claims of the pericope itself. Through Mark's reshaping of traditional material, Mk. 6:7–13 maintains a double focus on Jesus as authorizing agent and on the Twelve as those whom he commissions to play an active role in the eschatological New Exodus event. As Mark reports Jesus' sending them forth and their own missionary results, the passage provides critical clues to understanding Markan discipleship in its high-water moment.[3] Finally, on the basis of these findings, the present chapter concludes with a brief reassessment of ideal Markan discipleship, which is based in this passage not primarily on the disciples' supernatural abilities or on their correct Christological understanding, but rather on their faithfully carrying forward Jesus' own kingdom-of-God enterprise, as they mediate God's healing and triumph over the δαιμόνια.

Narrative context

Between Jesus' parabolic instruction (Mk. 4:1–34) and the sending out of the Twelve (Mk. 6:7–13), several episodes from Jesus' ministry demonstrate his miraculous power as well as his mixed reception among those who witness it. As Jesus embarks on a journey beyond the boundaries of Israel proper, he extends the reach of his gospel proclamation in a way that evokes amazement even in the Decapolis (Mk. 5:20); closer to home,

Gospel of Mark: Socio-Rhetorical Commentary [Grand Rapids, MI: Eerdmans, 2001], 427), but rather an important testimony to their occasional success.

[2] The fact that Mark takes notice of Jesus' inability to do deeds of power (Mk. 6:6) just before the episode recounting the disciples' successful missionary journey (Mk. 6:7–13) may constitute the text's strongest rebuttal to Weeden's theory of a heretical "divine man" Christology (*Mark: Traditions in Conflict* [Philadelphia: Fortress Press, 1971]). Rather than indicating either overt or implied censure of the disciples, the evangelist unreflectively assumes that both Jesus and his followers perform miracles as a constituent part of their demonstration of God's in-breaking kingdom.

[3] Robert C. Tannehill, "The Disciples in Mark: The Function of a Narrative Role," *JR* 57 (1977): 393, acknowledges "the similarity of their role to his."

similar astonishment gives way to deep-seated offense, as the "prophet without honor" experiences the brutal reality of hometown rejection (Mk. 6:1–6a).

While the scholarly consensus affirms Mark's use of traditional material in this section of the gospel, agreement breaks down when it comes to identifying precise limits of the pre-existing traditions. Various positions on this issue have been staked out, for instance, by Kuhn and Keck, who believe Mark has incorporated an existing collection of stories found in Mk. 4:35–5:43 and 6:32–52;[4] by Marcus, who suggests that the pre-Markan material may have included the boat scene found in Mk. 8;[5] and by Achtemeier, who isolates not one but two series (catenae) of miracle stories.[6] In any case, by embedding the disciples' missionary venture within this collection of wonder-working stories, Mark implies an important continuity between Jesus' miraculous powers and his followers' subsequent demonstration of the "mystery" of God's rule.

Consideration of the passage's narrative context will focus on two passages that overtly mention Jesus' disciples and lay groundwork for our understanding of their missionary journey. First, I shall consider the interaction between Jesus and his companions in the sea-crossing story (Mk. 4:35–41), which provides a transition from Jesus' parabolic instruction to his dynamic disclosure of God's power. In a second preparatory step, I shall examine the Markan story of Jesus' hometown impotence (Mk. 6:1–6) as a prelude to his sending out of the Twelve. In both incidents, Jesus' deeds of power adumbrate God's coming reign upon the earth, and both assign the wonder-working task both to Jesus and, by extension, to his disciples.

The first sea crossing (Mk. 4:35–41)

Immediately on the heels of his seashore teach-in, Jesus invites the disciples to cross in the boat to the "other side" (Mk. 4:35). In a noteworthy twist, the story conveys the rather awkward notion (for Mark) that the *disciples* take Jesus with *them* (παραλαμβάνουσιν αὔτὸν ὡς ἦν ἐν τῷ πλοίῳ, Mk. 4:36).[7] Then, while he sleeps in the stern, a great wind stirs,

[4] Heinz-Wolfgang Kuhn, *Ältere Sammlungen in Markusevangelium* (Göttingen: Vandenhoeck & Ruprecht, 1971), 191–213; also Leander E. Keck, "Mk. 3,7–12 and Mark's Christology," *JBL* 84 (1965): 346–7.

[5] Joel Marcus, *Mark 1–8: A New Translation with Introduction and Commentary*, AB 27 (Garden City, NY: Doubleday, 2000), 256.

[6] Paul J. Achtemeier, "Toward the Isolation of Pre-Markan Miracle Catenae," *JBL* 89 (1970): 265–91.

[7] In the gospel's three other instances that use the verb παραλαμβάνω in relation to Jesus as his followers, it is Jesus who serves as the verb's subject (Mk. 9:2; 10:32; 14:33).

rocking the boat as well as the disciples' confidence. Faced with such an apparent threat, the disciples' first recourse is to awaken their teacher, whom they accuse of indifference by asking, "Do you not care that we are perishing?" (Mk. 4:38). Jesus in turn responds first to the natural forces, commanding them, "Peace; be still" (Mk. 4:39), and then to his paralyzed followers, returning fire with two indicting questions of his own: "Why are you cowardly? Do you not yet have trust?" (Mk. 4:40).[8]

Taken together, Jesus' queries sound a note of pointed reproach that befits the emerging Markan theme of (faulty) discipleship, but what is the basis of his censure? On what grounds have they fallen short of his expectations in this predicament?

Traditionally, interpreters depend on the next verse's Christological question ("Who is this then . . . ?," Mk. 4:41) to explain the nature of the "faith" Mark's Jesus has found lacking in the disciples. That is, they do not yet trust Jesus, either as a divinely empowered thaumaturge[9] or as the one who grants access to divine assistance in time of need.[10] Presumably, if they possessed (ἔχετε, Mk. 4:40) that trust, they would not have exhibited the dread fear that accompanied their apparent peril at sea; after all, they had Jesus at their beck and call, available to rescue them on a whim. Certainly Augustine has this kind of Christocentric faith in mind as he gleans this advice from the story: "Rouse him, then; . . . This is the moment to awaken Christ."[11]

As prevalent as such an understanding may be, its sharply Christological focus fails to explain adequately Jesus' own response to his disciples. In the story at hand, it is the disciples' importunity, articulated in their appeal for his help, that evokes Jesus' rebuke, not their lack of trust in his command over the raging sea. Indeed, under closer scrutiny, the passage portrays the disciples' failure as a matter of their lapsed trust in God's

[8] David Rhoads and Donald Michie have detected the verbal ties between the parable in Mk. 4:26–9, which speaks of the sower who "sleeps and rises," with this report of a Jesus who "sleeps" and is "aroused" by the disciples (*Mark as Story: An Introduction to the Narrative of a Gospel* [Philadelphia: Fortress Press, 1982], 109). In both cases, the one sleeping seems to be trusting God as the sovereign provider. Cf. Joel Marcus, *The Mystery of the Kingdom of God*, SBLDS 90 (Atlanta: Scholars Press, 1986), 180–1, who emphasizes instead the passage's reflection of the "Markan community's experience of Christ's absence from them."

[9] E.g. Martin Dibelius, *From Tradition to Gospel*, rev. 2nd edn., trans B. Lee Woolf (London: James Clarke, 1971; orig. 1933): "belief in the power of the miracle-worker" (79).

[10] E.g. C. E. B. Cranfield, *The Gospel According to Saint Mark: An Introduction and Commentary*, CGTC (New York: Cambridge University Press, 1977), 175; William L. Lane, *The Gospel According to Mark*, NICNT (Grand Rapids: Eerdmans, 1974), 177.

[11] Augustine, Sermons 63, in *Patrologia Latina*, ed. Jacques-Paul Migne (Paris: Migne, 1844–64), 38:425.

sovereignty over the storm at sea, a command demonstrated reliably in and through Jesus but available to his companions as well.

In the first place, the story starkly contrasts Jesus' own response to the storm with that of his disciples. On the one hand, the narrative emphasizes through elaborate verbal detail Jesus' posture of repose: καὶ αὐτὸς ἦν ἐν τῇ πρύμνῃ ἐπὶ τὸ προσκεφάλαιον καθεύδων (Mk. 4:38a).[12] Despite the surrounding conditions (including a windstorm and engulfing waves, Mk. 4:37), Jesus sleeps. Much like the one who sows the seed of the kingdom only to "sleep and rise night and day" (Mk. 4:27), entrusting its care to God, Jesus' slumber implies a simple reliance on God's dominion even over the sea.

The disciples, depicted in pointed relief, do not share Jesus' restful confidence. Indeed, Mark's story employs finite verbs (ἐγείρουσιν, λέγουσιν, Mk. 4:38b) to convey their anxious if indirect plea for Jesus' help.[13] Notice that their very solicitation of his aid prompts Jesus' ensuing reprimand: they have neither emulated Jesus' secure trust in God's domination of demonic powers of chaos (cf. Gen. 8:1; Pss. 74:13–14; 104:4–9; 107:25–30) nor anticipated his authoritative quelling of those powers.[14]

Even more telling is the word Mark's Jesus uses to describe the disciples' cowardice. By asking why they are timid (δειλοί), Jesus describes a condition frequently contrasted with battlefield bravery. One elucidating example can be found in Deut. 20:8 (LXX), where such cravenness serves as grounds for dismissal from military service: "Is anyone afraid or cowardly (δειλός)? Let that one go back to his house, lest he make his brother's heart as cowardly as his."[15] In other words, such timidity in the face of adversity is not just unbecoming; it is dangerously contagious. Thus when Jesus accuses his disciples of cowardice, he finds their battle-readiness lacking, their hearts softened to the struggle in which they are fully expected to participate.

[12] Vincent Taylor, *The Gospel According to Saint Mark: The Greek Text with Introduction, Notes, and Indexes*, 2nd edn. (Grand Rapids, MI: Baker, 1981; orig. 1950), 276, appropriately attributes Jesus' peaceful demeanor to his trust in God's care; Joachim Gnilka, *Das Evangelium nach Markus*, 2 vols., EKKNT 2 (Zurich: Benziger; Neukirchen: Neukirchener Verlag, 1978–79), I:195, understands it as evidence of Jesus' own sovereignty. Yet throughout Mark's gospel, Jesus' "sovereignty" remains grounded in God's kingly rule.

[13] Rudolf Pesch, *Das Markusevangelium*, 2 vols., HTKNT 2 (Freiburg: Herder, 1976), I:272.

[14] Paul J. Achtemeier, "Person and Deed. Jesus and the Storm-Tossed Sea," *Int* 16 (1962): 169–76, cites the following Jewish literature in support of the view that the wind and sea embody demonic forces: *2 Enoch* 40:9; 43:1–3; 69:22; 4 Ezra 6:41–2; *Jub.* 2:2.

[15] In a case of inner-biblical exegesis, 1 Macc. 3:56 echoes the Deuteronomic provision for exclusion from military duty.

In view of these observations, the passage presents a vivid portrait of Jesus as quintessential embodiment of trust in God's dominion. Even in the midst of a storm, he reclines at rest, confident of Yahweh's victory in the apocalyptic showdown at hand. For their part, the disciples fail their calling both in their anxiousness and in their lack of resolve when confronted by a hostile sea. In this reading, we may paraphrase Jesus' censure this way: "Why are you cowering [in this battle against the sea's demonic force]? Do you not yet possess trust [in God's eschatological victory even over the wind and sea]?" Apparently the disciples' culpability lies not precisely in their mistrust of Jesus; after all, they do turn to him for help. Rather, they prove unable fully to trust the reality of God's rule that Jesus repeatedly and unhaltingly demonstrates.

Finally, the episode's wider context helps to explain the disciples' deficiency in terms of their refusal to trust the triumph Jesus has proclaimed, as well as the kingdom authority he has conferred upon them (Mk. 3:15). I have already discussed, in conjunction with Jesus' programmatic preaching (Mk. 1:14–15), that Jesus' summons to repentance and trust in the kingdom of God intends to evoke full assent to God's sovereignty that has "drawn near." Even as recently as Jesus' previous encounter with "those around him with the Twelve," Jesus asserts without qualification that ὑμῖν τὸ μυστήριον δέδοται τῆς βασιλείας τοῦ θεοῦ (Mk. 4:11). As discussed in the preceding chapter, what has been entrusted to Jesus' followers is the reality of God's dominion, which remains enshrouded in mystery. It is this reality that serves as the seed to be scattered indiscriminately and the lamp to be placed prominently.

For the Markan disciples and their heirs in Mark's community, to trust Jesus is to emulate his confidence and participation in divine victory over cosmic adversarial forces like the storm at sea. That trust entails faith *in* Jesus to the extent that it brings confidence in his access to God's power, yet for Mark, that trust is no passive matter. In this passage, the disciples fall short as they cower in the face of their foe rather than trusting God's impending rule. In this light, their decidedly Christological question "Who is this then?" signals not just their inadequate grasp of Jesus' identity *per se* but also their refusal to trust the decisive power he wields and has in turn imparted to them (e.g. Mk. 3:15).

The first sea-crossing story, then, exposes the disciples' failure to depend fully on God's command over the wind and the waves. If this deficiency arouses Jesus' ire, Mark's narrative has laid the groundwork for understanding it as his frustration over the disciples' own stymied power, which in turn stems from their lack of faith. Already these followers have aligned themselves with Jesus' program; already they have borne witness to his authoritative teaching and power; already they have been both empowered for and entrusted with a critical role in the enactment of God's triumphant reign upon the earth. Yet here they find themselves at a loss, passively clamoring for a bailout. It is no wonder, in light of this development, that Mark's story continues with reports of healings and exorcisms that provide something of a remedial course in discipleship for those who have been so paralyzed in the face of the opposition.[16]

Jesus at home (Mk. 6:1–6)

Once Jesus' campaign has ventured as far as the Decapolis, he makes his way home, joined again by his disciples. This hometown encounter, reported in Mk. 6:1–6, supplies a striking reminder that even Jesus' wonder-working abilities depend not just on his own trust in God's provision, but also on the trust of those who stand in need of healing.[17] In other words, the power at Jesus' disposal becomes effectual only when others align their expectations with the divine victory from which that power emanates.

Indeed, Mark reports that the crowd's refusal to believe his witness to that kingdom impairs Jesus' performance of miracles when he returns home, presumably to Nazareth. Here, the Markan story shifts its emphasis to Jesus' teaching, rather than his healing, a move that simply preserves the gospel's consistent linkage between Jesus' word and deed. But the response to his teaching in this case is rather surprising. Instead of the general public acclaim expressed in Mk. 1:27–8, the hometown crowd voices sarcastic incredulity; rather than being overcome with wonder and awe, they are scandalized (ἐσκανδαλίζοντο, Mk. 6:3) by the notion that one known among their own ranks would demonstrate such "wisdom" along with "deeds of power" (Mk. 6:2)

As the brief report of Jesus' stay at home continues, the impact of such "cognitive dissonance" – the radical discontinuity between the community's expectations for an "artisan's son" and the visible outcome of his career – carries grave implications for the "success" of Jesus' mission. Mark reports that Jesus was "unable (οὐκ ἐδύνατο) to do any deed of

[16] The intercalated healing stories found in Mk. 5:21–43 supply a telling reminder of the dynamic interplay between Jesus' healing powers and the full trust of those who stand in need of it. Both the hemorrhaging woman and Jairus apparently display the very faith that the disciples have lacked (Mk. 5:34, 36). Though the object of their trust remains unspecified, we may infer that it encompasses both particular confidence in Jesus' abilities and a larger belief in his divine authorization as agent of God's power.

[17] Dietrich-Alex Koch, *Die Bedeutung der Wundererzählungen für die Christologie des Markusevangeliums* (New York: De Gruyter, 1975), 147.

power there," (Mk. 6:5), a striking claim only somewhat mitigated by the phrase, "except that (εἰ μή) he laid his hands on a few sick people and cured them" (Mk. 6:5). Further, the closing summary reiterates the people's unbelief (τὴν ἀπιστίαν αὐτῶν) as the basis of Jesus' own amazement.

This story of Jesus' diminished power plays an important narrative role in the unfolding gospel drama in at least two respects. In the first place, it confirms Mark's consistent correlation between faith and deeds of power (see, e.g., Mk. 2:5; 5:34; 9:23). As Guelich puts it, even if faith is not effectual for healing, Jesus' "miracles do not take place in the absence of faith."[18] Problematic as this connection has become for subsequent interpreters, it is important to notice that the evangelist presupposes rather than ponders it.

A second observation follows from the first: despite his inability to do any deed of power in Nazareth, Jesus appears undeterred and resumes his own missionary journey, making his way "around the encircling villages teaching" (Mk. 6:6b).[19] As has been the case from the beginning, the good news that drives Jesus' ministry will not be thwarted. Resistance, and refusal to trust the gospel message, does not in Mark's view impede Jesus' progress; rather, it may spur the mission on.

Between the disciples' private instruction of Mk. 4 and their sending out in Mk. 6:7–13, then, Mark's gospel provides a glimpse not only of several impressive incidents of Jesus' healing power but also of some of the harsher realities of his mission. In the episodes mentioned here, both the disciples (Mk. 4:40) and the townspeople (Mk. 6:5) exhibit the condition Mark calls ἀπιστία, as both lack the requisite trust that Jesus' arrival really does establish the full unleashing of God's dominion on the earth. Notably, Jesus does not cower when he encounters such a lack of faith. Instead, he proceeds on his mission with increased boldness, equipping those who "have ears" with the "good news" message of God's kingdom, which lurks on the horizon.

[18] Robert A. Guelich, *Mark 1–8:26*, WBC 34A (Dallas: Word, 1989), 311.

[19] Most interpreters (e.g. Ernest Best, *Following Jesus: Discipleship in the Gospel of Mark*, JSNTSup 4 [Sheffield: JSOT Press, 1981], 190; Karl-Georg Reploh, *Markus – Lehrer der Gemeinde: Eine redaktionsgeschichtliche Studie zu den Jüngerperikopen des Markus-Evangliums*, SBM 9 [Stuttgart: Katholisches Bibelwerk, 1969], 51; Gnilka, *Markus*, I:236) link the report of Jesus' continued teaching in Mk. 6:6b more closely with the subsequent commissioning (Mk. 6:7–13) than with the preceding hometown encounter (Mk. 6:1–6a). The likelihood that Mark has inserted this phrase, together with the view that Markan seams often introduce new passages, supports this view. Yet, strictly in terms of content, the clause can be viewed equally as a reaction to Jesus' rejection at Nazareth and as a prelude to his sending of the Twelve; thus it may be most judicious to view Mk. 6:6b simply as a Markan hinge intended to move the narrative from one episode to the next.

The calling and sending out of the Twelve: Mark 6:7–13

As Mark positions the material, Jesus' impaired ministry in his hometown leads directly to his calling together and sending forth of the Twelve, whom he has formed as an eschatological entity in Mk. 3:13–15. Just as the initial summons of the Twelve to the mountaintop follows episodes of mounting tension with the religious authorities (Mk. 3:1–6), Mark's placement of the apostolic venture at this juncture hints, even if proleptically, at Jesus' own succession plan. The greater the threat to his person or the greater the resistance to his mission, the more prominence and authority he confers upon the disciples.[20]

If Mark's redactional hand is evident in the passage's strategic placement at this point in the story, the evangelist also appears to have left traces of editorial influence in his treatment of the traditional account. Several factors lead interpreters to the broad consensus view that an account of the disciples' missionary venture is rooted in the life of the historical Jesus. To begin with, the story's broad attestation[21] belies the view that the evangelists themselves first spun the tale.[22] Moreover, such an account makes coherent sense of the early Christian belief that the disciples are called to perpetuate the witness not just of the risen, exalted Christ but also of his own eschatologically charged earthly mission.

Yet to affirm the likelihood that this mission account derives from a pre-Markan tradition only sharpens the inquiry into the ways in which Mark has shaped its expression here. A review of the vocabulary and structure of the material included in Mk. 6:7–13 suggests that Mark's own narrative frame supplies an overarching interpretive lens through which two conjoined sets of missionary instructions come more clearly into focus.[23] As we shall see, the Markan claims that both precede and

[20] Many interpreters have noticed that the explicit discipleship passages (Mk. 1:16–20; 3:13–19; 6:7–13) launch the major subsections of the gospel's first half (Marcus, *Mark 1–8*, 379; Guelich, *Mark 1–8:26*, 316).

[21] Commentators detect between two and four separate accounts, including at least as "more or less independent forms" (Hahn, *Mission*, 41) Mk. 6:7–11 and Q (Lk. 10:2–12), but perhaps also special material unique to both Matthew and Luke.

[22] E.g. T. W. Manson, *The Sayings of Jesus: As Recorded in the Gospels According to St. Matthew and St. Luke* (London: SCM Press, 1949), 73–4; Martin Hengel, *The Charismatic Leader and His Followers*, trans. J. Grieg, SNTW (New York: Crossroad, 1981), 74.

[23] Gunther Schmahl, *Die Zwölf im Markusevangelium* (Trier: Paulinus, 1974), 73, assigns to the sayings in Mk. 6:8–11 "eine dienende Funktion." But cf. Hahn, *Mission*, 43–4, who suggests that the introduction of Mk. 6:7 constitutes a secondary growth. Mark's deliberate redaction, though, surely reflects his particular interpretive "spin" on the traditional material.

follow the traveling guidelines cast the mission of the Twelve as an early glimpse of the coming dominion of God.[24]

The structure of the passage itself demonstrates thematic and verbal relationships that follow a basic ABB′A′ form:

A: Jesus initiates mission (Mk. 6:7)
  B: Jesus instructs: "on the way" (Mk. 6:8–9)
  B′: Jesus instructs: "in the house" (Mk. 6:10–11)
A′: Mission report (Mk. 6:12–13)

As I consider each section in turn, I shall examine the ways in which Mark's report reiterates and expands the pattern of discipleship detected earlier in the gospel. The disciples' own practice of the authority given to them provides an important witness, for Mark, to the collective demonstration of God's kingdom beginning to take shape both in Jesus' life and in the lives of those who trust that reign.

Calling together and sending out (Mk. 6:7)

In the pericope's opening verse, Jesus continues in his role as a strong protagonist. Through the use of three finite verbs, προσκαλεῖται, ἤρξατο, and ἐδίδου, Mark attributes to Jesus actions that are calculated and purposeful. The verse's measured language and repetitive structure indicate that Jesus is here master of a momentous turning point in Mark's gospel. Moreover, the verse's string of paratactic clauses crescendoes not just in length but also in gravity, so that Jesus' dispensing of "authority over the unclean spirits" serves as the culmination of this encounter:

> **καὶ** προσκαλεῖται τοὺς δώδεκα **καὶ** ἤρξατο αὐτοὺς ἀποστέλλειν δύο δύο **καὶ** ἐδίδου αὐτοῖς ἐξουσίαν τῶν πνευμάτων τῶν ἀκαθάρτων. (Mk. 6:7)

As we shall see, the significance of the commissioning as introduced by Mark preserves the gospel's tension between Jesus' resolute command of the storyline and his relentless determination to engage his followers in his mission.

The opening verb προσκαλεῖται recalls for the gospel audience Jesus' inaugural action in Mk. 3:13, where he "calls together" those whom he

[24] In the gospels' "fusion of the 'Jesus tradition' and 'community formations,'" Hengel detects a "conscious awareness . . . of the 'continuity' between Jesus' activity and the later activities of the community" (*Charismatic Leader*, 83).

wishes to appoint formally as the Twelve. As it does frequently throughout Mark's gospel, the use of the present indicative form of the verb appears to signal a narrative transition at this juncture.[25] Still, since the verb προσκαλεῖται occurs in the present indicative in Mark only in these two "call" episodes, this "Markan doublet" also stands out as a vivid reminder of a momentous calling.[26] Besides a change of scene, then, Mark's use of the present tense preserves the summoning of the Twelve as a living memory that may well intend to shape his contemporary community's present expression of discipleship.[27]

The significance of Mark's word choice here, though, derives from more than just its tense. Throughout the second gospel, the participial form of the verb consistently depicts "calling together" as an initial summons that precedes weighty action. In most instances, it is Jesus who convenes his hearers to deliver an authoritative pronouncement; frequently, those whom he gathers are his own followers (e.g. his disciples/the Twelve: Mk. 8:1, 34; 10:42; 12:43; the crowd: Mk. 7:14; 8:34).[28] Even when Pilate "summons" the centurion (Mk. 15:44), he does so as an authoritative figure engaged in official action.

Such usage gains confirmation throughout the LXX and elsewhere, since the verb προσκαλέομαι implicitly ascribes authority to the one who beckons, as well as importance to the task which generally follows that summons. For instance, Gen. 28:1 casts a father's call to his son as the occasion for both a blessing and a command: προσκαλεσάμενος δὲ Ἰσαακ τὸν Ἰακωβ εὐλόγησεν αὐτὸν καὶ ἐνετείλατο αὐτῷ. In other instances, Esther summons a king's servant (Esth. 4:5), while *T. Reub.* 4:9 speaks of Pharoah's wife convening magicians in her powerful but unsuccessful effort to lead Joseph astray. Finally, Sir. 13:9 overtly attributes the summoning act to an influential person through the clause, προσκαλεσαμένου σε δυνάστου. In each case, the language signals a deliberate and

[25] On the role of the "historical present" in marking transition, see Marcus, *Mark 1–8*, 80, who cites C. D. Osburn, "The Historical Present in Mark as a Text-Critical Criterion," *Bib* 64 (1983): 486–500; see also Buist M. Fanning, *Verbal Aspect in New Testament Greek* (Oxford: Clarendon, 1990), 226–39.

[26] See Reploh, *Markus*, 54; also Schmahl, *Die Zwölf*, 74. But cf. Best, *Following Jesus*, 191, who ascribes both occurrences to underlying tradition.

[27] Best, *Following Jesus*, 194, affirms Mark's application of the tradition to his own setting but unnecessarily restricts it to those designated as "missionaries," since the passage "obviously envisions a journey of some considerable length." Marcus, *Mark 1–8*, 390, maintains that the passage has been deliberately crafted to promote the Markan community's identification with the commissioning, but he seems more judicious in his refusal to confine that commissioning to a select group.

[28] One notable exception is Jesus' apparent convening of the scribes in Mk. 3:23 to respond to their charges with parabolic instruction.

authoritative act. Thus the verb προσκαλεῖται in this Markan commissioning functions to establish Jesus' decisive command over this pericope; he calls together whom he desires, and he maintains a dominant influence over the gathering's outcome.

The second in Mk. 6:7's series of three καί-clauses features a distinctively Markan construction in its combination of the aorist ἤρξατο with the infinitive ἀποστέλλειν.[29] Typically, Mark employs this construction (ἤρξατο + infinitive) to signal a momentous shift in narrative action.[30] For instance, after Jesus cleanses the leper in Mk. 1:40–5, Mark reports that the healed man ἤρξατο κηρύσσειν πολλά (Mk. 1:45), a development that in turn directs Jesus' mission to the countryside. A similar "new beginning" occurs in Mk. 5:20, where Mark uses the same expression, ἤρξατο κηρύσσειν, to describe the Gerasene demoniac's open proclamation of Jesus' healing powers, a proclamation that again occasions Jesus' departure (Mk. 6:1). The construction sounds a more menacing note in Mk. 8:11 when the Pharisees ἤρξαντο συζητεῖν αὐτῷ; though here they only seek a sign from heaven, the reader has already learned of their mounting plot against Jesus (Mk. 3:6).

Most often, though, Mark employs the construction "began to" + infinitive to herald a new juncture in Jesus' ministry – specifically, his pausing to offer instruction. The seaside teaching of Mk. 4 opens with the expression, πάλιν ἤρξατο διδάσκειν (Mk. 4:1), implying that instruction is one of Jesus' trademark practices. Again, teaching emerges as Jesus' first response to the masses in Mk. 6:34, where Mark's observation of Jesus' compassion leads to the following pronouncement: ἤρξατο διδάσκειν αὐτοὺς πολλά. Finally, Mark introduces Jesus' teaching about the way of discipleship through the clause ἤρξατο διδάσκειν αὐτούς (Mk. 8:31). Each of these Markan instances of ἤρξατο + infinitive effectively freeze-frames the action, so that all eyes are on Jesus as his mission begins a new episode.

Yet besides heralding a significant narrative juncture, the infinitive ἀποστέλλειν hearkens back to Mk. 3:14–15, where Jesus has commissioned the Twelve to be "sent out." Thus Jesus' "beginning to" send them out here fulfills the second purpose established on the mountaintop.[31]

As we have seen, the intervening narrative has afforded Jesus' followers the chance to live out their calling "to be with him." Remaining in his company since that formative moment, the disciples have gained privileged

[29] The combination appears some twenty-six times in Mark, most of which Matthew and Luke omit. See Reploh, *Markus*, 54.

[30] BAGD, 111, 2β. [31] Reploh, *Markus*, 54.

instruction (Mk. 4:1–34) as well as first-hand exposure to the demonstrable power that accompanies Jesus' kingdom proclamation. Especially in light of Jesus' recently compromised abilities, the time seems more than ripe in the Markan narrative for the disciples to take up the mantle of authority they have been given three chapters earlier.

Finally, although the finite verb is in the aorist tense,[32] the primary thrust of this expression lies with the present infinitive ἀποστέλλειν; it is the act of "sending out" that conveys the purpose of Jesus' inaugural act here. But in what sense are we to construe Jesus' sending forth of a group of emissaries? On the one hand, Mark's gospel frequently employs the verb ἀποστέλλειν to emphasize Jesus' preeminent authority with respect to the one(s) he sends. For instance, he "sends" demons into a herd of swine (Mk. 5:20); later in the story, he "sends" a healed blind man home (Mk. 8:34) with precise instructions not to go into the village. In both cases, Jesus' sending can be seen as a magisterial act, one in which he exhibits his own dominant sway over the storyline.

Yet for Mark the act of sending seems equally to imply the sender's *delegation* of authority. A case in point can be found in Mark's Parable of the Wicked Tenants (Mk. 12:1–12), where the vineyard owner repeatedly "sends" individuals – three servants and a beloved son – as those authorized to collect his due from the tenants. In each case, the parable underscores the full authority with which the owner has endowed his emissaries; indeed the tenants' crime consists in their not respecting that authority but instead seeking to destroy it. And in both Mk. 1:2 and 9:37, Mark explicitly identifies God as the "sender" of both John and Jesus as agents of God's gospel scheme. These instances together indicate that the verb ἀποστέλλειν forges a close connection in authority and mission between sender and agent.[33]

When Jesus begins to "send" his disciples forth in Mk. 6:7, then, the Twelve become full participants in their teacher's own eschatological agenda, endowed with the same authority that has characterized Jesus' own ministry to this point. From the outset, they have been enlisted as "fishers of humans" (Mk. 1:17), echoing Yahweh's prophetic promise to "send many fishers."[34] At the formal establishment of the Twelve,

[32] Best lays too much interpretive weight on the aorist here, when he claims that "no idea of iteration is contained in [ἤρξατο]" (*Following Jesus*, 198). Certainly what one "begins," one can "begin again" (cf. Mk. 4:1) to do.

[33] Commentators have frequently noted the Mishnah's explicit claim that one's "agent is like himself" (*m. Ber.* 5:5).

[34] On the role of fishers within the scheme of God's eschatological sovereignty, see above, chapter 2, 59–62.

Jesus has named their being "sent out" as a main pillar of their calling (Mk. 3:14).[35] Now they are ready to embark on an enterprise Witherington calls "the war against the powers and principalities."[36] Contrary to Best's insistence that "much of Jesus' activity, in particular in its soteriological aspects, is peculiar to him and not continued by anyone,"[37] we find the disciples poised to play an integral part in the continuation of Jesus' ministry upon the earth. Indeed, as Jesus sends out the Twelve, he emulates God's sending the son (see Mk. 9:37; 12:6), thereby conveying an "unbroken continuity" from Jesus through the original disciples to the Markan community itself.[38]

The claim that Jesus sends out the Twelve "two by two" may well reflect pragmatic concerns even while it affirms the Old Testament's tradition of authenticating testimony by at least two witnesses. Whether the phrase δύο δύο derives from the historical ministry of Jesus or from the missionary practice of the early church, it seems to reflect at least two aspects of missionary travel.[39] In the first place, travel conditions in the ancient world would have influenced the practice of shared journeys for the purpose of safety and companionship.[40] Yet probably undergirding this specification in Mark, notably lacking in Matt. 10:5 and Lk. 9:2, is the Old Testament's legal requirement for two witnesses to authenticate a testimony (e.g. Deut. 17:6; 19:15; Num. 35:30).[41] As a result, to designate the pairing of missionaries lends a measure of gravity to their witness; as Stock maintains, the Twelve "haben nichts Eigenes zu sagen, sie haben einen Auftrag auszurichten und zu bezeugen."[42] Admittedly, the Old Testament itself does not employ the concept of double testimony in conjunction with travels; yet, as Jeremias has shown, rabbinic literature (e.g. *b. Sanh.* 26a, 43a) frequently refers to two official delegates sent out together.[43] Thus the Twelve, sent out by twos, proceed in their journey charged with a message of verifiable truth as fully authorized agents of

35 See above, chapter 3, 87–93. 36 Witherington, *Mark*, 153.

37 Best, *Following Jesus*, 204. 38 Reploh, *Markus*, 57.

39 Missionary travel throughout the New Testament often reflects this practice. See, e.g., Matt. 10:2–4, which lists the disciples in pairs; see also Acts 13:1–3.

40 Joachim Jeremias, "Paarweise Sendung im Neuen Testament," in *Abba: Studien zur neutestamentlichen Theologie und Zeitgeschichte* (Göttingen: Vandenhoeck & Ruprecht, 1966), 138.

41 A wide array of NT passages reflect a similar practice: e.g. Matt. 18:16, 26:60; Jn. 8:17; 2 Cor. 13:1; Heb. 6:18, 10:28 (which cites "the law of Moses").

42 Klemens Stock, *Boten aus dem Mit-Ihm-Sein: Das Verhältnis zwischen Jesus und den Zwölf nach Markus*, AnBib 70 (Rome: Biblical Institute, 1975), 87. He unnecessarily denies, though, the influence of more pragmatic factors in the pairing of the Twelve.

43 See Jeremias, "Paarweise Sendung," 136–8, for a more exhaustive catalogue of rabbinic passages indicating this pattern.

the one who sends them. Moreover, the effectiveness of their testimony carries weighty implications for their hearers, whose response would seal their destiny.[44]

If the narrative movement builds from Jesus' calling together of the Twelve to his sending them out "two by two," the verse's greatest rhetorical force can be found in its final clause, in which Jesus empowers the Twelve for their missionary journey. Even at first glance, the clause's length implies that, of Jesus' three acts in this introductory verse, his meting out "authority over unclean spirits" represents the culmination of their commissioning. Here Jesus deliberately and completely confers upon the Twelve a measure of his own authority so that they too might bear witness to God's dawning dominion.

Yet before I consider the power Jesus confers upon the disciples, I should briefly note a silent but salient feature of this commissioning act, as Mk. 6:7 omits mention of proclamation that elsewhere typifies the Twelve's task. Already we have seen that the gospel's initial commissioning episode (Mk. 3:13–19) reports a balanced, twofold purpose to Jesus' sending out of the Twelve: to proclaim (κηρύσσειν, Mk. 3:14) and to have authority to cast out the daimonia (ἔχειν ἐξουσίαν ἐκβάλλειν τὰ δαιμόνια, Mk. 3:15). And even the present passage's concluding summary of achievements will assign a primary function to the Twelve's preaching activity in its report that ἐξελθόντες ἐκήρυξαν ἵνα μετανοῶσιν (Mk. 6:12). What, then, are we to make of its absence in Mk. 6:7?

While commentators frequently overlook this omission, Witherington suggests that the text's emphasis on authority over the unclean spirits implies that "this, more than the preaching, manifested that the kingdom had come in power"; moreover, he insists that, for Mark, the "inbreaking eschatological time is dynamic, not merely a matter of proclamation."[45] Yet such a claim flies in the face of Mark's consistent witness to an "inbreaking eschatological time" heralded by proclamation (e.g. Mk. 1:14–15; Mk. 3:15; Mk. 6:12); indeed, such a proclamation that proves just as "dynamic" as do the deeds of power. It may simply be the case that Mark views word and deed as inseparable (see Mk. 1:39), so that apostolic preaching is assumed rather than overtly stated as a part of this missionary endeavor.

Still, the evangelist devotes most careful attention to Jesus' conferral of authority upon the Twelve: καὶ ἐδίδου αὐτοῖς ἐξουσίαν τῶν πνευμάτων

[44] Stock, *Boten*, 87, calls it a matter of "Leben und Tod," while Morna D. Hooker, *A Commentary on the Gospel According to St. Mark*, BNTC 2 (London: A. & C. Black, 1991), 156, speaks of judgment on those who refuse to hear. See below for a fuller discussion of these implications.

[45] Witherington, *Mark*, 210.

τῶν ἀκαθάρτων. Even the verb ἐδίδου suggests the weighty import of Jesus' empowerment of the disciples. In the first place, while Mark's use of the imperfect tense here may well express the repeated action required to give to each of the six pairs authority over unclean spirits,[46] additionally it accentuates the continuous nature of Jesus' "giving" action. Within Mark's own setting, the imperfect ἐδίδου conveys an episode without end, an ongoing "giving" that maps this paradigmatic equipping of the Twelve onto the experience of the evangelist's own community.[47]

It comes as no surprise that the verb δίδωμι here characterizes Jesus' commissioning act, since the language of "giving" pervades the second gospel. Already the "insider" status described in Mk. 4:11 depends on what has been "given" to Jesus' companions: υμῖν τὸ μυστήριον δέδοται τῆς βασιλείας τοῦ θεοῦ (Mk. 4:11). Throughout the narrative, the act of giving – whether performed by God, Jesus, or Mark's community – constitutes a core reality of God's dominion, as consistently the verb conveys not a mere transfer of possession but a trust established for the sake of others. In Jesus' "giving" of authority to the Twelve, Mark not only highlights Jesus' own authority[48] but also defines the nature of that authority as a power to be shared.

If Jesus' "giving" of authority in Mk. 6:7 implies the shared nature of the ἐξουσία, the modifying genitive phrase τῶν πνευμάτων τῶν ἀκαθάρτων more explicitly portrays that authority as a demonstrable power over God's adversaries in an eschatological showdown. The phrase echoes and reiterates the mountaintop commissioning in Mk. 3:15, where the "authority to cast out δαιμόνια" serves as the second purpose for which the Twelve are to "be sent out." Once again, the evangelist here highlights the supernatural battle that precedes God's impending victory. In this commissioning, Jesus endows his followers with the requisite weaponry for that battle, as they continue the campaign of binding the strong man already launched so successfully by Jesus (see Mk. 3:22–7).

Within first-century Jewish thought, the removal of "unclean spirits" relates closely to the establishment of God's uncontested reign upon the earth. An early adumbration of this kind of eschatological triumph can be found in the vision of Zech. 12–14, which expresses the hope that, "on that day," a fountain will flow from Jerusalem "to cleanse them from sin and impurity" (Zech. 13:1). Moreover, in the subsequent verse, the prophet bases eschatological hope on Yahweh's promise to remove "the unclean spirit" (Zech. 13:2). Within the Qumran Community Rule, a similar image

46 See Taylor, *Saint Mark*, 303, who admits this inference is "not certain."

47 Stock, *Boten*, 88. Cf. Robert P. Meye, *Jesus and the Twelve: Discipleship and Revelation in Mark's Gospel* (Grand Rapids: Eerdmans, 1968), 112; Lane, 207.

48 Hooker, *Mark*, 156.

of divine cleansing from "the defilement of the unclean spirit" (1QS 4:21–2) signifies God's determination to end "the existence of injustice" at "the appointed time" (1QS 4:18). Significantly, Mark ascribes to Jesus – and by extension to the Twelve – the authority to do the work of God by subduing the forces of the Evil One. Theirs is a calling to demonstrate that the "appointed time" has been fulfilled (Mk. 1:15); their enactment of "authority over the unclean spirits" in turn lends credence to God's dominion on the earth.[49]

Even within the passage's opening verse, then, momentum builds in anticipation of the Twelve's role as fully authorized ambassadors for God's coming dominion. In each of the clauses that compose Mk. 6:7, Jesus maintains a leading role as he convenes, begins to send, and confers his own authority upon the Twelve. Yet essential to his "leadership" in this passage is Jesus' resolute intent to continue his work through those who have aligned their lives with the "good news" of God's sovereign victory. Especially in light of his thwarted activity in the preceding pericope, the sending forth of Jesus' followers reflects the Markan view that, any appearance of debilitating opposition to the contrary, God's purposes will prevail.[50] That Mark crafts this verse as the narrative introduction to specific missionary instructions indicates his desire to emphasize the "gospel" purpose to which they have been called and for which they have now been commissioned.

Instructions "on the way" (Mk. 6:8–9)

Scholars generally concur that the specific missionary guidelines found in Mk. 6:8–11 derive from discrete strands of traditional material that the second evangelist has woven together.[51] The synoptic parallel accounts found in Matt. 10:9–14 and Lk. 9:3–6 – possibly reflecting the influence of Q material – share many details with the Markan passage, including a list of items forbidden for the missionaries' journey as well as an injunction

[49] An interesting point of contrast can be found in *T. Benj.* 5:2, which enjoins the reader to "continue to do good" so that "the unclean spirits will flee from you." In this view, the human performance of "good" expels unclean spirits, whereas in Mark and in the above-cited literature, that expulsion comes through divine intrusion into the human realm.

[50] Though more suggested than developed, this pattern of Jesus' failure followed by the disciples' success may reflect both the earliest church's response to the crucifixion and the later Markan community's response to persecution. In both instances, the defeat does not hold final sway; out of apparent disaster arises a vivid witness to God's claim of ultimate triumph.

[51] So Taylor, *Saint Mark*, 302; Guelich, *Mark 1–8:26*, 319. But contrast Hahn, *Mission*, 41–6; also Pesch, *Markusevangelium*, I:326, who attributes the passage to a pre-Markan redactor's combining of two traditions.

to shake dust from their feet in inhospitable places.[52] It is in the divergences among gospel accounts, though, that we detect traces of Mark's redactional handling that are consistent with the second gospel's recurrent themes and imagery. Specifically, Mark's version of this material depicts the sending out of the Twelve in terms that recall Israel's Exodus event.

Structurally, the set of missionary sayings can be grouped under two topical headings: instructions "on the way" (Mk. 6:8–9) and sayings addressing the missionaries' staying "at home" (Mk. 6:10–11). The introductory formulae καὶ παρήγγειλεν αὐτοῖς (Mk. 6:8) and καὶ ἔλεγεν αὐτοῖς (Mk. 6:10) clearly signal each thematic subset of guidelines.

I begin with a review of the "packing list" that Jesus provides for the Twelve as they embark on their travels. As we shall see, especially in contrast to the accounts found in Matthew and Luke, the second evangelist crafts these instructions in a manner which casts the Twelve as active participants in the New Exodus return from exile. In turn, these directions preserve the gospel's double focus on both the full assurance of God's sovereignty and its manifestation through the utter trust of those who affirm it.

Rhetorically, the instructions begin with a succinct directive to take nothing "on the way" (Mk. 6:8), an austere command only somewhat mollified by an ensuing list of permissible and forbidden items.

> καὶ παρήγγειλεν αὐτοῖς ἵνα μηδὲν αἴρωσιν εἰς ὁδὸν εἰ μὴ ῥάβδον μόνον, μὴ ἄρτον, μὴ πήραν, μὴ εἰς τὴν ζώνην χαλκόν, ἀλλὰ ὑποδεδεμένους σανδάλια, καὶ μὴ ἐνδύσησθε δύο χιτῶνας.

Despite the inclusion of allowable accoutrements, the initial charge ἵνα μηδὲν αἴρωσιν establishes a rigorous tone that governs the instructions that follow. Just as the narrative frame of Mk. 6:7 has depicted Jesus as the authoritative agent of God's dominion over the spiritual sphere, this call to depart empty-handed reiterates the claim, so typical for Mark, that the task of enacting that dominion means trusting God for material provision as well.[53]

The modifying phrase εἰς ὁδόν resonates with Mark's use of Deutero-Isaianic imagery found in the gospel's opening lines, where the "way" in the wilderness provides the staging ground for the coming of the

[52] See Marcus, *Mark 1–8*, 386–7, figure 12, for a helpful chart of the synoptic parallel accounts of the Missionary Instructions.

[53] Ibid., 389.

Lord.[54] By describing the Twelve's travels as a journey "on the way," Mark implicitly imputes to them a role – not unlike that of John the Baptist – as those who "prepare the way of the Lord."

The particular items Jesus permits the Twelve to take "on the way" together indicate that Mark means to portray their mission in terms of Israel's anticipated New Exodus. Particularly illuminating is the fact that, in Mark's account, Jesus deliberately amends his instructions to take "nothing" by allowing the Twelve to carry "a single stick" (ῥάβδον μόνον). Since even this item is forbidden in the Q account, Mark would appear to intend its inclusion. But why?

Scholarly conjectures about the possible role of the "single stick" range from the pragmatic to the symbolic. Some interpreters, for instance, emphasize the staff's defensive use against bandits and wild animals[55] and detect noteworthy points of contact between this allowance and the roughly contemporary practice of the Essenes as reported by Josephus.[56] According to his account, members of the sect took on their journeys nothing (οὐδὲν μὲν ὅλῶς) except arms against bandits (*J.W.* 2.125). Yet several factors suggest that this motive of self-preservation constitutes an over-reading of the Markan text. First, the ῥάβδος is not specifically mentioned by Josephus as a means of defense; second, unlike Josephus, Mark does not specifically cite the threat from which a ῥάβδος might provide necessary protection. Even more tellingly, the Markan passage's dominant focus on the decisive establishment of God's reign seems inconsistent with a reading that permits the Twelve to hedge their bets, just in case God's protective care proves insufficient.

Curious, too, is the fact that Mark's account allows a ῥάβδος while the Q account forbids it. If the opening command to "take nothing on the way" (Mk. 6:8) demonstrates the austerity of this missionary venture, why would Mark not follow the lead of the tradition and intensify the rigors of itinerant Cynic philosophers[57] by denying the use of a walking stick?[58]

[54] Joel Marcus, *The Way of the Lord: Christological Exegesis of the Old Testament in the Gospel of Mark* (Louisville: Westminster/John Knox Press, 1992), 47, calls the motif a "controlling paradigm" for the interpretation of Mark.

[55] E.g. Daryl Dean Schmidt, *The Gospel of Mark with Introduction, Notes, and Original Text* (Sonoma, CA: Polebridge Press, 1991), 79.

[56] Both Witherington, *Mark*, 210, and Hahn, *Mission*, 45, view the staff as allowable because, in Hahn's words, it "did not ensure the means of subsistence." Interpreters in this camp drive an unnecessarily sharp wedge between the missionaries' physical protection and their sustenance, deeming their self-reliance acceptable in the first instance and forbidden in the second.

[57] Epictetus mocks the Cynic for "his provision-bag and his staff and his big mouth" (Arrian, *Discourses of Epictetus* 3.22.50).

[58] Gerd Theissen, "Wanderradikalismus: Literatursoziologische Aspekte der Überlieferung von Worten Jesu im Urchristentum," *ZTK* 70 (1973): 259. See below for further comparison of the lists.

Here Mark's contradiction of the synoptic parallels found in Matthew and Luke suggests a less pragmatic and more symbolic role for the ῥάβδον μόνον as the single item the Twelve are permitted to carry.

Vital clues about the implied role for the missionaries' "single stick" can be found in the sacred stories of Israel which serve as backdrop for so much of Mark's gospel story. Within the Exodus narrative, the ῥάβδος serves as a vehicle of authoritative power wielded by both Moses and Aaron. For these noted figures, the staff provides an emblem of their divinely ordained calling as God's chosen leaders. Through a ῥάβδος, God confirms Moses' own authority (Exod. 4:3), and later, God causes Aaron's staff to blossom (Num. 17:8) as an endorsement of his leadership. In both cases, the staff provides an emblem not just of human leadership but also of God's prerogative in selecting Israel's leaders.

Yet in the Exodus story, the staff also offers repeated reminders that God is at work to implement God's agenda within human history. From the moment of Moses' calling, God explicitly commands Moses to carry the "staff, with which you shall perform the signs" (Exod. 4:17); throughout Moses' tenure, God works through the staff to mediate both curse against the Egyptians during subsequent plague episodes (Exod. 7–8, 10) and miraculous assistance for the people in the crossing of the sea (Exod. 14:16) and the provision of water (Exod. 17:5, 9). In the hands of God's chosen leaders, then, the staff provides not simply protection or assistance for the one who carries it; rather, it repeatedly mediates, through authorized leaders, God's demonstrable provision for God's people. While Mark makes no mention of the missionaries' use of the staff to perform miracles, they do wield its symbolic power as, in the tradition of Moses and Aaron, they become vessels of God's power at work on a formative journey.

Important though this exception may be, Guelich is correct to affirm that "actually, Jesus instructs the Twelve more about what not to take than what to take."[59] For each allowance – for the missionaries to carry (a "single staff") and to wear ("laced-up sandals") – is followed in Mark's account by specific prohibitions, lending a somewhat stringent tone to these instructions for "the way." At least to some extent, Mark invokes earlier tradition when he cites the specifically banned items: with Luke, Mark mentions bread, a provision bag, and silver (cf. Lk. 9:3); Matthew similarly outlaws coins for money belts as well as a provision bag (Matt. 10:9–10). As noted above, the collective witness may well reflect a deliberate differentiation, on the part of Jesus or his followers, from the

[59] Guelich, *Mark 1–8:26*, 322.

Cynic-Stoic preachers who did allow "bread" and a "beggar's bag."[60] In contrast to the philosophers' ideal of self-sufficiency, the Markan saying implies the missionaries' dependence on God.

Though admittedly a later witness, some rabbinic traditions forbid entering the Temple Mount while carrying several items, including a walking stick, overshoes, and a money bag (*m. Ber*. 9:5). Thus Manson infers fittingly that the traditional exclusion of travel items signals not random austerity but the very sacred nature of the journey the Twelve will take.[61] If the Markan form of the sayings reflects a revision of contemporary Jewish practice, though, the Twelve's implied itinerary – journeying from town to town – contrasts sharply with the view of Jerusalem as primary destination for those sent on God's mission. Indeed, when Jesus and his entourage *do* approach Jerusalem in Mark's gospel, what they find is not holiness but corruption and violent resistance.

A second pairing of a permitted item with a forbidden one repeats the rhetorical pattern, still dominated by the "nothing" of Mk. 6:8, that emphasizes what the Twelve will lack on their journey. Since Mk. 6:9 features a shift in verb form, from the third-person plural αἴρωσιν of the previous verse to the second-person plural imperative ἐνδύσησθε, we may be dealing here with a seam exposing different strands of tradition. In any case, such a dramatic grammatical break lends an emphasis to the verse that draws our close attention.

Mark's apparent combination of the traditional items may be reflected in the fact that, like the staff, "laced-up sandals" (ὑποδεδεμένους σανδάλια) play an important role in the Exodus story, where in the Passover liturgy of Exod. 12 they symbolize preparedness for participation in God's way through the wilderness.[62] Moreover, Mauser has noted that Exod. 12:11 mentions both sandals and walking staff, while Deut. 29:5–6 feature bread and sandals, as well as clothes (which Mk. 6:9 also mentions).[63] Such a lexical convergence confirms the underlying Exodus motif discussed above and further depicts this set of instructions as equipping the Twelve for their own participation in God's miraculous deliverance.[64] Thus the itemized list points beyond a simple injunction to

[60] See Hengel, *Charismatic Leader*, 28; Paul Hoffmann, *Studien zur Theologie der Logienquelle* (Münster: Verlag Aschendorff, 1972), 246–7.

[61] Manson, *Sayings*, 181.

[62] Ernst Lohmeyer, *Das Evangelium des Markus* (Göttingen: Vandenhoeck & Ruprecht, 1951; orig. 1937), 114.

[63] Ulrich Mauser, *Christ in the Wilderness: The Wilderness Theme in the Second Gospel and Its Basis in the Biblical Tradition* (London: SCM Press, 1963), 133–4, argues convincingly that the evangelist deliberately reshapes traditional material so that Mk. 6:8–9 echoes the wilderness experience.

[64] Best, *Following Jesus*, 190, suggests that a Markan provenance different from Q's best explains the discrepancy which permits a staff and sandals in the case of the second gospel.

trust in God's provision toward a more implicit summons to the enacting of God's long-awaited victorious return.[65]

With the injunction not to "put on two tunics" (Mk. 6:9), the packing (and non-packing) list provided in this passage is complete. Again, the direction sounds an ascetic note, since travelers often wore two layers for protection against harsh wind and cold (cf. Josephus, *Ant.* 17.136). Like the allowance of a "single staff," this limiting of garments may suggest that the missionaries are to be equipped with bare essentials only, so that the odd expression μὴ ἐνδύσησθε δύο χιτῶνας simply confirms the degree of rigor first introduced with the opening command to take nothing on the way. Finally, though more suggestively, the specific barring of "two tunics" may also recall OT passages which affirm God's miraculous preservation of Israelites' garments during their epoch of wilderness wanderings (Deut. 8:4; 29:5).[66]

In this first set of traveling instructions, then, Jesus permits only a single staff, laced up sandals, and a single tunic for the missionary journey the Twelve are poised to take. As we have seen, these restrictive guidelines equip the missionaries suitably to travel on the "way of the Lord," so that their dependence on God's provision resonates with the Israelites' own prototypical wilderness journey. Already in Mk. 6:7 Jesus has appointed and empowered the group as collective agents of God's in-breaking kingdom; here Jesus continues to wield magisterial authority as he sets the terms of their mission. With these instructions, the Twelve stand equipped both spiritually and physically for their authorized participation "on the way" in a wilderness wandering that vividly demonstrates God's power unleashed on the earth. In the next section, I shall consider his ensuing directions concerning the Twelve's reception as they set out on their journey.

Instructions "at home" (Mk. 6:10–11)

A second set of Jesus' directions to the Twelve, introduced by the typically Markan phrase καὶ ἔλεγεν αὐτοῖς, continues the direct address established

But it is precisely the items' combination in Exod. 12:11 that supports the view that Mark is telling his story through the lens of God's past deliverance of the people.

[65] Ched Myers, *Binding the Strong Man: A Political Reading of Mark's Story of Jesus* (Maryknoll, NY: Orbis, 1988), 213, identifies putting on of sandals as a "Markan metaphor for discipleship." Similarly, Lohmeyer, *Markus*, 114, emphasizes their state of preparedness for the journey.

[66] Marcus, *Mark 1–8*, 389. See also E. Power, "The Staff of the Apostles: A Problem in Gospel Harmony," *Bib* 4 (1923): 245, who suggests that a second garment would have provided shelter, so that its exclusion would have reiterated the Twelve's reliance on God, through others' hospitality, for shelter instead.

in Mk. 6:9b but shifts the domain of concerns from provisions for the journey itself to the group's conduct upon arrival at various destinations along "the way." While the guidelines apparently presume the Twelve's hospitable reception in many quarters, they also anticipate in explicit detail the unmistakable reality of resistance to their mission. Indeed, Jesus' rather caustic call for a witness directed toward resistant factions underscores the prophetic nature of the Twelve's mission and its weighty implications for those whom they address.[67]

The sayings' structure reveals this dynamic tension between hospitality and rejection, as the two responses are cast in stark antithesis to each other:

> καὶ ἔλεγεν αὐτοῖς, Ὅπου ἐὰν εἰσέλθητε εἰς οἰκίαν, ἐκεῖ μένετε ἕως ἂν ἐξέλθητε ἐκεῖθεν. καὶ ὃς ἂν τόπος μὴ δέξηται ὑμᾶς μηδὲ ἀκούσωσιν ὑμῶν, ἐκπορευόμενοι ἐκεῖθεν ἐκτινάξατε τὸν χοῦν τὸν ὑποκάτω τῶν ποδῶν ὑμῶν εἰς μαρτύριον αὐτοῖς.

I shall consider each response in turn before suggesting their relationship to one another and to their setting in Mk. 6.

The second set of instructions begins by addressing the tenure of the Twelve's stay in a home: "when you go into a home (εἰς οἰκίαν), there remain until you go out from there" (Mk. 6:10). Several features of this verse reveal underlying assumptions about missionary activity that warrant close consideration.

In the first place, the verse identifies the "home" (οἰκία) as the missionaries' primary destination. Indeed, the Twelve's anticipated arrival at a home implies that there, in a home, they will find the survival items excluded from their journey.[68] Notably, in contrast to Matthew's predominant concern with entry into a "town or village" (Matt. 10:11), both Mark and Luke first address the entrance into a home and only later extend the instructions to a "place" (Mk. 6:11), "village" (Lk. 9:6), or "city" (Lk. 10:10). What does the mention of "home" as the apostles' outpost contribute to our understanding of Mark's account of their journey?

To begin with, the entrance εἰς οἰκίαν explicitly links the Twelve's itinerant missionary journey with Jesus' own tendency, in Mark's gospel, to enter a home in conjunction with his demonstration of God's coming

[67] Once more, the prophetic nature of the apostles' missionary journey comports with their designation early on as eschatological "fishers," discussed above in chapter 2.

[68] According to Josephus (*J.W.* 2.125), the Essenes take nothing for their journey because of assumed communal hospitality as well as the appointment of agents, in every city, to provide "clothing and necessities (ἐσθῆτα καὶ τὰ ἐπιτήδεια)" to strangers. Myers thus seems correct in his estimation that the disciples also depend upon hospitality, taking on the sociological status of "sojourner in the land" (*Binding the Strong Man*, 213).

dominion. For instance, when Jesus leaves the synagogue in Capernaum, Mark reports ἦλθον εἰς τὴν οἰκίαν Σίμωνος καὶ Ἀνδρέου (Mk. 1:29), where he heals Simon's mother-in-law; it is in Levi's "home" (Mk. 2:15) that Jesus enfranchises tax collectors and sinners by dining with them; and later, when traveling through the region of Tyre, Jesus enters εἰς οἰκίαν (Mk. 7:24) – into a "home" where he accedes to a mother's desperate plea to heal her daughter. Jesus' missionary practice, then, establishes the home as a paradigmatic locale for his "gospel" demonstration.[69] The assumption that, once the Twelve are sent out as Jesus' authorized and empowered emissaries, they will enter a home further confirms that their journey is to be understood as an extension of his earthly ministry.

Yet within Mark's gospel, the word "home" often signifies more than a physical structure or destination for itinerant kingdom-of-God preachers; it represents a cohesive social unit that provides an important identity marker for its members. In two instances, Jesus' teachings employ the image of "household" as a symbolic referent: in Mk. 3:25–7, Jesus instructs his hearers that the durability of a household depends both on its unity (its not being "divided against itself") and on the freedom of its head (its "strong man" not being bound). Near the end of the apocalyptic discourse of Mk. 13, Jesus again appeals to the household metaphor to reiterate God's impending arrival (Mk. 13:34–5). In both cases, the word οἰκία designates a domain or sphere of influence which Jesus (and, by extension, his followers) would mold to the pattern of God's rule.

Such an understanding of the οἰκία certainly reflects the early Christian practice, common by Mark's time, of gathering as house-churches for worship and fellowship. For those nascent communities, allegiance to Jesus engendered rejection at home and, increasingly, at synagogue.[70] Rather than bloodline or even ancestral religion, these home-based groups were bound together through their affirmation of God's coming kingdom, evinced in and through the life and death of Jesus, an affirmation that entailed as well a graphic remapping of reality.

To construe Mark's use of οἰκία with reference to a sociological pocket of reception or rejection of God's dominion makes better sense of a redundancy in the verse that is frequently overlooked by translators. On the face

[69] In the gospel's second half, a home provides the setting for Jesus' teaching in Mk. 9:33 and 10:10, as well as for another significant meal with an outcast in Mk. 14:3.

[70] Elizabeth Struthers Malbon, "*TE OIKIA AUTOU*: Mark 2.15 in Context," *NTS* 31 (1985): 292, points out that the Markan emphasis on the "house" represents a "narrative manipulation of . . . architectural symbols" that provides "a way of responding meaningfully to . . . historical realities" like the destruction of the Temple and the community's expulsion from the synagogue.

of it, the instruction in Mk. 6:10 offers the somewhat ludicrous suggestion that Jesus' hearers remain in the house until they depart from the house: ὅπου ἐὰν εἰσέλθητε εἰς οἰκίαν, ἐκεῖ μένετε ἕως ἂν ἐξέλθητε ἐκεῖθεν.

Such a nonsensical injunction understandably prompts most interpreters to infer that each "there" (ἐκεῖ and ἐκεῖθεν) refers to a different place. In the first instance, they claim, ἐκεῖ designates "the house" overtly mentioned in the preceding clause, while the second "there" refers to the town where the house is located: "there [that is, in that house] remain until you depart from there [that is, that town]"). As is frequently the case, scholars here may well be following Matthew's lead as clarifying interpreter of Mark.[71] Once again, in response to Mark's apparent obliqueness, readers of his gospel depend on a later – and admittedly clearer – evangelist to settle the score.

Yet besides the questionable appeal to Matthew's interpretive skills, another problem arises when we follow this reading to its conclusion. To interject "that town or village" as referent for the second "there" establishes the duration of the apostles' in-home stay as the dominant concern of the instruction. As a result, by limiting their stay to only one home in a given community, Jesus deliberately precludes the missionaries' search for more favorable accommodations[72] as well as the townspeople's jealousy over the privilege of hosting such reputable guests.[73] Yet the *Didache* specifically forbids missionary visits spanning more than two to three days in one home (*Did.* 11–13).[74] Though readers such as Guelich reconcile this apparent contradiction by distinguishing between missionaries "establishing a witness in a community" and those visiting previously planted churches,[75] such a distinction lacks evidential support.

Because the common reading of Mk. 6:10 requires a referent not yet explicitly mentioned in the text, and because it suggests a practice specifically prohibited in early Christian practice, it may serve us well to reconsider the Markan verse as it stands, problematic pleonasm and all. Perhaps a more fruitful approach to the "nonsense" of this verse would be to take

[71] Matt. 10:11 begins this way: "Whatever town or village you enter . . ."

[72] So Pesch, *Markusevangelium*, I:329. Also Theissen, who links the prohibition against moving from house to house with the appearance of a desire for material gain ("Wanderradikalismus," 259).

[73] So E. Haenchen, *Der Weg Jesu: Eine Erklärung des Markus-Evangeliums und der kanonischen Parallelen* (Berlin: Alfred Töpelmann, 1966), 232.

[74] *Didache* 11 pronounces a missionary who remains three days to be a "false prophet'; *Did.* 12 instructs those who remain longer than three days to "work and eat." Both provisions appear to militate against members of the early Christian community taking financial advantage of their brothers and sisters.

[75] Guelich, *Mark 1–8:26*, 322.

at face value the claim that the missionaries are to "remain [in that house] until they depart from [that house]."

Once both occurrences of "there" (ἐκεῖ/ἐκεῖθεν) point to the household hosting the missionaries, exegetical weight shifts from the duration of the home visit to the activity enjoined during their tenure in that place: the command μένετε, "remain." As a result, the instruction concerns not the quantitative timespan for the visit, but the qualitative nature of the stay.

A review of the verb's semantic range, both within Mark's gospel and outside it, seems to confirm this hunch. Within Mark's gospel, the verb μένειν appears only here and in Jesus' command to his disciples, in the Garden of Gethsemane, to "remain and keep watch" (Mk. 14:34), where it implies not just physical presence but the active allegiance that accompanies that presence. At the critical hour in the garden, Jesus urges his disciples to "abide" with him not merely to keep him company, as it were, but deliberately to affirm their affiliation with him. Notably, in Jesus' apocalyptic discourse of Mk. 13, the verb's compound form ὑπομένω conveys endurance that leads to salvation: "The one enduring to the end, this one will be saved" (Mk. 13:13). Although the lexical witness in Mark's gospel is admittedly sparse, the verb seems to convey an active, rather than passive, presence – a physical location that entails personal engagement and affiliation.

Elsewhere in the NT canon, the fourth gospel's language of "abiding" reflects a similar semantic thrust that implies identity formation through active allegiance. John's Jesus repeatedly urges his followers to "remain" in a manner which conveys their relational affiliation with him through a variety of figurative residences: "abide in my word" (Jn. 8:31); "abide in me" (Jn. 15:4); "abide in my love" (Jn. 15:9–10). And in the LXX, the verb frequently functions figuratively to connote active loyalty rather than physical location, as is the case in 2 Macc. 8:1, where Judas rallies those who have "remained in the Judaism."

To read Jesus' command to "remain there" as an active missionary strategy not only makes more sense of the redundant language but also confirms the role of the household throughout Mark's gospel. For when the "house" that the missionaries enter denotes a social domain or sphere of influence, the command for them to "abide there" entails actively aligning with the welcoming household so as to "lay a foundation" (cf. 1 Cor. 3:10) of allegiance. In and through their "abiding" in the house, the missionaries' eschatological proclamation of God's dominion takes root and begins to bear fruit.

This added nuance of "remaining" as relational engagement gains further confirmation through the following verse's negative depiction of an inhospitable reception of a place which "does not welcome . . . or does not listen" (Mk. 6:11). The saying implies that a favorable encounter would entail a household's welcoming and listening to the Twelve (Mk. 6:11), actions that reflect not just the missionaries' physical presence in the home but the influential sway of their "abiding" there. Notably, Mark's account seems to equate the word τόπος in Mk. 6:11 with the οἰκία named in the previous verse, as the evangelist seems to sketch a house-by-house itinerary rather than the town-by-town itinerary found in Q.

The fact that the welcoming and listening acts constitute the basis of the household's assessment appears consistent with the Markan interest in an apocalyptic differentiation between those who align themselves with God's reign and those who deny it. Elsewhere in the second gospel, Jesus enjoins hearers to become childlike in their "reception" of the good news of God's kingdom (Mk. 9:37; 10:15). That is, they are to order their very reality according to the priorities of that kingdom. Further, to "receive" a messenger in the ancient world entailed a measure of hospitality that reflected more than passive politesse; to receive a visitor entails a willingness to embrace the message brought by actively "listening" to it.[76]

As a result, Jesus instructs the Twelve that, "in whatever place [or house]" they encounter a refusal to welcome and to listen to them, they should journey out from there and shake the dust from under their feet as a witness toward them (εἰς μαρτύριον αὐτοῖς, Mk. 6:11). What is the point of such deliberate removal from those who have refused to respond favorably to the missionaries?

The tradition of shaking dust from one's feet has been linked to Jewish practice described, for instance, in *m. Ohol.* 2:3 and *b. Ber.* 19b, where sojourners essentially break ties with those who have aligned their lives with a reality other than Yahweh. Whether the dominant thrust here is to deny the missionaries any further responsibility for their hearers' salvation[77] or to subvert any potential future salvation to those hearers,[78] the action certainly constitutes prophetic severance from those who do not welcome Jesus' emissaries and thus do not receive their message of God's dominion.[79]

The prophetic act itself gains magnitude through the modifying prepositional phrase, εἰς μαρτύριον αὐτοῖς. The shaking of dust from the feet

76 This phrase is seen by many as a Markan insertion, based on its apparent absence from Q as well as Mark's ongoing interest in the "hearing" of the word, as depicted for instance in Mk. 4. See, e.g., Marcus, *Mark 1–8*, 388.

77 Cranfield, *Saint Mark*, 201.

78 Gnilka, *Markus*, I:240.

79 Reploh, *Markus*, 53, 58, takes the matter farther than the text's own claims when he asserts that this act anticipates God's final and decisive judgment against them.

thus denotes a "witness" for the unwelcoming parties the missionaries encounter, but in what respect? At issue is the reading of the ambiguous dative pronoun αὐτοῖς, which some interpreters construe as a dative of advantage,[80] while others infer a sense of disadvantage.[81] Certainly the very act of shaking dust from one's feet implies a measure of judgment, as it symbolizes the deliberate disengagement from the party left behind. Additionally, as Strathmann has pointed out, the dative with μαρτύριον consistently carries a sense of disadvantage in literature outside the New Testament.[82]

Yet Jesus' insistence that the healed leper show himself to the priest εἰς μαρτύριον αὐτοῖς (Mk. 1:44) lacks a clear sense of indictment, and even the prophecy of believers' testimony before governors and kings (Mk. 13:9) seems more concerned with the strength of their witness than the destiny of those who observe it. In light of these Markan uses, the dative pronoun αὐτοῖς may in this case simply designate the gallery before whom the dust-shaking occurs, with the phrase's emphasis lying on the "witness" itself. Jesus' command for the apostles to shake the dust from their feet, then, may call for a crystal-clear display of their allegiance – a "witness" – to be viewed by those who have denied that allegiance. For although Mark's apocalyptic worldview includes judgment as a concomitant feature of God's coming kingdom, the timing and the outcome of that judgment ultimately rests not with the disciples but with the Son of Man (Mk. 13:26–7).

In the instructions found in Mk. 6:10–11, Jesus shifts his focus from the Twelve's traveling provisions to the very purpose of their mission, which is to stake the claim of God's impending reign upon the earth. On the one hand, Jesus anticipates their being welcomed when he urges them to "abide" within a household so that its members might be enfolded into their gospel mission. On the other hand, he devotes even more attention to the setting in which they are neither welcomed nor heard; in that case, they are to cut off ties with the household and move out from there. That the negative reception both echoes Jesus' own rejection at home (Mk. 6:1–6) and anticipates his destiny in Jerusalem establishes clear ties between the Twelve's experience and that of Jesus.[83] To the extent that the Markan community meets with indifference or hostility in its own missionary engagement, they too confront the harsh reality

80 E.g. Taylor, *Saint Mark*, 305; Lane, *Mark*, 209.

81 E.g. Guelich, *Mark 1–8:26*, 323; Marcus, *Mark 1–8*, 384.

82 H. Strathmann, "μαρτύριον," in *TDNT* 4 (1967): 502–3.

83 As Myers puts it, "the political destiny of those who proclaim repentance and a new order is always the same" (*Binding the Strong Man*, 217).

that, in some quarters, the "good news" of God's dominion falls on deaf ears.

Mission accomplished (Mk. 6:12–13)

For all Mark's mounting concern with suffering and rejection, it is striking to note that his crafting of traditional material does not conclude with the failure of the apostles' mission in some places. Instead, the evangelist introduces an elaborate narrative summary of the Twelve's missionary venture.[84] What is more, Mark emphasizes through his report their remarkably successful continuation of Jesus' own enterprise.[85] Together, these closing clauses enumerate in detail both the nature and outcome of the group's missionary venture:

> καὶ ἐξελθόντες ἐκήρυξαν ἵνα μετανοῶσιν, καὶ δαιμόνια πολλὰ ἐξέβαλλον, καὶ ἤλειφον ἐλαίῳ πολλοὺς ἀρρώστους καὶ ἐθεράπευον.

Notably, this itemized report of their effectiveness surpasses any expectations established in their prior commissioning (Mk. 3:13–15 and 6:7). As a result, Mark underscores not just the full measure of Jesus' authorization, but also the expansive nature of the Twelve's missionary journey.

As the first activity attributed to the Twelve in this Markan summary, their call for repentance introduces a missionary task not named in Mk. 6:7, where they were only "sent out" and given "authority over unclean spirits." Earlier in this chapter, I have briefly discussed the possibility that Jesus' "sending out" of the Twelve tacitly implies the preaching task. As his authorized emissaries, they would naturally embark on a mission patterned after his, which from the outset of Mark's gospel features kingdom-of-God proclamation (Mk. 1:14–15). Moreover, within the Markan narrative, when Jesus first constitutes the Twelve, he explicitly stipulates preaching as the first component of their missionary task (Mk. 3:15).

To maintain, as Hahn does, that the "preaching of God's Kingdom turns out no longer to have been of dominating importance for the Marcan

[84] Taylor, *Saint Mark*, 306, itemizes the vocabulary that is typically Markan, including ἐξελθόντες, ἐκήρυξαν, μετανοῶσιν, δαιμόνια, ἐξέβαλλον, ἀρρώστους, ἐθεράπευον, plus the verses' repeated use of the paratactic καί.

[85] The admitted awkwardness of this close link between Jesus and his followers supports, on the criterion of embarrassment, the authenticity of Jesus' commission of the Twelve to perform precisely the same tasks that have marked his own ministry. See Hahn, *Mission*, 46; Hengel, *Charismatic Leader*, 74–5.

church"[86] is to overlook the pride of place that Mark gives to proclamation in this report. Indeed, Mark's omisssion of the preaching task in Mk. 6:7 may simply reflect an underlying assumption that missionary work automatically entails verbal proclamation, whereas the "authority over unclean spirits" requires Jesus' deliberate conferral of power. Finally, the report that "they proclaimed that all should repent" (Mk. 6:12) provides an antidote to the rejection Jesus has anticipated in the previous instruction even as it forges an important link both with John the Baptist (Mk. 1:4) and with Jesus himself (Mk. 1:14–15).[87]

Moreover, there can be little doubt that the content of this proclamation, even for Mark, does not precisely concern Jesus' messiahship but rather the same "gospel" message heralded by both John and Jesus: the coming kingdom of God.[88] Like their precursors in preaching, the apostles aim to elicit repentance that entails a turning away from the old age and a turning toward a new age in which the early light of God's reign is dawning. In turn, this reorientation of life "makes the way" for the Lord's coming triumph over the powers of the δαιμόνια, whose sway over the world – with all its sickness and suffering – is nearing its demise.

Following Mark's report of their preaching enterprise, the Twelve's list of net results continues. Indeed the casting out of many demons dramatizes the power of God unleashed to unseat the adversary.[89] Notably the phrase δαιμόνια πολλὰ ἐξέβαλλον (Mk. 6:13) also departs from a strict repetition of the Twelve's authorization in Mk. 6:7, where they have been given "authority over the unclean spirits." Here, though, that authority becomes actualized in the vivid report of their "throwing out" the demons. Again, the language resonates with Mark's account of the Twelve's initial commissioning in Mk. 3:15. By inserting the word πολλά, though, Mark intensifies his report of their staggering success.

86 Hahn, *Mission*, 44. He bases this view on the fact that Mk. 6:7 lacks the proclamation component.

87 This link anticipates the ensuing account of John's death, which Myers finds "to create an essential narrative interrelationship between the mission and fate of Jesus, his disciples, and John" (*Binding the Strong Man*, 213). See below, chapter 6, for a more detailed discussion of this interrelationship.

88 Hoffmann, *Studien*, 239; Taylor, *Saint Mark*, 306. Even William Wrede notices that Jesus "authorizes [the Twelve] *only* to preach repentance and to drive out demons" (*The Messianic Secret*, trans. J. C. Grieg [Cambridge: James Clarke, 1971; orig. 1901], 11, emphasis added), though he appeals to the messianic-secret motif to explain this "limitation." Apparently following Wrede, Jack Dean Kingsbury maintains a sharp divide between the pre- and post-Easter messages (*The Christology of Mark's Gospel* [Philadelphia: Fortress Press, 1994; orig. 1983], 74).

89 In his resolute denial of an apocalyptic thrust to the second gospel, Best understands this as an "act to conquer existing evil," not one intended "to threaten apocalyptic evil" – a distinction that seems alien to Markan thought (*Following Jesus*, 9).

The third component of the mission, the anointing with oil of many sick ones, introduces language that is quite unusual to Mark as well as rare in the entire New Testament. While the use of oil for medicinal purposes was apparently common in the first-century world (cf. Isa. 1:6; also Josephus, *J.W.* 1.657), only here do the gospels refer to oil as a means for healing.[90] Still, its mention in Mk. 6:13 seems consistent with the anointing with oil mentioned in Jas. 5:14–15, where the practice serves as an outward expression of God's healing power rather than a cure in and of itself.[91]

Perhaps even more substantial than the verse's reference to anointment with oil is its reiteration of the Twelve's quantifiable success: they anointed πολλοὺς ἀρρώστους (Mk. 6:13). Again, the poignant juxtaposition between the outcome of Jesus' venture in his hometown, where Mark reports Jesus' inability to heal any except ὀλίγοις ἀρρώστοις (Mk. 6:5), and the Twelve's effectiveness implies that they have, for the moment anyway, eclipsed Jesus as dispensers of divine power.[92] What is more, this brief narrative summary forges the same link between proclamation and healing as is implied in Mk. 6:1–6. Where the seed of God's coming reign takes root, its fruitfulness is staggering; where it meets active or passive resistance, it languishes.

It seems no accident, then, that Mark closes his report about this highly effective missionary outing with explicit reference to the Twelve's effective healing. To this point in the narrative, Mark's gospel has used the verb θεραπεύω four times, each time to report Jesus' own healing activity (Mk. 1:34; 3:2, 10; 6:5). That Mk. 6:13 presents the second gospel's final report of "healing" seems to complete the gospel's depiction of the Twelve's fully authorized mission.

Implicit in this final observation is the suggestion, encountered throughout these opening chapters of Mark's gospel, that Jesus'

[90] Lk. 10:34 mentions the Samaritan's use of oil (together with wine) on the injured man's wounds prior to bandaging them, though the oil serves only as a salve in the healing process.

[91] Similar language of "anointing" can be found in Acts (4:27; 10:38), where the practice refers to Jesus' own anointment at baptism with the Holy Spirit. See Marcus, *Mark 1–8*, 384, who suggestively asks if the "anointing" of the sick somehow "reactivated the spiritual anointment . . . received at baptism."

[92] As Marcus points out, John 14:12 makes this claim explicitly: "the one who trusts in me will also do the works that I do and indeed will do greater works than these" (*Mark 1–8*, 385). Mark's inclusion of those "greater works" within the time frame of Jesus' earthly ministry seems calculated to achieve a twofold purpose: to lend more historical legitimacy to Mark's own community and to insist doggedly that their calling of empowered discipleship remains grounded in an active relationship with the risen Christ, who promises to "go before" them (Mk. 14:28; 16:7).

earthly ministry concerns at least in part his empowerment of devoted followers to carry on his purpose when he is no longer able to do so. Such a transmission of authority, initiated by Jesus himself, can also be detected in the subtle shift that takes place from Jesus to the Twelve as subject of the verbs. As discussed above, Jesus remains the primary figure throughout the opening narrative scene, where he "calls together," "begins to send them out," and "gives them authority." His prominence in the passage continues as Mark underscores that it is Jesus who "commands" (Mk. 6:8) and Jesus who "speaks" (Mk. 6:10). Especially in light of Jesus' sweeping narrative dominance throughout Mk. 6:7–11, Mark's concluding summary presents a distinct shift in focus as it tallies the Twelve's successes. To the careful attention Mark has devoted to their being "with him," this passage adds a complementary glimpse of their prophetic role as participants in Jesus' own kingdom-of-God agenda. Within the Markan community, just as the cross graphically depicts the cost of their discipleship, the resurrection preserves the possibility of a living Jesus who continues to empower his followers as fully authorized agents of God's in-breaking dominion, equipped to fulfill their office as God's "fishers" in an eschatological age.

Conclusion

Mark's account of this successful missionary venture develops several facets of the evangelist's portrait of discipleship that I have detected in earlier gospel passages. Indeed, Mk. 6:7–13 sketches something of an "ideal scene" in which Jesus' followers exercise the authority conferred upon them as agents of his own kingdom-of-God mission. At this point in the gospel story, we glimpse more clearly than ever Jesus' intent for the life of discipleship – a standard against which the Markan disciples will be judged.

(1) Though not yet clearly cruciform in shape, resistance to Jesus as agent of God's coming rule has appeared on the horizon, even compromising his own ability to assert God's power during his hometown stay. Against this increasingly ominous backdrop, Mark recounts a story of missionary success. In turn, the missionary journey situated within the historical time frame of Jesus' own mission serves also to adumbrate the post-resurrection work of Jesus' followers as heirs to his agenda. This "succession plan," reported in the sending out of the Twelve, functions both synchronically within the Markan narrative and diachronically within Mark's historical setting, where the evangelist seems intent on

convincing a weary and oppressed community of the continuing calling to discipleship.

(2) In continuity with both John's and Jesus' ministries, the Twelve reach an apex of service when they participate fully in the demonstration of God's coming kingly reign. Thus they go forth proclaiming the "good news" of that dominion not simply as propositional truth but as a power to be wielded in the apocalyptic showdown with adversarial forces. It is their utter trust in the dynamics of God's dominion, including ample provision of needs, healing, and subduing of the δαιμόνια, that makes the "way" for the seed of God's kingdom to take root and bear fruit.

(3) The resistance they encounter is an inevitable component of that apocalyptic battle. While suffering and sacrifice are not yet the dominant concerns that proceed from affirming God's rule, they will prove to be its inescapable consequences. Thus the groundwork is laid in this passage not just for the power of discipleship but also for its cost, a cost that looms ever larger as the gospel proceeds.

(4) The final outcome is assured. While the sovereignty of God may be provisionally contested within the human realm, Mark remains convinced that God's victory is imminent. While the "now" of Jesus' earthly ministry as well as Mark's community serves as a proleptic prelude to that final triumph, there can be no doubt, in this evangelist's story, that the full disclosure of God's reign is coming – and soon.

6

DISCIPLESHIP AS (TRANSFORMING) PRESENCE: THE WILDERNESS FEEDING IN MARK 6:30–44

Introduction

As is clear from its witness in the four canonical gospels, the feeding of the five thousand is a story deeply embedded in the tradition preserved and passed along within the nascent Christian community. In Mark's account, Jesus' miraculous multiplication of the loaves and fish performed before the masses nicely balances the gospel's earlier report of Jesus' teaching the "great crowd" (Mk. 4:1): just as his instruction has modeled the "sowing of the word," Jesus' feeding act constitutes a deed of power that provides a foretaste of God's coming dominion.

Yet, as has been true from the outset of his ministry, when Jesus feeds the hungry crowd, he does not operate alone. Indeed Jesus' dynamic interaction with his followers in Mk. 6:30–44 further elaborates the Markan portrait of discipleship, as readers glimpse in this episode what it means to be "with him." As we shall see, Mark's retelling of the feeding miracle employs imagery from Israel's scriptural tradition to depict God's eschatological abundance in the face of scarcity. And while Jesus presides over the meal, he also enlists and empowers his disciples as agents of the miraculous feeding of the masses.[1] Once again, discipleship as presence entails the full participation of Jesus' followers in the dawning reality of God's rule, a reality that in this case entails the satisfaction of human need.

The passage's pertinence to the present discipleship inquiry can be demonstrated from a variety of perspectives.[2] To begin with, the story's

[1] Klemens Stock fittingly calls this episode "ein neuer Höhepunkt für das Wirken Jesu durch seine Jünger am Volk" (*Boten aus dem Mit-Ihm-Sein: Das Verhältnis zwischen Jesus und den Zwölf nach Markus*, AnBib 70 [Rome: Biblical Institute, 1975], 109).

[2] On the basis of comparative philosophical and wisdom material, Whitney Taylor Shiner argues against reading this story as "anything other than an account of a miracle performed by Jesus" (*Follow Me! Disciples in Markan Rhetoric*, SBLDS 145 [Atlanta: Scholars Press, 1995], 219). Earlier in his monograph, though, Shiner notes important aspects of Mark's report that differ from the analogous literature (on the gospel's portrait of Jesus as a member

narrative context supplies important interpretive clues that accent the disciples' role as participants in the eschatological banquet in the wilderness. Since the feeding narrative follows the intercalated account of the Twelve's success and John's demise, its placement in Mark's narrative signals an "essential narrative interrelationship" linking the "mission and fate of Jesus, his disciples, and John."[3] By the same token, many details of Herod's banquet meal elaborately juxtapose the "apparent"[4] ruler's feast, which culminates in a gruesome death, with the provision of plenty that demonstrates, for Mark, the nature of God's kingly rule.[5]

Narrative context

Much has been made of Mark's insertion of the macabre flashback about John's death into the more triumphant report of the Twelve's successful missionary journey. The insertion itself is signaled by the Markan redactional frame flanking it: at one end is the summary report of the Twelve's activities following their commissioning (Mk. 6:12–13), and at the other end we find a typically Markan summary of "all [the disciples] had done and taught."[6] Between these bookend reports of the Twelve's heroic endeavors lies the grotesque tale of John the Baptist, beheaded at the behest of Herod to satisfy a vow to his daughter. As we shall see, attempts to explain Mark's arrangement here solely in terms of a narrative interlude allowing time for the Twelve to accomplish their mission[7] miss the adept interplay of disparate storylines, an interplay through which the evangelist scores important theological points and ultimately sets the stage for the ensuing feeding narrative.

of a community rather than as a lone hero like Apollonius of Tyana, see 125), so his appeal to outside criteria here seems to work against his own claims and, more importantly, to muffle the text's subtleties.

[3] Ched Myers, *Binding the Strong Man: A Political Reading of Mark's Story of Jesus* (Maryknoll, NY: Orbis, 1988), 213.

[4] Part and parcel of Mark's apocalyptic viewpoint is the discrepancy between the way things appear and the truer reality that is coming into view. For an explicit reference to "seeming" rulers, see, e.g., Mk. 10:42: "You know that the Gentiles' apparent rulers lord it over them . . . ." C. F. Stone, III, detects in this verse an allusion to Isa. 11:10 LXX that confirms its eschatological and messianic overtones (see "Allusion to Isa. 11.10 LXX in Mark 10.42b," *NTS* 48 [2002]: 71–83); further, he maintains that Mk. 10:42–5 is "applicable to church leadership in the interregnum" (71).

[5] Ben Witherington, III, *The Gospel of Mark: A Socio-Rhetorical Commentary* (Grand Rapids, MI: Eerdmans, 2001), 217, emphasizes this contrast.

[6] Karl-Georg Reploh, *Markus – Lehrer der Gemeinde: Eine redaktionsgeschichtliche Studie zu den Jüngerperikopen des Markus-Evangeliums*, SBM 9 (Stuttgart: Katholisches Bibelwerk, 1969), 52.

[7] See, e.g., Rudolf Bultmann, *The History of the Synoptic Tradition*, trans. John Marsh, rev. edn. (Peabody, MA: Hendrickson, 1994; orig. 1921), 301–2.

Herod hears . . . (Mk. 6:14–16)

Most commentators attribute the narrative link found in Mk. 6:14–16 to Mark's heavy editorial, if not creative, influence.[8] These verses do provide a vital transition from the report of the Twelve's deeds of power to the tale of John's death, even if Hooker is correct in her estimation that Mark accomplishes it "somewhat clumsily."[9] Indeed, it is the evangelist's rather artless shift from the report of the Twelve's mission to Herod's preoccupation with Jesus that exposes the first accomplishment of Mark's narrative strategy in this passage.

The episode opens abruptly with the claim, "King Herod heard (ἤκουσεν) of it, for his name had become apparent" (Mk. 6:14). In its present narrative context, the report mentioned refers clearly to the Twelve's repentance proclamation, their expulsion of demons, and their healing of many (Mk. 6:12–13). Less obvious is the connection between the missionaries' activities and Jesus' own notoriety. Some interpreters detect in this shifting emphasis from the Twelve to Jesus' "visibility"[10] evidence of a pre-Markan saying originally connected to a report of Jesus' own deeds of power; in this view, the second evangelist has severed that connection through the present arrangement of material.[11]

But such a speculative move is not necessary here. The text's seamless affiliation of the disciples' activities with Jesus' "name" is entirely consistent with their designation as "sent ones."[12] As I have noted in the previous chapter, Jesus' deliberate conferral of authority upon the Twelve has established them as his fully sanctioned emissaries. When Mark transfers

[8] For the view that Mark has, in these verses, cast a tradition of popular views of Jesus' ministry within the context of Herod's execution of John, see Ernest Best, *Following Jesus: Discipleship in the Gospel of Mark*, JSNTSup 4 (Sheffield: JSOT Press, 1981), 192; Vincent Taylor, *The Gospel According to Saint Mark: The Greek Text with Introduction, Notes, and Indexes*, 2nd edn. (Grand Rapids, MI: Baker, 1981; orig. 1950), 308; Eduard Schweizer, *The Good News According to Mark* (Atlanta: John Knox Press, 1970), 132; Joachim Gnilka, *Das Evangelium nach Markus*, 2 vols., EKKNT 2 (Zurich: Benziger; Neukirchen: Neukirchener Verlag, 1978–9), I:244. Less convincing is Rudolf Pesch, *Das Markusevangelium*, 2 vols., HTKNT 2 (Freiburg: Herder, 1976), I:332, whose view of Mark as "conservative redactor" leads him to the (inevitable) conclusion that the traditions were already conjoined in the pre-Markan tradition.

[9] Morna D. Hooker, *A Commentary on the Gospel According to St. Mark*, BNTC 2 (London: A. & C. Black, 1991), 159.

[10] The word φανερός appears only here and in Mk. 3:12 and 4:22; it consistently refers to the clarity with which Jesus and his mission are evident, not just "known" in a cognitive sense.

[11] See Martin Dibelius, *Die urchristliche Überlieferung von Johannes dem Täufer* (Göttingen: Vandenhoeck & Ruprecht, 1911), 82–3.

[12] See, e.g., Reploh, *Markus*, 55–6; Gunther Schmahl, *Die Zwölf im Markusevangelium* (Trier: Paulinus, 1974), 81.

attention from the work of the Twelve to Jesus' reputation, then, we infer a tacit reminder that whatever constitutes *their* mission, as Marcus puts it, "redounds to *his* glory."[13]

Another important narrative move is required, though, to link those deeds of power with the story of John the Baptist's death. Mark supplies it by appealing to the court of public opinion, where Jesus' identity can be explained according to three prominent theories: Jesus is either John *redivivus*, Elijah returned, or a "prophet like one of the prophets of old" (Mk. 6:14b–15).[14] While in Mark's view none of these possibilities adequately accounts for the powers unleashed through Jesus (and his followers), we may infer from their mention here that Mark intends to align Jesus with the cast of eschatological personages associated with the dawn of God's reign upon the earth.[15]

This transitional unit concludes with the repeated affirmation of Herod's "hearing" (Mk. 6:16), which prompts his attribution of the reported δυνάμεις to John's resurrection power.[16] With this verdict, Mark has paved the way for an elaborately crafted flashback report of the Baptist's death, a bifocal episode that adumbrates the destiny of Jesus and his followers even as it depicts a kingly banquet that will serve as a foil to the feeding story that follows. At the center of these discrete narrative functions lies the figure of Herod, whose temporary dominion entails both impotence and death; in stark contrast, God's rule, inaugurated and embodied by Jesus, will be characterized by abundance in the face of scarcity and life in the wake of death.

A kingly banquet (Mk. 6:17–29)

While the retrospective tale of John's demise, which begins with Mk. 6:17, reflects only modest editorial touches,[17] its redactional placement serves the evangelist's thematic purposes in two significant ways. For it is here, in the account of the banquet itself, that the intercalated

[13] Joel Marcus, *Mark 1–8: A New Translation with Introduction and Commentary*, AB 27 (New York: Doubleday, 2000), 398 (emphasis added).

[14] It is not necessary to infer, as do Pesch, *Markusevangelium*, I:332 and Gnilka, *Markus*, I:244–5, that Mk. 8:28 confirms an underlying tradition, since it cites the same three popular assessments of Jesus' identity. An equally viable possibility is the view that the second evangelist deliberately forges thematic ties between Jesus and these prophetic personages.

[15] In this respect, Marcus observes that these theories are "on the right track," even if they each "contain an element of miscalculation" (*Mark 1–8*, 399).

[16] If we have here an intratextual echo of Jesus' pronouncement against those who "hear" in vain (Mk. 4:12), Herod stands across the apocalyptic divide from those whose hearing prompts understanding.

[17] Examples of language possibly reflecting Markan editing include the phrase ἡδέως αὐτοῦ ἤκουεν (Mk. 6:20) and the Markan favorite, εὐθύς (Mk. 6:27).

structure achieves its two-part aim: to spell out the personal threat faced by those aligning themselves with God's dominion; and to juxtapose an elaborate depiction of Herod's kingly banquet with the wilderness feast hosted by Jesus and the disciples in the ensuing feeding narrative.

Already I have noted in the previous chapter that Jesus' instructions to the Twelve in Mk. 6:10–11 envisage not only pockets of hospitable reception but also a refusal, in other quarters, to "welcome" or to "listen" (Mk. 6:11). And although Mark's account of their journey ends on a successful note, the story of John's beheading provides a stark reminder that the stakes of the missionary endeavor are high; even proclaiming God's rule on the earth sets Jesus' followers at odds with the "powers that be."

Commentators have made frequent mention of the story's verbal and thematic ties with earlier accounts of Jewish martyrdom as well as with the passion narrative itself. In particular, the Markan account affirms John's upholding of the law as the basis for his imprisonment, an allegiance elsewhere attributed to Jewish martyrs such as Azariah (2 Chron. 24:20–2), Eleazar (2 Macc. 6:18–31), and the Maccabean brothers (2 Macc. 7).[18] Once he has been detained, John then becomes a victim of Herod's mishandled power. Thus, the Markan passion narrative also seems to lie behind this account in which demonic forces have somehow taken hold of the powers that be – even those who on some level affirm the martyr's innocence. What both the Maccabean stories and the passion narrative demonstrate is that for Mark, deeds of power and rejection by worldly authorities go hand-in-hand as constituent aspects of the kingdom-of-God program.[19] Even Herod's rather favorable disposition toward John[20] cannot thwart the adversarial forces that would threaten God's dominion.

[18] See Detlev Dormeyer, *Die Passion Jesu als Verhaltensmodell: literarische und theologische Analyse der Traditions- und Redaktionsgeschichte der Markuspassion* (Münster: Verlag Aschendorff, 1974), 43–7. Cf. Tessa Rajak, "Dying for the Law: The Martyr's Portrait in Jewish-Greek Literature," in *The Jewish Dialogue with Greece and Rome: Studies in Cultural and Social Location* (Leiden: Brill, 2001), 99–133, who notes the absence of "martyrdom" terminology in the Jewish-Greek literature and cautions against reading Jewish-Greek martyrologies through the lens of later Christian thought. Notably, Rajak's summary of thematic emphases in 2 and 4 Maccabees, as well as in the writings of Philo and Josephus, indicates that a willingness to die "for the law" in many instances manifests itself in a refusal to eat unclean food (see 126–9); while in the present Markan episode John does not die precisely for this reason, the lavish feast where his head is presented on a platter may reflect an implicit snubbing – even mockery – of Jewish dietary laws.

[19] For a discussion of the implications for Mark's own community, see Mary Ann Tolbert, *Sowing the Gospel: Mark's World in Literary-Historical Perspective* (Minneapolis: Fortress Press, 1989), 197–8.

[20] Mk. 6:20 reports that Herod "liked to listen to him." Moreover, Marcus, *Mark 1–8*, 394, suggests that the explanation for Herod's arrest of John, διὰ Ἡρῳδιάδα, may indicate a protective motivation.

Yet just as the grisly episode casts an ominous shadow on the Twelve's missionary success, it also provides a literary foil to the feeding narrative that follows. The stories share the setting of a meal where guests' appetites are satisfied, as well as a dominant character who responds to the petition of those close to him.[21] In these two stories, we find parallel accounts of kingly banquets.

Yet beyond these points of surface contact, the contrast between Herod's and Jesus' conduct is striking. In the first place, Herod accedes to the whims of his wife and daughter, revealing the deficient nature of his own authority (see Mk. 10:42). By contrast, Jesus subverts the disciples' inclination to "send [the crowds] away" (Mk. 6:36), trumping their request with an authoritative counterproposal: "you give them something to eat" (Mk. 6:37). Moreover, while both stories revolve around "giving," the nature of the object and the purpose of the distribution in the respective passages stand sharply at odds: on the one hand, Herod's soldier "gives" John's head to the girl who in turn "gives" it to her mother (Mk. 6:28); on the other hand, Jesus "gives" the broken bread to the disciples who in turn set it before the people (Mk. 6:41). Finally, perhaps the sharpest contrast between the two banquets can be found in their outcome: whereas the story of Herod's feast ends with John's burial, Jesus' feast ends with a report of staggering surplus.

In summary, Mark has strategically positioned the tragic tale of John's beheading so that it relates both to the apostles' work that surrounds it and to the wilderness feast that follows it.[22] On the one hand, the account's setting and claims issue a foreboding reminder of the high stakes that come with wielding the "powers" associated with God's dominion on the earth. On the other hand, Mark includes this decidedly dim portrait of an earthly king whose flimsy and destructive rule functions as narrative foil to the elaborate provision that typifies the dominion of God. Through his portrayal of the dynamic clash of these "powers," Mark reassures hearers that, despite appearances to the contrary, God's sovereignty is ultimately assured.[23]

[21] See Robert M. Fowler, *Loaves and Fishes: The Function of the Feeding Stories in the Gospel of Mark*, SBLDS 54 (Chico, CA: Scholars Press, 1981), 120, for a list of comparable details.

[22] Camille Focant, "La Tête du prophète sur un plat, ou, L'Anti-repas d'alliance (Mc 6.14–29)," *NTS* 46 (2001): 334–53, views the meal additionally as a parody of Jesus' last supper shared with his disciples. In this mixture of analepsis and prolepsis, Focant maintains, the evangelist deliberately introduces the suffering motif within the report of missionary success. While the Passover meal does hover on the narrative horizon, I deem the dominant point of contrast to lie closer at hand with the feeding narrative.

[23] Marcus, *Mark 1–8*, 397, maintains that the flashback "points to the paradox that the miraculous successes of Christian missionaries are made possible by the suffering death of

The wilderness feeding: discipleship as presence

Turning to the feeding narrative itself, this study will examine the disciples' prominence as Jesus' active interlocutors, as those who prompt his miraculous feat, and as those whom Jesus involves in the feeding itself. Of even more significance is the disciples' transformation from helpless figures who perceive a problem but propose an inadequate solution ("send them away") to empowered participants in God's eschatological feast. Against the backdrop of Israel's sacred lore, Mark crafts traditional material in a manner that underscores the disciples' role in the feeding narrative. In the end, to "be with him" at this narrative juncture entails the disciples' active involvement in the same kingdom-of-God reality that Jesus so consistently proclaims and demonstrates.

The first Markan feeding narrative has long been construed as a dramatic witness to Jesus' miraculous command over natural resources.[24] As Ephrem the Syrian marvels, "That which [people] effect and transform in ten months with toil, his ten fingers effected in an instant."[25] Form-critical analysis that finds the feeding itself (Mk. 6:32–44) to be a "gift miracle"[26] lends further credence to the view that the story primarily displays the divine powers of the one who dispenses the gift. And those who claim that the passage reverberates with Eucharistic overtones similarly underscore its momentous claims about Jesus' sacramental presence.[27]

Jesus, to which the death of the Baptist points." Yet two details urge caution in too quickly abandoning the narrative's own pre-Easter time frame: (1) the Markan introduction to this story links the disciples' powers to John's destiny, not Jesus'; and (2) the text itself assumes those powers are operative prior to Jesus' own death.

[24] Peering through this sharply ground Christological lens, Quentin Quesnell states that the only certain connection between the feeding narrative and the ensuing sea crossing is "that both are marvelous incidents in the life of Jesus" (*The Mind of Mark: Interpretation and Method through the Exegesis of Mark 6,52* [Rome: Pontifical Biblical Institute, 1969], 62).

[25] *Saint Ephrem's Commentary on Tatian's Diatessaron: An English Translation of Chester Beatty Syriac MS 709*, with introduction and notes by Carmel McCarthy, JSS-Sup 2 (Oxford: Oxford University Press for the University of Manchester, 1993), 191.

[26] E.g. Gerd Theissen, *The Miracle Stories of the Early Christian Tradition*, trans. Francis McDonagh, ed. John Riches, SNTW (Philadelphia: Fortress Press, 1983), 103.

[27] E.g. Quesnell, *Mind of Mark*; Alkuin Heising, *Die Botschaft der Brotvermehrung: zur Geschichte und Bedeutung eines Christusbekenntnisses im Neuen Testament* (Stuttgart: Katholisches Bibelwerk, 1966); Bastiaan Martinus Franciscus van Iersel, "Die wunderbare Speisung und das Abendmahl in der synoptischen Tradition (Mk. VI.35–44 par VIII.1–20 par)," *NovT* 7 (1964): 167–94. On the other hand, George H. Boobyer, "The Eucharistic Interpretation of the Miracles of the Loaves in St. Mark's Gospel," *JTS* 3 (1952): 161–71, dismisses eucharistic parallels because of significant differences (see also Gnilka, *Markus*, I:267; Pesch, *Markusevangelium*, I:352), and Paul J. Achtemeier, "The Origin and Function of the Pre-Markan Miracle Catenae," *JBL* 91 (1972): 198–221, suggests that Mark has deliberately muted eucharistic echoes found in the miracle tradition he has adopted. I shall consider this issue in greater detail below.

Exegetical findings from the previous chapters, though, suggest a reading of this passage that moves beyond its disclosure of Jesus' divine identity. Once attention turns toward the role of the disciples in the feeding narrative itself, we find that, at least in Mark's rendering, this story exhibits distinctive traits that explicate for his fledgling community what it means to advance Jesus' Christological cause through the demonstration of God's dawning dominion. Once again, Mark's account of the feeding of the five thousand portrays discipleship within the context of Jesus' own messianic mission.

To explicate both Christological and ecclesiological implications of the first Markan feeding story, we must pay close attention to its literary antecedents within Israel's sacred lore. On the one hand, Stegner has noted the broad narrative parallel between the Markan feeding story and the Exodus wilderness events: "Jesus and the disciples cross the sea to the wilderness place, and then the hungry are fed; in Exodus the Israelites cross the sea, wander in the wilderness, become hungry, and are fed with manna."[28] In both stories, the narrative progresses from the problem of hunger to the solution of a miraculous feeding. And, as we shall see, several verbal details found in the Markan account combine to portray this wilderness feeding as a dramatization of the kind of kingly banquet anticipated in the eschatological age.

Yet just where the Markan feeding story diverges from this Exodus typology, we can detect echoes of a complementary biblical tradition found in 2 Kings. In the disciples' participation in the event, in their sharing of their own resources, and especially in the overabundance of the provision, Mk. 6:30–44 both resembles and develops the story of a miraculous feeding associated with the prophet Elisha.

This study of the feeding story, then, will explore Mark's own transmission of traditional material in light of Israel's sacred writings. A preliminary comparison of the story's parallel account in John's gospel will expose thematic nuances that reflect Mark's interest in depicting Jesus' interaction with his disciples. Then the study will move through each of the episode's five scenes, noting along the way the resonance between this story and the Jewish scriptures it recalls. As we shall see, Mark draws on streams of complementary precursor texts to renarrate the feeding of the five thousand in terms of God's eschatological wilderness provision. In addition, Mark suggests, through the details and movement of the pericope, a thematic emphasis on Jesus' direct involvement of his disciples as

[28] William Richard Stegner, *Narrative Theology in Early Jewish Christianity* (Louisville, KY: Westminster/John Knox Press, 1989), 58.

he presides over that feast. As a result, Mk. 6:30–44 provides a dramatic glimpse of discipleship as both presence and practice; in their being "with him," Jesus' followers have no choice but to be swept up in their leader's vivid demonstration of God's coming kingdom.[29] Once again, questions of Christology and discipleship here converge.

Preliminary remarks: literary comparison as evidence of Markan emphasis

Especially given the likelihood that Mark and John compiled their written accounts independently of one another,[30] both their shared features and their rather striking divergences provide a helpful starting point for detecting the evangelists' redactional emphases.

To begin with, both evangelists describe a scene that moves from the problem of hunger to the solution not just of sufficiency but of leftovers. Along the way, they share many details as well as narrative patterns, as the following chart indicates:

	Mark	John
Crossing of the sea/lake	6:32	6:1
Followed by a "great crowd"	6:34	6:2
Jesus "sees" the multitude	6:34	6:5
The people need to eat	6:36	6:5
The disciple(s) report(s) the insufficiency of "two hundred denarii"	6:37	6:7
Resources at hand = five loaves and two fish	6:38	6:9
Jesus orders the people to sit down	6:39	6:10
Jesus blesses (Mk.)/gives thanks (Jn.)	6:41	6:11
The people are satisfied (Mk.)/filled (Jn.)	6:42	6:12
The disciples fill twelve baskets with remnants	6:43	6:13
The crowd is numbered as five thousand men	6:44	6:10

Such a high incidence of shared narrative details only casts in starker relief the evangelists' distinctive hermeneutical moves with respect to two prominent features:

[29] As Witherington observes, the event "was to reveal to the disciples Jesus' true character, and also their true calling to serve the people" (*Mark*, 219). The task undertaken here is to recognize Mark's presentation of a more organic relationship between Jesus' "character" and the disciples' "calling."

[30] Since both Mark and John combine the feeding and the sea-crossing stories, the gospels' literary relationship is rather hotly disputed with regard to this material. The options include the following: (1) the evangelists worked independently with independent, but overlapping, sources; (2) they worked independently, but with a shared "signs source"; (3) John depended on (though freely adapted) Mark. While the shared details enumerated here indicate common dependence on a similar source, it is more difficult to determine with certainty whether or not that source was identical.

(1) Narrative setting: in John's narrative, after a great crowd has followed Jesus, he "went up on a mountain and there sat down with his disciples" (Jn. 6:3). Mark not only adds and emphasizes the wilderness setting (ἔρημον τόπον: Mk. 6:31, 32, 35) but declares it as Jesus' original destination: following John's death and the successful report of the disciples' missionary activity (Mk. 6:30), Jesus urges them, "Come away by yourselves to a wilderness place and rest a while" (Mk. 6:31). This verse and its repetition in Mk. 6:32 continue the wilderness theme programmatically pronounced in Mk. 1:2–3 (see also Mk. 1:12–13, 35, 45) – a theme discussed above as emblematic of the prophetic hope of "eschatological victory in the wilderness."[31] Within Mark's unfolding narrative, the withdrawal to a wilderness place reflects Jesus' concern for the disciples in light of their successful (but exhausting) missionary activity as well as the more somber reflection on the implications, for Jesus and his entourage, of the Baptist's death.[32]

(2) Role of the disciples: from the outset, Mark's attention to the disciples attunes us to what is perhaps the most resounding dissonance between the two gospel narratives. Throughout his account, Mark repeatedly casts these followers as prominent players in the drama in at least three respects. First, it is the disciples who articulate the problem of the hungering crowd;[33] by contrast, John's voice-over emphasizes Jesus' own prescience: "for he himself knew what he would do" (Jn. 6:6). Second, Mark's Jesus responds to the disciples by imploring them to feed the crowd, despite their sarcastic protest of inadequacy, while John's story parodies the disciples' obtuseness by attributing to Philip a pat answer: "Two hundred denarii would not buy enough for each of them to get a little" (Jn. 6:7). And third, Mark reports that after blessing and breaking the loaves, Jesus "gave them to the disciples to set before

[31] Joel Marcus, *The Way of the Lord: Christological Exegesis of the Old Testament in the Gospel of Mark* (Louisville: Westminster/John Knox Press, 1992), 26.

[32] See, e.g., Marcus, *Mark 1–8*, 405: "John's death prompts Jesus to devote more concentrated attention to the disciples who will take his place after his own death." Also Robert H. Gundry, *Mark: A Commentary on His Apology for the Cross* (Grand Rapids, MI: Eerdmans, 1993), 322: "By highlighting the apostles, [the setting] stresses the degree to which Jesus' power has been extended."

[33] Representing a prevalent view in Markan scholarship, Robert A. Guelich contends that "this miracle story begins a series in which the disciples' lack of understanding . . . becomes more pronounced." He adds, "It stands in ironic tension with their preceding mission . . . The opening dialogue between the disciples and Jesus (6:35–8) reveals their confusion" (*Mark 1–8:26*, WBC 34A [Dallas: Word, 1989], 338). The view developed here identifies that same "ironic tension" (between success and confusion) within the feeding narrative itself.

the people" (Mk. 6:41);[34] in John's account, the disciples recede into the landscape's background, while Jesus distributes the loaves to the crowd.

Comparison of the two gospel accounts has identified several features that reflect Mark's narrative concerns: from the tradition, he has preserved the basic plotline of surplus provision in response to scarcity as well as many distinctive narrative details; in contrast to John, he has either accentuated or introduced both the wilderness setting and the narrative role of the disciples. Having laid the groundwork by considering Mark's handling of the feeding-story tradition, I now turn to the heart of the study, which examines the second evangelist's interpretive appropriation of much older traditions drawn from Israel's sacred lore.

The structure of Mark 6:30–44: from privilege to service

The interaction between Jesus and his disciples plays a pivotal role in the narrative progression of Mark's feeding of the five thousand. Both in its structure and in verbal details, the story sketches the disciples' subtle but significant transformation, as their role evolves from that of privileged protection to that of self-giving service.[35] Thus the dynamics of this passage in which the disciples are "with Jesus" confirm and reiterate the pattern of discipleship discussed above in chapter 4, where Jesus instructs his disciples not simply to bask in their special status but to perpetuate his own mission by disseminating the word of God's coming kingdom.

Mark's account of the feeding story features five distinct movements, each representing a discernible step in the disciples' transformation. The following chart demonstrates the dynamic interaction, in word and deed, that characterizes the major subsections of Mk. 6:30–44; throughout the passage, the participants ("key players") exchange vigorous banter even as their actions carry forward this story of surplus feeding.

[34] As Mark's earliest interpreter, Matthew emphasizes through repetition the disciples' role: "Taking the five loaves and the two fish, [Jesus] looked up to heaven, and blessed and broke the loaves, and gave them to the disciples, and *the disciples* gave them to the crowds" (Matt. 14:19).

[35] Shiner maintains that the disciples' dominant role is "to establish for the listener the magnitude of the miracle that Jesus performs" (*Follow Me!*, 218), though he does concede that they are "mediators between Jesus and the crowd" (221). Fowler cites the disciples' "antagonism to Jesus" in Mk. 6:36–8 as evidence of a "serious disjunction between their ministry and his" (*Loaves and Fishes*, 116). Neither interpreter seems to take seriously the constructive role the disciples play in this story.

	Key players	Their actions
1) Mk. 6:30–2	“apostles”	gather around Jesus to report what they have done and taught
	Jesus	commands them to come to a wilderness place, alone
	[together]	embark toward a wilderness place alone
2) Mk. 6:33–4	“many”	recognize and come toward Jesus/disciples
	Jesus	has compassion and begins to teach
3) Mk. 6:35–8	disciples	command Jesus to send the crowds away
	Jesus	commands disciples to feed them
	disciples	question the feasibility of Jesus’ command
	Jesus	questions their on-hand resources
	disciples	produce five loaves and two fish
4) Mk. 6:39–41	Jesus	commands the crowd to rest upon the grass
	crowd	sit down by groups of hundreds and fifties
	Jesus	takes loaves, blesses, breaks, gives to the disciples
	disciples	set the loaves before the crowd
	Jesus	divides the fish among them all
5) Mk. 6:42–4	“all”	ate and were satisfied
	[disciples?]	take up twelve baskets of remnants

As we shall see, Mark’s redactional touches effectively portray this feeding story as a prime example of discipleship as presence, since through lively interchanges with Jesus, those who are “with him” come to participate fully in his practice of God’s eschatological provision in the wilderness.

Scene one: Jesus and the disciples alone (Mk. 6:30–2)

The opening scene[36] provides a rather belabored transition to the story of Jesus’ provision for the multitudes. At the outset, only Jesus and his “apostles” are in view, and the passage opens with a summary of the group’s gathering around Jesus to report “all which [the apostles] did and taught” (Mk. 6:30); after the lengthy digression about John’s death (Mk. 6:14–29), Mark resumes the storyline in a manner that casts the

[36] From a form-critical perspective, interpreters differ widely on where the transitional “summary report” gives way to the “miracle story” proper, with some dividing the passage after Mk. 6:31 (e.g. Schweizer, *Good News*, 135–6; Pesch, *Markusevangelium*, I:345); some after 6:32 (e.g. K. Kertelge, *Die Wunder Jesu im Markusevangelium. Eine redaktiongeschichtliche Untersuchung*, SANT 23 [Munich: Kösel, 1970], 130); some after 6:33 (e.g. Daryl Dean Schmidt, *The Gospel of Mark with Introduction, Notes, and Original Text* [Sonoma, CA: Polebridge Press, 1991], 186–90; Bultmann, *Synoptic Tradition*, 231); some after 6:34 (e.g. Taylor, *Saint Mark*, 318). The present inquiry seeks not a hard-and-fast distinction between transition and story but an interpretive assessment of Mark’s transitional framing of the ensuing feeding account.

mission of the Twelve (Mk. 6:7–13, 30) as backdrop for the feeding narrative. For, while the chapter's retrospective reflection on John's destiny has foreshadowed the grisly implications of Jesus' apocalyptic mission, the evangelist now turns attention to the more positive side of that mission.[37]

Moreover, Mark's addition of "teaching" to the list of the apostles' activities may well signal a redactional interest in "the essential relationship between the mission of the Twelve and Jesus' mission."[38] Typically in Mark, it is Jesus whose work is characterized by teaching, while the proclamation task is shared by a wide range of characters, from John, to the disciples, to the benefactors of Jesus' healing acts. As a result, this summary report of the *disciples'* didactic activity serves as the gospel's unique instance in which Jesus' followers carry on this facet of his ministry; here Mark notes all that they had "done and taught," thus establishing continuity between Jesus' teaching ministry and the apostles' mission.[39]

Jesus responds to the apostles' report with a command that is quite consistent with the intimate, and somewhat protective, relationship Mark portrays between this master and his followers: δεῦτε ὑμεῖς αὐτοὶ κατ' ἰδίαν εἰς ἔρημον τόπον καὶ ἀναπαύσασθε ὀλίγον (Mk. 6:31). In the first place, the vocative δεῦτε echoes Jesus' initial call to discipleship (δεῦτε ὀπίσω μου, Mk. 1:17)[40] and so reiterates his leadership of this band of followers. In this way, the call to rest can be seen as a constituent part of discipleship.[41]

But just as significant is Jesus' impulse, quite prevalent throughout the gospel, to "circle the wagons," changing direction just when the success of his mission begins to weigh heavily on his entourage. At the outset of his ministry in Capernaum, for instance, Simon's report of the pursuing

[37] Fowler, *Loaves and Fishes*, 116, finds this "seemingly auspicious beginning . . . [to be] totally obliterated" by the disciples' ensuing lapses, which depict them as "intractable and blind." As I shall emphasize below, the disciples' culpability does not prevent them from ultimately heeding Jesus' command to "give [them] something to eat" (Mk. 6:36).

[38] Guelich, *Mark 1–8:26*, 339.

[39] For examples of Mark's prior depiction of Jesus as a teacher, see, e.g., Mk. 1:21; 2:13; 4:1 6:6b. Robert P. Meye calls this shift toward the disciples' teaching ministry "unique and interesting" and uses it to support his view of the gospel as a "didache to be learned and followed by the Marcan Church." (*Jesus and the Twelve: Discipleship and Revelation in Mark's Gospel* [Grand Rapids, MI: Eerdmans, 1968], 60.)

[40] See Stock, *Boten*, 102.

[41] Wilhelm Egger aptly links this call to rest to a dominical saying underlying Matt. 11:28–9, where Jesus promises rest to his followers (*Frohbotschaft und Lehre: Die Sammelberichte das Wirkens Jesu im Markusevangelium* [Frankfurt am Main: Knecht, 1976], 126–7); cf. Gundry, *Mark*, 328, who believes Matthew composed the verses. If we cannot decisively determine the literary origin of Jesus' call to rest, we can affirm the persistent thematic balance, in gospel accounts of discipleship, between activity and rest.

throngs elicits Jesus' resolve to "go on to neighboring towns" (Mk. 1:38), while the escape motif grows even more explicit when Jesus commands his disciples to prepare a boat, "so that they would not crush him" (Mk. 3:9).

The emphatic ὑμεῖς also signals a relational emphasis on the closeness shared between Jesus and his disciples. Indeed, as we shall see below, the use of the pronoun in the command to "give them something to eat" (Mk. 6:37) underscores the evangelist's dominant concern with the disciples' role in the story. Elsewhere in the second gospel, the construction similarly reflects Jesus' assumption that the disciples have closely aligned their lives with his (Mk. 7:19; 8:29). Thus this emphatic command reflects his deliberate intent to provide an opportunity to rest and eat for those closest to him.

Central to the exposition of these introductory verses is the repetition (and inversion) of the combined phrases "alone" and "to a wilderness place":

> δεῦτε ὑμεῖς αὐτοὶ κατ᾽ ἰδίαν εἰς ἔρημον τόπον . . .
> (Mk. 6:31)
>
> . . . εἰς ἔρημον τόπον κατ᾽ ἰδίαν
> (Mk. 6:32)

In one sense, these two phrases constitute a "double statement"[42] in that they separately bear witness to the same reality. If so, their repetition in Mk. 6:31–2 compounds the emphatic effect, as Mark drives home Jesus' desire that the disciples escape from the fray of their missionary activity, just as Jesus himself has withdrawn from the public eye in Mk. 1:35 and 1:45 and will remove himself further in Mk. 6:45–6.

Yet, in another sense, Mark's use of the phrase εἰς ἔρημον τόπον provides an important thematic transition to the kind of wilderness experience God's people have experienced in Israel's sacred tales. Though some interpreters explicitly deny the link,[43] this Markan anomaly suggests the evangelist's emphasis on the "wilderness place" as staging ground for

[42] This is the category to which Frans Neirynck assigns them (*Duality in Mark: Contributions to the Study of the Markan Redaction*, BETL 31 [Leuven: Leuven University Press, 1972], 95).

[43] Guelich attributes this detail to the pre-Markan tradition and dismisses the notion of "an identity or even a typology" that draws on wilderness imagery (*Mark 1–8:26*, 339–400). For Guelich, the phrase simply denotes the isolated locale associated with this miracle story, and though he does acknowledge the importance of wilderness imagery in the gospel's opening chapter (cf. 18, 38), he denies its role here with little explanation.

God's kingdom provision.[44] While the narrative transition thus preserves an ironic tension between Jesus' intended program for the disciples' seclusion on the one hand and their subsequent involvement with the crowd on the other, the catch phrase "in the wilderness" links the preceding summary with the feeding miracle itself. But what does this location indicate?

Rather predictably, Wrede explains all of Jesus' retreats from the public domain in terms of the messianic-secret motif. That is, Jesus removes himself from the press of the crowds because he wishes to conceal his true identity until after the resurrection.[45] Yet not only does the Markan text lack any specific mention of this purpose, but the withdrawal itself occurs within the context of a highly public ministry.

Further, in the present passage Jesus suggests a removal toward "a wilderness place" in order to provide not concealment but rest (Mk. 6:31). And once the events conspire against that restful purpose, the outcome of Jesus' "retreat" to the wilderness – the overabundant feeding of five thousand men – serves not to restrict but to amplify public acclaim for Jesus' miraculous powers. Thus Mauser's reading of Mark seems more substantiated by the evidence: he claims that the journey "toward a wilderness place" is "not meant to conceal but rather to reveal Jesus' true character" through the disclosure of "the eschatological function of the Son of God to fulfil his mission *in the wilderness*."[46]

The significance of the wilderness as the setting for God's activity "upon the earth" is evident in myriad LXX passages, beginning with the Exodus story itself. First, it is worth noting that Exod. 16:3 contains the LXX's only verbal linkage of "wilderness" and "bread" in the same verse, as the people complain to Moses: "Would that we had died in Egypt . . . when we ate bread (ἄρτους) to the full. For you have led us into this wilderness (ἔρημον) to kill this whole assembly with hunger."

Yet if wilderness imagery garners its original significance from the Exodus narrative, the reinterpretation (or "inner biblical exegesis") of that tradition in later biblical texts develops the motif eschatologically, as the wilderness becomes the place where the kingdom of God begins to take root. For instance, Deutero-Isaiah repeatedly depicts the wilderness

44 Rikki E. Watts, *Isaiah's New Exodus and Mark* (Tübingen: Mohr Siebeck, 1997), 179. Here, then, Mark continues to sound a theme established from the gospel's outset (see Mk. 1:4, 13).

45 William Wrede, *The Messianic Secret*, trans. J. C. Grieg (Cambridge: James Clarke, 1971; orig. 1901), 135–6.

46 Ulrich Mauser, *Christ in the Wilderness: The Wilderness Theme in the Second Gospel and Its Basis in the Biblical Tradition* (London: SCM Press, 1963), 143, n. 2 (emphasis added).

as the place where God acts decisively to restore the people that has been devastated through exile. Isa. 43:19 offers the promise: "I am about to do a new thing; now it springs forth, do you not perceive it? I will make a way in the wilderness and rivers in the desert." In a host of exile-based texts, the wilderness becomes the staging ground for God's deliverance.[47]

At least some strains of post-biblical Jewish thought apparently carried forward this expectation that the wilderness would be the site of God's decisive redemption. Though his assessment of their activity is less than favorable, Josephus provides a glimpse of activists who lured followers into the wilderness where they might hope to witness signs of God's coming salvation (*J.W.* 2.258–63). And certainly the Qumran community views its own wilderness setting as the place from which God's eschatological deliverance will come.[48]

In at least two respects, then, the feeding story's opening scene offers interpretive guidelines that are vital to the exposition of the ensuing miracle story. First, as becomes increasingly clear in the unfolding plotline, the narrative proceeds from a starting point that focuses not on Jesus' relationship to the crowds (though that interaction will take center stage in the ensuing scene) but on his relationship to the disciples. Indeed, this story supplies a vivid glimpse of what it means to be "with him" as a constituent part of the call to discipleship. Just as Jesus has initially summoned the fishers with the words δεῦτε ὀπίσω μου (Mk. 1:17), here he bids them, δεῦτε ὑμεῖς αὐτοὶ κατ' ἰδίαν (Mk. 6:31); just as Jesus has, to this point, served as preeminent teacher with authority, here too they have "taught." In these verbal ties linking Jesus' activity with the report of the apostles' mission, the transitional verses of Mk. 6:30–2 lay the groundwork for understanding even Jesus' miraculous feeding as a matter of both Christology and discipleship.

Yet, as we have seen, the "wilderness place" setting also paves the way for a dramatic exposé of God's incursion into the human realm. Beneath Jesus' surface concern to escape the demands of public life lies the expectation that God is about to do something very public indeed, an expectation conveyed through wilderness imagery and confirmed as the story unfolds. Ironically, though Jesus and his disciples will not achieve the kind of "rest" one might envision in a secluded setting, they will

[47] See, e.g., Isa. 40:3; 41:18; 42:11; 44:26; 51:3.

[48] Among details in the QL that comport with this "New Exodus in the wilderness" theme are the following: the covenanters' self-identification as "penitents of the wilderness" (1QM 1:2); their view of their role in clearing in the "wilderness a highway for . . . God" (1QS 8:12–16); and their organization in groups that correspond numerically to Pentateuchal accounts of Israel's sub-division during the proto-wilderness epoch (1QS 2:21ff.).

participate in the New Exodus event that takes place in a wilderness setting.[49]

Scene two: Jesus responds to the crowds (Mk. 6:33–4)

While Jesus and his companions apparently reach their physical destination (the wilderness place), they do not gain the solitude they have sought. Instead, once the group has set out for that undisclosed location in order to evade the masses, the narrator widens the lens to describe in vivid detail a crowd of persistent pursuers:

> καὶ εἶδον αὐτοὺς ὑπάγοντας καὶ ἐπέγνωσαν πολλοὶ καὶ πεζῇ ἀπὸ πασῶν τῶν πόλεων συνέδραμον ἐκεῖ καὶ προῆλθον αὐτούς. (Mk. 6:33)

Certainly the verse here sets the stage for the ensuing miracle by bringing the multitudes into view. Yet, under closer scrutiny, several details draw our attention both to the crowd's persistence and to the disciples' continued presence.

Interpreters dispute the historical authenticity of the information conveyed in Mk. 6:33. While some deny the account's plausibility on both geographical and pragmatic grounds[50] and so underscore the verse's theological rather than historical intent, others suggest that the verse need not indicate a complete east–west crossing. To them, Mk. 6:33 may simply depict a crowd traveling quickly around the periphery of a cove crossed more slowly by boat.[51] There is no need to render a decisive conclusion on the historical likelihood here to appreciate the report's consistency with Mark's story, which so often finds Jesus' course altered by contingent circumstance, especially in response to human need (e.g. Mk. 2:1–12; 5:21–43; 6:48). Just as the apostles' report in Mk. 6:30 has evoked Jesus' summons to a "wilderness place," so here the crowds take charge of the action; indeed their unrelenting pursuit ultimately shapes the story's outcome.

Moreover, the report of the crowd's flurry of activity (εἶδον, ἐπέγνωσαν, συνέδραμον, προῆλθον) stipulates αὐτούς as the object of their pursuit. It is not just Jesus whom they see and seek; it is the entire band

[49] See William L. Lane, *The Gospel According to Mark*, NICNT (Grand Rapids, MI: Eerdmans, 1974), 225.

[50] See, e.g., Thierry Snoy, "La Rédaction marcienne de la marche sur les eaux (Mc. VI:45–52)," *ETL* 44 (1968): 205–41; Fowler, *Loaves and Fishes*, 65–6.

[51] E.g. Pesch, *Markusevangelium*, I:349.

of Jesus with his disciples who have together been acclaimed, we infer, for their deeds of power.[52]

As the episode unfolds, though, Mark's Jesus steps once again onto center stage, since it is he who first responds to the masses who have pursued his cohort. Above I have noted that the crowd's "seeing" launches their journey toward Jesus and his disciples. But here it is Jesus whose "seeing" precedes his own conduct toward his pursuers: καὶ ἐξελθὼν εἶδεν πολὺν ὄχλον . . . (Mk. 6:34a).

If these verses constitute the transition toward Jesus' miraculous provision of food, Mark's account notably omits any mention of physical hunger as a problem to be solved.[53] Instead, Mark recounts Jesus' visceral reaction to the crowd, together with an explanatory clause accounting for that response: καὶ ἐσπλαγχνίσθη ἐπ' αὐτούς, ὅτι ἦσαν ὡς πρόβατα μὴ ἔχοντα ποιμένα (Mk. 6:34b).

Besides the recurrence of Jesus' compassion as a motive for the second feeding story (Mk. 8:2), the two other Markan uses of verb σπλαγχνίζω are tied closely to Jesus' demonstration of miraculous powers. Jesus' healing of a leper in Mk. 1:40–5 is preceded by a report of his compassion (Mk. 1:41),[54] and the father of the boy with the spirit implores Jesus to "have compassion" and to offer help (Mk. 9:22).[55]

This time, though, Jesus' compassion does not immediately prompt the performance of a miracle; instead, here it leads to his instruction. Yet, for Mark, wonder-working and teaching represent two facets of the same overarching reality: both activities characterize Jesus' demonstration of God's coming kingdom in word and deed (see Mk. 1:26–7). Indeed, this convergence fits well the gospel's Mosaic typology, since Moses'

52 See Lane, *Mark*, 225.

53 Gnilka points out the contrast here with Mk. 8:2, where Jesus' compassion is motivated by the crowd's hunger (*Markus*, I:259).

54 While an impressive list of manuscripts, including ℵ, A, B, C, K, L, bear witness to this reading, we should acknowledge the more difficult (and therefore not easily dismissed) reading of D, which replaces σπλαγχνισθείς with ὀργισθείς. While acknowledging the difficulty in adjudicating between the two options, Bruce M. Metzger, *A Textual Commentary on the Greek New Testament: A Companion Volume to the United Bible Societies' Greek New Testament,* 3rd edn. (London and New York: United Bible Societies, 1971), 65, suggests that the scribal change to ὀργισθείς may be attributed either to confusion about the underlying Aramaic or to the stern tone of the participle ἐμβριμησάμενος that appears later in the passage (Mk. 1:43).

55 See W. D. Davies and Dale C. Allison, *A Critical and Exegetical Commentary on the Gospel According to Saint Matthew*, 3 vols. (Edinburgh: T. & T. Clark, 1988–97), II:479, who present a similar conclusion with respect to the wider synoptic tradition (e.g. Matt. 15:32; 14:14; 20:34; Lk. 7:13).

mediation of the Torah and his mighty deeds both attest God's power at work through him.[56]

Of all verses in this pericope, Mk. 6:34b most nearly approximates "scriptural citation" in the clause: ὅτι ἦσαν ὡς πρόβατα μὴ ἔχοντα ποιμένα. In Num. 27:17, Moses offers this petition to Yahweh: "appoint someone over the congregation who shall go out before them and come in before them, who shall lead them out and bring them in, so that the congregation of the Lord may not be *like sheep without a shepherd*" (Num. 27:16–17). The staggering need that Moses detects is the community's leadership vacuum.

This discernable deficiency, it turns out, crops up repeatedly throughout the OT scriptures. Beginning with this reference to Joshua's leadership, the image "becomes a proverbial metaphor for the people suffering either through lack of strong leadership . . . or through evil rulers."[57] In 1 Kings, for instance, the prophet Micaiah predicts disaster at Ramoth-gilead: "I saw all Israel scattered on the mountains, like sheep that have no shepherd" (1 Kgs. 22:17). Later prophecy reverberates with similar language, as in the case of Zech. 10:2: "Therefore the people wander like sheep; they suffer for lack of a shepherd." Similarly, reflecting on the failings of Israel's leadership, the prophet Ezekiel posits God as the eschatological shepherd: "I myself will search for my sheep and will seek them out" (Ezek. 34:11). Thus the phrase characterizing the crowds as "sheep without a shepherd" reverberates not from one sounding in Israel's scriptures but from the collective witness of the interpretive tradition that portrays Moses and Moses-like figures as eschatological bearers of the "rod" and "staff" (Torah) that would shepherd God's people.[58]

To see Mark's Jesus as the one who assumes that leadership role proceeds quite naturally from the story's wilderness imagery and from the interpretive tradition that emphasizes Moses' prophetic lawgiving.[59] It is quite fitting, in this respect, that Jesus' first recourse should be to "teach

[56] Marcus, *Mark 1–8*, 417. [57] Ibid., 406.

[58] Thus Dale C. Allison, *The New Moses: A Matthean Typology* (Edinburgh: T. & T. Clark, 1993), who notes this feature "could make Jesus Mosaic" (239). Also, and more emphatically, Marcus, who contends that it is the "Mosaic aspect of the shepherd image that is most emphasized in our passage" (*Mark 1–8*, 406). Such texts as Ps. 119:176 and *2 Apoc. Bar.* 77:15, both of which connect sheep/shepherd imagery with law/commandment, certainly support the view that God has used Moses' paradigmatic leadership to guide an errant people.

[59] Guelich correctly discerns in the image of the eschatological shepherd "the Christological key to this miracle story in which Jesus provides food and table fellowship for the multitude" (*Mark 1–8:26*, 340).

them many things" (καὶ ἤρξατο διδάσκειν αὐτοὺς πολλά, Mk. 6:34b; cf. Mk. 4:1).[60] Moreover, this apparently editorial summary of Jesus' instruction advances the gospel's consistent portrait of Jesus' mission as one characterized by word and deed.[61]

To this point in the story the crowds have pursued Jesus and his disciples and have elicited a compassionate response, a diagnosis of their condition, and a front-line remedy for that condition. Only after the disciples perceive the crowd's physical hunger will Jesus shift gears to address it; his first impulse is to address, through teaching, their spiritual needs.

Scene three: Jesus responds to the disciples (Mk. 6:35–8)

At the heart of this passage lies an animated conversation boldly initiated by Jesus' disciples but decisively concluded by Jesus himself. Again, the players in view have shifted, as the crowd fades into the background while Jesus' followers step forward to identify a problem and propose a commonsense – even compassionate – solution. As has been the case in the episode's first two scenes, the story's plot moves forward only when Jesus responds to others' initiative. Yet in his reply, Jesus again assumes command of the narrative, transforming his disciples from spokesmen for scarcity to providers of abundance.

Already Jesus has answered the crowd's plight by teaching. Since we may infer that the masses have earnestly sought him in order to learn from him – his acclaim is based at least in part on his authoritative teaching – Jesus' instruction provides precisely the kind of direction the masses so desperately need.[62] But perhaps growing weary (remember, they never did get the chance to "rest a little"), Jesus' disciples approach their master with the perfect plan. Just as Jesus has recognized the disciples' nutritional needs in Mk. 6:30, they in turn address the crowd's physical privation.[63] "Since already evening has arrived," they say, "and the place is a wilderness and the hour is late,"

> ἀπόλυσον αὐτούς, ἵνα ἀπελθόντες εἰς τοὺς κύκλῳ ἀγροὺς καὶ κώμας ἀγοράσωσιν ἑαυτοῖς τί φάγωσιν. (Mk. 6:36)

[60] Hooker plausibly suggests the possibility of reading πολλά as a temporal adverb: "at length" (*Mark*, 166).

[61] Cf. Gnilka, *Markus*, I:259, who imposes an artificial fissure on the text when he maintains that Mark has subordinated the miracle to the teaching.

[62] Guelich, *Mark 1–8:26*, 340, maintains that in this act, Jesus has "fulfilled [the crowd's] wishes."

[63] Stock, *Boten*, 108.

At first blush, such a proposal exhibits not just an admirable concern for the hungering masses but a highly feasible and pragmatic action plan. What is more, the command to "send them away" equally addresses the needs of Jesus' own entourage, whose members have not yet gained the solitude that Jesus himself had envisioned for them.

Yet the caring and judicious nature of the disciples' suggestion is altogether lost on their leader, who answers with a succinct – if utterly unpragmatic – command of his own: δότε αὐτοῖς ὑμεῖς φαγεῖν (Mk. 6:37). As Marcus has observed, the emphatic pronoun ὑμεῖς may introduce a deliberate contrast with the disciples' proposal that the people obtain food "for themselves" (ἑαυτοῖς).[64] In addition, this terse imperative features the second use, in this passage, of the emphatic ὑμεῖς to convey Jesus' particular interest in his band of followers. Notably, however, while Jesus has earlier articulated their relational status as a *privilege* meriting restful withdrawal from the public eye, here he invokes that status as a *call to serve* the masses. Indeed Jesus' insistence that the *disciples* feed the crowds may well provide the interpretive key to this story of Christology and discipleship.

Especially those readers of this passage who focus exclusively on Jesus' miraculous powers tend to overlook the weighty significance of Jesus' retort. What are we to make of Jesus' expectation that the disciples should feed the crowds? Reflecting on the Lucan parallel (Lk. 19:10b–17), Jack Dean Kingsbury suggests this response:

> Shortly before, as Jesus sent out the twelve, he endowed them, too, with power and authority to preach the kingdom and to heal (9:1–2) . . . Precisely because the twelve have been endowed with power and authority, Jesus expects them to do as he has commanded and feed the five thousand . . . Within this episode, the twelve fall short of Jesus' expectations because they fail to view the situation as he does and to comprehend it aright: They do not realize that they have at their disposal the authority to do as Jesus does.[65]

To take seriously Jesus' rebuttal to his disciples affirms his expectation that they will wield that authority. After all, the command to feed the masses comes in the Markan narrative immediately on the heels of a glowing report of their success in just such an enterprise.

[64] Marcus, *Mark 1–8*, 418.

[65] Jack Dean Kingsbury, *Conflict in Luke: Jesus, Authorities, Disciples* (Minneapolis: Fortress Press, 1991), 118.

What is more, Israel's scriptures, which so influence Mark's telling of the Jesus story, freely correlate God's activity on earth with the actions of God's people. As an example of this interpenetration of divine and human horizons, post-exilic Isaiah depicts God's restorative act through language that recurs in Mark's feeding story. To begin with, the plural substantive ἔρημοι conveys the devastation that has taken place in Israel as a result of the exile,[66] and it is precisely in this place that Yahweh promises to confirm his rule. So, for instance, Isa. 61:4 utters this vision of hope: "They shall build up the ancient ruins (ἐρήμους) . . . they shall repair the ruined cities (πόλεις ἐρήμους)."

Perhaps even more to the point at hand, Isa. 58:9b–12 expresses the ethical underpinnings of such a promise:

> If you remove the yoke from among you,
> the pointing of the finger, the speaking of evil,
> if you give (δῷς) to the hungry your food (ἄρτον)
> and satisfy the needs of the afflicted,
> then your light shall rise in the darkness . . .
> The Lord will continually guide you and satisfy your needs in parched places . . .
> Your ancient ruins (αἱ ἔρημοι) shall be rebuilt . . .
> you shall be called the repairer of the breach,
> the restorer of streets to live in.

Within this interpretive trajectory, the problem posed by wilderness desolation finds its solution to be in part dependent on the actions of God's people. Thus Jesus' prophetic command to "give to them something to eat" may well extend this ethical injunction to those who have ostensibly adopted the perspective of possibility that proceeds from God's dominion.

This prophetic backdrop, which interlaces claims about God's coming redemption with its ethical implications for God's people, provides an interpretive bridge for understanding Jesus' command for the disciples to "give them something to eat." For whereas both the "original" and the eschatological manna events showcase God's provision of "something from nothing," Jesus expects the disciples to feed the crowds out of their reserves. Indeed in this feature, we can detect echoes of another prophetic biblical tradition: the story of Elisha, a servant, and a miraculous multiplication of loaves.[67]

[66] The motif of God's restoration of "desolate places" can be found throughout Isaianic prophecy. Besides passages mentioned here, see, e.g., Isa. 44:26, 51:3; 62:4.

[67] Many scholars have commented on the resemblance between these two stories, including Davies and Allison, *Saint Matthew*, II:482.

Within the unfolding drama of the Elisha narrative cycle found in 2 Kings lies the cryptic story of a "man from Baal-shalishah" who brings an array of foodstuffs to the "man of God" during a time of famine. Their brief encounter occupies a mere three verses, and its placement in the midst of much more elaborately recounted events – such as the reviving of the Shunammite woman's son earlier in the same chapter – helps the story fade into the background of the Elisha cycle. Yet even its brief plot and succinct wording exhibit affinities with the first Mark feeding story.[68] Indeed, just where the Exodus typology "breaks down" – especially in the role of supporting characters and in the outcome of abundance – we find the most striking parallel features in the Elisha narrative.[69]

Such common background in the relationship between master and servant/disciples paves the way for a Markan plotline that closely parallels the elements of the Elisha feeding account:[70]

	2 Kings	Mark
Statement of need	(4:38)	6:34–5
Command to feed	4:42	6:37a
Protest of inadequacy	4:43a	6:37b
Appeal to divine	4:43b	6:41a
Feeding and results	4:44	6:41b–4

Both passages move from a similar problem (vast nutritional need) to a similarly surprising solution (not just sufficiency but abundance). Along the way, the leading figure first commands his servant/disciples to provide for the masses, next entertains predictable protests, and then overrules

[68] The narrative kinship that Mark's gospel shares with the Elijah/Elisha cycle has been examined by Wolfgang Roth, *Hebrew Gospel: Cracking the Code of Mark* (Oak Park, IL: Meyer-Stone Books), 1988, who argues that the storyline present in 1 Kgs. 17–2 Kgs. 13 serves as the "conceptual-narrative paradigm" for the second gospel. Roth perhaps goes too far in his claim to have "cracked the code" of Mark and especially in his view of the feeding stories as haggadic midrashim on 2 Kgs. 4:42–4. Yet he does offer the helpful reminder that the gospel was composed not only in a historical context but also in relation to the "primary matrix of early Christian reflection and writing: the Hebrew Scriptures" (3). Indeed, even scholars who maintain closer connections between Mk. 6:32–44 and the Exodus narrative concede the Elisha story as a narrative backdrop. See, for example, Marcus, *Mark 1–8*, 407: "Despite the similarity to the manna miracle . . . the analogy is imperfect, because the food does not come out of nothing . . . This feature derives from a different OT source, the stories about Elijah and Elisha . . . and especially 2 Kgs. 4:42–4."

[69] It should be noted here that to detect in the Elijah/Elisha cycle a complementary precursor text is not to go so far afield after all. Allison reviews the biblical and extra-biblical evidence that identifies Elijah as a "second Moses" and finds that "Elijah was overlaid with Moses' features largely because his life and ministry were understood to correspond to Deut. 18:15 and 18: he was in the line of the prophets like Moses" (*New Moses*, 45).

[70] This chart is my own version of similar charts found in Davies and Allison, *Saint Matthew*, II:482, and Marcus, *Mark 1–8*, 415–16.

objections by appealing, overtly or implicitly, to God. Ultimately, both the servant and the disciples perform the task conferred upon them: they "give to them/the people [something] to eat."

Chief among the stories' parallel features is the figure who stands at the center of the text. In Mark's gospel, the baptism of Jesus by John (noted by many as an Elijah-like character) serves as the authorization and starting point for Jesus' ministry. Thus, according to Roth, "the beginning of Jesus' public activity corresponds to that of Elisha."[71] Both will proceed on a mission that entails miracle-working as a vivid demonstration of God's rule upon the earth.[72] But critical to understanding these divine emissaries is another shared feature of the two miracle stories: neither Elisha nor Jesus acts alone. Just as Elisha enlists the help of his "servant" in the feeding of the one hundred, Jesus looks to his disciples to provide for the five thousand.

Particularly striking is the close verbal resemblance that Jesus' command to his disciples shares with Elisha's command to his servant:

4 Kgdms. 4:42	δότε	τῷ λαῷ		καὶ ἐσθιέτωσαν
Mk. 6:37	δότε	αὐτοῖς	ὑμεῖς	φαγεῖν

This parallel structure casts in stark relief Mark's insertion of the emphatic pronoun ὑμεῖς; as I have discussed above, the pronoun apparently reflects the special relationship the disciples share with their master. In light of the Elisha story, Jesus' charge for his disciples to "give them something to eat" must be viewed not as a deliberate foil to his provision, but as a straightforward expectation that his followers will, like Elisha's servant, serve a meal to the hungry.

To take seriously Jesus' command for his disciples to feed the people introduces an important and neglected dimension into the discussion of the disciples' failure. For if we encounter within this story the Markan motif of Jesus' "fallible followers," it can be located most precisely in their impotent response to Jesus' command:

> ἀπελθόντες ἀγοράσωμεν δηναρίων διακοσίων ἄρτους καὶ δώσομεν αὐτοῖς φαγεῖν; (Mk. 6:37b)

Notably, neither the disciples' language nor their outlook has changed as a result of Jesus' imperative, as the highlighted verbs simply repeat the rhetorical framework of their initial proposal that the crowds "go

71 Roth, *Hebrew Gospel*, 11. Above I have examined the Elijah/Elisha narrative as template for Jesus' initial call to discipleship

72 Ibid., 9: "the train of events set into motion by Elisha's commissioning by Elijah . . . eventually led to the reestablishment of the Lord's sovereignty."

away," "buy," and "eat." (Mk. 6:36).[73] Impaired by their assessment of inadequate resources, the disciples fail to perceive what God would do *through them* at this wilderness meal. Here their reply reveals not that they misunderstand Jesus' identity, but that they fail to embrace Jesus' call to provide food for the crowd.

Once again, the scriptural backdrop casts helpful light on Mark's own theological agenda. In the first place, the disciples' complaint of insurmountable dearth sounds distinctly like the problem voiced by the grumbling Israelites in Exod. 16. There, the band of freed slaves boldly accuses Moses, "you have brought us out into this wilderness to kill this whole assembly with hunger" (Exod. 16:3). Like the Israelites, the disciples murmur against their leader in the wilderness, because they are convinced that ample food is lacking.

If Jesus' followers sound like God's people after the first Exodus event, they also seem to ignore the possibilities promised in Second Isaiah's vision of an eschatological wilderness feast. Notably, Mark's language here hints, if only allusively, at the eschatological wilderness feast depicted in Isa. 55, as the following chart illustrates:[74]

Isaiah 55:1	Mark 6:37
. . . you that have no money,	Are we to go and buy . . . bread,
come, buy and eat.	and give it to them to eat?

While the prophet summons his hearers to participate in a feast provided "without money and without cost" (Isa. 55:1), Jesus' disciples maintain that the only way to "give them something to eat" is to enter the marketplace and spend money they do not have. In this respect they have failed to grasp Jesus' message of sufficiency, even abundance, that is in evidence when one trusts the hopeful promise of God's coming kingdom.

Finally, the disciples' dispute elaborates the vague incredulity expressed by Elisha's servant: "How shall I give this before a hundred men?" (2 Kgs. 4:43). While the servant responds to his master's unfeasible command with the interrogative pronoun מָה/τι, Jesus' disciples offer a sarcastic retort that sheds full light on their perspective of scarcity. As a result, Mark highlights their shortcoming, which consists in an obtuse unwillingness to trust God's provision in the face of apparent lack.

Yet perhaps the story's greatest surprise consists in Jesus' response to the disciples' failure on this note, for Jesus neither adopts their insufficient

[73] Gnilka, *Markus*, I:260, aptly recognizes in their proposal a glimpse at their misunderstanding.

[74] Richard Schneck, *Isaiah in the Gospel of Mark, I–VIII*, BIBAL Dissertation Series 1 (Vallejo, CA: BIBAL Press, 1994), 154.

outlook nor dismisses them so he can demonstrate God's power apart from them. Instead, he solicits their own resources by asking, πόσους ἄρτους ἔχετε; ὑπάγετε ἴδετε (Mk. 6:38). In this narrative twist, Jesus' question reflects a notable departure from the Elisha story, where the loaves and grain to be shared belong to a peripheral figure and are readily available at the story's outset. By contrast, Jesus' disciples in the Markan story play an even greater role in the feeding: not only are they to work the miracle of serving dinner to the throngs, but they are also to rely on their own resources to do so.

Ultimately, the story's transformation of the disciples from foils to agents of Jesus' visionary solution occurs when they return with a report of their inventory. Though Jesus has commanded them only to tally their loaves, the disciples supplement their "five loaves" with "two fish." In this rather modest narrative detail, they have taken a first step toward participation in the eschatological feast Jesus seems determined to orchestrate.

Besides simply expanding the menu to be served to the crowds, the disciples' offering of fish calls to mind, if only suggestively, the occasional mention of fish within the proto-wilderness story as well as its anticipated reenactment. For, as Marcus has demonstrated, both biblical and post-biblical texts mention "fish" as a dietary counterpart to God's provision of manna.[75] Within the biblical tradition, to be sure, the association is a negative one, as the grumbling Israelites lament their deprived state: "If only we had meat to eat! We remember the fish (ἰχθύας) we used to eat in Egypt for nothing . . . but now our strength is dried up, and there is nothing to eat at all but this manna" (Num. 11:4–6). When God promises meat in staggering and sickening amounts, Moses challenges God's feeding abilities: "Are there enough flocks and herds to slaughter for them? Are there enough fish in the sea to catch for them?" (Num. 11:22). Later traditions such as *2 Apoc. Bar.* 29:4 announce the eschatological hope that "Behemoth will reveal itself from its place, and Leviathan will come from the sea . . . And they will be nourishment for all who are left." Since these references are scant, and in the case of *2 Baruch* also late, we should exercise caution about reading too much into the disciples' addition here.

Still, though the story will lend prominence to the "five loaves" perhaps because of their important symbolism,[76] we should not gloss too glibly over the disciples' introduction of fish to be provided in the ensuing miraculous feeding. At the very least, the introduction of fish functions at the narrative level to demonstrate the disciples' own initiative; Jesus has

[75] Marcus, *Mark 1–8*, 410–11. [76] Ibid., 407.

asked about loaves, and they have provided both loaves and fish. In this instance they seem to have turned from the perspective of scarcity that plagued them just two verses earlier and to trust in the more expansive vision of God's eschatological provision in the wilderness. In this sense, the disciples here heed Jesus' opening summons to "repent, and believe in the gospel" (Mk. 1:15).

Scene four: the wilderness feeding (Mk. 6:39–41)

Once Jesus and his disciples have concluded their assessment of available resources, the narrative focus widens again to include the entire crowd. In Mk. 6:39–41, the story reaches a climax, as Jesus steps forward to preside over the feeding of the multitude. Notably, for the first time in this scene, Jesus initiates the actions rather than responding to his interlocutors, and a close examination of his deeds reveals a portrait of one who authoritatively performs a deliberate task.

Again, the story contrasts with its Exodus precursor in seemingly significant ways. For instance, whereas the wilderness account portrays both the leader Moses and the people of Israel as passive recipients of the explicitly divine and strikingly miraculous feeding, Mark's feeding of the five thousand finds both Jesus and his disciples in the foreground of the feeding action. The actions of Jesus throughout the narrative depict a strong protagonist who directs the unfolding plot.[77]

Notice the following series of actions: Jesus commands the disciples to "give them something to eat" (Mk. 6:32); he asks about their resources (Mk. 6:38); he orders the people to sit down in the green grass (Mk. 6:39); taking the loaves and fish, he looks up to heaven and blesses and breaks them and gives them to the disciples to set before the people (Mk. 6:41); and he divides the two fish among them all (Mk. 6:41). Yet although Mark portrays Jesus as a formidable presence in this scene, his select group of followers appears with him in the foreground, working actively with their leader to supply the meal by multiplying the loaves. I turn attention now to the nature of the meal that is shared before returning to the collaborative partnership that characterizes Mark's account of the feeding.

Under careful examination, several details included in Mark's rather methodical report of the feeding event together confirm the story's earlier, more muted sketch of this meal as an eschatological wilderness banquet.

[77] Guelich, *Mark 1–8:26*, 339: "[The disciples] remain in the scene, but Jesus emerges as the primary subject of what follows." I would simply add that a quick review of the battery of Jesus' actions reveals that, in most cases, he involves the disciples in his work.

To begin with, Jesus orders his disciples to have the people "recline" in preparation for the feast (Mk. 6:39a). As Jeremias has argued, while such an action in the ancient world was associated with banqueting in general, in a Jewish context it suggested the particular celebration of a festival meal, especially the Passover meal.[78] At the very least, we can infer from Mark's account that this command for the people to recline signals a ceremonial celebration of a significant meal.

When Jesus further specifies that the people should recline "group by group" (Mk. 6:39), Mark's carefully crafted choice of words highlights the elaborate nature of this meal. Not only does the distributive phrase συμπόσια συμπόσια appear to reflect an underlying Semitism, but its lexical meaning also conveys an important facet of the crowd's participation in this feast. Although the word occurs here as a NT *hapax legomenon*, its use may reflect an appropriation – and radical transformation – of contemporary secular language. Etymologically, συμπόσια means "drinking together" and is employed in Greek thought as a gathering for the purposes of philosophical instruction.[79] Moreover, Stein has demonstrated that the Jewish seder meal had adapted features of the Greek symposium, so that the word use here may reflect the convergence of Mark's Jewish and Greco-Roman settings.[80] Drawing on Exodus imagery, the evangelist expresses this wilderness gathering as an event imbued with theological significance.

The rather odd mention of "green grass" as the gathering site for the meal has been explained variously as a vestige of first-hand recollection,[81] a reference to the eschatological age characterized by a fertile wilderness,[82] the springtime Passover setting,[83] or an elaboration of Jesus as the "shepherd" who leads the sheep "in green pastures."[84] In fact, such a variety of allusions need not be mutually exclusive, since even personal recollection may combine with the detail's other dimensions to stage the feeding as an eschatological event demonstrating God's dominion in which even the wilderness blossoms.

[78] Joachim Jeremias, *Eucharistic Words of Jesus* (Philadelphia: Fortress Press, 1966), 48–9, relies on rabbinic literature to distinguish between the first-century Jewish practice of sitting for common meals and reclining for ceremonial meals. Though his sources are later, they probably reflect the Jewish people's earlier appropriation of Greco-Roman habits for their own religious purposes.

[79] E.g. Plato's *Symposium*.

[80] S. Stein, "The Influence of Symposia Literature on the Literary Form of the Haggadah," *JJS* 7 (1957): 13–44.

[81] Schmidt, *Mark*, 191; Taylor, *Saint Mark*, 321.

[82] Gerhard Friedrich Erlangen, "Die beiden Erzählungen von der Speisung in Markus 6,31–44, 8,1–9," *TZ* 20 (1964): 18–20.

[83] Gnilka, *Markus*, I:260.

[84] van Iersel, "Die Wunderbare Speisung," 188.

This image of a fertile wilderness where God subverts scarcity in favor of abundance can be found in the passage's second, and somewhat redundant, mention of the crowd's configuration, as the following verse reports, καὶ ἀνέπεσαν πρασιαὶ πρασιαί (Mk. 6:40). Again, Mark employs a distinctive term to express the careful subdivision of a massive crowd into groups described metaphorically as "garden beds" – an agricultural image which in rabbinic literature depicts the lining up of students before their teacher.[85] An even more apposite parallel for the Markan setting can be found in the QL, which portrays the end-time chosen people as a "shoot of the eternal planting" in the desert (1QH 8:5–11).

Such an eschatological bent is reflected too in the numbering of groups of "fifties and one hundreds" (Mk. 6:40). Precisely the same terms describe the military camps of Israelites in the wilderness in Exod. 18:21, 25 and in Deut. 1:15, though the OT texts add groups of thousands on the one hand and tens on the other. And beyond the biblical era, these figures appear in Qumran documents to specify the sectaries' end-time groupings (1QSa 2:11–22), which Allison claims "sought to reproduce the organization of Israel's wilderness period."[86]

The story's detailed exposition of the crowd's posture, their arrangement, and their environment, then, casts the multitudes in the role of guests at God's kingly banquet. In their pursuit of Jesus and his disciples, the masses have sought spiritual nourishment in the form of instruction; now, and in response to the disciples' original concern, they are poised to partake in a meal that will supply their physical cravings. After carefully seating the crowds, Mark turns attention to the host and his assistants who together mediate God's miraculous feeding, "without money and without cost" (Isa. 55:1).

The nature of that feeding is the subject of Mk. 6:41, which serves as the moment toward which the entire feeding story presses. Here all eyes are on Jesus, who has called forth the disciples' on-hand reserves and now presides over their distribution to the people. Yet it is here too that close attention to the text reveals a critical role for the disciples, who become an extension of Jesus' ministry to the multitudes.

What can we infer from Jesus' actions at this critical narrative juncture? To begin with, several features of the verse reflect contemporary Jewish practice, where the *pater familias* would take bread in hand to begin a commonplace meal. The view that Jesus' looking "up toward heaven"

[85] See Marcus, *Mark 1–8*, 408, following J. Bolyki, "Menge–Tischgemeinschaft–Gruppe," *Communio Viatorum* 24 (1992): 20–6.

[86] Allison, *New Moses*, 239.

represents a departure from normal Jewish piety and thus reflects a special request for special help in the performance of a miracle[87] ignores the evidence from first-century literature which describes a similar posture (e.g. Lk. 18:13; Josephus, *Ant.* 11.56). Thus we have no solid grounds for doubting that Jesus here follows current custom as he begins a meal by blessing the God who has provided the bread (see *m. Ber.* 6:1).

A more pressing question, though, is whether Mark's account of Jesus' actions provides an adequate basis for construing this meal as a veiled but deliberate reference to the Eucharist. Certainly, the language and phrasing found in Mk. 6:41 closely parallel the Last Supper liturgy reflected in Mk. 14:22, Lk. 22:19, and 1 Cor. 11:24.[88] Moreover, the preliminary details that Mark's feeding story shares with the Last Supper narrative (Mk. 14:17–23) – specifically the late hour and the reclining posture – seem to indicate that the evangelist perceived the two meals in relation to one another.

Telling against a precisely Eucharistic reading of the Markan feeding narratives, though, are the stories' noteworthy differences. For instance, Mk. 6:30–44 lacks any mention of wine as well as any direct claims about Jesus' relationship to the bread (i.e. "this is my body").[89] And in terms of didactic focus, whereas the Eucharistic meal makes direct reference to Jesus' self-giving sacrifice, the feeding narrative attributes the loaves at hand to the disciples, not Jesus. Thus while the Jewish meal provides a common pattern upon which both the feeding and the Last Supper narratives are structured, we need not conclude that the miracle of the loaves is meant precisely to suggest a Eucharistic liturgy.[90]

To deny that Mark here specifically intends to portray a Eucharistic meal, however, does not mean we should overlook the interrelated nature of the two meals. Ironically, the feeding story's divergence from the Last Supper account suggests important interpretive links between the two. For instance, the disciples' provision and distribution of their own loaves suggests that they here anticipate Jesus' pattern of self-giving sacrifice.[91]

[87] See, e.g., Pesch, *Markusevangelium*, I:352–3.

[88] See Marcus, *Mark 1–8*, 410, figure 15, for a chart that presents the verses in parallel.

[89] For a discussion of the differences, see especially Boobyer, "Eucharistic Interpretation," 161–71; also Gnilka, *Markus*, I:261.

[90] Against Marcus, *Mark 1–8*, 409, it seems plausible, and supported by the literary witness to non-eucharistic meals (e.g. Acts 27:35), that the later evangelists' faithfulness to the tradition of Mk. 6:41–2 reflects the fixed pattern of Jewish meals rather than that of the Last Supper liturgy.

[91] Jouette M. Bassler has suggested that, because the gospel's second half increasingly emphasizes Jesus' self-sacrifice, the "implied reader" can retrospectively "recognize what was opaque [earlier in] the narrative: that on some inchoate level the loaves referred to

At the heart of the story's feeding act lies a carefully nuanced report of Jesus' continued interaction with his disciples as those who "give them something to eat." Already I have noted the parallel structure of a master's command for his servants to feed the people. But Mark's description of the feeding itself, found in Mk. 6:41, features yet another discernible departure from the Elisha story. On the one hand, both miraculous accounts hinge on the transformation of the servant/disciples who will provide for the hungry crowds. But how is that change accomplished? In the Elisha feeding, the prophet relies on the authority of the "word of the Lord," expressed through the citation formula כֹּה אָמַר יְהוָה/τάδε λέγει κύριος (2 Kgs. 4:43) to convert the servant and thus address the people's need.

But the Markan feeding story strays from this pattern in two respects. In the first place, Jesus appeals to God in a manner that is as dramatic as it is subtle:

> καὶ λαβὼν τοὺς πέντε ἄρτους καὶ τοὺς δύο ἰχθύας ἀναβλέψας εἰς τὸν οὐρανὸν εὐλόγησεν καὶ κατέκλασεν τοὺς ἄρτους καὶ ἐδίδου τοῖς μαθηταῖς αὐτοῦ ἵνα παρατιθῶσιν αὐτοῖς, καὶ τοὺς δύο ἰχθύας ἐμέρισεν πᾶσιν. (Mk. 6:41)

By "looking up toward heaven" and by "blessing" the loaves and fish, Jesus expresses through action and posture his gratitude toward the One who has provided the meal. The involvement of God in this feeding enterprise is beyond question; here Jesus offers his companions a tacit but profound reminder of the King who presides over this feast.

Moreover, while Elisha fades into the background as his servant carries out his command, Jesus remains front and center, actively working alongside his disciples to meet the need before them. The emerging portrait of discipleship is one of vital participation in which Jesus empowers the Twelve to perform the miracle (to be "sent out") not in his stead but working in concert (being "with him") with this eschatological shepherd (see Mk. 3:14).[92]

Jesus' broken body" ("The Parable of the Loaves," *JR* 66 [1986]: 168). The claim here, supported by the narrative development in the gospel's central section, seems to underscore the disciples' *participation* in Jesus' self-giving mission, not just their *recognition* of it.

[92] Stock notes the disciples' "vermittelnde Stellung zwischen Jesus und dem Volk" (*Boten*, 108) and describes it this way: "die Jünger bestimmt sind zum Dienst am Volk und wie sie für diesen Dienst ganz und gar von Jesus abhängig sind" (109). Witherington calls it "on-the-job training" (*Mark*, 219).

The imperfect verb ἐδίδου conveys the prolonged time frame of Jesus' "giving" of loaves to the disciples;[93] less clear is whether the repetition occurs throughout the entire feeding or simply long enough for each of the Twelve to be supplied with bread. Following Schweizer, Marcus opts for the former and translates the phrase "[he] kept giving them to the disciples."[94] Yet Mark uses the exact same imperfect form of the verb earlier in the chapter to describe a parallel imparting of power from Jesus to the disciples: "He called the twelve and began to send them out two by two, and gave (ἐδίδου) them authority over the unclean spirits" (Mk. 6:7). Both the proximity of this verse and its thematic interest in the disciples provide important interpretive clues for our understanding of Jesus' "giving" in Mk. 6:40, where once again, Jesus deliberately involves his followers in a dramatic demonstration of God's kingly rule.

As the narrative's zenith, the feeding itself thus provides a critical snapshot of the evangelist's portrait of discipleship as a collective extension of Jesus' own divinely sanctioned mission. In the previous section, we detected the disciples' initiative toward the people in a time of need as well as their faithful response to Jesus' call for resources. Here as the people are fed, the disciples join Jesus as mediating agents of God's eschatological provision. Having moved beyond their initial perspective of scarcity, the disciples step forward in Mark's story as useful (if flawed) vessels, active participants in the wilderness banquet that Jesus inaugurates and over which he so authoritatively presides.

Scene five: a satisfied crowd (Mk. 6:42–4)

The episode reaches its denouement with the concluding report about the crowd's satisfaction, the overabundance of the provision, and the numbering of the men fed. In each detail, the feeding's outcome could be said to surpass any measure of sufficiency; indeed, the rhetorical force of this summation only underscores the magnitude of this wilderness feeding.[95]

[93] As James Hope Moulton notes, the "augment throws linear action into the past" (*A Grammar of New Testament Greek*, 3rd edn. [Edinburgh: T. & T. Clark, 1930], 128).

[94] Marcus, *Mark 1–8*, 409. He also notes that the word "unlike other verbs in the passage, is in the imperfect tense, perhaps to indicate the repetition of the action because the supply of eucharistic loaves is never exhausted" (410). Maximilian Zerwick takes it a step further to claim that the imperfect deliberately stresses that "the multiplication thus took place in the hands of Our Lord Himself " (*Biblical Greek*, trans. Joseph Smith [Rome: Pontifical Institute, 1963], 91).

[95] According to Roth, *Hebrew Gospel*, 8, since "[m]ore people are fed, a larger number of servants are used, more is left over, and fewer loaves are used," Mark's Jesus "manifestly accomplishes a greater feat [than Elisha does] since he does so with fewer loaves and

Notably, the first basis on which the feeding act is assessed is the satisfaction of the crowds. The point of the story, at least as Mark reports it, concerns not the proper understanding of Jesus' identity but the feeding of the people. The report that "all ate and were satisfied" (Mk. 6:42) may fulfill the promise not only of Deut. 8:10 ("and you shall eat and be full"),[96] but also that of God's satisfying presence expressed poetically in Ps. 132:14–15 (131:14–15, LXX): "This is my resting place forever; here will I reside, for I have desired it. Its provisions I will surely bless; its poor I will satisfy with loaves."

The surfeit of loaves becomes evident in the following verse in our story, where Mark reports, "they took up twelve baskets full of broken pieces and of the fish" (Mk. 6:43). The evangelist leaves unspecified the antecedent for the pronoun "they," which could indicate that Jesus and the disciples, or even the people themselves, take up the twelve baskets of fragments.[97] While the quantity may simply indicate that each of the Twelve filled his own travel basket with remnants, the fact that Mark specifically mentions the number probably continues the passage's portrait of an end-time gathering that affords a special role to the twelve tribes as well as its Exodus typology (cf. the twelve springs of water at Elim, Exod. 15:27a).

I should note one final respect in which Mark's account departs significantly from the Exodus parallel, and it is in turn a point at which the story resonates once again with the Elisha narrative. The Pentateuchal wilderness account explicitly stresses the sufficiency of the manna, as the narrator claims, "But when they measured [the manna] with an omer, those who gathered much did not have more than enough, and those who gathered less did not have too little. They gathered as much as each one needed" (Exod. 16:18). Against this backdrop of miraculous adequacy, Mark's feeding story culminates in a markedly different outcome: the scene ends with the collection of "twelve baskets full of broken pieces and of the fish" (Mk. 6:43), sketching an indelible image of lavish abundance.

Conclusion

While Mk. 6:30–44 has traditionally been read and interpreted as a Christological tale meant to expose Jesus' messianic identity as he presides over

sustains more people." We should exercise caution, though, in attributing this intensified miracle to a motive of "one-upmanship" on the part of the evangelist.

[96] See Marcus, *Mark 1–8*, 421; Schmidt, *Mark*, 83.

[97] Gundry sees the disciples' involvement in this collection as an anomaly: "Apart from the disciples' bearing witness to this superabundance . . . their role is kept in the shadows" (*Mark*, 326).

this miraculous feeding, the present study of the text as well as its precursor traditions has demonstrated the story's tightly interwoven themes of Christology and discipleship. I may summarize the findings with respect to the variegated literary backdrop against which Mark has crafted this version of a familiar story.

(1) A comparison of the Markan story with its parallel account in Jn. 6 has illuminated the dynamic role the second evangelist assigns to Jesus' disciples in this episode. While John casts the feeding of the five thousand as a deliberate showcase for Jesus' stupendous prescience and powers, Mark's rendering sketches a much more lively interaction between a master (who ultimately presides over the narrative) and his servants (whom he ultimately transforms into co-workers for the task). The disciples first mention the crowds' hunger; the disciples supply their own loaves for the feeding; the disciples expand the feast's menu; and the disciples mediate the miracle. While Jesus presides over the meal in a magisterial manner, he also insists unrelentingly that his followers participate actively in the feeding miracle.

(2) The Exodus motif provides indispensable interpretive clues as well. On the one hand, Mark's narrative shares with the Exodus feeding story a plotline that progresses from hunger to divine provision. Moreover, key images and verbal ties such as a wilderness setting, the image of a sheep without a shepherd, and the numbering of both loaves and groups prompt the reader to understand this wilderness feeding as a reenactment of that formative scriptural event. And within that narrative context, Mark portrays Jesus as a Moses-like leader who shepherds God's people both by instruction and by demonstrating God's saving power in the wilderness.

Yet while the Exodus tradition dramatizes God's provision of "something from nothing," Mark's feeding story leaves no doubt about the source of the supply of loaves and fish that feed the crowd. And in contrast to the first wilderness feeding's emphasis on sufficiency, Mk. 6:30–44 ends on a note of staggering surplus. Thus in addition to its resonance with the Exodus paradigm, the Markan story offers its own hermeneutical commentary on the eschatological wilderness meal.

(3) In a complementary fashion, the Markan feeding miracle exhibits undeniable parallels with the Elisha narrative found in 2 Kgs. 4. Especially in its emphasis on the servants' role, the use of resources at hand, and the overabundance of food, the stories' similarities are too striking to be a matter of coincidence: both bear witness to the claim that a limited human appraisal of reality is not ultimately to be trusted. Where there are both ample hunger and restricted quantities, God mysteriously introduces kingdom bounty. Taken together, both the Markan passage and the Elisha

episode undermine any conventional understanding of resource allocation while offering the hope of abundance to all who contend with apparent lack. In this way, the Elisha paradigm offers a model not found in the Exodus tradition.

Yet Mark departs from the Elisha storyline in significant respects as well. Perhaps most noteworthy is the relationship between the respective leaders and their bands of followers. For while Elisha recedes from view once his servant is summoned to feed the one hundred men, Mark's Jesus remains not just present with his disciples but at the head of the table, both directing and participating fully in the staggering provision of excess loaves and fish for the hungering crowds. Mark's story is no passing of the baton from one leader/shepherd to another; Mark portrays the transmission of divine power in terms of participation, as Mark's feeding account finds the disciples working side-by-side with their master. Thus this story holds together the parallel strands of the disciples' calling to be "with Jesus" and to be "sent out" (see Mk. 3:14).

These synthetic findings, then, point the way toward a fuller appreciation of Mark's story, particularly as it sheds new light on our understanding of the gospel's portrait of discipleship. By weaving the eschatological feast motif together with the apostles' active participation, Mark effectively stages not just the in-breaking kingdom of God but also Jesus' fruitful collaboration with those who have answered his call to discipleship. As portrayed in Mark's gospel, the feeding of the five thousand offers a compelling witness both to the messianic purpose of Jesus and to the transforming power of his presence for those who would join in his work.

7

DISCIPLESHIP AS (FOILED) PRACTICE: THE MOTIF OF INCOMPREHENSION IN MARK 6:45–52[1]

Introduction

Immediately following the miraculous feeding in the wilderness, Jesus dismisses both his co-workers and the crowds and goes up to the mountain to pray. In their being-with-Jesus, the disciples have been transformed into agents of God's staggering surplus of food for the masses; in the wake of such success, Jesus now purposefully removes them from his presence. As we shall see, Mark recounts the second sea-crossing story (Mk. 6:45–52) in a manner that depicts that sea-bound journey as a second "sending out": just as in Mk. 6:7–13 they have effectively wielded the authority of God's dominion upon the earth, here Jesus compels them to embark on a sea crossing as fully endowed agents of that same dominion over the sea. As Origen puts it, "The Savior thus compelled the disciples to enter into the boat of testing and to go before him to the other side, so to learn victoriously to pass through difficulties."[2]

But this time, in stark contrast to Mark's account of their first missionary journey (Mk. 6:12–13), the disciples fail the test miserably, proving unable in this instance to display the authority over demons they have so effectively demonstrated earlier. Their downfall, moreover, entails a double lapse. In the first place, as they are tormented while rowing, the disciples exhibit incompetence against the threat of an adversarial wind, which in Mark's apocalyptic mindset represents the opposing powers of the present evil age. Yet such a weakness is only compounded as Jesus offers a second-chance reminder of the strength available to them. With their fearful outcry, the disciples rebuff Jesus' attempt to empower them.

Ultimately, Mark's editorial conclusion goes so far as to signal the disciples' failure as the interpretive crux of the outing: "For they did

[1] This chapter represents an expansion of my article originally published as "'Concerning the Loaves': Comprehending Incomprehension in Mark 6.45–52," *JSNT* 83 (2001): 3–26.

[2] Origen, *Commentary on Matthew* 11.5, in *The Ante-Nicene Fathers: Translations of the Writings of the Fathers down to AD 325*, 5th edn., ed. A. Menzies (Grand Rapids, MI: Eerdmans, 1978), 10:435.

not understand concerning the loaves, for their hearts were hardened" (Mk. 6:52). Their incomprehension "concerning the loaves," Mark seems to suggest, explains both their initial paralysis at sea and their failure to grasp Jesus' best effort to address their plight.

In this chapter, I shall examine the second Markan sea-crossing story with particular attention to its rendering of discipleship as *practice* – practice which in this case falls undeniably short. More precisely, I shall consider the nature of the disciples' incomprehension: if this passage represents a "negative" example of discipleship,[3] in what ways does Mark portray and underscore their lapses? As we shall see, the enigmatic claim of Mk. 6:52, "for they did not understand concerning the loaves," links the disciples' failure to the preceding pericope in a way that casts that failure in terms of their intended role within Jesus' own proclamation of God's coming kingdom.[4]

The incomprehension motif

The significance of the second Markan sea-crossing story (Mk. 6:45–52) as a critical clue to the theme of incomprehension in the second gospel has not been overlooked by scholars, for many have recognized that the verse includes the first use of the verb συνίημι to characterize the disciples: οὐ γὰρ συνῆκαν ἐπὶ τοῖς ἄρτοις.[5] Moreover, this first explicit mention of their "not understanding" has been widely affirmed by interpreters as evidence of the evangelist's increasing narrative disapprobation toward Jesus' followers.[6] Even scholars such as Focant who prefer to categorize

[3] See David M. Rhoads, "Narrative Criticism and the Gospel of Mark," *JAAR* 50 (1982): 418, who credits Weeden with focusing interpretive attention on the gospel's negative portrayal of the disciples. Even those who do not adopt wholesale Weeden's polemical reading affirm what is at best a mixed representation of the disciples.

[4] My approach here resembles Quentin Quesnell's: "Working only from the immediate context of the pericope and of the preceding pericope to which the verse itself refers has not given a satisfactory meaning for 6,52" (*The Mind of Mark: Interpretation and Method through the Exegesis of Mark 6,52* [Rome: Pontifical Biblical Institute, 1969], 68). Thus, my investigation builds on the findings about discipleship in Mark's gospel prior to this point in the story.

[5] The verb's only prior occurrence in the gospel can be found in Mk. 4:11, where it characterizes "those outside" in sharp contrast with those identified as ὑμῖν, or Jesus' inner circle.

[6] In addition to Theodore J. Weeden's detection of a three-stage progression from imperceptivity to misconception to rejection ("The Heresy That Necessitated Mark's Gospel," *ZNW* 59 [1968]: 145–58), see Camille Focant, "L'Incompréhension des disciples dans le deuxième évangile," *RB* 82 (1975): 185; also David J. Hawkin, "Incomprehension of the Disciples in the Marcan Redaction," *JBL* 91 (1972): 496, for similar construals of the disciples' mounting obduracy.

more narrowly the disciples' faltering responses to Jesus find in Mk. 6:52 a patent example of their incomprehension.[7]

Yet despite this widespread consensus about the passage's indispensable role in understanding Mark's portrait of discipleship, the pericope itself belies any clear construal of the incomprehension motif. In its allusion to "the loaves," Mk. 6:52 both hints at the nature of the disciples' misunderstanding *and* refuses to pinpoint exactly what it is that they have failed to grasp. Perhaps for this reason, Haenchen introduces the pericope as "einer der überlieferungsgeschichtlich interessantesten Abschnitte in den Evangelien."[8]

The elusive and perplexing nature of this verse has captivated the interpretive imagination of countless exegetes who have produced a range of tenable if not wholly convincing proposals about the precise meaning of this reference to the disciples' incomprehension. Foremost among attempts to decipher Mk. 6:52 is Quentin Quesnell's monograph *The Mind of Mark*. Based on the centrality of bread, not fish, in the early Christian Eucharist, Quesnell contends that the disciples have misunderstood the eucharistic implications of the feeding.[9] While this thesis has garnered significant support among interpreters, Quesnell himself identifies what can be considered its Achilles' heel:

> 6,52 introduces certain points which may be parts of larger themes (the non-understanding, the bread, the hardened hearts). It does not simply touch on these in passing, but drags them in, apparently without need, and adds them to a scene which seemed to make perfectly good sense in itself and to have its own point and form.[10]

In other words, Mark's own interpretation as presented in Mk. 6:52 (or at least in Quesnell's reading of it) complicates rather than clarifies the relationship between the disciples' sea voyage itself and this concluding diagnosis of their incomprehension.

Other, less exhaustive studies have suggested various interpretive options for Mk. 6:52. For instance, Matera posits that the disciples failed

[7] Focant argues that "il est abusif de vouloir tour ramener au thème de l'Incompréhension proprement dite" ("L'Incompréhension," 163). He distinguishes three terms, "la crainte," "l'étonnement," and "l'incompréhension" and sees only the last as characterizing blamable human behavior.

[8] E. Haenchen, *Der Weg Jesu: Eine Erklärung des Markus-Evangeliums und der kanonischen Parallelen* (Berlin: Alfred Töpelmann, 1966), 251.

[9] Quesnell, *Mind of Mark*, 268–70. [10] Ibid., 66–7.

to "recognize Jesus as the Shepherd Messiah,"[11] while Lane suggests that the disciples' failure to understand the miracle of the loaves prevented them from recognizing "Jesus' identity as the sovereign Lord who walks upon the waves of the sea."[12] Some scholars openly concede frustration at the verse's apparent impenetrability; Marcus calls Mk. 6:52 "difficult to understand,"[13] while Taylor claims that it may indicate "embarrassment on the part of the narrator."[14]

Underlying this wide range of possible readings lies a critical, though not yet sufficiently examined, presupposition: the notion that what the disciples have misunderstood concerns the identity of Jesus. As Schmahl puts it, "Das Thema des Jüngerunverständnisses führt also bei Markus hin zur Kernfrage des Evangeliums überhaupt, zur Frage nach der Person und Sendung Jesu: das Thema ist selber ein *christologisches* Motiv."[15] Certainly in the wake of Wrede's immense influence over twentieth-century readers of Mark's gospel, such a Christological focus is understandable. After all, Wrede's study sifted the second gospel's content according to post-resurrection claims about Jesus' messianic identity with the result that every Markan motif, including the disciples' incomprehension, came to be assessed in relation to Christological revelation or concealment.[16]

In the case of Mk. 6:45–52, though, this approach has raised more questions than it has answered. Indeed, several features of the narrative seem to undermine the view that it functions primarily to showcase Jesus' identity. For instance, despite the apparent Markan emphasis on Jesus' "volition,"[17] it is a volition consistently thwarted in the story by the disciples' own ineptitude. Though Jesus "compels" the disciples to proceed without him, their plight later motivates him to come toward them; though he intends to pass them by, their fearful response prompts him to join them

[11] Frank J. Matera, "The Incomprehension of the Disciples and Peter's Confession," *Bib* 70 (1989): 156, n. 5.

[12] William L. Lane, *The Gospel According to Mark*, NICNT (Grand Rapids, MI: Eerdmans, 1974), 236.

[13] Joel Marcus, *Mark 1–8: A New Translation with Introduction and Commentary*, AB 27 (Garden City, NY: Doubleday, 2000), 427.

[14] Vincent Taylor, *The Gospel According to Saint Mark: The Greek Text with Introduction, Notes, and Indexes*, 2nd edn. (Grand Rapids, MI: Baker, 1981; orig. 1950), 331.

[15] Gunther Schmahl, *Die Zwölf im Markusevangelium* (Trier: Paulinus, 1974), 125.

[16] Notably, even examples of the disciples' empowerment, according to William Wrede, are to be attributed to a "variant of the actual Markan tradition in the following form: that the messiahship was in general hidden but that the disciples and especially Peter recognised the secret" (*The Messianic Secret*, trans. J. C. Grieg [Cambridge: James Clark, 1971; orig. 1901], 239).

[17] See Marcus, *Mark 1–8*, 429.

on the boat. Besides, even Mark's editorial explanation of the disciples' failure does not focus explicitly on Jesus' Christological identity.

Taken together, then, these observations suggest that, when it comes to the Markan motif of incomprehending disciples, it may be time to regrind our interpretive lens. Perhaps in framing the question so narrowly as to ask what his followers have misunderstood *about Jesus*, we have not yet seen clearly the text's own clues to the enigma of Mk. 6:52. Without denying Mark's consistent Christological interest, this chapter probes Mk. 6:45–52 by asking, more simply, what the disciples have misunderstood.

Already, the preceding chapters of this study have laid the foundation for the present investigation by establishing the prominent role Mark's Jesus affords the disciples in his own mission. As we have seen repeatedly, Mark portrays Jesus' Christological purpose in the context of his dynamic relationship with his followers, as he draws them into his eschatological enterprise. Even where the second evangelist brings Jesus' messianic identity into view, as is the case in the first sea-crossing story (Mk. 4:35–41), he depicts Jesus as the exemplary embodiment of the kind of full-fledged trust in God's dominion that Jesus expects to find in his disciples.[18] Further, the fact that Mark includes in his gospel narrative the account of the disciples' successful missionary journey (Mk. 6:12–13) strongly undermines the notion that they remain entirely reliant on his presence for the dispensing of God's power.[19]

To expand the inquiry into the disciples' incomprehension "concerning the loaves" in a way that takes into account their relationship to Jesus builds on the cumulative findings of this study. Consistently we have recognized the intimate relationship Mark establishes between Jesus' own mission and purpose and that of his disciples – put differently, between Mark's Christology and his portrait of discipleship. Once we abandon the presupposition that proper discipleship proceeds necessarily from a proper Christological understanding of Jesus' identity,[20] we are in a position to affirm, with Kee, that neither "conceptually nor in literary ways is it possible . . . to draw an absolute distinction in Mark between Jesus and his followers, or in theological terms, between christology and ecclesiology."[21] Only when we view these two concerns as intimately intertwined

[18] See above, chapter 5, 138–42, for a discussion of this passage.

[19] Lane seems to overlook Mk. 6:7–13 when he claims that the disciples' absence from their master necessarily means "they find themselves in distress" (*Mark*, 235).

[20] For examples of this working assumption, see, e.g., Frank J. Matera, *What Are They Saying about Mark?* (New York: Paulist Press, 1987), 54.

[21] Howard Clark Kee, *Community of the New Age: Studies in Mark's Gospel* (Philadelphia: Westminster Press, 1977), 143.

can the gospel's "obvious christological thrust"[22] be most fully grasped. And just as that Christological thrust cannot be understood apart from the community Jesus calls to participate in his mission,[23] neither can the motif of incomprehension be explained by exclusive appeal to Jesus' Christological identity. As we shall see, for Mark, to "understand" Jesus entails more than acknowledging Jesus' status as God's suffering messiah; it is to be caught up in his apocalyptic gospel mission, to be enlisted in his vivid demonstration of God's rule, which is encroaching on the world.

Narrative context

Following the evangelist's own interpretive clues, investigation of the incomprehension motif in Mk. 6:45–52 begins with a brief review of the story's theological and literary ties to the preceding feeding account. Since even the fourth gospel links the two episodes (Jn. 6:1–21), their close-knit relationship seems both entrenched in the tradition and vital to our understanding of the respective passages.[24] In this section, I shall consider various explanations for the two stories' linkage as well as the interpretive leverage gained by discerning their connection.

To begin with, several awkward details combine to suggest that the feeding and sea-crossing stories recount episodes that originally existed independently within the Jesus tradition lore. That is, their episodic chronology more probably derives from an editorial conjoining of originally separate stories. Perhaps the most obvious seam can be found in the implausible combination of temporal settings: already the lateness of the hour has prompted the feeding (Mk. 6:35), which, given the number of participants, presumably lasts for hours; yet the disciples have time to set sail and arrive in the middle of the sea before the setting of the sun

22 John R. Donahue, *The Theology and Setting of Discipleship in the Gospel of Mark*, The 1983 Père Marquette Theology Lecture (Milwaukee, WI: Marquette University Press, 1983), 2.

23 See Joel Marcus, *The Way of the Lord: Christological Exegesis of the Old Testament in the Gospel of Mark* (Louisville: Westminster/John Knox Press, 1992), 123: "Mark pictures Jesus not just as an individual but as a figure with collective dimensions . . . The [Markan] church is the community of those chosen to be with Jesus in the way of the cross (8:34) but also in the new life of empowerment that is found as they tread that difficult and treacherous path."

24 On the probable literary independence of Mark and John, see Raymond E. Brown, *The Gospel According to John*, AB29 and 29A (Garden City, NY: Doubleday, 1966–70), 236–50, 252–4. More recently, see D. Moody Smith, *John among the Gospels*, 2nd edn. (Columbia, SC: University of South Carolina Press, 2001). While acknowledging scholars' increasing tendency to detect some form of literary relationship between John and the synoptics, Smith concludes that John's independence remains a "better working hypothesis for exegesis" (241).

(Mk. 6:47). Together with the likelihood of John's literary independence from Mark, this seam appears to imply that both evangelists found the stories previously linked, either as part of a larger miracle cycle[25] or simply as a mutually interpreting narrative doublet.

If the second evangelist has adopted this feeding/sea-crossing narrative pattern from pre-existing tradition, we can credit Mark with a distinctive redactional emphasis in the transmission of that tradition. Though an impressive number of scholars would confine Mark's contribution mainly to the editorial explanation of Mk. 6:52,[26] we should not overlook details included in the Markan account that bear the imprint of distinctive Markan themes. For instance, Mark appears to continue his depiction of a New Exodus in the passage's reference to the "mountain" as Jesus' destination for prayer (Mk. 6:46; see Mk. 3:13; 9:2); within Exodus, the "mountain of God" designates the location where Moses' most direct interactions with Yahweh occur.[27] In addition, Marcus detects in several of Jesus' actions (compelling, dismissing, intending) Mark's editorial interest in emphasizing "certain theological, and especially Christological, aspects of this tale."[28]

Yet there is another, complementary aspect that emerges as central to Mark's exposition of these pre-joined stories: the disciples' active engagement in the divine drama. As Denis has observed, in both cases, the disciples "ont un rôle actif, chose rare dans les récits de miracles."[29] Already we have seen that Mark's account of the miraculous feeding features their dynamic transformation from doubters of God's provision to participants in it. As Jesus has presided authoritatively over the long-awaited wilderness banquet, he has affirmed his close kinship with Yahweh as kingly host even as he has summoned – indeed, commanded – his followers to collaborate with him in giving the people "something to eat." Thoroughly resonant with the Exodus portrait of God's provision in time of need, the feeding narrative has depicted in living color the power associated not just with Jesus' presence but also with the new template of possibility that his presence provides those who would trust in the "gospel of God" (Mk. 1:15).

[25] See Paul J. Achtemeier, "The Origin and Function of the Pre-Markan Miracle Catenae," *JBL* 91 (1972): 198–221.

[26] See Taylor, *Saint Mark*, 330–1; Dietrich-Alex Koch, *Die Bedeutung der Wundererzählungen für die Christologie des Markusevangeliums* (New York: De Gruyter, 1975), 107; Robert A. Guelich, *Mark 1–8:26*, WBC 34A (Dallas: Word, 1989), 347.

[27] See above, chapter 3, 79–83.

[28] Marcus, *Mark 1–8*, 429.

[29] Albert-Marie Denis, "La Marche de Jésus sur les eaux: contribution à l'histoire de la péricope dans la tradition évangélique," in *De Jésus aux évangiles*, ed. I. de la Potterie (Gembloux: Duculot, 1967), 233–5.

Against this narrative backdrop, I turn to consider the second sea-crossing story, where revelation and rescue work in tandem to disclose not just Jesus' messianic identity but also the very reign of God. For Mark, "understanding" is more than a matter of cognitive affirmation of propositional truth; it is a matter of life-orientation, trust, and the new reality of God's dominion as evinced in and through Jesus.

What, then, joins the two stories and supplies interpretive handles for the texts' emerging incomprehension motif? Already I have discussed in detail the imagery Mark employs to cast the miraculous feeding episode in the hues of the Exodus story; what we shall see as I turn to the storm-at-sea passage is that once again, Mark's account draws on Israel's sacred literature to convey God's miraculous saving power at the disposal of those who trust God's rule. As Kee notes, the "twin motifs of God's command over the waters and his feeding his own in the desert appear frequently in the Psalms . . . [and] also in the later prophetic tradition, where the events of the Exodus serve as the model for the awaited eschatological redemption of the chastened, renewed nation."[30] If Mark's "gospel" content is formed and shaped within the framework of this eschatological expectation, these dual accounts of bread provision and sea crossing can best be understood as participatory events in which God's impending reign is gaining a foothold among those who have repented and trusted in its "good news."

The way has been paved, in the first Markan feeding narrative, for a Christological reading of the sea-crossing story that carries weighty implications for discipleship.[31] If Mark's story in that case serves a Christological purpose, its snapshot of Jesus' identity also finds his band of followers in the foreground of his mission work.[32] Such an observation only underscores the findings thus far: the disciples' significance lies not only in their nearness to Jesus marked by companionship and special instruction; it lies also, and perhaps more importantly, in the way he

[30] Kee, *Community*, 112; also Marcus, *Mark 1–8*, 428.

[31] Klemens Stock cites the verbal and narrative parallel between Mk. 1:35 (καὶ ἀπῆλθεν εἰς ἔρημον τόπον) and Mk. 6:32 (καὶ ἀπῆλθον ἐν τῷ πλοίῳ εἰς ἔρημον τόπον), as evidence that "Jesu Anfangswirken und das Anfangswirken der 12 in Verbindung miteinander gesehen werden sollen" (*Boten aus dem Mit-Ihm-Sein: Das Verhältnis zwischen Jesus und den Zwölf nach Markus*, AnBib 70 [Rome: Biblical Institute, 1975], 104).

[32] Stock emphasizes not only the disciples' "vermittelnde Stellung zwischen Jesus und dem Volk" (ibid., 108) but also their utter dependence on him: "die Jünger bestimmt sind zum Dienst am Volk und wie sie für diesen Dienst ganz und gar von Jesus abhängig sind" (109). Denise Steele likewise stresses the disciples' dependence, but expresses the gospel's ideal portrait of "self-in-relation" as a "loving and maturely trusting partnership with him in his demanding project" ("Having Root in the Self: Human Fruition and the Self-in-Relation in the Gospel of Mark" [Ph.D. diss., University of Glasgow, 2002], 266).

equips them to preach and to exercise authority to cast out demons – in a word, to do the things he does. The singular focus of Jesus' message, both in word and deed, is the nearness of God's kingdom, and he deliberately scatters the seed of that message not alone but both *along with* and *through* those whom he has called.

The second sea crossing as failed discipleship

The disciples' transformation into those who both trust and participate in the surplus provision of God's wilderness feast, then, provides the interpretive framework within which to read the story of the second sea crossing, an observation confirmed by the pericope's concluding verse. While in Jesus' *presence*, his disciples have been equipped and enlisted as authorized agents in the miraculous feeding of the multitudes; now, apart from him, the disciples find themselves poised to *practice* the same dawning hope of God's kingdom as they embark for the "other side" of the sea.

But as the story unfolds, the disciples fail miserably. Confronted by a "tormenting" force, they appear powerless; reminded by Jesus of his equipping presence, they are paralyzed by fear; apparently failing to recall their own part in the feeding miracle, their comprehension is emphatically blunted. As a result, the disciples depend ultimately on Jesus' command over the wind and waves, as he joins them in the boat. Once they are again in his presence, the storm subsides.

Yet to overemphasize the outcome of the story, which certainly depicts Jesus' godly authority over the sea's adversarial forces, misses its larger, more nuanced portrait of discipleship as foiled practice. Indeed, close scrutiny of each of the passage's three sub-units highlights the purpose of the sea-bound outing, which in turn provides a critical clue to this portrait of lapsed discipleship. In Jesus' deliberate removal of the disciples, in his intent to "pass them by," and in his setting foot on the boat, the disciples display incomprehension at every turn in a manner that contrasts markedly with their more favorable profile in the multiplication of the loaves.[33]

[33] Patrick J. Madden maintains that Mark's editorial activity, evident in the characteristic καὶ εὐθύς (Mk. 6:45) and the phrase ἐπὶ τοῖς ἄρτοις (Mk. 6:52), strengthens the ties between the feeding and sea-crossing stories "to heighten the theme of the lack of understanding on the part of the disciples" [*Jesus' Walking on the Sea: An Investigation of the Origin of the Narrative Account*, BZNW 81 (Berlin and New York: De Gruyter, 1997), 103]. This study takes that view a step further to inquire about the nature of that misunderstanding in light of the feeding miracle.

"To go before . . .": a second sending forth? (Mk. 6:45–7)

The pericope's opening section manifests the great care taken by the evangelist to set the stage for the ensuing encounter at sea. On the surface level, these three verses achieve an important narrative scene change from an event involving a sizable crowd to a more private affair. But Mark's choice of words depicts that transition as highly purposeful and no mere happenstance; its deliberately crafted language portrays this sea-crossing story as a second instance in which Jesus "sends out" those whom he has called and equipped.

Even the opening verse is replete with vocabulary that once again casts Jesus in a commanding role within the narrative as he discharges first the disciples and then the crowd. For example, Mark reports that Jesus "compelled" the disciples to embark without him: καὶ εὐθὺς ἠνάγκασεν τοὺς μαθητὰς αὐτοῦ ἐμβῆναι εἰς τὸ πλοῖον (Mk. 6:45a). In this (only Markan) use of ἀναγκάζω, I infer a pronounced sense of urgency or at least strong direction on Jesus' part.[34] But what is the cause of this exigency? Lane attributes the "hurried dismissal [to an] outburst of enthusiasm which followed the feeding of the multitude,"[35] yet this reading seems based more on the influence of the fourth gospel's account (cf. Jn. 6:14–15) than on Mark's, which fails to mention the crowd's response. Since the passage demurs from explaining Jesus' vehement insistence that the disciples depart, then, we may safely conclude only that the story here conveys Jesus' resolute removal of his followers. His "compelling" them constitutes a deliberate act that carries implications both for his dominant stature within the story and for those whose destiny he seems intent on shaping.

Indeed, this purposeful removal of the disciples from Jesus' presence introduces a noteworthy – if often neglected – dynamic that draws attention to the passage's portrait of discipleship. Since Jesus first called the four fishers in Mk. 1:16–20, they have consistently accompanied him in his work. True, Mark's Jesus does function occasionally without his entire entourage in the first half of the gospel (e.g. the healing of Jairus's daughter, Mk. 5:37–43); yet in Mk. 6:45 we find only the second instance of Jesus' intentional dismissal of the group from his presence. Moreover, since in the first instance (Mk. 6:7–13) Jesus deliberately sends his disciples out as his emissaries, the Markan narrative pattern opens the way

[34] BAGD, 52.

[35] Lane, *Mark*, 234–5. Similarly, Taylor attributes the choice of words to the vague "tension of Messianic excitement" (*Saint Mark*, 327), another explanation that over-reads the text itself.

for a similar intent at this juncture. In keeping with the discipleship pattern identified in both Mk. 1:16–20 and 3:13–15 (see above, chapters 2 and 3), the disciples have, for the most part, "come after" Jesus; they have remained "with him." At this point, Mark's potent language describing the removal of his followers from Jesus implies that here the secondary facet of their calling will take place, a facet that proceeds quite naturally from their having just been transformed while in his "presence."

A pair of infinitive phrases specifies two actions that serve as objects of the finite verb ἠνάγκασεν. Jesus compels the disciples not just to board the boat but also to "go ahead to the other side" (καὶ προάγειν εἰς τὸ πέραν, Mk. 6:45). The verb προάγειν introduces a striking word choice that further substantiates the view of this episode as a second "sending out."

Two dimensions of Jesus' urging the disciples to "go before" him appear to confirm the import of this journey as a missionary outing. In the first place, Jesus' initial call to discipleship found in Mk. 1:17 summons his followers to "come after me." Later, at the mountaintop commissioning, he establishes the Twelve for the primary purpose of continuing in his presence (ἵνα ὦσιν μετ' αὐτοῦ, Mk. 3:14) – a purpose that reflects a subtle shift in status from followers to companions. The developing storyline leading up to Mk. 6:45, then, suggests that Jesus' "compelling" the disciples to "go before" him suggests the maturation of the disciples as fully authorized agents of Jesus' mission. Subtle though the development may be, Mark's description of the followers' spatial relationship to Jesus has evolved from the initial "coming after" Jesus, to being "with him," to now going "before him." Implicit in the language, then, is the claim that these disciples-in-training are now poised to carry on their master's task.

Indeed the present passage's view of the disciples' "going before" Jesus appears all the more suggestive because it counterbalances the sense of the verb προάγω in the gospel's second half, where it is Jesus who consistently "goes before the disciples" (Mk. 10:32; 14:28; 16:7). As Marcus puts it, in Mark, "Christian discipleship is a matter of following Jesus in the way of the cross (8:34; 10:52) or of being with him (cf. 3:14), not of going before him."[36] What are we to make, then, of this instance in which discipleship is a matter of "going before him"?

Those who dismiss this anomalous instance as an insignificant narrative detail will miss an important facet of the story's portrait of failed

[36] Marcus, *Way*, 42–3, though he concedes that Jesus does order them to do so in Mk. 6:45 (43, n. 115).

discipleship as well. The fact that the disciples "prove to be incapable of carrying out this command [to go before him] and are helpless"[37] without Jesus constitutes a lapse on their part that occurs in advance of their misconstruing his identity. Their unsuccessful venture at sea apart from Jesus' presence does not nullify his original intent that they might "go before" their master. Put differently, despite the disciples' eventual failure, Jesus sends them ahead with the full expectation that they wield the power necessary to assert God's apocalyptic dominion over the demonic forces at sea.

Once Jesus has so purposefully sent the disciples on ahead, attention returns to the crowd, whom Jesus dismisses (ἀπολύει) without fanfare. Not only does this act achieve the narrative purpose of a scene change, but the verb ἀπολύει echoes the disciples' command in Mk. 6:36 to "send them away." With more than a hint of irony, Mark's Jesus has at last heeded the disciples' imperative to release the crowds, though notably "at Jesus' timetable rather than their own."[38]

The intervening verses, though, have demonstrated that the difference between the disciples' command and Jesus' dismissal of the crowds amounts to more than just a matter of "timetable." Far more striking than the temporal delay are the momentous events that have transpired in the meantime, as Jesus has transformed his followers' wholly inadequate proposal into their successful participation in God's wilderness provision for the multitudes. Only after the ample satisfaction of the crowd's hunger – and only after the disciples have both witnessed and joined in the miraculous feeding – does Jesus disperse the masses.

Mark further underscores Jesus' intentional removal from the disciples by a protracted and detailed account of their respective whereabouts. First, Jesus "takes leave" of an unspecified αὐτοῖς (Mk. 6:46), whose antecedent most commentators locate in the last word of the preceding verse, ὄχλον.[39] The apparent disagreement in number between the plural αὐτοῖς and the singular ὄχλον has led Guelich to suggest the pronoun originally represented the disciples.[40] Such speculation is not warranted, however, since frequently Mark refers to the crowd – itself a singular noun – with a plural personal pronoun (see Mk. 2:13; 3:9, 32; 4:1–2; 6:34; 7:14; 8:2–3; 9:15; 15:8). Further, the sequence of events relayed by Mk. 6:45–6 seems to constitute two separate actions: (1) Jesus sends forth

[37] Ibid., 43. [38] Marcus, *Mark 1–8*, 430.

[39] See Taylor, *Saint Mark*, 328: "It is improbable that αὐτοῖς refers to the disciples rather than the multitude."

[40] See Guelich, *Mark 1–8:26*, 349: "we may have here a remnant of the story's original introduction."

the disciples, an action apparently completed before (2) Jesus dismisses, and then takes leave of, the crowd.

With both the disciples and the crowd now removed from the scene, Mark reports that Jesus "went up on the mountain (εἰς τὸ ὄρος) to pray" (Mk. 6:46b). Both Jesus' destination and his prayerful purpose contribute further to our understanding of the narrative setting for the disciples' sea-crossing itself. Within Mark's gospel, this is the only instance in which Jesus goes alone to the mountaintop. Already I have discussed the significance of the location for the commissioning of the Twelve in Mk. 3:13–19; later, in Mk. 9:2–8, Peter, James, and John will witness Jesus' transfiguration atop a "high mountain" (Mk. 9:2). Just as each of these encounters features discipleship as a prominent concern, so here too does Jesus' departure to the mountain carry weighty implications for those closest to him.

Moreover, within Mark's own scriptural landscape, the "mountain" figures prominently in God's encounters with key leaders. Consistently the Old Testament affirms the mountaintop as the domain from which God "shines forth" (Deut. 33:2; Hab. 3:3), and figures like Moses (Exod. 3; 6; 33) and Elijah (1 Kgs. 19) find themselves on "the mountain" when God chooses to appear before them. That Jesus here journeys to the mountaintop to pray suggests that he will there find communion with the Source of his own gospel mission.

But within Mark's narrative, just as those who venture to the mountaintop meet there an empowering presence, so too Jesus' act of prayer bespeaks more than his own personal encounter with God.[41] For elsewhere in Mark's gospel, prayer offers a means of human access to the full expression of God's dominion. For instance, in Mk. 11:24–5, Jesus instructs his disciples about the potent efficacy of prayer, which depends on the suppliant's trust in God's provision. Later, at the Mount of Olives (another encounter on a mountain), Jesus' prayer of anguish steels him for his difficult and treacherous path, even as he again instructs his disciples to pray for similar faithfulness (Mk. 14:34, 38–9). In both cases, prayer functions to prepare the petitioner for full disclosure of God's kingdom. Thus Jesus' prayer here extends beyond a demonstration of "where the

[41] Sharyn Dowd, *Reading Mark: A Literary and Theological Commentary on the Second Gospel*, RNTS (Macon, GA: Smith & Helwys, 2000), 69, cites Philostratus' *Life of Apollonius* to support the view that Jesus' prayer here constitutes a defense against charges of practicing magic: "A magician conjures the gods with spells, but a religious person entreats them with prayers." Those charges, however, are nowhere in view within the second gospel.

source of Jesus' authority is to be found,"[42] as it encompasses the broader horizon of God's dominion.

After mentioning Jesus' prayer atop the mountain, this opening section culminates in Mk. 6:47 with a scan of the horizon at eventide: καὶ ὀψίας γενομένης ἦν τὸ πλοῖον ἐν μέσῳ τῆς θαλάσσης, καὶ αὐτὸς μόνος ἐπὶ τῆς γῆς. Since the preceding verses have already designated locations for both the boat and Jesus, Mk. 6:47 reiterates through redundancy the physical and spiritual divide between Jesus and his disciples. At this point, all of the characters are in place, ready for the action of the story to follow.

The use of the noun θάλασσα in place of the more common (and more precisely accurate) λίμνη is consistent with Markan topographical terminology, since the second evangelist refers repeatedly to the Galilean body of water as θάλασσα. But what are we to make of such a setting? Certainly the sea/lake plays a complex and prominent role in Mark's narrative, especially in the first half of the gospel.[43] It was along the shores of the sea that Jesus first "saw" Simon, Andrew, James, and John (Mk. 1:16–20), as well as Levi son of Alphaeus (Mk. 2:13–14), then called them to "come after me." And repeatedly in the first eight chapters we read of Jesus and his disciples crossing from one side to the other and teaching along the shores of the sea/lake (see also Mk. 3:7; 4:1; 4:35–41; 5:21; 6:32; and 8:13).[44] Thus the "sea" provides a thematic and geographical point of reference for the epoch of Jesus' Galilean ministry.

Yet, especially in light of the recurrent quelling of demons and disease in this "wonder working" phase of Jesus' mission, modern readers should not neglect the pervasive ancient view of the sea as the place where evil powers tend to hold sway.[45] For Mark's audience, the sea entails more

[42] Eduard Schweizer, *The Good News According to Mark* (Atlanta: John Knox Press, 1970), 142. Especially in light of the Mosaic typology, it seems important to affirm that God's authoritative endowment concerns not just the leading figure but the people who benefit from that leadership.

[43] Of the word's nineteen appearances in the gospel, all but two (Mk. 9:42; 11:23) appear in the gospel's first half.

[44] Many scholars point to the Sea of Galilee as a metaphorical dividing line between Jewish and Gentile territory. Representative of this view is Séan Freyne, who writes, "within Mark's gospel the various sea journeys mediate between the oppositions represented by the Jew/gentile portrayals" ("Galilee, Sea of," in *The Anchor Bible Dictionary*, II, ed. David Noel Freedman [Garden City, NY: Doubleday, 1992], 900). But not always: despite the named destination of Bethsaida, this sea crossing finds the disciples landing at Gennesaret, a Galilean region (Mk. 6:53).

[45] An interesting confirmation of this underlying assumption can be found in the preceding chapter of Mark, where the "legion" of unclean spirits inhabit a herd of swine that then drowns in the sea (Mk. 5:1–13). Their failed petition not to be driven "out of the countryside" (Mk. 5:10) seems to reflect a desire, thwarted by the power of Jesus, to retain a foothold on the land. See Marcus, *Mark 1–8*, 345, 352.

than a spatial location; it is a spiritual domain as well. As Freyne points out, "in Ancient Semitic and Jewish mythology the sea is associated with evil monsters, of whom Yahweh is Lord."[46] Similarly, Malbon maintains that Mark "presupposes the connotation of the sea as chaos, threat, danger, in opposition to the land as order, promise, security."[47]

Two complementary streams of Jewish tradition converge to depict the sea as the battlefield on which God's dominion will be victoriously established. In the first place, the Exodus motif which links the feeding and sea-crossing stories portrays the sea as the place where God's saving activity is most clearly manifest. Stegner views the rich interpretive traditions spawned by the Exod. 14 account of that Red Sea rescue as the armature around which this sea crossing has been constructed.[48] While it may be going too far to designate Mk. 6:45–52 – or even the pre-Markan tradition on which it is based – as a "Christian Passover celebration,"[49] it would be remiss to neglect the living memory of the sea as the locus of God's saving intervention on behalf of his people (see, e.g., Isa. 51:10; Ps. 78:13).

This living memory in turn provides the basis for the mounting eschatological hope for the New Exodus in which God's dominion will be firmly established. Together with the Exodus motif of the sea as the staging ground for God's decisive rescue, then, Israel's interpretive traditions draw on Canaanite mythology to construe the sea as the seat of demonic forces, as the place where Leviathan dwells. For instance, Isa. 27:1 pronounces that, "On that day, the Lord with his cruel and great and strong sword will punish . . . Leviathan the twisting serpent, and he will kill the dragon that is in the sea." Further, Ps. 74 combines wilderness and sea motifs in a vivid depiction of God "working salvation in the earth" (Ps. 74:12):

> You divided the sea by your might;
> you broke the heads of the dragons in the waters.
> You crushed the heads of Leviathan;
> you gave him as food for the people in the wilderness.
>
> (Ps. 74:13–14)

[46] Freyne, "Galilee," 900. Likewise, see Lane, who notes that "the sea, like the wilderness, was regarded as the dwelling place for demons" (*Mark*, 233, n. 133).

[47] Elizabeth Struthers Malbon, "The Jesus of Mark and the Sea of Galilee," *JBL* 103 (1984): 376.

[48] William Richard Stegner, "Jesus' Walking on the Water: Mark 6.45–52," in *The Gospels and the Scriptures of Israel*, ed. Craig A. Evans and W. Richard Stegner, JSNTSup 104 (Sheffield, England: Sheffield Academic Press, 1994), *passim.*

[49] Stegner, "Jesus' Walking," 227.

Clearly, in the psalmist's view, God's dominion "in the earth" entails the dramatic quelling of opposing forces in the sea and the provision of food for people in the wilderness.

Finally, literature more contemporary to Mark's gospel evinces an intensification of eschatological hope that reflects a similar view of the sea as a domain where evil resides. Several passages of the Qumran Hymns Scroll, for instance, invoke storm-at-sea imagery to depict eschatological distress (e.g. 1QH 3:6, 12–18; 6:22–5; 7:45). Moreover, Marcus explains this imagery with historical reference to Mark's contemporary audience when he notes that "the distress of the Markan disciples at sea would probably remind the Markan community of the eschatological affliction and bewilderment they themselves were experiencing in the wake of the persecutions associated with the Jewish War."[50] Similarly, Stegner observes, "Jewish Christianity apparently linked the chaos motif with the demonic and powers of darkness,"[51] adducing John's Revelation as evidence of an apocalyptic juxtaposition of the old age dominated by the dragon (Satan) – the "embodiment of chaos" – and the new age in which the sea is no more (Rev. 21:1).

Together, then, the resonant imagery found in Jewish apocalyptic thought, Mark's own historical setting, and the gospel's depiction of a mission to "bind the strong man" (Mk. 3:27) converge to suggest that this stormy voyage entails a showdown with the demonic powers that reside in the deep. As the disciples embark "on the sea," they do so fully authorized to demonstrate God's decisive victory over the powers of chaos typically found there. While Tannehill seems on target in his assessment that "Jesus' wonders were an integral part of the outburst of hope for overcoming evil,"[52] we may extend that claim to the disciples, whose successful wonder-working (Mk. 6:12–13, 30) establishes the expectation that they too might demonstrate this "outburst of hope" even apart from Jesus.

Two prominent features, then, emerge from a close examination of Mk. 6:45–7. First, the narrative's measured, frame-by-frame account of Jesus' deliberate removal from the disciples combines with the insistence that they "go ahead of" him to suggest that this second sea-crossing story also constitutes the second "missionary journey" of the disciples. In the first, they have laid claim to God's dominion within the human sphere, where they have preached, healed, and cast out demons; now

[50] Marcus, *Mark 1–8*, 431. [51] Stegner, "Jesus' Walking," 229.

[52] Robert C. Tannehill, "The Gospel of Mark as Narrative Christology," *Semeia* 16 (1979): 62.

they go forth to assert God's dominion by subduing the adverse spiritual powers associated with the sea. In preparation, the disciples have been twice empowered – at their commissioning and their sending forth (Mk. 3:13–15 and 6:7–9). What is more, their collaboration in the wilderness provision (Mk. 6:32–44) has transformed Jesus' followers from ardent defenders of inadequacy to active participants in God's extravagant feast. The time is ripe for Jesus to send them out; his prayer on the mountaintop may even afford the disciples the power of his presence *in absentia*.

Second, if Jesus has purposefully discharged the disciples, their sea-bound route would imply for Mark's readers not just the prominent geographical feature bordering Galilee but also its more spiritual connotation as nature's hosting site for the demonic sphere. In the middle of the sea, the gospel's apocalyptic saga will continue, as those aligned with Jesus – and thus with God's coming reign – encounter the evil forces resident there. At least on one level, this sea voyage provides an opportunity for the disciples to exercise the authority, conferred on them by Jesus, over the evil spirits and thus again to play a leading role in that "outburst of hope." As the opening scene comes to a close, the stage has been set for Jesus' disciples to demonstrate God's decisive victory over the sea just as that claim has already been staked upon the earth.[53]

"The wind was against them . . .": empowering epiphany (Mk. 6:48–50)

If Jesus has sent the disciples on ahead with confidence in the authority he has given them over the sea's demonic threat, the story's next verse provides a first glimpse of their failure. What Jesus sees when he scans the horizon is not the successful quelling of the storm at sea, but a boat full of men tormented in their rowing against an opposing gale. In the interchange that ensues, Jesus launches an initial rescue effort, as he comes toward the stranded disciples, intending to "pass them by." In this section, I shall consider Jesus' primary response to his followers' predicament as they labor against the contrary wind.

The section opens with a participial phrase that conveys Jesus' perspective: καὶ ἰδὼν αὐτοὺς βασανιζομένους ἐν τῷ ἐλαύνειν (Mk. 6:48a). In typically Markan fashion, it is Jesus' first "seeing" that engenders his saving action: the calling of the disciples (Mk. 1:16, 19; 2:14), the healing of the paralytic (Mk. 2:5), and the feeding of the multitude (Mk. 6:34)

[53] Steele puts it thus: "Jesus is here setting the disciples a task which he hopes they will successfully fulfil" ("Having Root in the Self," 139, n. 120).

all begin with a report of Jesus' first "seeing."[54] Thus it is appropriate that, once all the characters are in place (Mk. 6:47), Jesus' penetrating observation sets the story in motion.

The report of Jesus' vantage point from the mountaintop conveys a subtle, and often neglected, dynamic at work in this passage. Above I have maintained that Jesus' journey to the mountaintop to pray implicitly pertains both to his own mission and to the disciples' present circumstance. The fact that his gaze is fixed even from afar upon those whom he has sent out into the "middle of the sea" reveals both his remarkable vision[55] and his continued interest in their progress. For the Markan disciples, and for the evangelist's community, this detail offers a pastoral reminder that, even when Jesus is physically absent from his followers, he retains a stake in their own tumultuous journey.

Indeed, when Jesus looks out to sea, the sight he glimpses is anything but smooth sailing, since the passage describes in rather graphic terms the disciples' impeded journey. Discharged as fully authorized agents of God's power, the boaters whom Jesus spies now appear "tormented in their rowing." Certainly the passive participle βασανιζομένους indicates that the disciples are victims of a contrary force rather than masters of it. Even if the tale does not specify the threat they face,[56] Jesus' disciples here find themselves clenched in the jaws of the sea's mighty gale.

The verb βασανίζω itself suggests that a demonic force animates the adversarial wind. Elsewhere in Mark's gospel, the same verb characterizes Jesus' treatment of the evil entity that has gripped the Gerasene demoniac in an apparent apocalyptic showdown (Mk. 5:7). And although some interpreters infer in the disciples' "tormenting" here only the rather mild misfortune of a wind hindering the rowers' intended progress,[57]

[54] Two other instances of Jesus' penetrating gaze merit mention: (1) the hemorrhaging woman, whom Jesus "sees" after she has been healed (Mk. 5:32); and (2) the rich man, whom Jesus first "sees" before uttering a staggering command (Mk. 10:21). While Jesus' vision in neither case leads directly to the "healing" of another person, both passages confirm the Markan tendency to portray "seeing/looking" as Jesus' first impulse when he becomes aware of those in need.

[55] Marcus, *Mark 1–8*, 423, cites Mk. 2:5 and 5:32 as examples of Jesus' supernatural vision; Rudolf Pesch, *Das Markusevangelium*, 2 vols., HTKNT 2 (Freiburg: Herder, 1976), I:360, points out the great distance separating Jesus from his disciples in this verse; and Joachim Gnilka, *Das Evangelium nach Markus*, 2 vols., EKKNT 2 (Zurich: Benziger; Neukirchen: Neukirchener Verlag, 1978–9), I:268, emphasizes the darkness of the hour. On the other hand, Taylor, *Saint Mark*, 328–9, suggests the mountaintop setting enhances Jesus' vision.

[56] Robert H. Gundry, *Mark: A Commentary on His Apology for the Cross* (Grand Rapids, MI: Eerdmans, 1993), 342, maintains that, in contrast with Mk. 4:37–9, the "narrative carries not even a hint of mortal danger."

[57] Ibid.

the verb's use in ancient literature regularly conveys the hostile intent of the tormenting power.[58] Particularly noteworthy are those instances in which βασανίζω describes the experience of those deliberately tortured as a part of the judicial process (cf. 2 Macc. 7:13; 4 Macc. 6:5; Josephus, *Ant.* 2.105; 16.232). The Maccabean martyrs, in particular, respond to the "tormenting" not as passive victims of brutal harrassment but as those who actively trust their God with their destiny (e.g. 2 Macc. 7:14). While the disciples at sea are not exactly passive either – after all, they continue at their oars for hours – they do appear to lack resolute confidence in God's victory over the sea.

Another feature of this story further depicts the "tormenting" as a testing of the disciples' trust that Jesus both anticipates and permits: its prolonged time frame.[59] When considering the passage's temporal markers (ὀψίας γενομένης, Mk. 6:47; περὶ τετάρτην φυλακὴν τῆς νυκτός, Mk. 6:48), interpreters most often view them as evidence of a redactional seam exposing the independent origins of the sea-crossing and feeding stories. Since the phrase ὀψίας γενομένης seems to correspond to the time frame in which the feeding narrative takes place (ἤδη ὥρας πολλῆς, Mk. 6:35), commentators such as Guelich detect a tension which "suggests that the two stories, each with temporal settings essential to their respective narratives, were originally unrelated."[60] Moreover, the discrepancy between the arrival of eventide in Mk. 6:47 and the mention of the "fourth watch of the night" in Mk. 6:48 has similarly been attributed to this story's conflation of two separate narrative strands, one epiphanic and another salvific in thrust.[61]

As I shall discuss in greater detail below, the story's discrete thematic interests in divine self-disclosure and rescue frequently converge in ancient literature.[62] Thus, I shall treat the passage as a coherently fashioned account. Still, a gaping temporal divide opens between the opening mention of dusk (Mk. 6:47) and Jesus' perceptive gaze, which occurs just before dawn (Mk. 6:48). What are we to make of such a protracted narrative chronology?

[58] BAGD, 134, especially sections 1 and 3.

[59] This feature has been noted in pre-critical exegesis. For example, John Chrysostom observes: "But whereas before they had Him in the ship when this befell them, now they were alone by themselves . . . [N]ow leading them to a greater degree of endurance, He . . . departs, and in mid sea permits the storm to arise, so that they might not so much as look for a hope of preservation from any quarter; and He lets them be tempest-tossed all the night, thoroughly to awaken, as I suppose, their hardened heart" (Homily 50 on Matt. 14:23–4).

[60] Guelich, *Mark 1–8:26*, 349. Also Haenchen, *Der Weg Jesu*, 252, n. 2.

[61] See L. Schenke, *Die Wundererzählungen des Markusevangeliums*, SBB 5 (Stuttgart: Katholisches Bibelwerk, 1974), 243–4.

[62] See below, 227–9.

In the first place, the delay underscores the duration of the struggle, a narrative feature that is regularly glossed over.[63] If already by the arrival of early evening, the disciples are "in the middle of the sea," their lack of forward progress as dawn presses in implies that they have "endured to the end" (Mk. 13:13) this clash with the forces of darkness. The possibility that Mark's community found itself in the throes of a similar "tormenting" – possibly relating either to events around the Jewish War or to the Neronian persecution – suggests that the sustained nature of the disciples' resistance would not have been lost on the gospel's earliest hearers; even after a long night's struggle, an "absent" Jesus "sees" and responds from afar.

Besides portraying such a prolonged front-line effort against the "tormenting" wind, the mention of the "fourth watch of the night" casts the episode within a horizon of hopeful anticipation. In the Exodus narrative, the Egyptians meet their demise in the sea precisely during the same "morning watch" (Exod. 14:24), a detail preserved in other biblical recollections of that formative saving event (Ps. 46:5; Isa. 17:14).[64] And as Marcus points out, later Jewish traditions similarly identify the hour just before dawn as the temporal setting within which God ushers in salvific help.[65] Among examples he cites is the following passage from *Joseph and Aseneth*:

> And as Aseneth finished her confession to the Lord, lo, the morning star rose in the eastern sky. And Aseneth saw it and rejoiced and said, "The Lord God has indeed heard me, for this star is a messenger and herald of the light of the great day." And lo, the heaven was torn open near the morning star and an indescribable light appeared. (14:1–3)[66]

As it makes way for the dawn's first light, then, the fourth watch of the night adumbrates the impending arrival of that "great day."

From his mountaintop vantage point, Jesus now sees the disciples' enduring struggle against the adverse wind. For over nine hours, they have rowed in vain, proving incapacitated by the sea's supernatural resistance

[63] Guelich, *Mark 1–8:26*, 349, mentions in passing (but does not comment upon) the fact that the disciples "had struggled most of the night and made little headway."

[64] See also Pinchas Lapide, "A Jewish Exegesis of the Walking on the Water," trans. G. W. S. Knowles, *Concilium* 138 (1980): 38–9, who claims, on the basis of *b. Sanh.* 94a, that early first-century Jewish exegesis employed Isa. 21:12 to interpret Exod. 12:42 messianically.

[65] Marcus, *Mark 1–8*, 423.

[66] H. F. D. Sparks, ed., *The Apocryphal Old Testament* (Oxford: Oxford University Press, 1984).

and thus finding themselves hindered in their mission to "go before" Jesus to reach the other side. In their powerlessness, the disciples' trust in God's dominion, which would unleash the authority Jesus has given them, proves inefficacious. Unable to subdue the storm, Jesus' followers reach a low point in their practice of discipleship that contrasts sharply with the acclaim of their missionary results reported in Mk. 6:12–13, 30; as they remain subject to a contrary wind, the disciples find themselves abandoned to a fate of futility, stymied in their progress, and at the mercy of forces over which they could have wielded God's authoritative power.

It is within this context that we may more fully understand Jesus' response to his followers. By the "fourth watch of the night," the time has come for a display of divine power through which chaos is subdued and tormenting ceases. So Jesus seizes command of the scene as he responds to the disciples' plight by "coming toward them," presumably somehow to address their difficulty.

It is interesting to note that up to this point the story shares several common features with the first sea-crossing story (Mk. 4:35–41): it is again evening, the destination is the other side of the sea/lake, the crowd is left behind, and a wind brings difficulty.[67] On the basis of these similarities, Best takes the two accounts to represent Mark's exhortative portrait of Jesus "as their risen Lord [who] comes continually to them when they are in need."[68] In effect, Best claims, it is Jesus' "presence" that Mark intends to stress, a presence which would have reassured Mark's community that Jesus continues to mediate divine assistance to them.

While Best may be on target when he finds here a message about Jesus' available presence to the evangelist's community, his reading fails to take into full account the epiphanic and apocalyptic nature of that presence, as well as its intended function.[69] As a result, the distinctive claims of this second sea crossing are forfeited to a generalized conception of Jesus' saving presence. For if Mark's story primarily offers his hearers a reminder of "how the presence of Jesus can bring calm,"[70] that reminder seems muted in this story when Jesus' seemingly empathetic response to the disciples is checked by a curious addendum: καὶ ἤθελεν παρελθεῖν

[67] C. S. Mann goes so far as to say: "if this narrative is not a doublet of 4:35–41, its purpose is wholly obscure" (*Mark: A New Translation with Introduction and Commentary*, AB 27 [Garden City, NY: Doubleday, 1986], 306).

[68] Ernest Best, *Following Jesus: Discipleship in the Gospel of Mark*, JSNTSup 4 (Sheffield: JSOT Press, 1981), 232.

[69] Best does not deal directly with Jesus' intent to "pass them by" but claims only that it is "the 'presence' rather than the 'epiphany' which is uppermost in [Mark's] mind" (ibid., 232).

[70] Ibid.

αὐτούς (Mk. 6:48). Because in its plainest sense, the claim that Jesus "intended to pass them by" works to undermine Jesus' saving impulse (which seems both to precede and to follow it), these four words have presented exegetes with a "notorious crux of interpretation."[71]

Some scholars collapse the apparent contradiction between Jesus' intent to "come toward them" on the one hand and "pass them by" on the other by taming ἤθελεν to read "he was going to," an aim thwarted by the disciples' fearful reaction.[72] But as Gundry points out, Mark uses this verb most frequently in cases where the "intended" action is at least achievable,[73] so that Snoy's argument is more compelling: "il vaut mieux entendre θέλω dans son acception courante de 'vouloir' comme dans les autres passages où Marc l'emploie et de façon générale dans le NT."[74] Moreover, this reading preserves Jesus' studied purposefulness conveyed throughout this episode.

If we take seriously Jesus' deliberate intent to "pass them by," though, what purpose might such an action convey to Mark's readers? To be sure, readers of the Septuagint would recognize in the verb παρέρχομαι "similar language used in an epiphany of God to Moses (Exod. 33:19–23; 34:6) and Elijah (1 Kgs. 19:11)."[75] As a result, many commentators suggest that Jesus means to reveal himself to his wind-tossed disciples. Indeed, Marcus demonstrates that this interpretive stance rests on firm ground by noting that the LXX of both Dan. 12:1 and Gen. 32:31–2 introduce the verb παρέρχομαι where it is lacking in the MT; thus the verb, he maintains, has become "almost a technical term for divine epiphany in the Septuagint"[76] – and, by extension, in the thought-world of first-century Jewish Christianity. For Mark and his hearers, Jesus' desire to "pass by" his disciples probably signals their master's first response to their distress: to disclose himself to them as an authorized agent of divine power.[77]

[71] Marcus, *Mark 1–8*, 426. [72] So Taylor, *Saint Mark*, 329.

[73] Gundry, *Mark*, 341, cites the following Markan uses: 1:40, 41; *3:13*; 6:22, 25, 26; *8:34*; 9:13, 30, 35; *10:43, 44*, 51; 12:38; *14:7*, 12, 36; 15:9, 12. Notably, the italicized verses speak of discipleship in terms of the deliberate "intent" of both Jesus and his followers.

[74] Thierry Snoy, "Marc 6,48: '. . . et il voulait les dépasser.' Proposition pour la solution d'une énigme," in *L'Evangile selon Marc: tradition et rédaction*, ed. M. Sabbe, BETL 34 (Leuven: Leuven University Press, 1988; orig. 1974), 349.

[75] Guelich, *Mark 1–8:26*, 350.

[76] Marcus, *Mark 1–8*, 426. See also John P. Heil, *Jesus Walking on the Sea: Meaning and Gospel Functions of Matt. 14:22–33, Mark 6:45–52 and John 6:15b–21*, AnBib 87 (Rome: Biblical Institute Press, 1981), 69–71.

[77] Based on the use of the infinitive παρελθεῖν in Amos 7:8 and 8:2, Harry Fleddermann argues that Mk. 6:48c "functions both in the sea-rescue miracle and in the epiphany" ("'And He Wanted to Pass by Them' [Mark 6:48c]," *CBQ* 45 [1983]: 394). But the parallel is weak:

Moreover, Mark's twofold description of Jesus "walking upon the sea" (περιπατῶν ἐπὶ τῆς θαλάσσης, Mk. 6:48; ἐπὶ τῆς θαλάσσης περιπατοῦντα, Mk. 6:49) only reiterates the motif of divine disclosure conveyed through the verb παρέρχομαι, since as Marcus notes, "in the OT and some later Jewish texts it is consistently God or his wisdom who walks on the waters of the sea and tramples its waves, thus demonstrating that he and no other is divine."[78] Moreover, Stegner demonstrates that the Jewish exegetical tradition viewed the sea as the place of definitive divine disclosure.[79] To support this claim, he cites both the *Mekilta* on Exod. 15:2c, which speaks of the Holy One who "revealed Himself at the sea,"[80] and *Pirqe deRabbi Eliezer* on Ps. 77:19, which claims that the people "saw the Holy One . . . walking before them"[81] through the sea. Hence Stegner concludes, "As the Israelites saw their God in the midst of the deliverance at the sea, so the disciples saw Jesus in delivering them from the windswept sea."[82]

To some interpreters, such an epiphanic emphasis seems at least partially inconsistent with the impulse toward rescue implicit in Jesus' coming "toward them" and in his embarking on the boat. Indeed, painstaking effort has been devoted to the task of separating narrative strands that the Markan redactor – or a predecessor – has presumably interwoven. This line of inquiry has produced an elaborate debate among interpreters about Mark's chief intent: do we have in this passage a rescue story that has been developed into an epiphany?[83] Or does the episode reflect an epiphany

the claim that Yahweh's "passing by" in Amos would have functioned primarily to avert destruction is not at all transparent in the text. What is more, the disciples in this case do not appear to be subject to the kind of travails of judgment that concerns the OT prophecy; their rescue is not a matter of delivery from the throes of God's judgment, but rather from the forces of an adversarial wind.

[78] Marcus, *Mark 1–8*, 432. Texts he adduces to support this claim include Job 9:8; Hab. 3:15; Ps. 77:19; Isa. 43:16; 51:9–10; Sir. 24:5–6. See also Richard B. Hays, "Can the Gospels Teach Us How to Read the Old Testament?" *Pro Ecclesia* 11 (2002): 409–11, for a sharply Christological reading of this allusion. Foremost on Mark's mind, Hays suggests, is not just the LXX of Job 9:8, which marvels at a God who "walks upon the sea as upon dry ground," but the entire passage, which mentions in v. 11 God's "passing by," as well as Job's "not understanding" God. Thus, Hays views Jesus' walking on the water as "a manifestation of divine glory [that] remains indirect and beyond full comprehension" (411).

[79] Stegner, "Jesus' Walking," 226–7.

[80] *Mekilta de Rabbi Ishmael*, ed. J. Z. Lauterbach, 3 vols. (Philadelphia: Jewish Publication Society of America, 1933–5), 2:25.

[81] *Pirqe de Rabbi Eliezer*, ed. G. Frielander (New York: Benjamin Blom, 1971), 330.

[82] Stegner, "Jesus' Walking," 227.

[83] So Martin Dibelius, *From Tradition to Gospel*, rev. 2nd edn., trans. B. Lee Woolf (London: James Clarke, 1971; orig. 1933), 100; also Tannehill, "Gospel of Mark," 64.

that has been reworked into a rescue story?[84] Yet such discrepant findings may suggest that it is the form-critical categories themselves that fail to yield decisive results about the fundamental thrust of this passage.

A more constructive way forward, I submit, recognizes that the rescue and revelatory motifs found in this passage reflect not competing but complementary claims. If we take at face value the grave implications of the participle βασανιζομένους as well as the initiative Jesus shows upon "seeing" the disciples' struggle on the one hand (the rescue motif), and Jesus' resolve to "pass them by" on the other hand (the epiphanic motif), we may ask how these emphases work together to elucidate Jesus' response to the disciples in a time of trial.

Other scholars have already advocated this "middle way," which rejects the hypothesis of a surgical splicing of traditional material. For instance, Theissen calls this episode a "soteriological epiphany,"[85] while Perkins notes that the form-critical debates on this matter "ignore the combination of epiphany and salvation in appearances of Yahweh (e.g. Ex 33:22; 34:5–6)."[86] Kingsbury elaborates the relationship between rescue and revelation even more suggestively when he contends that Jesus' intention to "pass them by" reflects an expectation that, given a visible reminder of his presence, the disciples will "recall . . . [their] authority to complete whatever mission [Jesus] gives them."[87]

Indeed, Kingsbury's admittedly provocative claim – that Jesus' self-disclosing *presence* aims to recall for his disciples the mission he has authorized them to *practice* – elucidates this "notorious crux of interpretation" in a manner that coheres with the passage's sacred precursors in the OT texts mentioned above. The stories of both Moses and Elijah provide clear literary antecedents that establish a helpful interpretive backdrop for Jesus' intent to "pass them by."

In the first place, Israel's sacred tradition depicts a God who "passes by" God's servants precisely at their point of deepest desperation. In the wake of the golden-calf episode and God's scathing indictment of the "stiff-necked people" (λαὸς σκληροτράχηλος, LXX; עַם־קְשֵׁה־עֹ֫רֶף, MT), Moses

[84] So Gnilka, *Markus*, I:267; Koch, *Wundererzählungen*, 105–6; Guelich, *Mark 1–8:26*, 346; Marcus, *Mark 1–8*, 428–9.

[85] Gerd Theissen, *The Miracle Stories of the Early Christian Tradition*, trans. Francis McDonagh, ed. John Riches, SNTW (Philadelphia: Fortress Press, 1983), 101, notes comparable stories in ancient literature that combine the motifs (e.g. *Homeric Hymns* 33:12; Aristides, *Hymn to Serapis* 33).

[86] Pheme Perkins, "Mark," in *The New Interpreter's Bible*, vol. VIII (Nashville, TN: Abingdon, 1995), 603, n. 264.

[87] Jack Dean Kingsbury, *Conflict in Luke: Jesus, Authorities, Disciples* (Minneapolis: Fortress Press, 1991), 100.

pleads urgently for an assurance of God's continued presence: "How shall it be known that I have found favor in your sight, I and your people, unless you go with us?" (Exod. 33:16). Indeed, Moses solicits visible confirmation of his clout when he petitions God, "Show me your glory, I pray" (Exod. 33:18). We should note that, for Moses, God's divinity is not in question; rather it is evidence of God's covenant commitment to God's people that Moses seeks.

In similar fashion, God's self-disclosure to Elijah occurs at a critical juncture in his prophetic career. Jezebel has just issued a death threat which has prompted Elijah's fearful departure "a day's journey into the wilderness" (1 Kgs. 19:4), where he first asks for God to take his life and then registers an utterly disconsolate complaint: "I alone am left, and they are seeking my life, to take it away" (1 Kgs. 19:10). In short, both heroic figures find their power and authority jeopardized in some measure; having responded to God's claim upon their lives, both Moses and Elijah find their mission thwarted and threatened. In both instances, God deigns to "pass by" as a reassuring act of self-disclosure.

Yet even more significant for the interpretation of this passage is the purpose of God's self-revelation. In neither case does the epiphanic moment provide a simple tonic for despondency; neither encounter with God functions primarily to prove God's identity; and, perhaps most importantly, neither prized revelation constitutes a miraculous deliverance for God's servant. Rather, the outcome of each encounter with God is to reinvigorate the chosen agent with a new passion for the mission to which he has been called. So Moses descends from the mountain with a radiant face, carrying in hand the re-created stone tablets of the covenant (Exod. 34:29), and thus reclaiming his leadership of God's wayward and recalcitrant people. And Elijah resumes his mission of asserting God's kingship by enlisting Elisha as understudy and heir to his power. In both cases, God's "passing by" revives despairing servants by reminding them of their divinely ordained authority.

The cumulative weight of the evidence suggests that the same is true in this Markan instance of Jesus' intent to "pass by" his disciples in their time of trial. Here Mark's Jesus means not merely to showcase his own divine identity but to respond to his followers' plight by reinvigorating them for their mission. As they have been "with Jesus," these seafaring emissaries have been granted demonstrable power associated with God's apocalyptic reign; indeed, his presence has transformed them into agents of that dominion. So in this instance, when Jesus "comes toward them" intending to "pass them by," he stages an epiphany designed to fortify them through a reminder of his presence for the leadership for which they have been called and equipped. Thus, rather than reflecting competing motifs of rescue and epiphany, Jesus' coming toward them and passing them by together suggest that Jesus' self-disclosure serves as a requisite step in addressing the disciples' plight. Like Moses and Elijah, the disciples could be expected to emerge from their encounter fortified for the battle against their apocalyptic adversary, the tormenting gale.[88]

But if Jesus' revelation aims to empower the disciples in their battle against the tormenting wind, the epiphanic thrust of the encounter is lost on them, as Mark reports:

> But when they saw him walking on the sea, they thought it was a ghost and cried out for they all saw him and were terrified (ἐταράχθησαν). (Mk. 6:49–50)

Notably, the same verb ταράσσω appears in Ps. 77:16 (LXX 76:17) – within the context of a passage which combines the motifs of Exodus and epiphany: "O God, when the waters saw you, they were afraid (ἐφοβήθησαν); the very deep was disturbed (ἐταράχθησαν)."[89] By thus characterizing their response, the evangelist introduces a deft touch of irony that grows more pronounced as the episode comes to a close. Here the disciples respond to Jesus' divine disclosure not as those who welcome as "gospel" God's kingly victory but as those aligned with the forces at odds with God's reign.

Somewhat surprisingly, though, Jesus neither directly criticizes the disciples' response nor accepts it unquestioningly.[90] Instead, he addresses their imperception and fear through this word of reassurance: θαρσεῖτε, ἐγώ εἰμι: μὴ φοβεῖσθε (Mk. 6:50). In language that rings a familiar scriptural note, Jesus articulates the message God repeatedly conveys to the people of Israel at critical junctures in the biblical story.

Careful consideration is warranted with respect to Jesus' self-identifying expression ἐγώ εἰμι: does the phrase merely counter the disciples' case of mistaken identity ("It's me, guys, not a ghost"), or does

[88] Notably, the Job passage that Hays cites lends credence to this view as well (see "Gospels," 410). Job 9:5 attributes to God alone the ability to "remove mountains," while Mark's Jesus instructs his disciples that their faith in God effectively gives them access to that same remarkable power (Mk. 11:22–4). If this kind of power belongs to God alone, Mark's Jesus repeatedly expects others to participate in its manifestation.

[89] Marcus, *Mark 1–8*, 431, notes that the Targum similarly "transfers the disturbance from the waters to 'the peoples.'"

[90] This "third-way" response on Jesus' part is consistent with his response to the disciples' equally untrusting assessment of the crowd's hunger in the feeding story. In this narrative, we may detect another subtle thematic link between the two stories – a link that expands the accounts' Christological claims to include Jesus' engaging interaction with his followers.

it signal Jesus' use of an established "self-revelatory formula"?[91] While Mark seems to demur here as elsewhere in the gospel[92] from an overt claim to Jesus' divinity, several features of this use of ἐγώ εἰμι tip the scales in favor of reading it as Jesus' allusive identification with the saving power of God. If the phrase on one level simply prompts the disciples to recognize their teacher, on another level it functions to recall for them God's sovereignty over the tormenting wind and waves.

In the first place, the LXX commonly employs ἐγώ εἰμι to translate the first-person pronoun אָנֹכִי/אֲנִי, and the phrase frequently appears as preamble to God's revelatory encounter with select leaders. The Genesis patriarchal narratives, for example, include episodes in which God addresses Abraham (Gen. 17:1), Isaac (Gen. 26:24), and Jacob/Israel (Gen. 31:13), in each case beginning the pronouncement with ἐγώ εἰμι. Similarly, the phrase introduces the God whom Moses encounters in the burning-bush episode (Exod. 3:6, 14). While these instances do not precisely equate the phrase ἐγώ εἰμι with the divine name (since they all supply a predicate), they do consistently employ ἐγώ εἰμι as the opening line of God's self-disclosure where God taps those leaders who would carry forward God's agenda.

Even more significant for the purposes of this passage are its thematic and verbal ties with exilic Isaiah's prophetic hopes for a New Exodus. For repeatedly in Deutero-Isaiah, the phrase ἐγώ εἰμι translates the bipartite אֲנִי־הוּא where the oracle pronounces God's coming triumph on the earth in and through his chosen people.[93] First, in two instances the LXX translates the Hebrew text's self-disclosure formula אָנֹכִי אָנֹכִי הוּא with the

[91] The phrase derives from Heinrich Zimmermann's view of the absolute ἐγώ εἰμι as "*die* alttestamentliche Offenbarungsformel" ("Das absolute ἐγώ εἰμι als die neutestamentliche Offbarungsformel," *BZ* 4 [1960]: 270, emphasis added) and is adopted, e.g., by Gnilka, *Markus*, I:270; Guelich, *Mark 1–8:26*, 351. Cf. Margaret Davies, *Rhetoric and Reference in the Fourth Gospel*, JSNTSup 69 (Sheffield, England: JSOT Press, 1992), 84–5, who calls for prudent caution in equating the phrase with the divine name, though she does acknowledge that, "in prophetic oracles, the Septuagint does translate the Hebrew for 'I (am) he' by the Greek ἐγώ εἰμι" (85). See below for further discussion of LXX Isaiah's relevance to this Markan passage.

[92] See, e.g., Mk. 1:11; 9:7; 14:36; 15:39, where the relationship between Jesus and God is characterized as father to son. Also cf. Mk. 10:18, where Jesus deliberately differentiates himself from God, who alone is "good."

[93] Cf. Catrin H. Williams, *I Am He: The Interpretation of "Anî Hû" in Jewish and Early Christian Literature* (Tübingen: Mohr Siebeck, 2000), *passim*, for a thorough study of the significance of אֲנִי־הוּא in the Hebrew Bible as well as in later Jewish exegesis. Her findings stress the importance of the phrase not just for identifying the one God – thus not as a proper name *per se* – but for pressing beyond God's identity to God's activity. As she puts it, "it is the nature and content of the claims attributed to God that makes them theologically signficant" for those invoking the "I am" phrase (307).

doublet ἐγώ εἰμι ἐγώ εἰμι, thus implying that the second occurrence of the Greek phrase serves as the predicate nominative for the first.[94] Moreover, with respect to the claims made by the prophet on Yahweh's behalf, Isa. 41:1–10 combines an emphasis on Yahweh's sovereignty among the nations (ἐγὼ θεὸς πρῶτος καὶ εἰς τὰ ἐπερχόμενα ἐγώ εἰμι, Isa. 41:4) with a command to "fear not" (μὴ φοβοῦ, Isa. 41:10). And perhaps most tellingly, the oracle of Israel's coming redemption envisioned in Isa. 43 casts God's self-revelation (ἐγώ εἰμι, Isa. 43:10, 25) and God's command to "fear not" (μὴ φοβοῦ, Isa. 43:5) within the context of a New Exodus in which the people will "pass through waters" (Isa. 43:2) accompanied by the God who "makes a way in the sea, a path in the mighty waters" (Isa. 43:16).[95]

Such a convergence of language and sea-crossing imagery, then, provides an important interpretive framework within which to view Jesus' response to the disciples in peril upon the waves. As Marcus puts it,

> When Jesus quells the power of the sea, strides in triumph across the waves, and announces his presence to the disciples with the sovereign self-identification formula 'I am he' . . . he is speaking in and acting out the language of Old Testament divine warrior theophanies, narratives in which Yahweh himself subdues the demonic forces of chaos in a saving, cosmos-creating act of holy war.[96]

As I have discussed above, the raging waters serve as a theater of battle where God's decisive victory will be won within the human sphere. While it may be going too far to understand "I am he" as God's proper name, the phrase does seem to echo the prophetic message of divine promise, so prominent in Deutero-Isaiah, that God's coming rule will overshadow all pretenders to power (cf. Mk. 13:6). And for the disciples as for the exiled people of Israel, that claim to God's sovereignty carries with it the implication that they will participate fully in that reign.

To this point, I have considered the sea crossing as an unsuccessful attempt at the full practice of discipleship. Jesus has sent his companions ahead, apparently in the hope that they might effectively subdue the demonic powers of the raging sea. Yet, despite valiant efforts in their rowing, the disciples continue to be tossed about, victims of the adversarial wind and waves. Implicit in their failure, I have suggested, is their lack

[94] See Isa. 43:25; 51:12. A third instance of a double ἐγώ εἰμι occurs in Isa. 45:19, where it translates אֲנִי יְהוָה; indeed this case may lend greatest weight to the notion that the LXX translator equated the phrase ἐγώ εἰμι with the divine name.

[95] See Heil, *Jesus*, 59.

[96] Marcus, *Way*, 144–5.

of trust in God's dominion and its triumphant power, which Jesus has already conferred upon them.

Importantly, we have seen that Jesus' first impulse is not to strip that authority but to revitalize it. Through an attempt at self-disclosure, Jesus has sought to recall for the disciples what God would do in and through them as advance agents of God's impending reign. If they miss the cue, we infer already something of their imperceptivity: they have misconstrued the power of the presence that would rescue them in a time of trial. As Mark's story unfolds, this obtuseness only grows more pronounced as the narrative moves toward resolution.

"Toward them into the boat . . .": failure overcome and explained (Mk. 6:51–2)

In the end, though the disciples fail to grasp the empowering presence of Jesus in word ("it is I; fear not") and deed (walking on water), Jesus does not abandon them to their own obduracy. Instead he embodies his message by stepping into the boat. As is true so often in Mark, "good news" words are accompanied by "good news" action.[97] Notice, too, that the wind does not cease in this story until the very moment when Jesus joins them.[98] In other words, neither his walking on the water nor his self-disclosure provides the remedy for the problem at hand; it is only when he is once more *with the disciples* that the storm at sea is tamed. Here again, the in-breaking kingdom hinges not simply on Jesus' identity, exposed with pomp and circumstance as he walks and talks upon the waves, but more definitively on his active involvement with his followers as he joins them in the boat.

In light of findings thus far, I turn at last to one of the most enigmatic verses in the entire second gospel. While there is debate about exactly where Mark's interpretation begins (Mk. 6:51c or 52), scholars generally agree that "Mark's explanation [for the disciples' astonishment] is given in 52."[99] As it brings full-circle the passage's initial transition from

[97] Other examples include the teaching at Capernaum coupled with the man possessed by an evil spirit (Mk. 1:21–7); the healing/forgiving of the paralytic (Mk. 2:1–12); and the Sabbath teaching along with the man with the shriveled hand (Mk. 3:1–5).

[98] Lane suggests that Jesus' "walking upon the water proclaimed that the hostility of nature against man must cease with the coming of the Lord, whose concealed majesty is unveiled in the proclamation 'I am he'" (*Mark*, 236). But in this account the wind dies down not while Jesus walks on the water but only after he is again with the disciples.

[99] Taylor, *Saint Mark*, 330. See also Guelich, *Mark 1–8:26*, 347. This widely held conclusion is based on such observations as these: (1) γάρ clauses are typical of Markan redaction; (2) incomprehension is not directly mentioned in the preceding passage; (3) Mark is

Mk. 6:30–44, this verse offers a unifying interpretation of the second sea-crossing story. I have noted above that most interpreters decode the riddle of Mk. 6:52 by focusing on Jesus' miracle working in Mk. 6:30–44 and thus read "the loaves" as a cryptic reference to the feeding story as a whole. In this view, had the disciples correctly appraised Jesus' divine nature, they would have recognized him as he approached the boat and would have trusted him to subdue the wind. After all, one who can miraculously reproduce five loaves so as to feed a crowd of five thousand men can certainly muster the wherewithal to trounce the waves.

Yet a close reading of the feeding narrative itself may supply a significant, though previously undetected, interpretive clue. What does Mark mean to say about the disciples' incomprehension "concerning the loaves"? Perhaps the phrase reflects not a metonymic reference to the multiplication of loaves and fish but rather a precise concern with the loaves themselves. After all, the feeding story itself makes a noteworthy distinction between the loaves and the fish: after Jesus blesses and breaks the loaves, he gives them τοῖς μαθηταῖς ἵνα παρατιθῶσιν αὐτοῖς (Mk. 6:41). Indeed this deliberate description of the disciples serving the loaves contrasts markedly with the sharing of fish: τοὺς δύο ἰχθύας ἐμέρισεν πᾶσιν (Mk. 6:41). What is it the disciples ought to have grasped "concerning the loaves"? Perhaps it is their own part in Jesus' mission and thus their own God-given authority over the evil spirits "tormenting" their rowing. For the disciples fail the test in this passage on more than one level: it is not just Jesus' self-disclosure that they mismanage; at least for the moment, they have also misappropriated the power he has entrusted to them. Even when he comes toward them to renew that authority, they can only cower in fear. Thus we may more fully explicate the disciples' incomprehension in this way: "For they did not understand that, just as Jesus had empowered them to distribute the loaves in his eschatological feeding enterprise, so now Jesus expected them to 'go ahead to the other side,' fully trusting in and authorized to claim God's dominion over the sea."

It is important to note that this reading of Mk. 6:52 reflects an expansion – not a denial – of more traditional Christological interpretations.[100]

elsewhere concerned with incomprehension; and (4) v. 51 offers a typical ending for a miracle story.

100 Scholars cannot be blamed for following the lead of the first sea-crossing story, which ends with the disciples' own Christological musing: "Who is this then . . .?" (Mk. 4:41). Similarly, the third sea-crossing story (Mk. 8:14–21) features Jesus posing a battery of questions reiterating the two feeding stories' abundant surpluses and is read by most scholars as Jesus' code language for self-disclosure. Yet, significantly, neither instance places the Christological claims on the lips of Jesus. For further discussion of Mk. 8:14–21, see chapter 8 of this work.

For if the disciples in Mark's account have failed to exercise the kingdom authority Jesus has conferred upon them, then they have failed to latch onto the mission and message of their teacher. Already, many interpreters have laid the foundation for this reading of Mk. 6:52 without explicitly linking the verse to the disciples' mission. In her discussion of the Sea of Galilee in Mark, Malbon asserts that while "the sea is a threatening entity [in the gospel], it is to be mastered, metaphorically, by Jesus' followers as it is mastered, spatially, by the Marcan Jesus."[101] In addition, several scholars emphasize the missionary nature of discipleship: Tannehill maintains that "the disciples should share in Jesus' mission and fate";[102] Best holds that the "twelve" in this gospel are "those engaging in more or less full-time missionary activity";[103] and Kingsbury claims, "discipleship has 'mission work' as its purpose."[104] Thus, the second sea-crossing story provides an important reminder that, for Mark, Jesus' Christological identity is worked out in relationship with his followers.

Finally, this reading of the incomprehension motif seems viable in part because it lends more integrity to the passage as a whole. If we see their misunderstanding as the disciples' failed demonstration of God's kingdom power, no longer must we maintain that this verse introduces a radical reinterpretation of the encounter at sea; no longer must we view the motifs of bread and incomprehension and hardness of heart as unrelated themes that, as Quesnell claims, Mark "drags . . . in, apparently without need, [adding] them to a scene which seemed to make perfectly good sense in itself."[105] Rather, against the backdrop of the disciples' full participation in the miraculous distribution of the loaves, their conduct when sent on the boat ahead of Jesus becomes reproachable not for failing to recognize Jesus' divine power but for failing to exercise the kingdom-of-God power at their own disposal. Finally, such a reading elucidates Jesus' actions: his initial sending away of the disciples, his intent to "pass them by," and finally his "Plan B" remedy of rescue.

The remaining phrase to consider in this concluding verse points not to the content of the incomprehension but to its origin. If their actions throughout this story indicate the presenting symptoms of the disciples' condition, the phrase ἡ καρδία πεπωρωμένη names the root cause of their misunderstanding. Hardened hearts are diagnosed three times in Mark's gospel: once describing the Pharisees (Mk. 3:5), and twice describing the

[101] Malbon, "Sea of Galilee," 374. [102] Tannehill, "Gospel of Mark," 65.
[103] Ernest Best, "Mark's Use of the Twelve," *ZNW* 69 (1978): 33.
[104] Kingsbury, *Conflict*, 91. [105] Quesnell, *Mind of Mark*, 67.

disciples (Mk. 6:52; 8:17).[106] Already the present discussion of Mk. 4 has noted that the second evangelist refuses to assign his characters to static categories, so it should not surprise us to see the narrator ascribe to the disciples the very trait that serves as the foundation of the Pharisees' plot against Jesus in Mk. 3. Though earlier in the story the disciples' actions have paralleled those of Jesus himself, here the story casts these followers in a role "not essentially different from his opponents."[107]

What does Mark accomplish by linking the disciples' obtuseness with their hardened hearts? Watts believes the point of this language is to cast the disciples in the role of "exiled Israel awaiting deliverance,"[108] and thus maintains that their "hardened hearts" reflect God's judgment upon them for not recognizing both Jesus' identity as Son of God and his destiny as Son of Man.[109] Yet despite this interpretive emphasis on cognition, Watts must finally concede that the "one thing that sets the disciples apart is not that they immediately understand, but instead when called they follow, even though hardly comprehending."[110] Such a complex portrait of the disciples, then, belies a simple diagnosis of their condition.

Perhaps we are better served, then, by recalling that Mark's apocalyptic mindset, so doggedly devoted to God's sovereignty, would perceive the divine hardening activity as the driving force behind the human condition. Rather than indicating a blamable offense, the phrase "hardened hearts" employs the divine passive simply to account for the disciples' shortcomings. As Matera puts it, "hardness of heart is not merely the result of moral failure, although it is often manifested through moral failure . . . Hardness of heart is a situation in which human beings find themselves in the face of God's revelatory action if God does not provide assistance to comprehend it."[111]

Certainly the condition is one that in Israel's scriptures explains resistance to God's activity within the human sphere. Just as Pharaoh's heart is hardened in opposition to God's rescue of the Hebrew slaves through Moses (e.g. Exod. 7:3, 13), even God's "holy people" themselves exhibit

106 Matera posits that, because in the two instances referring to the disciples, "Mark employs the passive form of the verb rather than the noun as in 3,5 . . . the hardening of the disciples' hearts should not simply be equated with the hardness of heart of the Pharisees and Herodians" ("Incomprehension," 157). Such a clear distinction belies Mark's tendency to preserve the complexity of characters who embody both faithfulness and incomprehension.

107 See Lane, *Mark*, 236.

108 Rikki E. Watts, *Isaiah's New Exodus and Mark* (Tübingen: Mohr Siebeck, 1997), 222.

109 Ibid., 223. 110 Ibid., 290.

111 Matera, "Incomprehension," 158–9. So Focant, who points to other NT uses of hardened heart ("L'Incompréhension," 166) and restates it as an "impuissance radicale à comprendre plutôt qu'un réfus délibéré et malveillant" (167).

that hardness of heart when they live "like those whom [God does] not rule" (Isa. 63:17). In both cases, the hardened heart can be attributed to a sovereign God; in neither case does the condition of a hardened heart ultimately thwart the purposes of that sovereign God.

So too in Mk. 6:45–52, where the concluding phrase attributing to the disciples a commonly shared "hardened heart" explains the underlying cause of their misunderstanding. Rather than serving as living, breathing agents of God's power over the sea, the disciples exhibit a condition more akin to rigor mortis.[112] Yet if here they resemble those more overtly opposed to God's plan, such as the Pharisees (Mk. 3:5), it is important to bear in mind that Jesus' followers continue on the way with him, even to the end. Thus while this concluding phrase pronounces a somber assessment of the disciples' state of heart, Jesus does not abandon them. In its stark expression of their compromised faithfulness, the disciples' "hardened heart" does not disqualify them from following Jesus, even if sometimes "at a distance" (cf. Mk. 14:54).

Conclusion

I have now examined passages that feature significant interaction between Jesus and his disciples. From the incipient call to follow and subsequent mountaintop commissioning, through the imparting of special parabolic instruction and the working of miracles, the disciples have played a vital role in the dawning dominion of God that is proclaimed and embodied by Jesus. If in this second sea-crossing story we encounter the gospel's first mention of the disciples' incomprehension, we gain interpretive leverage by examining this instance of obduracy in relation to the story's literary and historical contexts. The following observations both summarize my findings with respect to Mk. 6:45–52 and lay an important foundation for a synthetic understanding of discipleship in Mark.

(1) A second "missionary journey": evidence within the passage itself as well as within its broader narrative context has led to the conclusion that Jesus sends his disciples out on this sea-crossing voyage much as he sends them out on the missionary journey of Mk. 6:7–13. While the passage admittedly lacks explicit mention of the outing's purpose, factors such as Jesus' intentional dismissal of the group, their "going ahead" of him, and their prior successful demonstration of God's kingly rule together indicate that, as Origen observes early on, Mark's Jesus means this second

[112] Tannehill believes that the condition "is not minor and temporary but arises from the basic character of the disciples" ("Gospel of Mark," 69).

sea-crossing as an opportunity for the disciples to continue their witness to the "gospel of God."

(2) The disciples' failure: in Mark's account, not only do the disciples succumb to the tormenting powers of the sea, but they also fail to recognize Jesus' empowering presence when he comes toward them, intending to "pass them by" (Mk. 6:48). As reflected in Mk. 6:45–52, then, their misunderstanding does concern their inability to recognize Jesus, and thus is "Christological" in nature. Yet their lapse concerns less Jesus' identity *in and of itself* than it does his identity *in relationship with his disciples* as those he has called and enlisted in his mission. At least in this pericope, what they "did not understand" is their own divinely ordained authority over the adversarial force animating the storm at sea.

(3) "The loaves": I have discerned in Mark's reference to "the loaves" an important but commonly ignored confirmation of this construal of the disciples' failure. Without ruling out the phrase's probable Eucharistic implications for the Markan community, I have suggested that the reference to "the loaves" recalls the disciples' full participation in the feeding miracle itself (Mk. 6:41). In addition to Jesus' Eucharistic presence, then, "the loaves" signals the empowerment that Jesus' presence has entailed for the Markan disciples and so for Mark's own community.

(4) The "gospel of God": despite their uncomprehending "hardened hearts," the disciples do not suffer the fate of those abandoned to their own shortcomings. When Jesus' handpicked followers prove incapable of their high calling, their leader's first response is to come toward them. When they fail to lay claim to his empowering presence, Jesus' second response is to offer the enduring promise: "fear not; I am (once again) with you" (Mk. 6:50). The "good news" here, Mark seems to indicate, lies in God's assured victory, asserted convincingly by Jesus, even in the wake of human failure to trust in it.

PART IV

Conclusion

8

FURTHER THOUGHTS "ON THE WAY"

The preceding study of discipleship in the gospel of Mark has been deliberately limited in scope. Not only has the inquiry been confined to passages occurring within the gospel's first six chapters, but it has also concluded at the precise point where Mark's portrait of discipleship takes a turn for the worse, as the evangelist for the first time overtly ascribes incomprehension to Jesus' followers: "For they did not understand concerning the loaves, for their hearts were hardened" (Mk. 6:52). Thus the interpretive aims of this project have been modest; rather than an exhaustive treatment of discipleship in Mark, I have attempted primarily to delineate the contours of discipleship *as set forth from the gospel's outset*, a pattern that in turn provides a platform against which we might assess the disciples' impending failures as the story progresses. Perhaps the most striking outcome of this study has been this: at least in the gospel's opening chapters, faithful discipleship can best be understood not as the correct appraisal of Jesus' Christological identity, but as the disciples' collective participation in Jesus' Christological mission. As a way of concluding this study, I shall review its results before noting their implications for the interpretation of Mark.

Summary of findings

After setting the terms of the ensuing exegetical study in Part I, Part II has explored in great detail two passages that are foundational for understanding Mark's portrait of discipleship. In chapter 2, I have examined Jesus' initial call to follow, extended to four fishers (Mk. 1:16–20). Among the interpretive points identified there are the following. First, Jesus' purposeful selection of a band of followers comes on the heels of – and is thematically tied to – his opening proclamation of God's coming reign, the "gospel of God" (Mk. 1:15); as a result, this gathering of disciples should be viewed as a vital part of the apocalyptic scheme that Jesus announces. Second, and in light of that apocalyptic worldview, Mark's Jesus summons these four fishers for two distinct purposes: to "come after" him (presence), and to be made "fishers of humans" (practice). Drawing especially on prophetic imagery found in Jer. 16, the latter component of this initial call to follow confers upon the first disciples a significant role in God's impending rectification of the created order. So from the outset, these followers are to be fashioned as participants in Jesus' own "gospel" mission.

In chapter 3, we have seen that this pattern of presence and practice gains confirmation in the formal commissioning of the Twelve (Mk. 3:13–19), where Jesus summons to the mountaintop his inner coterie of followers and further elaborates their calling. In the first place, simply the numbering of twelve disciples telegraphs to the first-century Jewish world the expectation that Israel is about to be restored, in and through the actions of this group associated with Jesus. Moreover, the language of their commissioning both reiterates the presence and practice to which the first disciples have been called and emphasizes through rhetorical weight the latter aspect of that calling: Jesus will send them out "to proclaim and to have authority to cast out demons" (Mk. 3:14). In their "fishing" enterprise, the Twelve become more than just ardent spokesmen for the coming reign of God; they will wield its very power, in both word and deed. In a word, from this moment, Jesus authorizes them to do the things he does.

Absent from these formative encounters, we should note, is any indication that correct Christological beliefs serve as the prerequisite to discipleship. Neither does the Markan text itself suggest that, at this pre-resurrection narrative moment, the disciples' failure to comprehend Jesus' identity and destiny in any way hinders the fulfillment of their intended role. As a result, our estimation of discipleship in Mark must take seriously the passages in which Jesus' followers do fulfill their calling *both* to remain with Jesus *and* to carry forth his own "proleptic fulfillment of the triumph of God."[1]

[1] The phrase is J. Christiaan Beker's characterization of the "coherent center of the Gospel" in Pauline thought (*Paul the Apostle: Triumph of God in Life and Thought* [Philadelphia: Fortress Press, 1984; orig. 1980], 351). On the Pauline influence on Mark, particularly evident in their respective theologies of the cross, see Joel Marcus, "Mark – Interpreter of Paul," *NTS* 48 (2000): 473–87. To Marcus's concluding list of theological interests that appear in both Mark and the Pauline corpus, I would add the participatory role afforded Jesus' followers, whose narrative portrait in the second gospel appears to correspond to the Pauline theme of being "in Christ." On this motif, see, e.g., Albert Schweitzer, *The Mysticism of Paul the Apostle*, trans. William Montgomery (Baltimore: Johns Hopkins University Press, 1998; orig. 1931); also E. P. Sanders, *Paul and Palestinian Judaism: A Comparison of Patterns of Religion* (Minneapolis: Fortress Press, 1977), 549, who coins the

The remainder of the Markan episodes considered in this study follow the narrative terrain as it offers glimpses of discipleship in action, and with varying degrees of effectiveness. As a first instance of discipleship as *presence*, chapter 4 has examined the seaside teaching (Mk. 4:1–34). Here we find Jesus' followers portrayed as front-row observers of their master's proclamation of God's dominion, vividly illustrated through his parabolic instruction. What insights does this encounter yield for our construal of Markan discipleship? First, a group loosely defined as "those around him with the Twelve" (Mk. 4:10) presses Jesus for further clarification, and by doing so they attain insider status. Indeed, the inquiring spirit indicates not only that they are intrigued by Jesus' teachings, but also that they are willing to commit to those teachings as definitive for their lives. Second, Jesus reminds them of their "giftedness," in that they have been entrusted with the τὸ μυστήριον . . . τῆς βασιλείας τοῦ θεοῦ (Mk. 4:11). In turn, both the interpretation of the sower parable and the accompanying "parables of the kingdom" implicitly ascribe to the disciples a role in disseminating the "word," even in the face of apparent futility. Thus implicit even in this example of discipleship as *presence* is the expectation that the disciples, and their heirs in the Markan community, will continue Jesus' sowing activity.

Now fully authorized and thoroughly inculcated, the disciples begin their own missionary activity in Mk. 6:7–13, which serves as the focus of chapter 5. In the first place, I have noted the narrative placement of this episode at the precise juncture where Jesus' own powers have been compromised by his hometown's lack of faith (their ἀπιστία, Mk. 6:6a). Possibly in response to this setback, Jesus convenes the Twelve and reiterates the authority he has conferred on them in Mk. 3:13–15. And after receiving missionary instructions that employ New Exodus imagery, the apostles go forth to bear witness to the dawning reality of God's dominion. Indeed, the report that Mark supplies notes the burgeoning success of their activity, as the disciples "went out and proclaimed that all should repent. They cast out many demons, and anointed with oil many who were sick and cured them" (Mk. 6:12–13). Once again, Mark reports their unqualified effectiveness.

As the next step in the investigation, chapter 6 has examined the portrait of discipleship in a tale traditionally scrutinized for its Christological

term "participationist eschatology" to express the Pauline view that the "believer becomes one with Christ and that this effects a transfer of lordship and the beginning of a transformation which will be completed with the coming of the Lord." This description, especially with its emphasis on involvement with the risen Christ, along with its expectation for a future coming, seems not far from the mindset that permeates the second gospel.

implications: the feeding of the five thousand (Mk. 6:30–44). In this scene, as in the parabolic teachings of Mk. 4:1–34, close attention to Jesus' interaction with his followers reveals that even their being in Jesus' *presence* points toward their active *practice* of his own Christological agenda. In this case, Jesus directly involves the disciples in the feeding miracle first by commanding them, "you give them something to eat" (Mk. 6:37), and then, in response to their protests, by transforming them into participants in this eschatological wilderness meal. As we have seen, not only do the disciples draw on their own resources to supply the food, but they also work in concert with Jesus in the miraculous distribution of the loaves. In the face of scarcity, Jesus equips his band of followers to help him demonstrate the surfeit of God's coming kingdom.

The final, and perhaps most provocative, exegetical step comes in chapter 7, where I have considered the second Markan sea-crossing story (Mk. 6:45–52), with a keen eye to its portrait of discipleship. With the exegetical observations of this study's first five chapters serving as an interpretive springboard, many features of this storm-at-sea passage emerge in a new light. First, I have noted that the story's language and narrative context suggest the possibility that this episode constitutes a second "sending out" of the disciples. Yet this time, as they encounter the demonic forces of the sea, the disciples prove incapable of effective resistance; despite a night of struggle, they are still, by the hour just before dawn, "tormented in their rowing" (Mk. 6:48).

Further, I have maintained that Jesus' first response to their predicament, described by Mark as his intent to "pass them by" (Mk. 6:48c), makes most sense when understood in the context of God's tendency to "pass by" leading figures in the sacred lore of Israel. That is, the phrase conveys self-disclosure, but self-disclosure that renews God's leaders for their divinely ordained purpose. The fact that Jesus' followers misapprehend this encounter when they perceive him to be a ghost signals their disoriented perspective: just as they have failed to tame the wind, so too have they failed to recognize their master's empowering presence. Only when the disciples are again "with him" in the boat does the gale subside, a detail that suggests that their practice of discipleship depends not on their own miraculous abilities but on the authority derived solely from being with Jesus. In the end, it is this dynamic interplay of *presence* and *practice*, an interplay already evident in the distribution of the loaves, that the disciples misunderstand (Mk. 6:52).

These six focus passages together establish a narrative pattern for discipleship that has been all but ignored by recent Markan scholarship. Certainly, this pattern of presence and practice is intimately intertwined with

Jesus' own Christological mission. Yet, in the episodes reviewed here, Mark predicates true discipleship not on full knowledge of Jesus' precise identity but rather on his followers' full participation in his kingdom-of-God agenda. In both the praiseworthy and the reprehensible glimpses of discipleship examined in this study, a common theme has emerged: Jesus consistently expects his followers to wield authority that stems from God's sovereign dominion – not on their own as self-designated "divine men," but as those empowered by Jesus for the collective extension of his Christological witness. Thus where they emulate his paradigmatic exposition of God's rule, the disciples have properly grasped not just Jesus' true messianic identity but also their own call to participate in the new age of God that he proclaims and embodies. Where they fall short, they have failed to trust the prevailing promises of God's coming dominion.

Impact of findings

Despite the limited scope of this investigation, these findings carry weighty implications for reading the entire second gospel. In a way, more exegetical issues have been opened than resolved. In particular, four aspects of Markan research gain interpretive leverage from the cumulative findings thus far: the relationship between Christology and discipleship; the nature of the disciples' incomprehension; the overarching "gospel" storyline; and Mark's "word on target" for his community. Together, the synthetic observations that follow demonstrate that renewed attention to the pattern of discipleship exposed in the unfolding Markan narrative lends greater coherence to the second gospel as a whole and sheds important new light on several problematic features of the story.

Christology and discipleship

As noted in this study's opening chapter, Markan scholarship has frequently viewed the evangelist's Christological agenda as a "way in" to the gospel's portrait of discipleship.[2] In this common approach, well-executed discipleship hinges on a proper understanding of Jesus' suffering and dying messiahship. As a result, Witherington speaks for a host of interpreters when he claims that, for Mark, "true discipleship, based on true understanding of Jesus and his mission, was only possible after

[2] See above, chapter 1, for a discussion of the wide variety of Christological emphases that interpreters have detected in the second gospel.

Easter."[3] Despite the "way of the cross" teachings found in the gospel's central section, Jesus' followers fail to grasp the nature of his messianic mission and thus are portrayed as tradents of either flawed or insufficient Christology, which in turn precludes their faithful fulfillment of the discipleship calling.

As widespread as this understanding of Markan discipleship may be, this study's exegetical attention to the gospel's first six chapters has exposed its fundamental weakness: Mark's narrative begins with a positive portrayal of the disciples' calling and proceeds with a glowing performance review *before* it reports with increasing intensity the more sobering account of the disciples' flagrant failures. Moreover, where the disciples demonstrate rampant "success," they do so not by subscribing to a fully developed, post-Easter Christology but somewhat naively as authorized agents of God's coming kingdom.

Together, these findings warrant a careful remapping of the relationship between Christology and discipleship as portrayed in the second gospel, a relationship that lies at the heart of Mark's narrative. As demonstrated throughout this work, any inquiry into the implications of Jesus' messiahship for those who would follow must begin with the wider messianic program Mark imputes to Jesus. As we shall see, rather than denying Mark's interest in sketching Jesus in Christological hues, the interpretive results of this study expand the horizon of Mark's Christology so that it encompasses both Jesus' particular messianic role and his followers' intended function in the messianic age that he inaugurates.[4]

From the outset, we should recognize that Mark conveys Christological concerns in a nuanced and somewhat muted fashion and that Mark's Jesus himself does not explicitly solicit faith in himself. Indeed, Jesus' reticence about his own identity contrasts strikingly with his posture in John's gospel, since Mark lacks statements such as the "I am" sayings (see, e.g., Jn. 8:58; 10:7, 14; 11:25; 15:1, 5), claims to preexistence with God (see, e.g., Jn. 1:1–17; 17:5, 24), and the direct imperative to trust

[3] Ben Witherington, III. *The Gospel of Mark: A Socio-Rhetorical Commentary* (Grand Rapids, MI: Eerdmans, 2001), 441.

[4] It is not without significance that the findings here cohere with the assessment of Helmut Koester regarding the content of Q sayings: "The Jesus of the earliest formulation of [Q] proclaims the arrival of God's kingdom as a challenge to the disciples, who are asked to realize that their own existence belongs to a new eschatological moment" ("The Sayings of Q and Their Image of Jesus," in *Sayings of Jesus: Canonical and Non-Canonical*, ed. William L. Petersen, Johan S. Vos, and Henk J. De Jonge [Leiden: Brill, 1997], 154). My only quibble is with Koester's term "arrival"; with respect to Mark, and probably Q as well, I would substitute "palpable nearness."

in him (see, e.g., Jn. 14:1).[5] Readers of Mark's gospel encounter a Jesus who barely addresses the matter of his Christological identity.[6]

This pervasive demurral on the part of Mark's Jesus seems admittedly at odds, though, with the general tenor of a story that features Jesus as its clear focus. As I have noted throughout this study, Jesus consistently emerges not just as the protagonist, but also as a protagonist in full command of the narrative. It is Jesus, for instance, who first summons followers and promises to make them fishers of humans (Mk. 1:16–20). It is Jesus who convenes a mountaintop summit in order to appoint the Twelve and to empower them for their part in his mission (Mk. 3:13–15). It is Jesus who offers private instruction to his inner circle (Mk. 4:13–34), sends the apostles out on a missionary journey (Mk. 6:7–13), involves them, upon their return, in the miraculous feeding (Mk. 6:34–44), and finally addresses their lamentable failure at sea (Mk. 6:45–52).

Moreover, Mark's Jesus clearly enjoys a privileged relationship with God. Twice, a voice from heaven echoes both Ps. 2:7 and Isa. 42:1 in its acclamation of Jesus as God's "beloved son" (Mk. 1:11; 9:7); Peter names Jesus as ὁ Χριστός (Mk. 8:29), an identification that Jesus qualifies but does not deny; and the centurion utters a word of recognition when he claims that "truly, this man was God's son" (Mk. 15:39). With artful subtlety, Mark does advance Christological claims, carefully recasting the messianic role to include both the ignominious fate of death on a cross and, just over the horizon, the eschatological Son of Man seated at the right hand and coming in power (Mk. 14:62). Despite Jesus' own reticence on the matter, then, Mark's gospel does portray Jesus in a messianic light.

In addition, the more Mark's narrative presses toward full disclosure of Jesus' identity, the more Mark casts his followers as obdurate and even reprehensible. While the disciples' culpability in the feeding narrative may be only implied, Mark overtly attributes their alarm at sea to their incomprehension (Mk. 6:52). What is more, this mention of the

[5] Not that "faith/trust" plays a negligible role in Mark's gospel: to the contrary. Yet three observations shape our understanding of the nature of that faith: (1) nowhere does the narrative overtly mention Jesus as the object of that faith; (2) where faith's object is specified, it designates God (e.g. Mk. 11:22), or the "gospel" [of God] (Mk. 1:14) as that object; and (3) where "faith" finds no object, it obliquely refers to faith in Jesus only insofar as he is the one who "discloses God's sovereignty" (Christopher D. Marshall, *Faith as a Theme in Mark's Narrative*, SNTSMS 64 [New York: Cambridge University Press, 1989], 54). Put negatively, the nature of "faith" in Mark is never confined to belief in Jesus' identity as the suffering messiah.

[6] Indeed, he does so only before the High Priest (Mk. 14:62) – and there only after an initial silence (Mk. 14:61).

disciples' incomprehension only heralds the beginning of a downward spiral of discipleship. While I have identified a positive ideal for Markan discipleship in the pattern of presence and practice – in Jesus' expectations from the outset that his followers will participate in his mission – the unfolding narrative presents a widening chasm not just between Jesus' faithfulness and the disciples' faltering ways, but also between their own calling and their inability to fulfill it.

Indeed, on the boat again two chapters later, Jesus hurls a series of indicting questions and directly assails them for misunderstanding (Mk. 8:21: "Do you not yet understand?"). When Peter rebukes Jesus for suggesting an ignoble pattern of a suffering messiahship, Jesus calls him "Satan" (Mk. 8:33). And when the disciples prove unable to cast out a boy's unclean spirit, they are arguably party to the "generation of unbelief" (Mk. 9:19) that seems to hinder full disclosure of God's reign. Finally, in the passion narrative, they sleep in Gethsemane when Jesus has bid them to remain watchful (Mk. 14:37); Peter denies any affiliation with Jesus not once but three times; and even at the empty tomb, only three women represent a scant minority of faithful followers. Without a doubt, the disciples in Mark's gospel come under increasing fire as the story progresses.

The findings of this exegetical study, then, neither neglect the gospel's Christological concerns nor ignore its escalating censure of Jesus' disciples. Jesus *is* the protagonist of Mark's gospel – and a protagonist who is uniquely authorized, as God's son, to herald the onset of God's sovereignty. His followers *are* an increasingly obtuse group of supporting characters, characters who freely fall away, especially as they face the skyrocketing cost of following Jesus.

What then is the relationship between Christology and discipleship in the gospel of Mark? Simply put, Mark's Christology drives his portrait of discipleship in just this respect: true discipleship entails *both* full-fledged trust in the reality of God's coming rule, as evinced in and through Jesus, *and* active stewardship of the messianic power conferred by Jesus upon the disciples. As Marshall puts it, "Discipleship faith is ultimately faith in God (11:22) and participation in his eschatological activity, both as the companions of Jesus during his ministry, and as the community of Jesus . . . after his resurrection."[7] In the subduing of demons, in the healing of illness, in the forgiveness of sins, the disciples faithfully wield the authority of God's coming kingdom; so too in the way of the cross,

[7] Marshall, *Faith*, 175.

Jesus compels his followers to join in his frontal assault on the "seeming" powers (Mk. 10:42) by walking the path of self-denying servanthood, a posture that subverts and redefines the power structures of the present evil age.

Mark's Christology, then, can only be understood in light of the "gospel" mission that characterizes Jesus' life and death: his apocalyptic engagement with forces animated by God's adversary. And Mark's portrait of discipleship, despite its increasingly unflattering appearance, can only be understood in light of the fact that Jesus' Christological enterprise is not a solitary one. As he enlists others to follow him, learn from him, and carry forward his program of regime change, Mark's Jesus envisions true discipleship as the continuing vital witness to the kingdom of God he so authoritatively heralds.

As we have seen, this collective, community-based embodiment of an individual leader's cause finds literary antecedents within the Jewish scriptures. The Danielic Son of Man extends his power and authority to the community of the "holy ones" (Dan. 7:18, 22, 27), and Deutero-Isaiah assigns God's chosen servant a role consistent with that of faithful Israel (e.g. Isa. 42:1–9; 49:1–6; 52:13–53:12). Rather than forcibly distinguishing between God's anointed viceroy and those who acclaim him as such, Mark fashions his story by appeal to a familiar theme of the community's reflection, even embodiment, of its leader's priorities.

In the end, then, the "Christology" of Mark's gospel, fully grasped, does concern Jesus' identity as God's son, but it also entails a broader interest in his mission as harbinger of God's coming reign upon the earth, in both power and passion. Within the Markan narrative, Jesus' messianic purpose is to lead the charge in this dawning new age. But he does not proceed on his mission without enlisting others as agents of his authority, agents who remain dependent on Jesus' presence as they practice the kingdom power conferred upon them.

In turn, "discipleship" does entail Christological confession (see, e.g., Mk. 8:29), but it also carries a broader call to participate in the messianic kingdom Jesus inaugurates. Just as faithful discipleship will ultimately involve walking the way of the cross, it also entails the powerful disclosure of God's encroaching dominion. Where the disciples fall short, they do so not just by underestimating the cost of following Jesus, but also by underestimating (or not trusting) the authority he has unleashed in and through them to extend the good news of God's victory to all who would receive it. The ideal of discipleship in Mark's gospel, though it proves to be an elusive ideal, can best be seen as the full outworking of Jesus' own Christological mission. And as Jesus both initiates and authorizes his relationship with his followers, Mark defines discipleship in a manner that inextricably links the practice of God's kingdom with the continuing presence of Jesus, and vice versa.

The incomprehension motif

A second ramification of this study's results follows from the first and concerns the Markan motif of the disciples' incomprehension. For once we identify the contours of discipleship sketched from the gospel's outset – contours of presence and practice – we are better equipped to grasp its increasingly negative depiction of those whom Jesus has called to follow him. As we have seen, Mark portrays faithful discipleship not in terms of correct Christological confession but rather as active participation in Jesus' Christological purpose. In turn, then, the disciples' ineptitude must be assessed not strictly according to their beliefs about Jesus' messiahship, but more broadly in terms of their own participation in his gospel mission. When the disciples fail in Mark's account, they do so by cowering in the face of the hopeful prospect of God's kingly reign, by failing to exercise the powers conferred upon them by Jesus; thus the disciples increasingly misconstrue their role as a collective witness to God's apocalyptic rectification of the world.

Once we move beyond the concern of Jesus' Christological identity and purpose *per se* to consider the Christological implications for Markan discipleship, the gospel's motif of incomprehension can be more adequately considered. For to take seriously the composite portrait of discipleship found in the six passages studied here prompts us also to consider the possibility that the disciples' misunderstanding entails more than just the fact that Jesus *is* the Christ, and even more than just the strange messianic twist introduced by the passion. Rather, their incomprehension derives from the disciples' faltering grasp of Jesus' apocalyptic messiahship as it impinges upon their own lives. But does this expanded view of the disciples' incomprehension square with subsequent episodes that depict the group as decidedly obtuse? A brief consideration of two instances in which the disciples perform poorly will demonstrate the interpretive payoff of this approach for our grasp of the incomprehension motif.

To begin with, the third in the gospel's triad of sea-crossing stories (Mk. 8:14–21) provides an important test case as we reconsider the nature of the disciples' incomprehension. For here, when the disciples find themselves once again at sea just after the feeding of the four thousand (Mk. 8:1–10) and the Pharisees' demand for a sign (Mk. 8:11–13), Jesus utters his most scathing indictment yet of those who have so closely aligned their lives with his:

> Why are you talking about having no bread? Do you still not perceive or understand? Are your hearts hardened? Do you have eyes, and fail to see? Do you have ears and fail to hear?
>
> (Mk. 8:17–18)

Already I have examined the first sea-crossing story (Mk. 4:35–41) briefly and the second (Mk. 6:45–52) in greater depth.[8] In both cases, Jesus' disciples manifest attitudes and actions incongruent with the kind of trust in God's kingdom that Jesus both demonstrates and requires. In neither case, it should be noted, does Mark specifically attribute the disciples' lapse to a deficient Christology, as if they fail to grasp Jesus' wonder-working powers.

At issue this time is not an adversarial wind but the presence or absence of bread. Rather curiously, even at the outset of the story, the narrator describes the disciples' food supply in a somewhat paradoxical statement: "Now they had forgotten to bring any bread; and they had only one loaf with them in the boat" (Mk. 8:14). Then, in response to Jesus' warning about the Pharisees' leaven, they respond, "It is because we have no bread" (Mk. 8:16). Indeed, it is precisely this claim that provokes Jesus' ire, prompting him to ask why they are discussing having "no bread" (Mk. 8:17). Moreover, Jesus paints the disciples in the same Isaianic hues he has employed to describe "those outside" in Mk. 4:11–12: not perceiving or understanding; having hardened hearts; having eyes that fail to see; having ears that fail to hear. Finally he denounces them for failing to remember the two feeding accounts and, in particular, the abundance of leftovers the disciples have collected (Mk. 8:19–20).

What is the nature of the disciples' incomprehension in this third boat scene? Jesus' scathing indictment suggests that the disciples' misunderstanding extends far beyond the realm of Jesus' miraculous powers to the nature of God's dominion that he so powerfully demonstrates. On one level, they misconstrue Jesus' warning about the "leaven" of both Herod and the Pharisees, who have encountered the palpable evidence of God's coming kingdom and failed to "turn and trust in the gospel." This message, though, is lost on Jesus' companions, who are preoccupied with the question of available bread.

As a result, the story's narrative link with Mk. 4:11–12 (with its reference to motifs from Isa. 6) assigns the disciples themselves to "outsider"

[8] See above, chapter 5, 138–42; chapter 7, 212–37.

status, as their incomprehension here stems from their own inability to perceive the "mystery" of God's kingdom which is taking root and bearing fruit on the earth.[9] At this narrative juncture, they have twice witnessed the demonstration of abundance in the face of an apparent lack, a "mysterious" manifestation of God's coming reign, to be sure. So when the disciples stretch the truth of "one loaf" to claim "we have no bread," they have already abandoned the perspective of God's kingdom and opted, as it were, for the leaven of the Pharisees and of Herod. Jesus' ensuing battery of questions certainly confirms his own role in the miraculous provision, but the questions also press further to suggest the mysterious nature of God's rule, evident wherever surplus trumps deprivation. Thus in this passage too, the disciples' incomprehension derives from their misperception not just about Jesus' messianic status, but more broadly about the promises of God's coming rule, which carries drastic implications for their own perception of the world.

Though it does not qualify, strictly speaking, as an "incomprehension" story, another case of compromised discipleship provides a second test case for assessing the shortcomings of Jesus' followers. In Mk. 9:14–29, a father reports to Jesus that he has asked the disciples to cast a spirit out of his son, but that they proved impotent (οὐκ ἴσχυσαν, Mk. 9:18). Granted that the disciples have been both empowered for spirit-expulsion (Mk. 3:15) and successful in that activity (Mk. 6:13), the man's request is a reasonable one. Perhaps that is why Jesus seems so perturbed in his response: "O faithless generation, how much longer must I be among you? How much longer must I put up with you?" (Mk. 9:19).

Since Jesus laments the ἄπιστος nature of those involved in this thwarted exorcism,[10] the clear implication is that faith/trust is necessary

[9] On the thematic and interpretive connection between Mk. 8:14–21 and the parabolic instruction of Mk. 4, see Rikki E. Watts, *Isaiah's New Exodus and Mark* (Tübingen: Mohr Siebeck, 1997), 226–8; also Mary Ann Beavis, *Mark's Audience: The Literary and Social Setting of Mark 4.11–12*, JSNTSup 33 (Sheffield: Sheffield Academic Press, 1989), 103–14; John P. Heil, *Jesus Walking on the Sea: Meaning and Gospel Functions of Matt 14:22–33, Mark 6:45–52 and John 6:15b–21*, AnBib 87 (Rome: Biblical Institute Press, 1981), 136–40. In each case, the interpreter's view of the "mystery" revolves more tightly around the issue of Jesus' identity than I have claimed above (chapter 4), though Watts adds this caveat: "all this within the parameters of Israel's hopes and expectations concerning the inauguration of God's I[saianic] N[ew] E[xodus] reign (*Isaiah's New Exodus*, 228).

[10] Whether the father or the disciples are characterized by the term is debatable. Favoring the view that the "unbelief" can be located with the father is his subsequent plea, "Help my unbelief" (Mk. 9:24), as well as the gospel's prior claims that people's "unbelief" basically renders even Jesus impotent (Mk. 6:5–6). On the other hand, the passage's closing conversation, together with Mark's increasingly reproachful stance toward the disciples, leads many interpreters to identify them as the object of this censure too. Perhaps Marshall's

for the miracle to be successful. Indeed, other features of the passage reflect the pivotal dynamic of πίστις.[11] First, when the father petitions Jesus for help, a request he qualifies with the clause, "if you are able to do anything" (Mk. 9:22), Jesus answers emphatically: "If you are able! All things are able to be done for the one trusting (τῷ πιστεύοντι)" (Mk. 9:23). Second, in his candid admission that his own trust is tinged with mistrust, the father tacitly acknowledges that he lacks the efficacious faith required for a successful healing. And finally, when the disciples inquire about the cause of their failure, Jesus explains their inability to heal in this way: "this kind can come out only through prayer" (Mk. 9:29) – an act Mark's Jesus will define as a request made in full trust of God (Mk. 11:24). If this foiled exorcism does constitute a failed discipleship event, as the disciples prove unable to execute their authority to "cast out demons," what is at issue is not precise Christological confession but faith/trust in the Christological program devoted to the binding of the strong man (Mk. 3:27).

These two passages thus confirm two aspects of my findings on the incomprehension motif. First, within the unfolding Markan plot, we find evidence of flawed discipleship that extends beyond the trait of "incomprehension" itself to include the disciples' impotence, as well as themes of denial (Mk. 14:66–72) and absence (Mk. 16:1–8). Yet even more importantly, the failures derive not from a pre-resurrection vantage point that prevents their full recognition of Jesus' messiahship; rather their lapses are the direct result of their "hardened heart," which prevents them from perceiving God's kingdom power at work and from submitting to its service.[12]

Mark's Jesus has come to proclaim and to manifest a proleptic glimpse of God's kingly rule upon the earth; he has summoned followers to engage in that mission. To do so requires not simply their affirmation of Jesus as

view is most judicious; he infers that the term refers to "all who are present" (*Faith*, 118). Similarly, Camille Focant, "L'Incompréhension, des disciples dans le deuxième évangile," *RB* 82 (1975): 174-5.

[11] Indeed, Eduard Schweizer claims that this passage is "much more a treatise about unbelief and belief than a miracle story" ("The Portrayal of the Life of Faith in the Gospel of Mark," *Int* 32 [1978]: 389).

[12] See Heikki Räisänen, *The Idea of Divine Hardening: A Comparative Study of the Notion of Divine Hardening, Leading Astray and Inciting to Evil in the Bible and the Qur'an* (Helsinki: Publications of the Finnish Exegetical Society, 1972), who finds that the motif of divine hardening (1) derives from the wider landscape of God's sovereignty (see, e.g., 95); (2) is more prevalent in literature associated with apocalyptic sectarianism, that is, as a source of "courage in the battle" (see 93; also ch. 3); and (3) may address the early church's problematic "social experience," that is, "why so many people have rejected the Gospel" (90). All three factors help to explain Mark's inclusion of the theme.

messiah, nor even as a messiah who suffers, but their unflinching trust in the good news of God's power to reorder the very world as they know it (see Mk. 11:20–4). As Marcus puts it, with respect to Mk. 10:15, "These warriors enter into God's *basileia*, into his kingly power, by acknowledging their childlike dependence on him; and they stand awestruck before the mighty works of redemption that he performs through them in spite of – indeed, because of – their weakness."[13]

The unifying message of Mark's gospel

By expanding the notion of the disciples' "incomprehension" to include their generally increasing incapacity to "trust in the gospel" (Mk. 1:15) – to acknowledge that "childlike dependence" – we find ourselves in a position to reconsider the nature of that "gospel." Already, I have examined above[14] Jesus' programmatic proclamation of Mk. 1:15: "The time has been fulfilled and the dominion of God has drawn near; repent and trust in the gospel." At this point, the findings suggest that this "gospel" serves as the unifying message of Mark's story; in short, this "gospel of God" (Mk. 1:14) supplies the wider horizon within which Mark sketches his Christological portrait of Jesus.

We should note key features of this "gospel" before considering its interpretive payoff as the work's governing framework. In the first place, the "good news" to which Jesus bears impeccable witness is God's assured victory not just in the heavenly places but also within the sphere of human history. As we have seen in chapter 2, Mark's (and the early church's) coinage of εὐαγγέλ terminology reflects the Isaianic expectation that God's dramatic incursion into the human realm will liberate a people and reestablish God's righteous reign.[15] Indeed, the link for Mark is made explicit from the outset of his work, in the citation of the "prophet Isaiah" (Mk. 1:2–3) as the starting point and framework within which the story will proceed.

In turn, this dramatic disclosure of God's reign, according to Mark, involves a frontal assault against adversarial forces, in hand-to-hand combat that comes as a prelude to the full establishment of God's kingdom upon the earth.[16] In the tradition of Jewish apocalyptic thought, Mark's

[13] Joel Marcus, "Entering into the Kingly Power of God," *JBL* 107 (1988): 675.

[14] See above, chapter 2, 43–8.

[15] See, e.g., Peter Stuhlmacher, *Das paulinische Evangelium. Vorgeschichte* (Göttingen: Vandenhoeck & Ruprecht, 1968), I:236, for the identification of "gospel" with this notion of the "kingdom of God."

[16] As Rudolf Schnackenburg puts it, "This is not yet the cosmic manifestation of God's kingship but it is more than a hint or a promise . . . The basileia is essentially a revelation

worldview features a discernible chasm between those who have repented and trusted in God's rule on the one hand, and those still aligned with the powers of the present evil age on the other. Thus full disclosure of God's dominion comes only in the wake of necessary skirmishes in which God's agents battle mightily against the powers that be.

Onto the stage of this apocalyptic drama Jesus strides forth, endowed with the authority to quell opposing forces of sickness and demons and death itself; as God's "beloved son" (Mk. 1:11; 9:7), he is the figure who both proclaims and enacts the "gospel" of God's coming dominion. Thus we may speak of the good news of God's reign as the horizon within which to construe the "gospel of Jesus Christ": in Mark's view, he is not just its herald (as "proclaimer") but also its full embodiment (and thus "proclaimed"). Thus Mark's story announces the coming of God's long-awaited rule upon the earth, a rule that becomes most clearly manifest, even if proleptically, in the life, death, and resurrection of Jesus.

Though others have pointed to God's coming kingdom as the claim running through Mark's gospel,[17] the common tendency to read the entire narrative primarily in terms of precise Christological disclosure leaves out of account the broader, more cohesive understanding of the gospel landscape within which we might understand Jesus' identity in terms of his mission and purpose. Already I have noted Jesus' reticence concerning his own identity, a narrative feature that grows more intelligible if the evangelist purposely situates Jesus' life and death within the contours of the "gospel of God." Even the secrecy motif, which is highly problematic if Mark's dominant message is to proclaim *that* Jesus is the Christ, can be more easily explained if Mark's point is to depict Jesus' messiahship with direct reference to "what the Lord has done" (Mk. 5:19). While both Wrede and his critics[18] have attempted to reconcile Mark's post-resurrection, sharply Christological agenda with the narrative's rather muffled, pre-resurrection Christological claims, Jesus' efforts to prevent full disclosure of his identity cohere with his role as God's faithful servant

of divine power, even though it is not yet the complete manifestation of his glory" (*God's Rule and Kingdom*, trans. John Murray [Freiburg: Herder, 1963], 125).

17 With strikingly different emphases, this argument has been advanced, for example, by Schweitzer, who views as something of a tragedy Jesus' failed attempts to bring about the eschatological kingdom, and by Watts, who detects the framework of a New Exodus drama but focuses on Jesus as the true Israel.

18 See, e.g., Heikki Räisänen, *The "Messianic Secret" in Mark's Gospel*, trans. Christopher Tuckett, SNTW (Edinburgh: T. & T. Clark, 1990), 250–8, who proposes what he admits to be "simply a variation" of Wrede's view: the secrecy motif was developed by the evangelist himself to account for – and respond to – the rather non-Christological nature of competing traditions, such as those preserved in Q.

whose identity becomes most transparent in his most self-emptying act (Mk. 15:39). Simply put, once we challenge the prevailing assumption that Mark's gospel functions primarily to disclose Jesus' messianic *identity* with the claim that it depicts Jesus' messianic *mission*, the gospel's "secrecy motif" (detected by Wrede in myriad forms)[19] may well suit Jesus' own agenda, which is to focus attention on *God's* apocalyptic rectification of the world.[20]

This view of God's coming kingdom as Mark's unifying message carries a second interpretive payoff: it makes coherent sense of the gospel's two "halves." Interpreters have long viewed the stories of Jesus' powerful miracle-working in Mk. 1:1–8:21 as, at best, an insufficient portrait of Jesus and, at worst, a problematic foil to his true Christological identity as a suffering servant.[21] But within the schema of God's gospel, both Jesus' earthly mission and his passion demonstrate quite vividly his active staking of God's claim upon the world. From the beginning of his ministry, Mark's Jesus encounters adversarial forces in the form of sickness and demonic possession (Mk. 1:34), religious and political leaders (e.g. Mk. 3:5–6), even natural powers (e.g. Mk. 4:39). As he does so, he launches a decisive campaign against the powers that would prevent the full establishment of God's rule upon the earth.

In turn, the second half of the gospel can best be understood as the escalation of this same conflict. The cost of resisting the powers of the present evil age has indeed grown precious – as precious as life itself (Mk. 8:34–9:1; 10:42–5). Seen in this light, the wonder-working of the gospel's first half differs only in magnitude, not in substance, from the passion emphasis of the second half. In both cases, Jesus performs with authority the messianic role assigned to him; in both cases, he involves his followers in disclosing that messianic age; and in both cases, Jesus demonstrates that, all appearances to the contrary, God's rule has indeed "drawn near."

Thirdly, such a sweeping plotline makes sense of the diverse array of scriptural allusions that appear throughout the gospel. As we have seen, Mark deliberately casts his gospel narrative within the context of God's rule anticipated in Deutero-Isaiah (Mk. 1:2–3). Yet while some have maintained that Mark's story follows one dominant scriptural

[19] See ibid., 242–3, for a helpful list of sub-themes that Wrede had grouped together within the "messianic secret" motif.

[20] Thus the chasm between the historical and narrative worlds may not be so sprawling after all: ironically, Mark may preserve, even develop, authentic traditions of Jesus' reticence precisely in service of the evangelist's own Christological purpose.

[21] See above, chapter 1, for a discussion of these positions.

template – be it Isaiah,[22] the Exodus narrative,[23] or the Elijah/Elisha cycle[24] – a more fruitful approach finds in the intertextual nature of these echoes a broad scriptural grounding for the Markan story.[25] In retelling the story of Jesus' mission and destiny in a manner that interweaves disparate images and longings from Israel's sacred lore, the second evangelist portrays Jesus' palpable power within the biblical matrix of eschatological expectation for God's final triumph upon the earth. It is this dominant thematic emphasis that lends unity to the gospel itself.

Mark's "word on target"[26]

Finally, this study's findings about the intended nature and function of discipleship in Mark introduce promising interpretive possibilities concerning the evangelist's stance toward his own community. What is the nature of the relationship between the disciples in Mark's gospel – disciples who come under increasingly scathing critique – and the original audience to whom it was addressed?

As interpreters have attempted to answer this question, they have generally labored under the assumption of a wide epistemological chasm between the disciples' pre-Easter perspective and the Markan church's post-Easter vantage point.[27] As a result, while Jesus' original disciples may be forgiven for their incomplete assessment of Jesus' messiahship –

[22] Among those who view Isaiah as the dominant influence are Watts, *Isaiah's New Exodus*, who claims Mark's opening Isaiah citation functions "iconically," and Schneck, *Isaiah in the Gospel of Mark, I–VIII*, BIBAL Dissertation Series 1 (Vallejo, CA: BIBAL Press, 1994).

[23] See Otto Piper, "Unchanging Promises: Exodus in the New Testament," *Int* 11 (1957): 3–22; also Willard M. Swartley, "The Structural Function of the Term 'Way' (Hodos) in Mark's Gospel," in *The New Way of Jesus: Essays Presented to Howard Charles*, ed. William Klassen (Newton, KS: Faith and Life Press, 1980), 73–86.

[24] See Wolfgang Roth, *Hebrew Gospel: Cracking the Code of Mark* (Oak Park, IL: Meyer-Stone Books, 1988).

[25] Michael Fishbane's description of the developing Hebrew Bible can also be applied to NT writings, perhaps especially the gospels: "as long as the textual corpus remained open, Revelation and Tradition were thickly interwoven and interdependent" (*The Garments of Torah: Essays in Biblical Hermeneutics* [Bloomington, IN: Indiana University Press, 1989], 18).

[26] The phrase is Beker's apt description of Paul's hermeneutical task. Notably, Beker detects an "apocalyptic core" in Pauline thought that consistently points to "the imminent cosmic triumph of God" (*Paul the Apostle*, 19), which proves to be a central conviction of Mark.

[27] Of course, this assumption forms the crux of Wrede's reconstruction. Yet despite the efforts of subsequent interpreters to chip away at his views of the "messianic secret," the view of the passion as a turning point for Christological understanding has proven virtually unassailable. See, e.g., Räisänen, *Messianic Secret*, 244: "Wrede had a point: the resurrection marked a new epoch."

only fully disclosed at the empty tomb – their heirs in the Markan community should know better, should disavow their feeble grasp on true messiahship, and should take comfort in the reassurance that their own "way of the cross" conforms with Jesus' teachings to a degree never achieved by Jesus' own entourage. Thus scholars subscribing to both a "polemical" and a more "pastoral"[28] view of the gospel's discipleship portrait concur on just this point: faithful discipleship, impossible before the cross, is now attainable on the basis of Jesus' full Christological disclosure.

Yet, if we expand our understanding of Mark's Christology to include not just Jesus' identity but the contours of his apocalyptic mission as well, such a clear bifurcation of pre- and post-Easter perspectives seems to forge an unnecessary divide between Mark's narrative and the historical setting his gospel addresses. We can scarcely deny that the stakes around Jesus' messiahship grow higher as the story moves toward Calvary, yet Mark's very purpose in writing his gospel as a "passion narrative with extended introduction" may well have been to overcome that distinction. In setting forth an account of Jesus' earthly mission that features his disciples as prominent, if flawed, players in it, Mark appears to forge a close connection between those "historical," pre-passion followers and the latter-day, post-passion disciples in his own community. For Mark, neither the suffering nor the power that characterized Jesus' stay on earth were intended as an isolated glimpse of God's coming kingdom. In the evangelist's resolute insistence that Jesus involved his first followers in his own mission and destiny, we can detect his dream that his own community might carry forward the self-sacrificing demonstration of Jesus' "gospel" mission. Once again, I shall note several ramifications of this view of Mark's hermeneutical strategy.

First, and perhaps most provocatively, the "problematic" feature of Jesus' wonder-working ministry can be seen in the "unproblematic" light of the gospel itself once we view these episodes neither as remnants of flawed[29] nor as insufficient[30] Christology, but as a "call to arms" for Mark's own community. By so closely correlating the terms of discipleship with Jesus' own deeds of power, Mark's gospel suggests that Jesus'

[28] For a discussion of these respective approaches, see above, chapter 1, 5–9.

[29] See, e.g., Norman Perrin, "The Christology of Mark: A Study in Methodology," in *A Modern Pilgrimage in New Testament Christology* (Philadelphia: Fortress Press, 1974), 104–21; Theodore J. Weeden, "The Heresy that Necessitated Mark's Gospel," *ZNW* 59 (1968): 145–58.

[30] See, e.g., Robert C. Tannehill, "The Gospel of Mark as Narrative Christology," *Semeia* 16 (1979): 57–95; Jack Dean Kingsbury, *The Christology of Mark's Gospel* (Philadelphia: Fortress Press, 1994; orig. 1983).

call to "come after" him (Mk. 1:17) and to "be with him" (Mk. 3:14) remains inextricably linked to his promise to involve those followers in his own apocalyptic fishing expedition.

Together, Jesus' powerful words and deeds, along with the disciples' replication of them, represent a preliminary engagement of forces animating the present evil age. As Mark recounts their story to an audience that must still have awaited the full disclosure of God's coming kingdom, he may well have attempted to counter not their defective understanding of Jesus' identity but their lagging zeal for carrying forward the banner of Jesus' apocalyptic program of regime change. What Jesus' life, death, and resurrection authoritatively secured – the assurance of God's sovereign victory and coming reign – Mark's own community must fully trust, and by trusting, perform.

Once we recognize both Jesus' and the disciples' deeds of power as opening skirmishes in an apocalyptic battle, Mark's central section, constructed around three sets of passion predictions (Mk. 8:31; 9:31; 10:32–4), can be seen as an ominous adumbration of the escalating intensity of that eschatological engagement. In other words, the call to take up one's cross (Mk. 8:34) and to become a servant of all (Mk. 9:35; 10:44) both issue forth from Jesus' impending sacrifice, which will be accompanied by the very rending of the heavens (Mk. 15:38; cf. 1:10). If Mark's Jesus expects a similar destiny for his followers, Mark's message may well mean to convey to his hearers an exhortative message in two respects: (1) by understanding their present travails as a reflection, even an imitation,[31] of Jesus' own path, they might (2) be reassured that the outcome is assured, that those who endure to the end will be saved (Mk. 13:13).[32] The evangelist's storytelling efforts, it seems, intend to foster close ties between his own community's experience and the path walked by both Jesus and his followers a few decades earlier.

Long viewed as opposing claims, then, the deeds of power and path of suffering that characterize Mark's gospel may instead reflect complementary, if escalating, thrusts, both of which seem pressing for the

[31] Mark does not use "imitation" language *per se* (cf. 1 Cor. 11:1), though it has been noted throughout this study that he describes the disciples' actions in terms that repeat actions otherwise ascribed to Jesus. The pattern continues beyond the texts considered here, even to the point of the proleptic injunction to "take up the cross."

[32] If Mark's mention of impending persecutions reflect his own community's experience, as maintained, for instance, by Joel Marcus (*Mark 1–8: A New Translation with Introduction and Commentary*, AB 27 [Garden City, NY: Doubleday, 2000], 28–9), the case only grows stronger for reading both Jesus' paradigmatic suffering and its explicit application to his followers as a constituent but provisional step in the establishment of God's rule upon the earth.

evangelist. In both miracle and passion, Mark's "word on target" interprets his community's present, flawed reality – perhaps accompanied by waning trust in the "gospel of God" – in light of the more stolid conviction that, despite appearances to the contrary, the outcome of God's reign is assured. In Mark's story, this conviction takes on palpable human form as the sick are healed, the demon-tormented are set free, and the hungry are fed – namely, as Jesus' transforming presence manifests the power of God unleashed in the world. What is more, Jesus' destiny at the hands of powers that appear to prevail, that matrix of Roman and Jewish leaders, unleashes the self-sacrifice that provides the "ransom for many" (Mk. 10:45). And in the end, that power endures beyond the cross, in spite of his followers' lapses, in Jesus' resurrection promise to "go before you" (Mk. 14:28). Despite their doubt, their fear, their abandonment, the disciples are not left to their own devices but are swept up by a force larger than themselves, the "already-inaugurated explosion of God's power into the world,"[33] the very dominion of God. The paradox of Mark's gospel is this: for disciples of Jesus, and thus for "disciples" in Mark's hearing, hope lies finally not in anything they are able to do or not do, to believe or not believe, but rather in the immensely vulnerable act of Jesus' self-sacrifice, which fully exposes the firm hold of God's rule upon the earth.

Final thoughts

With Mark's introduction of the incomprehension motif in Mk. 6:52, the tide of discipleship within the second gospel begins to turn. Increasingly, Jesus' followers are objects of their master's withering critique, as they prove less and less capable of the kind of trust in God's coming rule that characterizes Jesus' mission and his sacrifice.

This study has attempted to reassess the disciples' initial successes and failures as Mark portrays them, particularly in relationship to the evangelist's Christological claims. In sum, my review of the evidence at hand commends a reading of Mark's gospel that balances the gospel's message of an active call to discipleship with its consistent reminder that the disciples, as well as their heirs in the Markan community, depend on the empowering presence of a risen Jesus who promises to "go before" them to the very end. Throughout the gospel, Mark's Jesus launches a frontal assault on the powers of the present age, as he asserts God's impending

[33] Marcus, "Kingly Power," 674.

apocalyptic victory. In turn, he deliberately engages his disciples in this inaugural activity. In the end, God's sovereignty is assured, so that any apparent defeat – be it incomprehension or desertion or even the humiliation of death on a cross – becomes subsumed within God's triumphant claim upon the world. For Mark, and for subsequent readers of his story, *this* is the "gospel of Jesus Christ."

BIBLIOGRAPHY

Aalders, Gerhard Charles. "Fishers and the Hunters." *EvQ* 30 (1958): 133–9.

Achtemeier, Paul J. "Person and Deed. Jesus and the Storm-Tossed Sea." *Int* 16 (1962): 169–76.

"Toward the Isolation of Pre-Markan Miracle Catenae." *JBL* 89 (1970): 265–91.

"The Origin and Function of the Pre-Markan Miracle Catenae." *JBL* 91 (1972): 198–221.

"'He Taught Them Many Things': Reflections on Marcan Christology." *CBQ* 42 (1980): 465–81.

Mark. 2nd edn. PC. Philadelphia: Fortress Press, 1986.

Allison, Dale C. *The New Moses: A Matthean Typology*. Edinburgh: T. & T. Clark, 1993.

Jesus of Nazareth: Millenarian Prophet. Minneapolis, MN: Fortress Press, 1998.

Ambrozic, Aloysius M. *The Hidden Kingdom: A Redaction-Critical Study of the References to the Kingdom of God in Mark's Gospel*. Washington: Catholic Biblical Association of America, 1972.

The Ante-Nicene Fathers: Translations of the Writings of the Fathers down to AD 325. 5th edn. Ed. A. Menzies. Grand Rapids, MI: Eerdmans, 1978.

Aune, David E. "A Note on Jesus' Messianic Self-Consciousness and 11QMelchizedek." *EvQ* 45 (1973): 161–5.

The New Testament in Its Literary Environment. LEC 8. Philadelphia: Westminster Press, 1989.

Baird, J. Arthur. "A Pragmatic Approach to Parable Exegesis: Some New Evidence on Mark 4:11, 33–34." *JBL* 76 (1957): 201–7.

Bassler, Jouette M. "The Parable of the Loaves." *JR* 66 (1986): 157–72.

Bauer, W., W. F. Arndt, F. W. Gingrich, and F. W. Danker, *A Greek–English Lexicon of the New Testament and Other Early Christian Literature*. 2nd edn. Chicago: University of Chicago Press, 1979.

Beavis, Mary Ann. *Mark's Audience: The Literary and Social Setting of Mark 4.11–12*. JSNTSup 33. Sheffield: Sheffield Academic Press, 1989.

Beker, J. Christiaan. *Paul the Apostle: Triumph of God in Life and Thought*. Philadelphia: Fortress Press, 1984; orig. 1980.

Best, Ernest. "Mark iii. 20, 21, 31–35." *NTS* 22 (1975–6): 309–19.

"Mark's Use of the Twelve." *ZNW* 69 (1978): 11–35.

Following Jesus: Discipleship in the Gospel of Mark. JSNTSup 4. Sheffield: JSOT Press, 1981.

Mark: The Gospel as Story. Edinburgh: T. & T. Clark, 1983.

Disciples and Discipleship: Studies in the Gospel According to Mark. Edinburgh: T. & T. Clark, 1986.

"Mark's Preservation of Tradition." In *The Interpretation of Mark*. Ed. W. Telford. 2nd edn. IRT 7. Edinburgh: T. & T. Clark, 1999; orig. 1977. 119–33.

Betz, Hans Dieter. *Nachfolge und Nachahmung Jesu Christi im Neuen Testament*. BHT 37. Tübingen: Mohr (Siebeck), 1967.

Black, C. Clifton. *The Disciples According to Mark: Markan Redaction in Current Debate*. JSNTSup 27. Sheffield: JSOT Press, 1989.

Blackburn, Barry. *Theios Aner and the Markan Miracle Traditions: A Critique of the Theios Aner Concept as an Interpretative Background of the Miracle Traditions Used by Mark*. WUNT 2.40. Tübingen: Mohr Siebeck, 1991.

Blevins, James L. *The Messianic Secret in Markan Research, 1901–1976*. Washington, DC: University Press of America, 1981.

Bolyki, J. "Menge–Tischgemeinschaft–Gruppe." *Communio Viatorum* 24 (1992): 20–6.

Boobyer, George H. "The Eucharistic Interpretation of the Miracles of the Loaves in St. Mark's Gospel." *JTS* 3 (1952): 161–71.

Boring, M. Eugene. "The Christology of Mark: Hermeneutical Issues for Systematic Theology." *Semeia* 30 (1984): 125–51.

"Mark 1:1–15 and the Beginning of the Gospel." *Semeia* 52 (1990): 43–81.

Bornkamm, Gunther. "μυστήριον." In *TDNT* 4 (1967): 814–17.

Bostock, D. Gerald. "Jesus as the New Elisha." *ExpT* 92 (1980): 39–41.

Boucher, Madeleine. *The Mysterious Parable: A Literary Study*. CBQMS 6. Washington, DC: Catholic Biblical Association, 1977.

Breytenbach, Cilliers. *Nachfolge und Zukunftserwartung nach Markus: Eine methodenkritische Studie*. ATANT 71. Zurich: Theologischer Verlag Zürich, 1984.

Bright, John. *Jeremiah*. AB 21. Garden City, NY: Doubleday, 1965.

Broadhead, Edwin K. *Teaching with Authority: Miracles and Christology in the Gospel of Mark*. JSNTSup 74. Sheffield: JSOT Press, 1992.

Brodie, Thomas L. "Jesus as the New Elisha: Cracking the Code." *ExpT* 93 (1981): 39–42.

Brown, Raymond E. *The Gospel According to John*. AB 29 and 29A. Garden City, NY: Doubleday, 1966–70.

"Parable and Allegory Reconsidered." In *New Testament Essays*. Garden City, NY: Image/Doubleday, 1968. 321–33.

Semitic Background of the Term "Mystery" in the New Testament. Philadelphia: Fortress Press, 1968.

"Jesus and Elisha." *Perspective* 12 (1971): 85–104.

Bultmann, Rudolf. *Theology of the New Testament*. 2 vols. New York: Charles Scribner's Sons, 1951–5.

The History of the Synoptic Tradition. Trans. John Marsh. Rev. edn. Peabody, MA: Hendrickson, 1994; orig. 1921.

Burkill, T. Alec. *Mysterious Revelation: An Examination of the Philosophy of St. Mark's Gospel*. Ithaca, NY: Cornell University Press, 1963.

Charlesworth, James H., ed. *The Old Testament Pseudepigrapha*. 2 vols. Garden City, NY: Doubleday, 1983, 1985.

Collins, Adela Yarbro. *The Beginning of the Gospel: Probings of Mark in Context.* Minneapolis: Fortress Press, 1992.
Collins, John J. *The Apocalyptic Imagination: An Introduction to the Jewish Matrix of Christianity.* 2dn. edn. Grand Rapids: Eerdmans, 1998; orig. 1984.
Cranfield, C. E. B. *The Gospel According to Saint Mark: An Introduction and Commentary.* CGTC. New York: Cambridge University Press, 1977.
Craigie, Peter C., Page H. Kelley, and Joel F. Drinkard, Jr. *Jeremiah 1–25.* WBC 26. Dallas: Word Books, 1991.
Cross, Frank Moore. *Canaanite Myth and Hebrew Epic: Essays in the History of the Religion of Israel.* Cambridge, MA: Harvard University Press, 1973.
Crossan, John Dominic. *In Parables: The Challenge of the Historical Jesus.* New York: Harper & Row, 1973.
The Historical Jesus. San Francisco: Harper, 1991.
Daube, David C. "ἐξουσία in Mk. i. 22 and 27." *JTS* 39 (1938): 45–59.
"Responsibilities of Master and Disciples in the Gospel." *NTS* 19 (1972–3): 1–15.
Davies, Margaret. *Rhetoric and Reference in the Fourth Gospel.* JSNTSup 69. Sheffield, England: JSOT Press, 1992.
Davies, W. D. and Dale C. Allison. *A Critical and Exegetical Commentary on the Gospel According to Saint Matthew.* 3 vols. Edinburgh: T. & T. Clark, 1988–97.
Delling, G. "πλήρης." In *TDNT* 6 (1968; orig. 1959): 459–62.
Denis, Albert-Marie. "La Marche de Jésus sur les eaux: contribution à l'histoire de la péricope dans la tradition évangélique." In *De Jésus aux évangiles.* Ed. I. de la Potterie. Gembloux: Duculot, 1967. 233–47.
Dewey, Joanna. *Markan Public Debate: Literary Technique, Concentric Structure, and Theology in Mark 2:1–3:6.* SBLDS 48. Chico, CA: Scholars Press, 1980.
Dibelius, Martin. *Die urchristliche Überlieferung von Johannes dem Täufer.* Göttingen: Vandenhoeck & Ruprecht, 1911.
From Tradition to Gospel. Rev. 2nd edn. Trans. B. Lee Woolf. London: James Clarke, 1971; orig. 1933.
Dodd, C. H. *The Parables of the Kingdom.* New York: Scribner's, 1961.
According to the Scriptures. London: Fontana, 1965; orig. 1957.
Donahue, John R. *The Theology and Setting of Discipleship in the Gospel of Mark.* The 1983 Père Marquette Theology Lecture. Milwaukee, WI: Marquette University Press, 1983.
Dormeyer, Detlev. *Die Passion Jesu als Verhaltensmodell: literarische und theologische Analyse der Traditions- und Redaktionsgeschichte der Markuspassion.* Münster: Verlag Aschendorff, 1974.
Dowd, Sharyn. *Reading Mark: A Literary and Theological Commentary on the Second Gospel.* RNTS. Macon, GA: Smith & Helwys, 2000.
Drury, John. *The Parables in the Gospels: History and Allegory.* London: SPCK, 1985.
Dupont, Jacques. "La Parabole du semeur." *Foi et Vie* 66 (1967): 3–25.
Egger, Wilhelm. *Frohbotschaft und Lehre: Die Sammelberichte das Wirkens Jesu im Markusevangelium.* Frankfurt am Main: Knecht, 1976.

Ehrman, Bart D. "The Text of Mark in the Hands of the Orthodox." *LQ* 5 (1991): 143–56.

Saint Ephrem's Commentary on Tatian's Diatessaron: An English Translation of Chester Beatty Syriac MS 709. With introduction and notes by Carmel McCarthy. JSSSup 2. Oxford: Oxford University Press for the University of Manchester, 1993.

Erlangen, Gerhard Friedrich. "Die beiden Erzählungen von der Speisung in Markus 6,31–44, 8,1–9." *TZ* 20 (1964): 10–22.

Evans, Craig A. *To See and Not Perceive: Isaiah 6.9–10 in Early Jewish and Christian Interpretation.* JSOTSup 64. Sheffield, England: JSOT Press, 1989.

Fanning, Buist M. *Verbal Aspect in New Testament Greek.* Oxford: Clarendon, 1990.

Farmer, William R. *The Synoptic Problem: A Critical Analysis.* Mercer, GA: Mercer University Press, 1981; orig. 1964.

Fay, Greg. "Introduction to Incomprehension: The Literary Structure of Mark 4:1–34." *CBQ* 51 (1989): 65–81.

Fee, Gordon D. *The First Epistle to the Corinthians.* NICNT. Grand Rapids, MI: Eerdmans, 1987.

Fishbane, Michael. *The Garments of Torah: Essays in Biblical Hermeneutics.* Bloomington, IN: Indiana University Press, 1989.

Fleddermann, Harry. "'And He Wanted to Pass by Them' (Mark 6:48c)." *CBQ* 45 (1983): 389–95.

Focant, Camille. "L'Incompréhension des disciples dans le deuxième évangile." *RB* 82 (1975): 161–85.

"La Tête du prophète sur un plat, ou, L'Anti-repas d'alliance (Mc 6.14–29)." *NTS* 46 (2001): 334–53.

Fowler, Robert M. *Loaves and Fishes: The Function of the Feeding Stories in the Gospel of Mark.* SBLDS 54. Chico, CA: Scholars Press, 1981.

Frei, Hans W. *The Eclipse of Biblical Narrative: A Study in Eighteenth and Nineteenth Century Hermeneutics.* New Haven: Yale University Press, 1993; orig. 1974.

Freyne, Seán. "The Disciples in Mark and the *MASKILIM* in Daniel. A Comparison." *JSNT* 16 (1982): 7–23.

"Galilee, Sea of." In *The Anchor Bible Dictionary*, II. Ed. David Noel Freedman. Garden City, NY: Doubleday, 1992. 900.

The Twelve: Disciples and Apostles: A Study in the Theology of the First Three Gospels. London: Sydney, Sheed & Ward, 1968.

Friedrich, G. "εὐαγγελίζομαι." In *TDNT* 2 (1964): 707–37.

Gamble, Harry Y. *Books and Readers in the Early Church: A History of Early Christian Texts.* New Haven: Yale University Press, 1995.

García Martínez, Florentino and Eibert J. C. Tigchelaar, eds. *The Dead Sea Scrolls: Study Edition.* 2 vols. Grand Rapids, MI: Eerdmans, 1997–8.

Gerhardsson, Birger. "The Parable of the Sower and Its Interpretation." *NTS* 14 (1967–8): 165–93.

Gibson, Jeffrey B. "Jesus' Wilderness Temptation According to Mark." *JSNT* 53 (1994): 13–34.

Gnilka, Joachim. *Die Verstockung Israels. Isaias 6:9–10 in der Theologie der Synoptiker.* Munich: Kösel, 1961.

Das Evangelium nach Markus. 2 vols. EKKNT 2. Zurich: Benziger; Neukirchen: Neukirchener Verlag, 1978–9.
Goldingay, John. "'Holy Ones on High' in Daniel 7:18." *JBL* 107 (1988): 495–9.
Grundmann, Walter. *Das Evangelium nach Markus*. THKNT 2. Berlin: Evangelische Verlagsanstalt, 1977.
Guelich, Robert A. *Mark 1–8:26*. WBC 34A. Dallas: Word, 1989.
Gundry, Robert H. *Mark: A Commentary on His Apology for the Cross*. Grand Rapids, MI: Eerdmans, 1993.
Haenchen, E. *Der Weg Jesu: Eine Erklärung des Markus-Evangeliums und der kanonischen Parallelen*. Berlin: Alfred Töpelmann, 1966.
Hahn, Friedrich. *Mission in the New Testament*. SBT 47. London: SCM Press, 1965.
"Das Gleichnis von der ausgestreuten Saat und seine Deutung (Mk. iv. 3–8, 14–20)." In *Text and Interpretation*. Ed. E. Best and R. McL. Wilson. Cambridge: Cambridge University Press, 1979. 133–42.
Hartman, Louis Francis and Alexander A. Di Lella. *The Book of Daniel*. AB 23. Garden City, NY: Doubleday, 1978.
Hawkin, David J. "The Incomprehension of the Disciples in Marcan Redaction." *JBL* 91 (1972): 491–500.
Hays, Richard B. *Echoes of Scripture in the Letters of Paul*. New Haven: Yale University Press, 1989.
First Corinthians. Interpretation. Louisville, KY: John Knox Press, 1997.
"Can the Gospels Teach Us How to Read the Old Testament?" *Pro Ecclesia* 11 (2002): 402–17.
Heil, John P. *Jesus Walking on the Sea: Meaning and Gospel Functions of Matt. 14:22–33, Mark 6:45–52 and John 6:15b–21*. AnBib 87. Rome: Biblical Institute Press, 1981.
Heising, Alkuin. *Die Botschaft der Brotvermehrung: zur Geschichte und Bedeutung eines Christusbekenntnisses im Neuen Testament*. Stuttgart: Katholisches Bibelwerk, 1966.
Henderson, Suzanne Watts. "'Concerning the Loaves': Comprehending Incomprehension in Mark 6.45–52." *JSNT* 83 (2001): 3–26.
Hengel, Martin. *The Charismatic Leader and His Followers*. Trans. J. Grieg. SNTW. New York: Crossroad, 1981.
Hoffmann, Paul. *Studien zur Theologie der Logienquelle*. Münster: Verlag Aschendorff, 1972.
Hooker, Morna D. *A Commentary on the Gospel according to St. Mark*. BNTC 2. London: A. & C. Black, 1991.
"Mark's Parables of the Kingdom (Mark 4:1–34)." In *The Challenge of Jesus' Parables*. Ed. Richard N. Longenecker. Grand Rapids, MI: Eerdmans, 2000. 79–101.
Horbury, William. "The Twelve and the Phylarchs." *NTS* 32 (1986): 503–27.
Iersel, Bastiaan Martinus Franciscus van. "Die wunderbare Speisung und das Abendmahl in der synoptischen Tradition (Mk. VI.35–44 par VIII.1–20 par)." *NovT* 7 (1964): 167–94.
Jeremias, Joachim. *Eucharistic Words of Jesus*. Philadelphia: Fortress Press, 1966.
"Paarweise Sendung im Neuen Testament." In *Abba: Studien zur neutestamentlichen Theologie und Zeitgeschichte*. Göttingen: Vandenhoeck & Ruprecht, 1966. 136–43.

Jerusalem in the Time of Jesus: An Investigation into Economic and Social Conditions during the Time of Jesus. Philadelphia: Fortress Press, 1969.
New Testament Theology. Part I. *The Proclamation of Jesus*. London: SCM Press, 1971.
The Parables of Jesus. Trans. S. H. Hooke. New York: Scribner's Sons, 1972.
Jesus' Promise to the Nations. Philadelphia: Fortress Press, 1982.
Juel, Donald. *Mark*. ACNT. Minneapolis: Augsburg, 1990.
Jülicher, Adolf. *Die Gleichnisreden Jesu*. 2nd edn. Tübingen: Mohr, 1910; orig. 1888.
Kähler, Martin. *The So-Called Historical Jesus and the Historic Biblical Christ*. Trans. Carl E. Braaten. Philadelphia: Fortress Press, 1964; orig. 1892.
Keck, Leander E. "Mk. 3,7–12 and Mark's Christology." *JBL* 84 (1965): 341–58.
"The Introduction to Mark's Gospel." *NTS* 12 (1965–6): 352–70.
Kee, Howard Clark. "The Function of Scriptural Quotations and Allusions in Mark 11–16." In *Jesus und Paulus*. Ed. E. Earle Ellis and E. Grässer. Göttingen: Vandenhoeck & Ruprecht, 1975. 165–85.
Community of the New Age: Studies in Mark's Gospel. Philadelphia: Westminster Press, 1977.
"Christology in Mark's Gospel." In *Judaisms and Their Messiahs at the Turn of the Christian Era*. Ed. Jacob Neusner, W. S. Green, and E. S. Freirichs. New York: Cambridge University Press, 1987.
Kelber, Werner. *The Kingdom in Mark: A New Place and A New Time*. Philadelphia: Fortress Press, 1974.
Kelber, Werner, ed. *The Passion in Mark*. Philadelphia: Fortress Press, 1976.
Kermode, Frank. *The Genesis of Secrecy: On the Interpretation of Narrative*. Cambridge, MA: Harvard University Press, 1979.
Kertelge, K. *Die Wunder Jesu im Markusevangelium. Eine redaktiongeschichtliche Untersuchung*. SANT 23. Munich: Kösel, 1970.
Kingsbury, Jack Dean. *Conflict in Luke: Jesus, Authorities, Disciples*. Minneapolis: Fortress Press, 1991.
The Christology of Mark's Gospel. Philadelphia: Fortress Press, 1994; orig. 1983.
Kittel, Gerhard, and Gerhard Friedrich. *Theological Dictionary of the New Testament*. Trans. and ed. Geoffrey W. Bromiley. 10 vols. Grand Rapids, MI: Eerdmans, 1964–76.
Klauck, Hans-Josef. *Allegorie und Allegorese in synoptischen Gleichnistexten*. Münster: Aschendorff, 1978.
Klein, Günther. *Die zwölf Apostel: Ursprung und Gehalt einer Idee*. Göttingen: Vandenhoeck & Ruprecht, 1961.
Koch, Dietrich-Alex. *Die Bedeutung der Wundererzählungen für die Christologie des Markusevangeliums*. New York: De Gruyter, 1975.
Koester, Helmut. "The Sayings of Q and Their Image of Jesus." In *Sayings of Jesus: Canonical and Non-Canonical*. Ed. William L. Petersen, Johan S. Vos, and Henk J. De Jonge. Leiden: Brill, 1997. 137–54.
Kuhn, Heinz-Wolfgang. *Ältere Sammlungen in Markusevangelium*. Göttingen: Vandenhoeck & Ruprecht, 1971.
Kümmel, Werner Georg. *Promise and Fulfillment: The Eschatological Message of Jesus*. Trans. Dorthea M. Barton. SBT 23. London: SCM Press, 1961.

Lambrecht, Jan. "Redaction and Theology in MK., IV." In *L'Evangile selon Marc: tradition et redaction*. Ed. M. Sabbe. BETL 34. Leuven: Leuven University Press, 1974. 269–307.
Lampe, Peter. "Die markinische Deutung des Gleichnisses vom Sämann, Markus 4, 10–12." *ZNW* 65 (1974): 140–50.
Lane, William L. *The Gospel According to Mark*. NICNT. Grand Rapids, MI: Eerdmans, 1974.
Lapide, Pinchas. "A Jewish Exegesis of the Walking on the Water." Trans. G. W. S. Knowles. *Concilium* 138 (1980): 35–40.
Levenson, Jon D. *Sinai and Zion: An Entry into the Jewish Bible*. New Voices in Biblical Studies. Chicago, New York, Minneapolis: Winston Press, 1985.
Liddell, H. G., R. Scott, and S. Jones. *A Greek–English Lexicon with a Supplement*. Oxford: Clarendon, 1968.
Lohmeyer, Ernst. *Das Evangelium des Markus*. Göttingen: Vandenhoeck & Ruprecht, 1951; orig. 1937.
Loisy, Alfred Firmin. *L'Evangile selon Marc*. Paris: Emile Nourry, 1912.
Lührmann, D. *Das Markusevangelium*. HNT 3. Tübingen: Mohr (Siebeck), 1987.
Lundbom, Jack R. *Jeremiah 1–20*. AB 21A. Garden City, NY: Doubleday, 1999.
Luz, Ulrich. "Das Geheimnismotif und die markinische Christologie." *ZNW* 56 (1965): 9–30.
"The Disciples in the Gospel According to Matthew." Trans. Robert Morgan. In *The Interpretation of Matthew*. Ed. Graham Stanton. Edinburgh: T. & T. Clark, 1995. 115–48.
Madden, Patrick J. *Jesus' Walking on the Sea: An Investigation of the Origin of the Narrative Account*. BZNW 81. Berlin and New York: De Gruyter, 1997.
Malbon, Elizabeth Struthers. "Fallible Followers: Women and Men in the Gospel of Mark." *Semeia* 28 (1983): 29–48.
"The Jesus of Mark and the Sea of Galilee." *JBL* 103 (1984): 363–77.
"*TE OIKIA AUTOU*: Mark 2.15 in Context." *NTS* 31 (1985): 282–92.
In the Company of Jesus: Characters in Mark's Gospel. Louisville: Westminster John Knox, 2000.
Mánek, Jindrich. "Fishers of Men." *NovT* 2 (1957): 138–41.
Mann, C. S. *Mark: A New Translation with Introduction and Commentary*. AB 27. Garden City, NY: Doubleday, 1986.
Manson, T. W. *The Teaching of Jesus: Studies of Its Form and Content*. Cambridge: Cambridge University Press, 1931.
The Sayings of Jesus: As Recorded in the Gospels According to St. Matthew and St. Luke. London: SCM Press, 1949.
Marcus, Joel. "Mark 4:10–12 and Marcan Epistemology." *JBL* 103 (1984): 557–74.
The Mystery of the Kingdom of God. SBLDS 90. Atlanta: Scholars Press, 1986.
"Entering into the Kingly Power of God." *JBL* 107 (1988): 663–75.
"'The Time Has Been Fulfilled!' (Mark 1.15)." In *Apocalyptic and the New Testament*. Ed. Joel Marcus and Marion L. Soards. JSNTSup 24. Sheffield, England: JSOT Press, 1989. 49–68.
The Way of the Lord: Christological Exegesis of the Old Testament in the Gospel of Mark. Louisville: Westminster/John Knox Press, 1992.
"Blanks and Gaps in the Markan Parable of the Sower." *BibInt* 5 (1997): 247–62.

Mark 1–8: A New Translation with Introduction and Commentary. AB 27. Garden City, NY: Doubleday, 2000.
"Mark – Interpreter of Paul." *NTS* 48 (2000): 473–87.
"Son of Man as Son of Adam. Part II: Exegesis." *RB* 110 (2003): 370–86.
Marshall, Christopher D. *Faith as a Theme in Mark's Narrative*. SNTSMS 64. New York: Cambridge University Press, 1989.
Marxsen, Willi. *Mark the Evangelist: Studies on the Redaction History of the Gospel*. Trans. James Boyce, Donald Juel, and William Poehlmann. Nashville: Abingdon Press, 1969.
Matera, Frank J. *What Are They Saying about Mark?* New York: Paulist Press, 1987.
"The Prologue as the Interpretive Key to Mark's Gospel." *JSNT* 34 (1988): 3–20.
"The Incomprehension of the Disciples and Peter's Confession." *Bib* 70 (1989): 153–72.
Mauser, Ulrich. *Christ in the Wilderness: The Wilderness Theme in the Second Gospel and Its Basis in the Biblical Tradition*. London: SCM Press, 1963.
Meier, John P. *A Marginal Jew: Rethinking the Historical Jesus*. 3 vols. Garden City, NY: Doubleday, 1991–2001.
Mekilta deRabbi Ishamael. Ed. J. Z. Lauterbach. 3 vols. Philadelphia: Jewish Publication Society of America, 1933–5.
Melbourne, Bertram L. *Slow to Understand: The Disciples in Synoptic Perspective*. Lanham, ND: University Press of America, 1988.
Metzger, Bruce M. *A Textual Commentary on the Greek New Testament: A Companion Volume to the United Bible Societies' Greek New Testament*. 3rd edn. London and New York: United Bible Societies, 1971.
Meye, Robert P. *Jesus and the Twelve: Discipleship and Revelation in Mark's Gospel*. Grand Rapids, MI: Eerdmans, 1968.
Moore, Stephen D. *Literary Criticism and the Gospels: The Theoretical Challenge*. New Haven: Yale University Press, 1989.
Moulton, James Hope. *A Grammar of New Testament Greek*. 3rd edn. Edinburgh: T. & T. Clark, 1930.
Mussner, F. "Gottes herrschaft und Sendung Jesu nach Mk. 1, 14f. Zugleich ein Beitrag über die innere Struktur des Markusevangelium." In *Praesentia Salutis. Gesammelte Studien zu Fragen und Themen des Neuen Testaments*. Düsseldorf: Patmos, 1967.
Myers, Ched. *Binding the Strong Man: A Political Reading of Mark's Story of Jesus*. Maryknoll, NY: Orbis, 1988.
Neirynck, Frans. *Duality in Mark: Contributions to the Study of the Markan Redaction*. BETL 31. Leuven: Leuven University Press, 1972.
Noth, Martin. "The Holy Ones of the Most High." In *The Laws in the Pentateuch and Other Studies*. Trans. D. R. Ap-Thomas. Edinburgh: Oliver & Boyd; Philadelphia: Fortress Press, 1966. 215–28.
Öhler, Markus. "The Expectation of Elijah and the Presence of the Kingdom of God." *JBL* 118 (1999): 461–76.
Origen. *On First Principles*. Trans. G. W. Butterworth. London: SPCK, 1936; reprint, Gloucester, MA: Peter Smith, 1973.
Osburn, C. D. "The Historical Present in Mark as a Text-Critical Criterion." *Bib* 64 (1983): 486–500.

Painter, John. *Mark's Gospel: Worlds in Conflict*. New Testament Readings. Ed. John Court. New York: Routledge, 1997.
Patrologia Latina. Ed. Jacques-Paul Migne. Paris: Migne, 1844–64.
Peisker, Carl Heinz. "Konsekutives ἵνα in Markus IV, 12." *ZNW* 59 (1968): 126–7.
Perkins, Pheme. "Mark." In *The New Interpreter's Bible*. Vol. VIII. Nashville, TN: Abingdon, 1995. 507–733.
Perrin, Norman. "The Christology of Mark: A Study in Methodology." In *A Modern Pilgrimage in New Testament Christology*. Philadelphia: Fortress Press, 1974. 104–21.
Pesch, Rudolf. "Levi-Matthäus (Mc 2,14/Mt 9,9; 10,3). Ein Beitrag zur Lösung eines alten Problems." *ZNW* 59 (1968): 40–56.
"Ein Tag vollmächtige Wirkens Jesu in Kapharnaum (Mk. 1,21–34.35–39)." *BibLeb* 9 (1968): 114–95.
Das Markusevangelium. 2 vols. HTKNT 2; Freiburg: Herder, 1976.
Piper, Otto. "Unchanging Promises: Exodus in the New Testament." *Int* 11 (1957): 3–22
Pirqe deRabbi Eliezer. Ed. G. Frielander. New York: Benjamin Blom, 1971.
Power, E. "The Staff of the Apostles: A Problem in Gospel Harmony." *Bib* 4 (1923): 241–66.
Quesnell, Quentin. *The Mind of Mark: Interpretation and Method through the Exegesis of Mark 6,52*. Rome: Pontifical Biblical Institute, 1969.
Räisänen, Heikki. *The Idea of Divine Hardening: A Comparative Study of the Notion of Divine Hardening, Leading Astray and Inciting to Evil in the Bible and the Qur'an*. Helsinki: Publications of the Finnish Exegetical Society, 1972.
Die Parabeltheorie im Markusevangelium. Helsinki: Finnische Exegetische Gesellschaft, 1973.
The "Messianic Secret" in Mark's Gospel. Trans. Christopher Tuckett. SNTW. Edinburgh: T. & T. Clark, 1990.
Rajak, Tessa. "Dying for the Law: The Martyr's Portrait in Jewish-Greek Literature." In *The Jewish Dialogue with Greece and Rome: Studies in Cultural and Social Location*. Leiden: Brill, 2001. 99–133.
Reploh, Karl-Georg. *Markus – Lehrer der Gemeinde: Eine redaktionsgeschichtliche Studie zu den Jüngerperikopen des Markus-Evangeliums*. SBM 9. Stuttgart: Katholisches Bibelwerk, 1969.
Rhoads, David, and Donald Michie. *Mark as Story: An Introduction to the Narrative of a Gospel*. Philadelphia: Fortress Press, 1982.
"Narrative Criticism and the Gospel of Mark." *JAAR* 50 (1982): 411–34.
Robbins, Vernon K. "Mark 1.14–20: An Interpretation at the Intersection of Jewish and Graeco-Roman Traditions." *NTS* 28 (1982): 220–36.
Jesus the Teacher: A Socio-Rhetorical Interpretation of Mark. Philadelphia: Fortress Press, 1984.
Roth, Wolfgang. *Hebrew Gospel: Cracking the Code of Mark*. Oak Park, IL: Meyer-Stone Books, 1988.
Sabbe, M., ed. *L'Evangile selon Marc: tradition et rédaction*. BETL 34. Leuven: Leuven University Press, 1974.
Sanders, E. P. *Paul and Palestinian Judaism: A Comparison of Patterns of Religion*. Minneapolis: Fortress Press, 1977.
Jesus and Judaism. Philadelphia: Fortress Press, 1985.

Schenke, L. *Die Wundererzählungen des Markusevangeliums*. SBB 5. Stuttgart: Katholisches Bibelwerk, 1974.
Schmahl, Gunther. *Die Zwölf im Markusevangelium*. Trier: Paulinus, 1974.
Schmidt, Daryl Dean. *The Gospel of Mark with Introduction, Notes, and Original Text*. Sonoma, CA: Polebridge Press, 1991.
Schnackenburg, Rudolf. *God's Rule and Kingdom*. Trans. John Murray. Freiburg: Herder, 1963.
Schneck, Richard. *Isaiah in the Gospel of Mark, I–VIII*. BIBAL Dissertation Series 1. Vallejo, CA: BIBAL Press, 1994.
Schulz, Anselm. *Nachfolgen und Nachahmen. Studien über das Verhältnis der neutestatmentlichen Jüngerschaft zur urchristlichen Vorbildethik*. SANT 6. Munich: Kösel-Verlag, 1962.
Schweitzer, Albert. *The Quest of the Historical Jesus: A Critical Study of Its Progress from Reimarus to Wrede*. Baltimore: Johns Hopkins University Press, 1998; orig. 1906.
The Mysticism of Paul the Apostle. Trans. William Montgomery. Baltimore: Johns Hopkins University Press, 1998; orig. 1931.
Schweizer, Eduard. "Die theologische Leistung des Markus." *EvT* 19 (1964): 337–55.
The Good News According to Mark. Atlanta: John Knox Press, 1970.
"The Portrayal of the Life of Faith in the Gospel of Mark." *Int* 32 (1978): 387–99.
A Select Library of the Nicene and Post-Nicene Fathers of the Christian Church. Ed. P. Schaff *et al*. Peabody, MA: Hendrickson, 1994; orig. 1887–94.
Shiner, Whitney Taylor. *Follow Me! Disciples in Markan Rhetoric*. SBLDS 145. Atlanta: Scholars Press, 1995.
Smith, C. W. F. "Fishers of Men: Footnotes on a Gospel Figure." *HTR* 52 (1959): 188–203.
Smith, D. Moody. *John among the Gospels*. 2nd edn. Columbia, SC: University of South Carolina Press, 2001.
Snodgrass, K. R. "Streams of Tradition Emerging from Isaiah 40:1–5 and Their Adaptation in the New Testament." *JSNT* 8 (1980): 24–45.
Snoy, Thierry. "La Rédaction marcienne de la marche sur les eaux (Mc. VI: 45–52)." *ETL* 44 (1968): 205–41, 433–81.
"Marc 6,48: '. . . et il voulait les dépasser.' Proposition pour la solution d'une énigme." In *L'Evangile selon Marc: tradition et rédaction*. Ed. M. Sabbe. BETL 34. Leuven: Leuven University Press, 1988; orig. 1974. 347–63.
Sparks, H. F. D., ed. *The Apocryphal Old Testament*. Oxford: Oxford University Press, 1984.
Standaert, B. H. M. G. M. *L'Evangile selon Marc. Composition et genre littéraire*. Nijmegen: Stichting Studentenpers, 1978.
Steele, Denise. "Having Root in the Self: Human Fruition and the Self-in-Relation in the Gospel of Mark." Ph.D. diss., University of Glasgow, 2002.
Stegner, William Richard. *Narrative Theology in Early Jewish Christianity*. Louisville, KY: Westminster/John Knox Press, 1989.
"Jesus' Walking on the Water: Mark 6.45–52." In *The Gospels and the Scriptures of Israel*. Ed. Craig A. Evans and W. Richard Stegner. JSNTSup 104. Sheffield, England: Sheffield Academic Press, 1994. 212–34.
Stein, Siegfried. "The Influence of Symposia Literature on the Literary Form of the Haggadah." *JJS* 7 (1957): 13–44.

Steinmetz, David C. "The Superiority of Pre-critical Exegesis." *Theology Today* 37 (1980): 27–38.

Stock, Klemens. *Boten aus dem Mit-Ihm-Sein: Das Verhältnis zwischen Jesus und den Zwölf nach Markus*. AnBib 70. Rome: Biblical Institute, 1975.

Stone, C. F., III. "Allusion to Isa. 11.10 LXX in Mark 10.42b." *NTS* 48 (2002): 71–83.

Strathmann, H. "μαρτύριον." In *TDNT* 4 (1967; orig. 1959): 502–3.

Streeter, B. H. *The Four Gospels: A Study of Origins*. London: Macmillan, 1924.

Stuhlmacher, Peter. *Das paulinische Evangelium. Vorgeschichte*. Göttingen: Vandenhoeck & Ruprecht, 1968.

Swartley, Willard M. "The Structural Function of the Term 'Way' (Hodos) in Mark's Gospel." In *The New Way of Jesus: Essays Presented to Howard Charles*. Ed. William Klassen. Newton, KS: Faith and Life Press, 1980. 73–86.

Tannehill, Robert C. "The Disciples in Mark: The Function of a Narrative Role." *JR* 57 (1977). 386–405.

"The Gospel of Mark as Narrative Christology." *Semeia* 16 (1979): 57–95.

Taylor, Vincent. *The Gospel According to Saint Mark: The Greek Text with Introduction, Notes, and Indexes*. 2nd edn. Grand Rapids, MI: Baker, 1981; orig. 1950.

Telford, William, ed. *The Interpretation of Mark*. 2nd edn. IRT 7. Edinburgh: T. & T. Clark, 1999; orig. 1977.

Theissen, Gerd. "Wanderradikalismus: Literatursoziologische Aspekte der Überlieferung von Worten Jesu im Urchristentum." *ZTK* 70 (1973): 245–71.

The Miracle Stories of the Early Christian Tradition. Trans. Francis McDonagh. Ed. John Riches. SNTW. Philadelphia: Fortress Press, 1983.

Thesaurus linguae graecae: Canon of Greek Authors and Works. 2nd edn. Ed. L. Berkowitz and K. Squiter. Oxford: Oxford University Press, 1986.

Thompson, Mary R. *The Role of Disbelief in Mark: A New Approach to the Second Gospel*. New York: Paulist Press, 1989.

Tolbert, Mary Ann. *Sowing the Gospel: Mark's World in Literary-Historical Perspective*. Minneapolis: Fortress Press, 1989.

Trocmé, Etienne. *The Formation of the Gospel According to Mark*. Trans. Pamela Gaughan. Philadelphia: Westminster Press, 1975.

Tuckett, Christopher M., ed. *The Messianic Secret*. IRT 1. Philadelphia: Fortress Press, 1983.

The Revival of the Griesbach Hypothesis: An Analysis and Appraisal. SNTSMS 44. Cambridge: Cambridge University Press, 1983.

Tyson, Joseph B. "The Blindness of the Disciples in Mark." *JBL* 80 (1961): 261–8.

Vermes, Geza. *Jesus the Jew: A Historian's Reading of the Gospels*. Philadelphia: Fortress Press, 1981.

Watts, Rikki E. *Isaiah's New Exodus and Mark*. Tübingen: Mohr Siebeck, 1997.

Weeden, Theodore J. "The Heresy that Necessitated Mark's Gospel." *ZNW* 59 (1968): 145–58.

Mark: Traditions in Conflict. Philadelphia: Fortress Press, 1971.

Weinfield, M. "Jeremiah and the Spiritual Metamorphosis of Israel." *ZAW* 88 (1976): 17–56.

Weiss, Johannes. *Jesus' Proclamation of the Kingdom of God*. Trans. and ed. R. H. Hiers and D. L. Holland. Philadelphia: Fortress Press, 1971.

Williams, Catrin H. *I Am He: The Interpretation of "Anî Hû" in Jewish and Early Christian Literature*. Tübingen: Mohr Siebeck, 2000.

Windisch, Hans. "Die Verstockungsidee in Mk. 4:12 und das kausale ἵνα in der späteren Koine." *ZNW* 26 (1927): 203–9.

Witherington, Ben, III. *Jesus the Seer*. Peabody, MA: Hendrickson, 1999.

The Gospel of Mark: A Socio-Rhetorical Commentary. Grand Rapids, MI: Eerdmans, 2001.

Wrede, William. *The Messianic Secret*. Trans. J. C. Grieg. Cambridge: James Clark, 1971; orig. 1901.

Wuellner, Wilhelm H. *The Meaning of "Fishers of Men."* Philadelphia: Westminster Press, 1967.

Zerwick, Maximilian. *Biblical Greek*. Trans. Joseph Smith. Rome: Pontifical Institute, 1963.

Zimmerman, Heinrich. "Das absolute ἐγώ εἰμι als die neutestamentliche Offbarungsformel." *BZ* 4 (1960): 266–76.

INDEX OF PASSAGES CITED

Old Testament

Apocrypha

Pseudepigrapha

New Testament

Dead Sea Scrolls

Rabbinic texts

Extra-canonical early Christian literature

INDEX OF MODERN AUTHORS

Lightning Source UK Ltd.
Milton Keynes UK
UKHW010311111218
333801UK00001B/7/P

9 780521 091398